by Edward Salim Michael
The Law of Attention, Nada Yoga and the Way of Inner Vigilance
(previously titled the Way of Inner Vigilance
Inner Awakening and Practice of Nada Yoga
The Suprême Quest
Obstacles to Enlightenment and Liberation
Fruits of Awakening
Awakening, a Matter of Life or Death
In the Silence of the Unfathomable

And also by *Michele Michael*
Journeys in Lands of Awakening and Sainthood

Originally published in French by Guy Tredaniel Editeur under the title "Le Prix d'un Destin Remarquable" © *Guy Tredaniel Editeur 2012.*

ISBN-13: 978-1503382589

www.edwardsalim-michael.org
www.meditation-presence.com

THE PRICE

OF

A REMARKABLE DESTINY

Michele Michael

THE PRICE

OF

A REMARKABLE DESTINY

The Life and Spiritual Journey of
Edward Salim Michael

Translated from the French by Tania Doney

To Vidji, our daughter

Contents

INTRODUCTION

Destiny was awaiting me on that December day in 1974, when I knocked at the door of a small room, part of the former servants' quarters, on the first floor of a smart apartment block in Paris's sixteenth arrondissement, where a "hatha yoga teacher", recommended to me by a friend, was to be found.

I had a premonition that something important lay ahead of me. The man who received me was around fifty years old; his gaze was deep and penetrating and his entire being radiated gentleness, nobility, and seriousness. This was how I met the man who would open a spiritual door for me and enable me to find the meaning of existence through a direct personal experience. We would follow the path together until his departure from this world at the end of November, 2006.

Some five years after I became his student, Salim, on my insistent request, embarked upon the writing of his first book, which he composed in English. As he never had been able to go to school, this was a real challenge for him and we worked together for four years before the book was published in Great Britain. I simultaneously undertook the translation into French and, subsequently, I helped Salim with the composition of his other works, which were all written directly in French.

The source of this biography is twofold: firstly, Salim's recollections and reflections, which I gathered from him, as well as the recounting of events which we lived through together until the end of his life; and, secondly, extracts from his books, which make it possible to retrace his spiritual path, the exercises he practiced, the inner experiences he had and the understandings he gleaned from them, which are expressed in his own words. Some passages are taken from videos of teachings recorded towards the end of his life.

It was only after much hesitation and reluctance that he agreed to confide his memories to me; only on my insistence did he consent, because I thought that his life and experiences could help and inspire seekers. The reason he agreed to answer my questions was that his life and teaching were so closely intertwined that one shed light on the other.

How can the whole of a life be condensed into a few hundred pages? How can words convey the intensity of events which were often dramatic? Nothing has been embellished or exaggerated—on the contrary. In fact, this story even under-represents the reality and many of the ordeals Salim went through are not included. He sometimes had difficulty in determining an exact chronology for certain events; therefore, any dates given should be considered indicative only. It should also be specified that reflections on music, spirituality, and existence in general, are the expression of his ideas, even if, for compositional reasons, they are not always directly attributed to him.

* * *

We live in a hyperactive world—and even more so nowadays, because of the frenetic activity created by the speed of communication methods—but we do not see that we are inwardly passive. Inner life and silence are non-existent; thus there is an extreme vulnerability when facing the difficulties of existence. Indeed, if our gaze is turned solely towards the outside, which attracts all our attention, we are powerless when suffering its storms.

Salim's life demonstrates the opposite. Not because he withdrew to the depths of a hermitage or monastery, but because he found an inner cloister, pursuing his inner practice with unwavering tenacity, even within the turbulence of external life.

As his inner path took priority, he was able to withstand external storms; he was able to ascend to rarely explored summits and acquire extremely enviable spiritual knowledge.

It is this path which we are going to travel with him in this biography where inner understandings will always have more importance than outside facts. The intensity of his practice will take him off the beaten track; he will find himself alone, without a master outside of himself.

All his life, Salim responded first to the inner call, without seeking either the approbation or the admiration of others. Facing the difficulties of all sorts that he encountered, he sought, he despaired, he fought, he, as he would say, "wasted a lot of time"; he had to find out how to overcome the resistance within himself, in a word, he was, as he liked to repeat, "tragically human." The efforts, the crucial importance of which he emphasizes in his books, he made alone, without any guide, with constancy and determination.

It was his life itself which constituted the range of experiences from which he drew his understandings and his teachings. He practically never read, but he meditated and practiced a tireless vigilance, thus succeeding in becoming connected with what he called the Superior Aspect of his nature to the extent "that it would have been as difficult for him to forget it as it had been difficult for him to remember it at the beginning."

Edward Salim Michael was not raised in any religion; his parents never read or quoted holy texts – his mother was herself illiterate and a foreigner, yet it is known that it is principally from the mother that the child becomes imbued with religion, connecting him to the society in which he lives. This lack of religious bearings drove him to find his own path within himself, beyond dogma, without cultural references, a path nevertheless embarked upon with the greatest rigor, based solely upon direct experience, without belief; that is what makes it so valuable in this modern world which is both deculturized and vulnerable to every type of fanaticism.

This cultural destitution was perhaps necessary to permit him to find by himself the spiritual laws common to various religions, not by compiling knowledge from books, but by direct experience without cultural or historical references.

A seeker's practice must, he would say, aim to allow him to know in himself, by a direct experience, the Primary Cause, the Source of Origin which is always present, as it is a-causal, a-temporal and a-spatial —whether it be called the Kingdom of Heaven, God, Buddha-Nature, Brahman, the Absolute, or the Infinite, it is the same thing. When this Source has been recognized, the seeker must fight to deepen this experience and render it permanent; only in this way can he attain liberation, nirvana, spiritual marriage, mystic union, salvation, which all represent the same thing: the ultimate goal of a quest.

Salim had a very particular veneration for Christ whom he regarded as a being without equal; he was not, however, a Christian in the sense habitually given to this word. For him, the Buddha was the one who had brought to the world the most rigorous and effective spiritual knowledge in terms of achieving the goal of a practice, yet he was not, strictly speaking, a Buddhist. He viewed the Bhagavad Gita as the holy book containing the highest spiritual truths and India as the cradle of spirituality in the world; nevertheless he did not consider himself a Hindu. Salim liked to say he was not Christian, Buddhist, or Hindu, but Christian, Buddhist and Hindu all at once, as he did not want a label which locks one into an immediate mental pattern.

Knowledge acquired at school is a transmission of human experience which develops through time and space. Erudition stems from memory; scientific knowledge calls for discursive intelligence—it is a kind of knowledge which is acquired by the "expansion" of learning. If someone studies mathematics and physics, he will follow the intellectual approach leading to the discoveries of the great scientists. Thus, these discoveries, translated into mathematical language, can be understood and subsequently transmitted to others.

It is a different matter when it comes to spiritual knowledge, which is acquired in discontinuous degrees, in leaps, not through an accumulation of data, but through a quality of experience. The path may be indicated, the means provided, but knowledge can only be grasped by a personal inner experience situated in other levels of consciousness.

Because this knowledge is independent of the senses, it is accessible independently of any intellectual erudition; this is why Salim was able to access it without ever having been to school and without book-based education. It requires individual sincerity and intuition and can be shared in words only up to a certain point; achieving it requires a personal effort which cannot be made for somebody else.

*   *   *

In Asia, it is often thought that having a fortunate destiny, good health, material success, renown, and success in one's undertakings is the result of "good karma". Yet, are not external and internal ordeals greater sources of awakening and maturity than an existence in which everything is easy, comfortable, and seemingly favorable?

Salim's life was extremely difficult and his spiritual achievements out of the ordinary. At the age of twenty-five, Salim had already attained the maturity brought about by suffering. He had suffered physically and morally since his childhood: physically, through knowing poverty, hunger, cold and, above all, through having been ill practically all his life; morally, through being subject to constant fear during his childhood, including his parents' continual arguments, then, at the age of nineteen, the trauma of the war for five years, the attacks on his music, its destruction, and solitude on the spiritual path. The fact of having been everywhere, throughout his existence, regarded as a foreigner, the fact that he had not been to school and that he did not know how to cope in the outside world, made life especially hard for him; it drew down upon him the scorn of people around him, sometimes even of those who were very close to him; all this, Salim lived through and overcame, thanks to the powerful spiritual experiences which lined his route.

He mentions, in his books, the necessity for an aspirant on the Path to become an extreme being; we will see the extent to which he himself was one. Possessing the rare ability to devote himself to anything he did with the passion of a great artist, he could have made Gustav Mahler's words his own: "I don't like those who grow slack, only those who push themselves interest me." He was a passionate being who gave himself to what he was doing, "with the whole of himself," composing, playing the violin, conducting, writing, teaching, and, of course, in his meditation, everything was an aid to, or an opportunity for, practice and spiritual experiences.

Salim was the living proof that it is possible not to be emotionally involved while being warm and attentive—warm and attentive because he was available in the present. He had succeeded in channeling and mastering his extremely sensitive and extremely emotional artist's temperament, thus enabling a feeling of intense reverence for the Sacred and infinite compassion for his fellow human beings to germinate within him. The desire to help others had become an integral part of his nature. If one sees somebody drowning, one keeps trying to offer a lifebelt to him; this is what Salim did to try to awaken seekers from the waking-sleep in whose depths they were plunged. He strove to share with them the pressing need to follow the path, and the seriousness such an approach implies.

This predominance of inner life over external life gave him a knowledge of the human being such that it was enough for him to see someone for a moment to know their spiritual potential. On the other hand, he lacked practical knowledge about the material world to an extent that is difficult to imagine. As he did not know how to cope with external life, he was disarmed, vulnerable in the face of life's demands, not only in our modern society, but even in the East. Therefore, he candidly admired, in others, their ordinary capacities to respond to the outside world.

Why did Edward Salim Michael experience such a difficult destiny? Is it necessary to suffer as he suffered in order to know and understand what he knew and understood? After reading about such a trying life, this is a question which naturally comes to the reader's mind.

Here is the response Salim gave to this question about the trials he had experienced in his life:

"In the past, people have said to me, 'it's your karma', in other words,

I had committed some foolishness in the past and, for that reason, I was to be 'punished' by the suffering I endure in this life.

"People do not understand the word, karma; did Christ commit foolishness in a former life to be crucified? Was this his 'karma'? Can that be said? And how many great mystics have had very hard lives?

"No, these are things one cannot ordinarily understand. Sometimes, before birth, one finds oneself before a fork in the road: either one has a normal life with normal difficulties and spiritual evolution will be slower, or one will experience great difficulties which will greatly accelerate this particular evolution which is the only thing that counts. And there are people who have something within them saying: yes, I am ready to do anything; I am ready to do anything for That, and, without even realizing it, like a spirited horse, they choose the second path."

If one examines the journey of the Buddha (who said, "I attained the goal after so much effort"), Milarepa (whose "meditation cushion did not grow cold"), Ramana Maharshi (who spoke of "the Herculean effort required to master urges to exteriorize"), Madame Guyon (whose entire path was to practice the annihilation of the self), and other great mystics, one is forced to admit that attaining spiritual heights is no easy task and that it requires extraordinary determination and self-sacrifice.

Salim was filled with the sense of mystery, with a state of questioning which he kept alive until his last day, with wonder before the Incommensurable, with deep reverential respect, and with absolute sincerity. Perhaps his destiny will lead readers to feel that life is infinitely more mysterious than they suspected.

Michèle Michael

THE BEGINNING OF THE PATH

LONDON – DECEMBER, 1949

His host showed him into a small room where stood a magnificent statue of the Buddha in the meditation posture, which was over a meter tall. The cleverly positioned lighting fell on his head, inlaid in the Indian style with small, sparkling, colored stones, which seemed to be swathed in a mysterious glow. The face with closed eyes radiated unutterable serenity and peace.

This vision impressed Salim to the greatest extent imaginable; he remained transfixed in front of the statue for a long moment, while Mr. Adie, who had not failed to notice Salim's deep emotion, stayed silently by his side. On returning home, Salim felt the irresistible need to put himself into the same posture as this Buddha, a posture he adopted without difficulty, and, with his eyes closed, he began to focus on a sound he heard inside his ears and head, without even knowing that what he was doing was called meditation.

He sensed that another world had just opened up to him. Since his childhood in Baghdad, he had carried within himself a burning inner questioning which, until that time, had remained unanswered.

Years later, when recalling the power of the impact this statue had upon him, Salim would say: "There is no doubt that a silent memory without words or images, coming from a spiritual practice already undertaken in a previous life, awoke within me, irresistibly impelling me to sit, and it guided me, particularly in that I took, as an aid to concentration, an inner sound that I discovered much later to be known in India by the name of Nada (Nada-Yoga)."

Chapter 1

A Childhood and Adolescence
in the East: 1921-1940

My favorite story.

"Please tell me my favorite story again; you know which one..." the little boy begged his grandmother. The grandmother replied: "But I've already told it to you, what more can I say?" Sitting at her feet, Salim seized her hand and, raising his head towards her, reiterated his request: "It doesn't matter, grandmother, tell it to me again please, I want to hear it again!" She always gave in in the end and started once again the story of the outstanding man who was his great-great uncle, which the young boy never tired of wanting to hear again.

He was, apparently, a great mystic immensely rich, who spent his days in meditation. He was extremely good and very generous; his servants adored him. Twice a week he hired cooks and treated all the beggars of Baghdad who came to his home throughout the day, in a seemingly interminable procession, to a meal. When one among them died, he would personally go and collect the body; he would wash it, carry out the funeral toilette, and bury it with his own hands.

Ordinarily, he would stay in a small room at the top of his vast dwelling. He would shut himself in for hours on end, with orders that he should not be disturbed under any circumstances and that, in any case, no-one was to enter without first knocking. One day, one of the servants, forgetting the rule, inadvertently opened the door and found the room completely immersed in a supernatural light, which frightened her so much that she fainted. The poor girl was terrified and, subsequently, never wanted to approach that part of the house again.

When, having become a centenarian, this great-great uncle felt his end drawing near, he summoned all his descendants, including those who lived in various far-away places. At that time, when it was necessary to contact a relative who lived far away, the only way of doing so was to dispatch messengers who travelled relatively slowly. It took nine months for the whole family to be assembled. The reunion took place in the inner garden, decorated with refreshing fountains which embellish the sumptuous homes of the East. When everybody stood attentively around him, this exceptional man calmly dictated his last wishes, fairly distributing a share of his immense fortune to each person in the presence of the others. He forgot no-one, including the servants, even granting them enough to support themselves until the end of their lives. Finally, when he had bequeathed all his possessions, he asked his wife to come and sit at his side on the divan and, in front of the entire intrigued gathering, who did not understand his attitude, he lay down, rested his head on his wife's knees, closed his eyes, then, with a strange smile upon his lips, he peacefully expired. His face reflected such serenity that it filled those who came to pay homage to him with wonder.

The whole town knew of his reputation for holiness and all the religious denominations mixed together attended his funeral. One can imagine the distress and sadness of all those people, of whom there were so many in Baghdad, whom life had not favored and who, for so many years, had benefitted from the boundless kindness of this extraordinary character.

This story fascinated Salim beyond all measure. Afterwards, he would go and hide himself in a secret nook to dream of the strange destiny of this admirable being and the mystery of the spiritual call.

The meeting of his parents in Baghdad – Salim's birth in England.

Following the break-up of the Ottoman Empire at the end of the First World War, Iraq found itself under British mandate. India was still the jewel of the Empire; Gandhi had already attracted attention, but Europe wanted to continue believing in the perennial nature of its colonial conquests. During that period, a cosmopolitan community comprising a mixture of Easterners and Westerners of various nationalities was living in Baghdad. It was in this particular atmosphere that Salim's parents met.

His mother, named Flora, was the next to last of thirteen children; she belonged to a well-off family of Anglo-Indian merchants originally from Bombay* who had settled in Baghdad. (Her own mother was from Poona, a city located around a hundred kilometers from Bombay where Salim would subsequently spend several years.) She was a young girl of great beauty, very much a dreamer and completely ignorant of the necessities of life. At that time, girls received little or no schooling; so she dreamed of her marriage, played with her sisters, and occasionally learnt a little French from some friends. So, she led a pleasant life and could not imagine the difficulties that awaited her. She fell in love with a young man of limited means, who also had the misfortune of a limp. The family vigorously opposed their union, preferring a wealthy suitor, far older than she, with a fine bearing, cultivated, and speaking several languages. The young girl complied and married the husband who had been chosen for her.

Salim's father, who was in his forties, had travelled extensively and spent a long time in the West, particularly in France. He was working in Baghdad when, as the years were passing, he decided to start a family, captivated by the graceful beauty of this fifteen-year-old girl. The new couple settled in the Iraqi capital. The young bride soon found herself pregnant. In Iraq, particularly in Baghdad, hygiene conditions were appalling: garbage, never collected, accumulated in the streets and a host of rats fed off it. The narrow alleys of the old city hardly ever saw the sun. With the exception of the main avenues, open sewers ran through trenches dug on either side of the road, giving off a terrible stench in the summer heat and attracting flies and red cockroaches which inevitably spread into the dwellings. Furthermore, at that time (according to what Salim later learned from his mother), the region

---

* Bombay was rebaptized Mumbai in 1995.

Salim's parents in England
1921

was not provided with hospitals. The mother-to-be was terrified at the thought of giving birth in such conditions and asked her husband to take her to England, where his brothers and sister lived, and where she knew sanitary conditions to be far better. Therefore, they went to Great Britain, where they moved in with her husband's sister.

The young sixteen-year-old Oriental felt terribly disoriented and disconcerted in this family with its very British manners, who did not understand her and, taking offence at her lack of manners, were unduly hard and cold towards her. Feeling deeply depressed and lonely, she cried incessantly in her room throughout her entire pregnancy, desperately feeling the absence of her own mother at such a critical time.

Salim was born in Manchester on November 30, 1921. It proved to be an extremely difficult delivery, as if the child, anticipating the trials which would be his lot in the existence that lay ahead of him, did not want to come into the world. His mother gave birth later than normal, after a ten month gestation. She was young and slender; the baby was very large. After hours of suffering for the mother and child, the newborn gave all the signs of being lifeless; sacrificing him was contemplated in order to save the life of the poor woman who was growing dangerously weak. However, the doctor decided to make a final attempt: the child was resuscitated, and so these were the coerced and forced beginnings of Edward Salim Michael in this life. His mother called him by his second name, Salim, which means "he who came out safe and sound," and which would later be the name under which he wrote his books, whereas his musical works would be published under the name of Edward Michael—this first name having been chosen by his father.

A second son, Victor, was born three years later. The parents remained in Great Britain throughout this period, during which Salim's father blithely spent all the money he had earned in Iraq. With his savings dissipated, he needed to find work; he thought that this would be easier for him in Baghdad where he had connections. His wife was delighted to return to the East; her family lived there and England had hardly been welcoming to her. Therefore, they set off for the Middle-East without regret.

Return to Baghdad. Poverty.

Things did not go exactly as Salim's father had imagined. Having lost contact with his old associates, he encountered more difficulties than expected in finding work. He ended up getting a badly-paid job in a hotel. The family then experienced a period of extreme poverty: they lived in squalid housing and practically never ate enough to satisfy their hunger, their everyday fare, sometimes for months at a time, reduced to a plate of rice and zucchini, for lunch and dinner.

There were frequent arguments in the house; Salim's mother bitterly recalled the happy days of her adolescence and, remembering the man she had not been able to marry, she reproached this husband who was imposed upon her with despair for the odious situation he had put her in with two children. The latter were witness to the lack of compassion which can arise in a couple, especially when separation is inconceivable. Their mother could not have managed alone in a country such as Iraq; what would she have done? In such places, there were no family benefits or any type of aid. Knowing herself to be a prisoner, she felt resentment which made her life, as well as that of the other members of the family, even harder to bear.

That time still evoked in Salim the memory of a worrying night when his father held him by the hand, followed by his mother and brother. They were walking in the streets of Baghdad not knowing where to sleep. His mother was crying and berating her husband; the two frightened children remained silent. Finally, they approached a police station and asked whether they could settle themselves near the entrance to avoid being attacked while they were sleeping.

A fascination with the stars.

Salim's life was unfolding at that time amidst deprivation and fear, while, at the same time, providing a wealth of profound, picturesque impressions, imparting curious premonitions to him now and then, which awoke in him he knew not what long distant enigmatic memory. In the mornings, when the sun rose and small pink clouds formed and then swiftly vanished, or at dusk, when the sky was spectacularly set aglow, the young boy experienced strange, troubling feelings that he was unable to describe, before the beauty of infinite space.

In the East, because of the heat, the houses, at that time, had flat roofs on which it was usual to sleep in the summer, despite the mosquitoes which feasted relentlessly. Before he fell asleep, Salim would gaze at the stars which shone softly above his head and he would feel embraced by an indefinable emotion. Fascinated, he contemplated the unfathomable depth of the darkness and the sparkling limpidity of the stars which seemed to deliver a message to him which he believed he alone understood.

His parents did not practice any religious rites; nevertheless, he was immersed in an atmosphere where references to God were omnipresent. Five times a day, the muezzin called the faithful to turn towards Allah, the All-Compassionate. Any greeting between neighbors or even mere acquaintances had to begin with an extremely long invocation of Heaven's blessings on the various members of the family. Hence, the reality of the Divine Presence was a matter of course for everybody.

As Salim had a naturally devotional temperament, every evening after a glance to make sure that the other members of the household were already asleep, he sat on his bed and, brushing his lips with his fingertips, blew God tender kisses. He would continue this unusual ritual for several minutes, sometimes as much as half an hour, until he finally felt that this time, the kiss was true, that it was, as it should be, conveyed with the whole of himself. Then, pleased with having done what was necessary, he would go back to bed and fall asleep.

A childhood under the sign of fear and death.

Baghdad was a fascinating but frightening city. At every moment, one was in contact with dangers of all kinds, which could prove fatal.

Over the years that the family spent in this city, they moved frequently, renting a small, Eastern-style, flat-roofed house for a while. However, the young woman's beauty aroused too much covetousness in the men of the neighborhood. As she was not a Muslim, she did not wear the hijab, and, as her husband was absent all day, the risk of her being assaulted was constant. The poor woman lived in permanent terror. When, after a certain time spent in one place, she started to feel too threatened, they would leave and settle in another neighborhood.

This constant fear that dwelt within her, she felt as much for her children as for herself. Indeed, the family also had to move to avoid Victor, then aged five, becoming the victim of a neighbor who had already tried to assault him sexually. His parents did not press charges because they would have been risking the man killing the entire family in retaliation.

Most Arabs, including children, were armed with knives. It often took little for one of them, believing he had been insulted, to take out his weapon and stab the unwary person without further ado. One constantly heard of missing children, young girls abducted, to be found raped and murdered, kidnappings, homicides, and so on.

Unless important people were involved, the police did not concern themselves with pursuing criminals, who, consequently, knew that their impunity was practically guaranteed, especially if they attacked ethnic or religious minorities. As a result, a group of young thugs lured a ten-year-old Armenian boy into an ambush and odiously battered and raped him without being worried in the slightest. Following this evil deed, these good-for-nothings, whose brutish force invoked fear in everyone who crossed their path, continued to parade around the area, without any shame.

With this background of constant danger, it was important for the children not to be seen as foreigners. Therefore, so that they would have a better chance of defending themselves if they were attacked, especially if they were on their own, only the local dialect was spoken at home, with the result that neither of the two sons ever benefited from their father's knowledge of languages.

Once, Salim's brother Victor, who was four years old at the time, got lost in the souqs. It was rare to recover a lost child. The parents, plunged into a state of extreme distress, paid criers to go across the market calling for the little boy. Salim, who was three years older, shared the anguish of his mother and father and trembled at the thought of never seeing his brother again. By some miracle, he was found. This event marked Salim deeply, imprinting him with a long-lasting fear regarding the dangers of the outside world.

On a number of occasions, in their successive homes, Salim's parents made a hiding place in a wall; they rehearsed putting him in there with his brother, giving him, as the elder of the two, explicit instructions. They told him that if they thought it necessary, they would put both of them into the hiding place and that under no circumstances were they to come out, even if they heard chilling cries from their father and mother, followed by a worrying silence. The six-year-old child who was being given such instructions wondered with anguish in the darkness of his hiding place: "But, if something terrible happens to my parents, where will I go?" This fear tormented him: "I wouldn't know where to go with my little brother if my parents were killed!"

Eastern-style mourning. A dangerous game. Public hanging.

Unlike the customs which prevail in the West, death was not concealed; it was omnipresent. One night, the family was woken with a jolt by the piercing, distraught cries coming from a neighboring dwelling where some Christian Armenians lived. A woman had died and the other female inhabitants of the house were expressing their despair in the Eastern way, that is, howling and pulling out their hair. These extremely intense displays would extend well beyond the funeral. At a burial, which for climatic reasons took place a few hours after the death, it was common to hear the funeral procession from a long way off due to the noisy lamentation of the bereaved who threw themselves onto the coffin. Some of them even wanted to take their own lives and had to be prevented from doing so by force. On that occasion, to avoid the children being witness to all this painful emotional outpouring, their mother took them to spend the next day with friends who lived in another neighborhood.

One day, as Salim was playing in the narrow alley next to where they were living at the time, he found a long, brand-new, wooden box, deposited not far from their home. He was enthusiastically playing at jumping onto it when his mother caught sight of him and shouted, "You wretch, it's a coffin; it's already got a body in it! If someone sees you, they'll cut you to pieces!" The child was paralyzed with terror, so much so that he could not get down from the funeral casket. In a single movement, his mother rushed towards him, took him in her arms and dashed into the house. By an amazing stroke of luck, no-one had seen them. As, in addition to this, the house was extremely insalubrious, the family left not long afterwards; it was to collapse on the new occupants three months later.

One day, when Salim was barely six years old, he was walking down the street at his father's side when his father suddenly started trying to attract Salim's attention. Feeling that this behavior was meant to prevent him from seeing something, the young boy became even more curious and, turning his head, discovered the spectacle of three bodies swinging at the end of a rope. The three men had been hanged in accordance with English custom and the corpses were left for thirty-six hours to be exhibited as an example. The hanging had been carried out by the sudden opening of a trap-door beneath the three corpses; consequently, the cervical vertebrae had been broken; their heads were tilted to one side at a strange angle, their eyes were rolled upwards, and their necks had been stretched into a grisly strip at least twenty centimeters long. The child remained haunted by the image of these three hanged men, whose bodies swayed slightly and turned in the wind from time to time. This sight impressed upon him a feeling of horror, which was later revived when he found himself confronted by the same horrifying scene on a number of occasions.

Thus, Salim's childhood unfolded in a somber atmosphere where the unexpected was very often a source of anxiety.

The River Tigris. An angelic presence. The murdered lover.

The young Salim was of a tranquil and solitary disposition. When his family lived for a while near the great River Tigris, he got into the habit of spending his days at the water's edge untiringly observing the permanent spectacle which played out there: the boats which came and went from one bank to the other; the large boats whose sails were rhythmically hauled in by groups of Arabs and Blacks; the animals that came to drink at sunset following and jostling each other in a picturesque parade of camels, cows, donkeys, and sheep. The river sometimes carried putrefied carcasses which infected the water and, without realizing it, Salim was given a lesson on the impermanence of existence and of all living creatures.

Often, while he spent hours contemplating the swaying of the palm trees in the breeze or the movement of the iridescent water whose wavelets broke on the grassy bank, an enigmatic silence flooded his being, arousing within him the impression that an angel stood behind him, observing him with infinite goodness. He was convinced of the presence of this celestial entity with whom he felt he had a particular relationship, which he would have been unable to explain. He saw her in his mind, always clad in a floating dress of a delicate sky-blue hue, with wings of the same color.

It was undoubtedly the memory of these hours spent listening to the lapping of the river's waters which provided him with the inspiration for one of the twelve spiritual tales included in his last book, Du fond des Brumes (From the Depths of the Mist).

While his brother had found some little playmates, Salim liked to remain alone near the river, even hiding when his mother called him for lunch. Tired of not getting a response, she eventually accepted that she would not see him come back until dusk, which did not prevent her from worrying about him with, it should be said, good reason. One day, when seven-year-old Salim was tranquilly walking by the water's edge with his young brother, an individual of about thirty, seeing that they were alone, suddenly pulled out, from beneath his djellaba, a knife which seemed enormous to the two little boys who owed their salvation only to the unexpected arrival of some kind Arab neighbors towards whom they ran.

On another occasion, while they were walking along the river bank with their mother in the scorching heat, they persistently complained of thirst, as children do. After their mother had tried in vain to reason with them, she reluctantly decided to ask for a little water from a local inhabitant who was outside on his doorstep. He immediately started to hurl abuse at her and, at that moment, Salim felt with a shock the fear that gripped his mother. She grabbed them by the hands and ran away, knowing that the man could throw them into the river or stab them without any passer by coming to their assistance.

As summer progressed, the river's water level would drop and small islands would emerge. Sometimes, rich Arabs gave parties on them. They went there in kouffas, a sort of small, round, tarred boat, steered with a boathook. They had food, musicians and dancers brought to the islands. Servants caught large freshwater fish, called "shabbout", for the occasion, which they split in two and grilled over a wood fire. At night, the glow of the braziers and the shadows of the dancers could be seen; the warm breeze carried the heady scents and the sound of the piercing chords of Oriental music, which Salim listened to with fascination.

One day, while he was contemplating the river as usual, Salim heard screams coming from the other bank. A teenager had had the misfortune to fall in love with a young girl from a clan other than his own and had ventured into her territory to catch a glimpse of his beloved who, in return, was smitten by him. The poor boy had just been taken by surprise and some furious men from the young girl's clan were chasing him. He hastily jumped into the water to escape them; the pursuers then took a kouffa and worked to bring the boat level with him. Having caught him, they beat him ruthlessly with planks until he lost consciousness and sank. In the meantime, on the bank, the women, who had feverishly watched the unfolding of this drama, let out strident cries of, "youh-youh" to express their joy in knowing that the young man had drowned. Transfixed, Salim witnessed this tragedy, his heart in his mouth.

Death of a dog. Artistic interests. Marriage of a little girl.

Salim's mother once again felt threatened by the covetousness of the men of the neighborhood; the family moved far away from the river and the child's escapades were at an end. From then on, he stayed in the house and spent his days in his bedroom, sitting by the window. One day, he noticed one of those poor scrawny stray dogs, frequently encountered in the East. Nobody cares about their fate; on the contrary, people throw stones at them as soon as they see them. The young boy befriended the animal, giving it his meager meal unbeknownst to his mother, until the day when a local police officer, having noticed the dog's regular passage in that area, pulled out a gun and shot it right in front of the horrified little boy. The poor animal's death throes lasted ten interminable minutes, during which its paws convulsed spasmo-dically. The policeman, who was proud of himself and his work, put his foot on the still-warm body while admiring onlookers gathered around him. Salim, his heart crushed by grief, looked upon the lifeless remains of his friend. All his life, he retained the image of that poor skeletal animal, whimpering in the dust before breathing its last.

Salim's artistic temperament pushed him towards drawing, which he adored. Not having any materials available to him, he discovered that crushing the small dark red carrots which grew in those regions enabled him to draw a line on the walls. So, he began surreptitiously to steal these vegetables from his mother and to practice his art everywhere, including on the walls of their house. His father quickly put an end to this unusual use of family provisions and, subsequently the budding artist had to make do with drawing on the dusty ground using anything he could find.

The family moved again. One of the dwelling's windows overlooked the courtyard of another house occupied by Arabs. Salim would see the women quarrelling among themselves there all day long and falling silent in fear when their husband came home. They lived in dread of being repudiated and thrown out onto the street with their children, at any moment, with no means to support themselves, while their lord and master wed a younger wife.

A marriage of this type took place in the neighborhood between an old man of over sixty and a little girl of eight. Salim, who heard the poor child crying out and sobbing throughout the wedding night, could not forget her wild look when he passed her in the street a short while later.

The chaikhanas. Beggars in Baghdad.

After years of effort, Salim's father took on new duties at the hotel and earned a better living. Conditions became less difficult for his family. Sometimes, he took the children in turns to the restaurant or the "chaikhanas," a sort of Arab café, where he showed them proudly to his acquaintances.

It was always a celebration for Salim when his father took him along. He particularly liked a chaikhana located by the Tigris. He derived unadulterated pleasure from observing the comings and goings of the waiters, the customers who tranquilly savored their "kahwa" (coffee), as well as the colorful, noisy crowd thronging in the neighboring street; furthermore, they played Arab music there which Salim always delighted in.

When he brought Salim with him, his father generally took a cab drawn by two horses which was the habitual means of transport in Baghdad in those days. Passengers were protected from the fierce heat of the sun by a canopy, but this was not the case for the poor animals who had to wait patiently for customers, sometimes for hours at a time, under the blazing sun, without their owner even giving them a little water to drink. These unfortunate beasts, the majority of whom were skeletally thin, were in a pitiful condition. When they did not go as fast as their master wanted, he would become angry and start to whip them hard to make them trot more quickly. Salim, who could not bear this cruelty, timidly asked his father to intercede with the coachman to treat his horses more gently. However, this request, on most occasions, was only rewarded with a stream of abuse from the driver, while he redoubled his blows to the flanks of his exhausted animals.

The Arabs very much appreciated the company of Salim's father. When he was with them, he had a manner of being that captivated the young boy. He discoursed and joked with them in a way that charmed them, adopting a demeanor that the child never saw in him at home, which was only a place of perpetual quarrels.

In the Middle East, custom dictates that parents are given the name of their eldest son. Hence, the Arabs called Salim's father, "Abou

Salim" and his mother "Oum Salim"—a custom which is psychologically devastating for the other sons, not to mention the daughters who have, so to speak, no recognized existence.

Salim was delighted by these excursions where he received impressions different from those of his everyday life in the family environment. He remained very quiet at the side of this elegant, jovial man, fascinated to see him laughing, enjoying himself, gambling in various games, telling stories that his Arab friends loved to hear; and in their turn, they would begin to recount all sorts of colorful anecdotes with typically Eastern loquacity.

Life was hard and pitiless in Baghdad: many destitute people roamed the streets calling on the charity of passers by. On one of these occasions, when Salim's father took him to lunch with him, as they arrived at the door of a restaurant renowned for its cuisine, two famished beggars, one about the same age as Salim and the other barely any older, ran towards them. The younger one, with all his limbs trembling, caught hold of Salim's arm. With an imploring look, they begged pitifully to be given a little food to eat. Not knowing what to do or say, Salim stood stock-still, transfixed, when the owner of the restaurant came out into the doorway and brutally chased them away.

As Salim was frozen to the spot, his father pulled him inside. Incapable of understanding why he could not share the food on his own plate with them and still feeling the child's trembling hand on his arm, he swallowed a few small mouthfuls of food with difficulty, while his father, not realizing his son's emotion, insistently encouraged him to eat the delicious meal that had been served for him.

Salim's father, who often reminisced nostalgically about the luxury of the years before his marriage, dreamed of returning to the affluence he had enjoyed at that time. In the hope of regaining this standard of living, he had been seized with a passion for gambling. He was finally tempted into purchasing three thoroughbred race horses, on whose acquisition he squandered a substantial sum of money. One rainy day, after a violent storm that had transformed the streets into torrents of mud, one of the horses slipped and fractured its pelvis. Everything possible was tried to save it, but, in the end, it had to be destroyed. Once again, Salim found himself confronted with suffering and death raising profound questions, to which no-one around him seemed able to respond.

His maternal grandmother. An attack of appendicitis.

Salim's maternal grandmother who had borne thirteen children, more than half of whom had died at a very young age, was separated from her husband; although the latter was a very wealthy man, he left her with no means of support. As she lived in extreme poverty Salim's mother tried to help her within the limits of her own ability to do so. When the professional situation of Salim's father improved and they were able to move into less cramped accommodation, they took her with them.

Salim loved her very much; she was very gentle and modest, as Indian women naturally are; she had a taciturn temperament and spoke very little, remembering, from time to time, with sadness and nostalgia, Bombay and her childhood in India.

Salim and his brother often fell ill; they caught, among other things, dysentery, a common and sometimes fatal pathology in countries with infected water and almost non-existent hygiene. When their mother saw them so ill, she would call a poor passer by, only too happy to offer small services for a little money, to carry them on his shoulders to the only doctor she knew in Baghdad, an Armenian who was a very kind man. It was necessary to wait several hours to see him, as a crowd flocked to his office. Patients had the habit of detailing, with a torrent of words and an overflowing of emotions typical of Eastern people, for the benefit of the other patients the afflictions that had brought them there; thus each of them shared the anxieties and the worries of all.

The doctor taught Salim's mother how to treat dysentery with a diet of yoghurt and white rice which proved to be fairly effective. As is often the case in hot countries, the two children would also regularly catch intestinal parasites which their mother would treat vigorously with laxative oil and a cure of onion and salt soups. In addition to these relatively benign illnesses, Salim also contracted serious illnesses, such as diphtheria and typhoid.

One day, the young boy began to complain of violent stomach pains. He had a very high fever and was delirious. The doctor immediately diagnosed an attack of acute appendicitis. At that time, there were no surgeons in Baghdad; the family would have had to go to Syria to find one, which would have meant a journey of at least forty hours. The doctor told Salim's father that there was no chance the child could hold on for so long. Time was of the essence. The pharmacist, who was a friend of the family and happened to be there, said to the distraught parents: "Listen, I've never operated on anyone, but I have studied anatomy extensively and I have a passion for surgery. If he is not operated on, your child will inevitably die; let me try!" Having no alternative recourse, the parents could not do other than agree albeit with extreme anguish. By some incredible miracle, the operation was a success. After the operation, Salim suffered from painful vomiting; his mother spent days and nights at his bedside while, lips dry and cracked from thirst, he deliriously begged in vain for water.

Beginning and end of schooling. A servant. Street storytellers.

At that time, children's toys could not be found for sale. Therefore, children were obliged to show some imagination. Victor, Salim's younger brother, proved to be extremely inventive in this regard and would make all sorts of objects which the two boys would sometimes play with together. He also displayed a gift for all things mechanical. Once, he took all the padlocks in the house apart to examine their mechanisms and understand how they worked. Of course, he was roundly told off, but, to everyone's astonishment, he succeeded quickly and without difficulty in reassembling them perfectly.

Although Salim and Victor's father was cultivated, as he was kept too busy by the necessity of earning a living and the incessant quarrels that transformed their home into a battlefield, he did not take the time to teach anything to his sons. Sometimes, when he was alone with them, he would teach them to read and write a few words of Arabic, but the two children were never able to acquire sufficient knowledge to be able to read books themselves. Apart from the Quranic schools of the mosques, there were no educational establishments. Nevertheless, their father found a small school run by orthodox nuns. In fact, it consisted of merely a single room in which twelve children, at most, from local Christian families, learned the rudiments of reading, writing, and arithmetic. Salim was delighted and the nuns adored him; he was naturally well behaved and studious. A few weeks after his arrival in this class, a bearded man wearing a tall black hat and a long black robe came to visit the school. Salim saw him talking to one of the sisters, pointing to him and looking at him in a hostile manner. Shortly afterwards, the sister approached him and told him, seemingly embarrassed, that she needed to speak to his father. To great sadness of the whole family, the two boys had to leave the school the next day. This was the first and only opportunity that Salim and his brother had of going to school.

The disparity in conditions between the rich who lived in luxury and the poor who were not even able to feed their children was very great. From time to time, a poor woman accompanied by a young girl aged around twelve, or sometimes even younger, would knock on the door of the family home asking if her child could be employed in exchange for a little food and a roof over her head. At that time, wages were derisory; servants were glad simply to be accommodated and fed; as for any meager salary they might receive, they would pay all of it over to their families in order to help them.

One day, a woman who was extremely impoverished asked Salim's parents to take her daughter, who was around seventeen years old, into their service. Salim's mother had known poverty too well herself not to feel compassion for this adolescent girl. As her husband's situation had sufficiently improved, she agreed to take the girl in. She knew that, without work, however modest it might be, the unfortunate girl would soon have no choice but to turn to prostitution to survive. The two boys quickly became attached to the young servant; she was extremely kind to them and obediently busied herself assisting their mother with the household chores. After only three months, while she was spending a few days with her family, she was suddenly taken ill and died in just a few hours without anybody ever knowing the cause. Salim and Victor, who had both become very fond of her, were very much affected by her death.

At that time in Baghdad, the only mode of escapism from day to day life were the evenings when professional storytellers would weave about their fascinated listeners the endless tales of the "Arabian Nights" or the countless stories about Mullah Nasreddin, a man both wise and mad, and famous throughout the Middle East. Salim loved listening to these storytellers. He would surreptitiously leave the house and slip silently into the circle of listeners, listening for all he was worth to the repertoire of moral, comic, absurd, but also, sometimes, very spiritual stories, with which he would later regale his students.

England. The Louvre. Return to Baghdad. Saint-Saëns.

After Salim's operation his mother, who had been convinced she was going to lose him, wanted to leave Baghdad for a more peaceful country with better healthcare facilities. She owned some jewelry* which she had bought with secretly-accumulated savings. One day she took it out and asked her husband to sell it to pay for their voyage to England (at that time by boat and train) where she believed her sons would be able to go to school and learn English. Salim was about eight years old at the time.

They passed through Paris, where their father took the children to the Louvre. Moving through the museum's rooms, they reached one lined with representations of a man nailed to a cross with blood running from his head, his hands, and his side. While his father passed tranquilly before these pictures, Salim felt himself seized by unutterable terror and asked himself: "But how can anyone do that to someone?" He retained a horrified memory of this; his father had not realized at all the effect that this sight had had on Salim.

Having arrived in London, they found accommodation on the second floor of a house, the first floor of which was occupied by a couple who also had two children. These children quickly made friends with Salim and Victor. From time to time, the two brothers would go and play in their friends' apartment, which had a piano. Salim was fascinated by this instrument, as well as by the phonograph on which he could listen to a few pieces of classical music recorded on wax cylinders.

Salim's memory for everything to do with music was quite remarkable. More than sixty years later, he happened to hear a piece of music on the radio, which, to his surprise, he recognized immediately as being one of those he had listened to in his neighbors' home in London when he was only eight years old. He did not know the name of the piece because it was one that is very rarely played; the program's presenter announced that it was the "Ballet Egyptien" by Alexandre Luigini who, apparently, was a brilliant student of Massenet's, but who has now practically fallen into obscurity.

The English episode would be of short duration, as, after a few months, the family was obliged to return to Baghdad. Salim's father, having gambled and lost all the money he possessed, believed he would find work there more easily than in Great Britain. In fact, he

---

* Jewelry in the Orient played a part that went beyond simple ornament. It was considered as a way to keep savings within easy reach and, particularly for the poorer classes who did not use the bank, it was a form of insurance against precarity.

did, by chance, find work with a British bus company, "The Nairn Transport Company", which operated the Baghdad to Damascus route. The buses, well equipped and luxurious for the time, could transport around a dozen passengers, mainly British or other Westerners, and their baggage. Sometimes, some of the passengers, weary at the end of a long journey undertaken in stifling heat, would get off the bus forgetting to take some of their possessions with them. The company would keep these objects for a year, after which time employees drew lots for them. It was in this way that, one day, Salim's father acquired a wind-up phonograph with classical music wax cylinders and needles that had to be changed after each use.

To his wonder, Salim heard an emotive voice emanating from the magical machine. It was a well known aria from the Saint-Saëns opera "Samson and Delilah", from the passage in which Delilah attempts to intoxicate Samson with words of love in order to draw from him the secret of his strength. For no apparent reason, Salim began to sob while listening to this music; he could not help wanting to listen to it again and again. He would later learn that it was this exact piece his mother had listened to many times while carrying him, during the time that she was so unhappy in England.

Among the other records were a number of works for violin, which Salim would play tirelessly. He had immediately been attracted to and seduced by the sound of this instrument. The performers, all famous virtuosos of the time, were called Kreisler, Heifetz and even Yehudi Menuhin who, at the age of fourteen, performed Max Bruch's concerto for violin and orchestra. While listening to this music, Salim would imagine himself in the role of the violinist, and would begin to depict the motions as if it was he who was playing. His father eventually said: "Maybe, one day, this boy will be a violinist."

Armenian massacres. Leaving Iraq.

Salim's father, who worked hard, was very much appreciated by the Englishman who owned the company. He was responsible for supervising the departure and arrival of every bus. The Baghdad-Damascus line, ran twice a week; departures were at six in the morning, meaning he had to leave home at four, while it was still dark. He had to make a forty minute journey on foot, through streets that often had little or no lighting, with the risks that implied in a country where murders were commonplace. Two evenings a week he also had to await the bus's return, and, consequently, returned home very late. The whole family, including Salim's maternal grandmother (who was now living with them) would be waiting in a state of dread. Salim's mother watched anxiously from the window so as to be sure she recognized her husband's clothes and gait in order to avoid opening the door to an intruder. A neighbor had once had the misfortune of opening the door too hastily to a prowler who had imitated her husband's voice and his manner of knocking at the door. The poor woman paid a heavy price for her mistake; she was raped before her throat was cut along with those of her children. In addition to all these dangers, it was not uncommon to find scorpions (whose stings were extremely dangerous) inside houses and sometimes even snakes.

Once again, Salim's father bought a horse and spent a lot of money on gambling. Fortunately, he was now earning a good living and his wife, without saying anything, was saving a little money when she had the chance, in readiness for any future difficulties. From time to time, he would take his oldest son to the races when his horse was running. The racecourse was an exclusive place, mostly frequented by the British; a brass band led by an English conductor would play overtures from famous operas and, while his father feverishly followed the race, the child, enthralled, would listen to the music.

Iraq had been under British mandate since 1920. Faisal I had become king in 1921. The country gained its independence in 1932. The king fell ill at that very time and left to undergo medical treatment in England where he died in 1933. His son Ghazi, hostile to the British and a fervent supporter of Arab nationalism, succeeded him. Immediately, horrific massacres of Armenians were perpetrated in the north of Iraq, where men, women, and children were exterminated. In Baghdad itself, bloodthirsty hordes hunted down anyone who might be Armenian, Jewish, or simply a foreigner, Westerner or not. A member of the neighboring Indian family was stabbed in the street. Salim and his family, terrified, owed their salvation only to some Arab friends. They trembled even more, retrospectively, when they discovered, over the following days, the spectacle of horror presented by some areas of the city. Salim's mother, taking out her meager savings, said to her husband: "We have escaped it, but we risk being murdered at every moment; let us leave this country, which is no longer under British mandate, before it is too late." Neighboring Syria, which was still under French administration, seemed safer. The whole family, grandmother included, and their baggage crossed the desert in a small rental car, all piled on top of each other.

Damascus, Alexandria, Palestine, Lebanon.

In Damascus, Salim discovered with wonder abundant vegetation, very different to that of Baghdad. The beauty of the mountain peaks standing out against the horizon remained engraved upon his memory. Despite all his efforts, Salim's father was unable to find work in Syria, so he decided to try his luck in Egypt. Therefore, the family set off for Alexandria and then went on to Cairo. Some evenings Salim's father would take him to the "chaikhanas," where he would talk with the Arabs and gamble for long hours, while his son watched him constantly, admiring unreservedly the way he joked with the Egyptian friends he was able to make so quickly and easily. He walked with such a naturally fine bearing that he never failed to attract looks from passers by. Thus, Salim felt extremely proud to be at his side.

His father became friends with an Egyptian who suggested they start a small business together in Palestine. Salim's mother, still concerned for the family's security, persuaded him to accept the offer which constituted an opportunity to settle in a region still under British rule and, therefore, likely to be safer. During their stay in Palestine, they moved constantly, from Haifa to Jaffa to Tel Aviv.

At the top of Mount Carmel, overlooking Haifa, stands the magnificent "Baha'i" temple, which has become the holy place of this religion, whose origins are in Islam and whose founders were two Shi'ite Iranians from the nineteenth century. Baha'is believe that religious truth is not absolute, but relative, that all the great religions are divine in their origins and that their goal is identical. This faith, which is now established in many countries, is considered by Islam to be heretical. From its beginnings, tens of thousands of believers have been executed in Iran where they continue to be persecuted today.

At that time, Haifa was still only a small town principally made up of two main streets cut into the mountainside and surrounded by olive plantations. The safety that the family was able to find there proved to be very much relative, as, one day, Salim, who was about twelve years old, went far enough from the house to find himself in an isolated spot where three men were busy digging the foundations of a new house. In a moment of inattention, he stumbled and fell into the excavation where the three men were working. In an instant, one of them rushed at him raising his pickaxe to smash Salim's head, looking at him with eyes that were cold and filled with inexplicable hatred, while one of the other two workers hurriedly exclaimed: "The poor kid, leave him alone, leave him alone!" Still fixing his potential victim with a merciless stare, the man slowly lowered his arm. Salim did not understand what force had stayed the murderous hand of this individual, who could so easily have killed and buried him in this deserted place without anyone ever knowing what had become of him. This dramatic incident and his assailant's icy stare would mark him indelibly.

This young boy, who was a dreamer and very sensitive, thus grew up in an atmosphere imbued with fear, traces of which remained with him throughout his life, even in the West, where the conditions of daily existence are nevertheless significantly different.

Music would beckon him from time to time, secretly calling to him. In Haifa, a neighbor had noticed Salim's fascination for this art, and when he was able to tune into the broadcast of a symphony or an opera on a European radio station, he would turn up the volume on his radio. While his family slept, Salim would stay on the balcony for hours on end, sometimes late into the night, listening to this music which invoked elevated and very troubling emotions within him.

In the neighborhood, a few music lovers had formed a small amateur classical orchestra and, for the first time in his life, Salim saw and heard a real band playing before him. He remained fascinated by this universe that had opened up to him, discovering, with wonder, the different instruments, especially the oboe, which, perhaps due to its oriental sound, particularly moved him.

His father bought him, at a public auction, a very cheap, old violin on which the young boy tried, in vain, to practice alone. His parents asked a violinist from the neighborhood, who played in the cafés, to give him some lessons. However, this apprenticeship was short lived, as, once again, the family had to move.

The majority of the Jews who were living in Palestine at that time were refugees who had principally come from Europe. They were, for the most part, extremely cultured but, to survive, had to take on manual work, as bricklayers, road-menders, or farmers. Among them were a number of scientists, artists, doctors, musicians, and poets. Due to the political situation at the time, foreigners were considered with suspicion and Salim's family was no exception; therefore it was not possible for them to integrate.

His business being far from as successful as he had hoped, Salim's father decided, after around two years, to try his luck in Lebanon. He knew a great deal about oriental carpets and resolved to go into that trade, but, once more, the business proved unprofitable. The family moved again to Jordan, then to Egypt, and once more to Palestine. Every move necessitated quickly learning to speak the local dialect and becoming familiar with the customs and way of life of each new place. Hence, Salim could not help keenly sensing the uncertainty and precarity of their existence.

Inner conflicts.

When he talked about this period, which saw him pass from childhood into adolescence, Salim would admit that it was a turbulent time for him and difficult to bear within himself. His parents' continual quarrels and the horrific stories that he constantly heard told around him made him more and more depressed.

The news that an exceptionally beautiful and fragile young woman, whom Salim knew, had been raped made a frightening impression on him. Following this drama, the victim had lost her mind and had to be committed to a psychiatric asylum. She was married and the mother of two children; it was sad to witness the grief that afflicted her whole family. Those establishments for the mentally ill that existed in that part of the world at the time were extremely dirty and badly maintained, not to mention the atmosphere that must have reigned within.

The stories of kidnapping and rape that Salim had heard incessantly since his early childhood, in the end, left an oppressive impression on him. He was now coming to the age of sexual awakening. However, these tragic stories and the committal of the young woman created, within him, an inner conflict. He called into question this aspect of nature which seemed incomprehensible to him both through the strength of its demands as well as the way in which certain people responded to it without worrying in the slightest about the consequences of their actions on their victims.

In addition to this questioning and these painful events, there reigned at that time, over the whole of this troubled region, an oppressive climate of permanent menace, which contributed to the worsening depressive state that was taking hold of Salim.

Salim 17 years old

Continual questions arose within him, without, for all that, receiving any response. He wondered keenly whether he had already existed before his birth and, if so, where he originally came from. He contemplated the meaning of physical existence, always at the mercy of unforeseen disasters and death, and about the fact that, despite the compassion and charity spoken of by the religions, atrocities were endlessly committed all around him. He could not help saying to himself: "Does God really exist?"

He was tormented by doubt, despite the inexplicable feelings of spiritual elevation that seized him at times to such an extent as to astonish him. Where did these feelings come from? Why could he not prevent himself from experiencing these devotional surges, in spite of these uncertainties which continued to arise within him and trouble him? He knew that it was of no use to talk to his parents about the many questions that were arising within him and disorienting him. They seemed unable to answer or, rather, the kinds of answers they had given him in the past had left him more perplexed than ever.

Having reached adolescence, Salim remained reserved. His health had improved considerably over the years and he had become surprisingly strong physically. Sometimes, during these perpetual peregrinations, he would come across some other boys here and there, who, to their surprise, even in a group of three or four, were unable to knock down this shy boy who would stand firmly upright, legs slightly apart, surprised by his own strength.

As business was still going badly, his mother who, as soon as she had succeeded in saving a little of money, had purchased some pieces of jewelry, took out her meager reserves once again so that the family could travel to England. Salim's maternal grandmother, who had always followed the family whenever they moved, did not want to go to the West where she knew she would find herself even more out of place. She decided to stay with another of her daughters.

Salim's father, who was no longer young, encountered difficulties in finding work, as Europe was then undergoing a severe economic crisis. Therefore, after having searched in vain for a job in Great Britain, he had to resolve himself to leaving his wife and children and setting out alone back to the Near East. He was able to send a little money from time to time, allowing them to survive, as best they could, for a few months until the time he joined them in London shortly before war broke out.

Salim had just turned eighteen. He felt completely out of place in a country where he understood neither the language, nor the extremely reserved attitude of its people. The reasoning and thought processes of Westerners were completely foreign to him. The climate, customs and atmosphere were too different to those of the East, a world that was both fascinating and terrifying, but one in which he had spent the whole of his childhood. As he was unable to read and write— something that had hardly bothered him until now—how would he be perceived by the English, especially in view of the fact that he also had Indian blood?

Chapter 2

England: 1940-1949.

The shock of military life.

After the poverty that had so often been the lot of his family in the East, after having escaped death many times, Salim was not, for all that, prepared for the shock he would undergo when, at the end of 1940, having just turned nineteen, he found himself, as a British citizen, enlisted in the ground staff of the Royal Air Force.

Having only been in Great Britain for a few months, he still spoke English very badly. When he presented himself at his stationing on his first day, Salim didn't understand the words of the sergeant who, for no apparent reason, was shouting ferociously at all the new arrivals. Salim then had to undergo a medical which took place with a lack of privacy that embarrassed him enormously. Then he had to immediately learn his regimental number by heart. He was asked to sign some forms and he had to admit, to his shame, that he did not know how to write.

The first evening, when he found himself in his barracks, surrounded by some thirty other airmen who were joking and exchanging words that were unintelligible to him. Salim, who felt completely lost, was flooded with anguish; he experienced the feeling of entering an incomprehensible and frightening world. When, at last, the order was given to go to bed and the light was turned out, he was finally able to let himself go and, under the covers, sobbed in despair.

After three months of intensive training, he was sent to a base where he stayed for the first three years of the war. It was a closed universe that included administrative buildings, a hospital, and four wings, each housing around two thousand men and comprising, in addition to the airmen's barracks, the officers' quarters. The men could get inebriated every night in the mess. The days were reserved for drills, maintenance of weapons, and fatigues.

The conscripts that Salim was surrounded by were, for the most part, vulgar, rude and brutal. As his knowledge of English improved, he understood that their sole subject of conversation was limited to sexuality, and anything related to it. Some of them would recall how they had given a venereal disease to a woman, "initiating her", as they called it, during their last period of leave. Most of them spoke "cockney," the slang spoken in working-class areas of London. Salim felt intuitively that their manner of half swallowing syllables denoted a kind of mental laziness that he would have to avoid at all costs.

He felt horribly alone and out of place, at the mercy of insensitive men who would throw at him, often with contempt, the words: "You are not one of us." Sometimes, they would play cruel tricks on him that he had no choice but to suffer in silence. Abusing his ingenuousness, they would claim to be passing on, on behalf of noncommissioned officers, orders that they had just wholly invented. On occasions, he would return exhausted from a night watch to find a dead rat in his bed. Some even derived perverse pleasure from relieving themselves in his shoes during the night, watching his face in the morning when he put them on.

In addition to his fellow airmen, Salim also had to face the aggression of some of the noncommissioned officers. When he had learned, rapidly, thanks to the sensitive ear of a future musician, to recognize the few terms spat out with fury by the warrant officers, he realized that, most of the time, every order was wrapped in insults and obscenities. These noncommissioned career officers had finally found, in the war, the chance of an outlet for their repression; the most mediocre of them were unequivocally sadistic. There was even a case where one man with a sensitive temperament, as a result of having been constantly harassed, committed suicide by putting his gun in his mouth and pulling the trigger; others lost their sanity in the end.

Military brutality.

Salim retained, in particular, a painful memory of one chief warrant officer with whom he had had some disputes and who conducted himself with unbelievable brutality. He was a small man and, to compensate for an evident complex, he would often choose to pick on airmen who had the misfortune of being taller than average. Every morning, at roll call, he would inspect the men. They had to stand to attention, sometimes in glacially cold conditions, for the whole duration of the inspection which he would perform with maniacal meticulousness, inflicting diverse punishments for jacket buttons being insufficiently polished or shoes not shining like mirrors.

One day, he set his sights on a particularly tall airman, a real giant, whose stature he must undoubtedly have taken as a personal affront. He began to insult the poor man in every possible and imaginable way, yelling at him without pause, when, suddenly, the airman began to undo his pants. Everyone was following this scene with curiosity, without understanding the reasons for his strange conduct. They soon saw him throw himself on the short noncommissioned officer who continued spitting his insults, lift him off the ground, and, wrapping his pants around his neck, begin to pull them tight with all his strength. The officer's eyes were bulging and his swollen tongue coming out of his mouth when an officer hastily gave the order to help him. It took no less than twelve men to overcome the deranged airman who had lost control of himself and was finally sent to a psychiatric asylum. Even after this incident, which had nearly proved fatal to him, the warrant officer did not, for all that, modify his behavior.

Caught between the persecution of his fellow airmen, and that of the noncommissioned officers, Salim lived in fear of not having understood or correctly carried out an order. He had to remain always alert in order to evade the airmen who were trying to stave off their boredom by using him as their whipping boy. Many years later, recalling this period, Salim could not help wondering how he managed to avoid both suicide and madness.

The shock of the air force was such that Salim's health began to deteriorate rapidly. He suffered from serious intestinal problems that manifested themselves in continual bouts of acute diarrhea. He finally became so ill that he had to be hospitalized on several occasions. In these times of war, anyone serving in the military really had to be very seriously ill for the military doctors to agree to admit him to hospital. Despite treatment, his health problems persisted, without the doctors understanding the cause. As soon as he experienced any slight improvement, he would be immediately sent back to his quarters.

The cold afflicted him perpetually. In fact, since his arrival in England, everything had seemed glacial: the climate, the language, the atmosphere, people's way of being and thinking, and, in comparison with the East, he deplored the monotony of western life. He would seek a little warmth in the mess where he would drink tea while the other airmen got drunk on beer.

The waitresses were known as W.A.A.F. (Women's Auxiliary Air Force); they were women who had signed up for voluntary service. They were very kind to Salim and one of them made it clear to Salim that she harbored more tender feelings for him. However, for Salim, who naturally felt great respect for women in general, it was out of the question for him to approach one of them unless he intended to make a serious commitment. As he was unable to count, when he had to pay for his food and drink, he would take out the handful of coins that represented his week's pay and hold it out to the waitress. He later realized that she had taken very little and she would also give him a few sweet treats, which he had great need of to compensate for his solitude.

A providential meeting: Squadron Leader Strover.

The air force, which was a merciless world of harshness and violence, would, paradoxically, be the means of Salim meeting someone who, subsequently, exercised a decisive influence over his destiny. One day, not long after his arrival, while a number of airmen, who had surrounded him, were amusing themselves by knocking him to the ground and kicking him from one man to another an officer walked past the gathering. Scandalized by the behavior of these men, he inquired, with severity, why they were acting in such a way. Taken by surprise, one of the airmen mumbled: "He's a bloody foreigner"; another, thinking to amuse the officer, added: "He doesn't know how to read, he's an idiot!" Their superior officer, who was around sixty-five years old and a chaplain, sharply reprimanded the men and told them: "If I ever catch you tormenting this boy again, you will have me to deal with! Now, fall out!" They saluted, embarrassed, and left casting filthy looks towards their victim.

The officer, turning back towards Salim who was still on the ground, thoroughly dazed, helped him gently to his feet and invited him to follow him to his office. He asked Salim some questions, and when he realized that he didn't speak English very well and that he really was unable to read or write, he immediately obtained permission for his protégé to spend two hours in his office every day. He began by teaching him to write his name, then to recognize the letters of the alphabet; he also taught him the four basic operations of arithmetic. After three months, during which Salim made rapid progress, the chaplain gave him work to do alone.

The human being completes the major elements of his intellectual apprenticeship before the age of eleven or twelve; past this age, he no longer has the same speed or the same flexibility of mind. Having acquired the indispensable bases during his first years of schooling, it is then possible for him to continue learning because his intellect has been functioning with a certain regularity since childhood. This was not the case with Salim; his intellect had never been called upon during the first nineteen years of his life and, once he had mastered the educational basics, which he assimilated very rapidly, he encountered subsequent difficulties in pursuing intellectual work of this nature. It is understandable that he was never able to acquire, in this area, the ease and automatic learning reflexes of those who had attended school from a very young age.

From the moment they met, the chaplain, who bore the rank of squadron leader and who was known as Padre Strover, took an instant liking to Salim. He was a career officer, very distinguished and cultured as were the majority of the high ranking British officers. He had been a pilot during the First World War. His plane had been brought down and, although pilots were not equipped with parachutes at that time, miraculously he had come out of it alive. Following this event, he had developed a deep faith and decided, while remaining in the air force, to become a chaplain.

Observing Salim's solitude, he invited him to visit him at home whenever he had a few hours off duty. This represented an unhoped for opportunity for the young man to meet beings of a rare quality, who had nothing in common with the airmen that surrounded him.

Music comes to Salim: a passion emerges: the beginnings of the composer.

Squadron Leader Strover lived with his wife (being an Anglican priest, he was allowed to marry) and their three sons who were ten, twelve and fourteen years old, in a small house near the base. Mrs Strover was a musician, she played the viola. Often, she would gather together a few other instrumentalists (violinists, cellists and pianists) at their home to play string quartets, quintets with piano, trios of strings or with piano, sonatas, etc. Their repertoire included works by composers such as Mozart, Beethoven, Brahms and Schubert. During these musical gatherings, which Salim attended with wonder, he made the acquaintance of Dr Padel, who was an amateur cellist, and his wife, a clarinetist; they quickly became faithful friends.

All the musicians were astonished by the surprising memory Salim displayed when it came to music. He was able to hum a tune that he had heard only once, and sometimes even entire phrases of an instrument playing in the background. Mrs Strover, impressed, thought it would be a great shame for someone so gifted not to develop his skills; she therefore decided to teach him musical theory herself.

Salim demonstrated an extraordinary facility in this field and made progress with astounding rapidity. He immediately understood the principles of notation and began writing short pieces himself almost at once. Mrs Strover procured a book by Stuart Macpherson on form and harmony in musical composition which she read to Salim explaining its contents to him. She showed him, on the piano, the difference between a major third and a minor third, between a perfect chord (or consonance) and an imperfect chord (or dissonance). She taught him the rules of harmony and stressed the importance of modulation. She then found a small book by Gordon Jacob on orchestration and, in the same way, read it to him explaining the capacities and limitations of each instrument and its place in the orchestra.

It all seemed strangely easy to Salim; he possessed an extremely sensitive ear and assimilated this knowledge with lightening speed, as if he already knew it and was, mysteriously, simply remembering. Initially, he encountered some difficulty with transposing instruments, that is to say those for which the notes written on the score are not those which are heard, such as clarinets, horns, and trumpets, but, very quickly, he was able to read increasingly complex orchestral scores.

While, for the majority of people, listening proves indispensable if they wish to discover a musical work—the codified notes on the paper only take on meaning, even for many musicians, once they are played on an instrument—for Salim, simply reading the score sufficed for him to hear the music internally; if it was a symphonic work, he would hear all the instruments simultaneously as well as the musical progression, which is not a privilege accorded to all composers, even the most famous. Musicians such as Chopin, Wagner and Ravel needed a piano to be able to compose.

Having acquired the bases of musical structure, Salim began writing symphonic pieces. Mrs Strover, who observed the fruits of her efforts with pride, regularly supplied him with music paper. Thanks to her, he had found a refuge far from the brutality of military life. Every free moment was consecrated to composition. He found his inspiration mainly in the sky, the stars, and the mystery of infinite space.

Writing music as an airman. A watch that ends badly.

The entirely military organization of the day left little time for leisure; moreover, it was difficult for Salim to isolate himself from others. He developed the habit, to the surprise of the other airmen sharing his barracks, of requesting, once a week, the night duty consisting of maintaining the fire in the coal burning stove in the kitchen. He was alone, he was tranquil, it was warm, and he could write his music. After a night without sleep, airmen were not, for all that, exempt from their obligations the following day, but Salim preferred to sacrifice sleep for composition.

Padre Strover had found him a job as waiter in the officers' mess during the day. There, he was relatively safe from other duties, and the tempers of the noncommissioned officers. He did, however, have to face the irascibility of drunken officers who would take issue with him without the slightest motivation. He was also given the role of liaison between the different wings of the camp and carried messages or letters between the buildings.

Nevertheless, he had to keep watch like the other airmen. Since his arrival in the air force, he had suffered constantly from acute intestinal problems; yet he still had to keep the full duration of his watch, which lasted for twenty-four hours at a stretch, at all costs. He was allowed to go and have a hot drink once every two hours. In winter, in addition to the fatigue, he had to face snow and glacial cold. This cold, which he could not accustom himself to, chilled him to the bone.

One night, exhausted by his long watch, Salim did not have the automatic reflex to salute a passing officer and was immediately severely punished. The punishment consisted, after twenty-four hours of watch and without having slept, of loading himself up with his full kit and running around the training ground, while a warrant officer followed him, obliging him to maintain a steady pace. When he was allowed to return to his barracks, he was so exhausted that he was not even capable of getting undressed and fell, like a stone, onto his bed. For once, his comrades took pity on him and, when he woke several hours later, he saw that someone had taken off his shoes and placed a cover over him. However, as the punishment did not end there, Padre Strover interceded with the chain of command to which his protégé was answerable, in order that he be given a reprieve.

Over the following days, the officer who had administered the punishment came across Salim carrying a letter. Surprised to see him when he believed him to be under military arrest, he summoned him with severity to accompany him to his office; full of worry, Salim followed him. The officer asked him coldly who had lifted the sanction. Naively believing that his benefactor could be blamed and punished, Salim did not want, at any price, to implicate him; he therefore refused to answer. Furious, the officer raised his voice, but Salim, although trembling all over, would not utter a word. Finally, his interrogator, determined to find out who had dared to contravene his orders, dismissed him with a stream of threats; undoubtedly he would have made enquiries, but, in any case, would have been unable to do anything to a military chaplain, especially one who held the rank of squadron leader.

Leave in London.

Salim was allowed leave, the duration of which was generally limited to two days. The camp was a long way from London; returning home meant spending practically all of his leave traveling and only spending a few hours there. Nevertheless, he was impatient to go home to his family, but, when he returned for the first time, it seemed to him, seeing his loved-ones again, that he had landed in a strangely distant universe. Could it be that so many events had come to pass in just a few months? He was no longer the same.

His brother Victor had started to attend literacy evening classes, funded by the state; he had also succeeded in finding a day job as an apprentice in a radio factory. His parents were still quarreling with renewed vigor. His father had worked here and there at the beginning of the war, but he was now over sixty and was no longer able to find work. His mother had therefore had to find work. She had been hired as a cleaner in a hotel and worked there until after the war.

Salim's family lived poorly, in a single room with an adjoining kitchen, in which there was a bath tub. The toilets, on the first floor, were shared by all the tenants. Salim was no more able to find the tranquility and solitude he needed so badly here, than at the barracks. As the journey to London was tiring and took up almost all of his leave, he would only return when he had seven consecutive days of leave, which was fairly rare.

During most of the war, the capital was subjected to constant bombing. As his mother obstinately refused to go down into the shelters, Salim would, when he was there on leave, stay with her in the apartment. One night, when he was at his parents' home, the bombing having been more intense than usual, he climbed, anxiously, onto the roof of the house to evaluate the consequences. Unconcerned by the shrapnel from the anti-aircraft gun shells that was falling dangerously around him, he discovered, astounded, an incredible reddish light which was illuminating from one side of the horizon to the other. One could see almost as clearly as in broad daylight! It was London that was burning, the docks in particular, which had been ravaged by fire. The family home was too far away for him to be able to distinguish the flames, but their glow, which flickered and flared was an eloquent sufficiency. He thought the entire city had been destroyed.

Later, the bombing raids were replaced by V-1s, auto-piloted flying bombs. The drone of the motor approaching would be heard first, then a silence heralding the imminent explosion. During one leave that he obtained following a spell in hospital, Salim was at his parents' apartment when a V-1 fell at the end of their street. For around ten seconds their own house rocked like a boat. His mother, terrified, was screaming in fear; he had the greatest difficulty in bringing her back to her senses.

Later still came the challenge of the V-2 rockets. These were the first long-range missiles. They travelled through the sky like huge shooting stars, with no sound to indicate their approach, and caused dreadful damage.

Leave did not really constitute a moment of respite for Salim and did not offer him the opportunity of regaining his strength. Only music helped him to escape from the military world that he was obliged to live in.

An unexpected encouragement.

At the end of 1942, after two years of musical work, Salim, one day, as he had always done, showed one of his pieces to Mrs Strover. She, taking the measure of the astonishing progress he had made in such a short time and without saying anything to him, sent the score into a competition being organized in London. Three months later, she had the joy of telling him that he had won a prize and that his composition, a Scherzo for orchestra of twelve minutes' duration, entitled "The Dionysia", would be played at the Albert Hall by the London Philharmonic Orchestra.

Thanks to Padre Strover, he obtained leave for the occasion and it was with the impression of living a dream that he boarded the train for the capital. The works of the three laureates selected were introduced by Michael Tipett, himself a well-known composer. Salim's work was less modern than the two others. Following the execution of the three pieces, the conductor, John Hollingsworth, turned to the audience and asked them which was the one they would like to listen to again. To Salim's great surprise and emotion, his composition was chosen. He was sitting in the front in his military uniform and the conductor pointed him out to the public who applauded him at length. At the age of twenty-one, this was an unprecedented experience and a tremendous encouragement for him to hear his music played before a London audience. From that day on, he continued to compose with ever greater fervor; it was undoubtedly this passion that saved him from the military machine and the culture shock that he had been suffering since his arrival in England.

A number of exceptional musicians, composers like Saint Saëns, César Franck, and, of course, Mozart, or performers such as Evgeny

Kissin, Clara Haskil, Herbert Von Karajan, and others, demonstrate, from their earliest childhood, a talent that is exceptional, incomprehensible even, if one does not take into consideration work done in other lives. Salim's abilities in terms of music emerged later, due to circumstances, but to have his first orchestral work win a prize and be performed by the London Philharmonic Orchestra just two years after beginning to study music comes close to prodigy.

After this significant event, he met a biologist who worked at the base's hospital. He was a young man, very kind, married and the father of two children. Salim became friends with him and would, as often as he could, take refuge in his laboratory to work quietly on writing his music. Of course, he needed a pretext to be authorized to stay there. So whenever the medical officer came into the room, he would pretend to be washing test tubes and the biologist would explain that he had requested the assistance of an airman to carry out these duties. This kind complicity did not, unfortunately, last very long, as, one day, his friend, refusing to stand by a doctor who had made a diagnostic error that had cost an airman his life, was transferred far away from the base. Salim learned of his death not long after.

Salim leaves the base. The dark year.

After this first base, where Salim had spent nearly three years, he was, to his great sadness, transferred far from Padre Strover and his wife, to another camp from where, a few months later, after the allies had landed in Normandy in June 1944, he was sent to the continent.

The true horror of the war hit him head on. This part of his life, however difficult that life was, would be the darkest of all; he never wanted to talk about it. Once, however, with a look filled with deep sadness, he told me that he had, on many occasions, been able to observe the extent to which the context of war could easily bring the most abominable of human impulses to the fore.

Faced with the behavior of certain individuals, Salim came to the conclusion that, in fact, some people, although possessed of a human body, did not yet belong to the world of humans. These non-human beings, encountered in all countries and among all races, prove themselves capable of committing the worst cruelties in cold blood without showing the slightest remorse. It is as though certain functions were absent in them, as if they were lacking psychological organs, thus preventing them from attaining the phase of the human. On the other hand, there may also exist beings—infinitely rarer—who have surpassed the human level and who, like Christ and Buddha, have chosen to sacrifice themselves by reincarnating themselves in a corporeal envelope in order to help humanity. Although inhabiting a human body, these entirely exceptional beings have reached a degree of evolution situated far beyond the world of humans.

Later, when he began a spiritual practice, Salim realized how vain it is to hope for an end to war in the world. Despite multiple peace conferences and endless statements of intent, as soon as his personal interests are at stake, the human being immediately forgets the grand principles he was supposed to defend. Furthermore, as Salim would later explain to his pupils, there exists, in every human being, an impulse to self-destruction that sometimes pushes him to act with murderous folly and even to pull as many others as he can in his wake, as this colossal global conflict demonstrated in such a sadly tangible way. Only, Salim would say, a personal inner transformation, sought by so few, could change the destiny of humanity.

Towards the end of the conflict, Salim was hospitalized several times in Belgium, Holland, and Denmark. In 1945, while he was in hospital again, in Germany this time, in Schleswig, two convalescent Polish officers came and sat on his bed one night, completely drunk. They told him, with amused chuckles, how they had caught a young German girl, aged around nineteen, and, having decreed that she was a spy, had, along with six English soldiers, raped her before killing and burying her. Terribly distressed, Salim passed a dreadful night. The following morning, he went to his superior to report what these two men had told him. A search was conducted immediately; the body of the young girl was indeed discovered in the spot where the two

Polish officers had, in their intoxicated state, bragged about having buried her. But what could be done? This was a time of war. The officer kindly advised Salim to keep quiet unless he wanted end up with a bullet in his back. Not one of the guilty parties to this ignoble act was troubled.

It is precisely in such circumstances, Salim would say, when someone finds himself in a situation where it is possible to cause suffering to another with complete impunity, that he finds himself confronted by hidden tendencies within himself, whose existence he was unaware of and which had never before had the occasion to manifest themselves.

Still in Germany, Salim was part of a small patrol that passed an elderly German couple in the street. The military men called them over and began to rob them of what little they had. The old man was wearing a watch which one of the men, wanted to take, but Salim, interposing himself between the two, prevented him from achieving his end. His comrade, furious, took aim at Salim and threatened to kill him there and then in front of the old couple who, terrified, held each other tightly. The airman cried angrily: "They've caused us enough harm! Wasn't it them who started it?" But Salim did not move an inch and replied: "If we do the same to them, then we are no better than they are!" The other, not at all convinced, reluctantly re-holstered his weapon. Nevertheless, Salim had to face reprisals when he returned to his barracks; he was beaten until he bled from his ears and from his head. Without being able to explain it clearly to the others, he firmly believed that we should never allow ourselves to do harm, even to those who have done harm to us. He felt the same certitude as Gandhi who said of the law of retaliation: "An eye for an eye only ends up making the whole world blind."

The war comes to an end.

Nearly five years had passed since Salim had been enlisted. He welcomed the news that the war had ended with unutterable relief.

He thought he would finally be able to leave behind this military environment in which he continued to suffer cruelly.

He was in Germany when the armistice was signed on May 8, 1945. He was sure that it would now only be a question of days before he was released. Contrary to his expectations, however, weeks passed, then months, and the much awaited order still did not arrive. The end of the year was approaching and he was still in the military, and still prey to constant health problems.

Finally, in January 1946 he was feeling such despair that he gathered all his courage and went to find the medical officer, to whom he declared: "As the war has now been over for more than six months, you no longer need me; I'm also very ill and I want to go home." The officer tried to temporize, but Salim, who was drawing from his distress the strength to remain inflexible, announced that he would not leave the room until arrangements had been made for his demobilization. Finally, at the end of a long and bitter discussion, the officer promised him that after having spent a final month under observation in a hospital in England to determine whether he would qualify for a disability pension, he would be free. He kept his word, and Salim was at last able to emerge from the nightmarish universe that the military world had been for him.

After his return to civilian life, it took him a long time to come to realize that he was no longer simply on leave and that he never had to return to his quarters. For years, he often had the same disturbing dream: he was still in the air force, despite the fact that he knew he should not be there, as, apparently, a Kafkaesque administrative problem was preventing him from regaining his liberty. He would wake every time in a state of anguish, distraught at the intolerable thought of finding himself once more under the military yoke. It took him a long time to overcome this fear, bound up in all that he had experienced over five years that had seemed to him to last an eternity.

His general condition had been so badly affected that he was granted a meager disability pension and, more importantly, free medical care for a certain duration, which was going to be of great help to him during the time he remained in England.

His health never recovered; throughout his life, until the age of sixty-eight when the cause was finally discovered, he continued to suffer from the same intestinal problems. Most of the time, as soon as he ate, he was flooded with abdominal pain. His body was shaken by spasms, he was seized by violent bouts of diarrhea and he was sometimes driven to vomit as if he had been poisoned. He found himself torn between the necessity to feed himself to survive and the suffering of his weakened body. He went from hospital to hospital, from examination to examination, from diet to diet, without success. Throughout all these years, he so often encountered such incomprehension from those around him and even the doctors, who seemed to blame him for their inability to discover the origins of his problems, that, on several occasions, he plummeted to the lowest depths of despair.

It is practically impossible to put oneself in the place of another. Unless one has oneself passed through a similar trial, it is hardly possible to imagine the Calvary that acute intestinal problems of this sort can engender. Salim lived in fear of going out in case he was struck by one of his crises of acute diarrhea which lasted for hours and left him exhausted. Whenever he had to go somewhere, he would force himself not to eat and when he had to undertake a journey, he would go without food for one or two days beforehand.

He would suffer for nearly fifty years from this affliction which robbed him of a career as a solo violinist and conductor. The fact that he was able to survive and pursue both his musical composition and his intense spiritual practice is testimony to the primacy of the mind over the body.

An unrecognized inner calling.

After the five years he spent in the army, Salim was physically and morally broken. Leaving his room one day, he saw a nearby church and a tree. He looked at them in a way that he had never looked at anything before in his life. He remained frozen to the spot, suddenly experiencing an entirely unusual state, plunged into a radiant inner silence.

This moment of intense inner presence possessed a very particular quality that had a specific effect on his being, without Salim, at the time, grasping its value. It engraved itself in an indelible manner on his memory as a moment imbued with an entirely different reality to that of the ordinary world. It was only later that he understood that it was, in fact, an inner call, and that this type of experience can occur in people who are not yet engaged in a spiritual practice to prompt them to feel that, apart from these moments which open onto another level of reality, ordinary life is nothing but ephemeral dreaming and illusion.

Le Rêve d'Himalec.

Immediately upon his demobilization from the air force, while he was extremely unhappy, Salim composed a piece that he would work on again later, and which, peculiarly, foretold his own destiny. It was a symphonic piece called "Le Rêve d'Himalec" (Himalec's Dream). The theme, highly symbolic, was about the forgetting of the original paradise, and the return to these Edenic lands. As an introduction to the orchestral score, Salim wrote the following text:

"In a garden of unimaginable beauty, lived beings gifted with intelligence, who lacked nothing. They were happy and the garden's walls protected them against all danger.

"One day, curiosity to know what lay beyond this Eden took hold of them and they went out from the garden. It would have been so easy for them to return, but they did not. They ventured further and lost themselves in the desert where they were the prey of all sorts of strange beasts and terrifying phenomena. Now absorbed by their endless struggles, they slowly but surely forgot their beautiful garden and, in the end, even the slightest trace of its memory disappeared from their minds.

"They continued to live in fear and in hate, and even came to fighting one against another, until, one day, one of them, perhaps because he had suffered more than the others, suddenly remembered the Garden and the path that led back to it. He began to fight and succeeded, at the cost of much effort, in returning to his paradise. And he took with him those who believed him. "

Salim's spiritual destiny was, in a way, contained within this story, which he believed he had invented in all its particulars.

The rise of the musician.

The passion with which he threw himself into music was, for Salim, a true benediction. It allowed him to escape from the despair that his experiences relating to the war had engendered in him, opening a door for him towards another universe, higher than the world of ordinary life. He came out of the war desirous, with all his being, to continue his music studies. The air force provided him, as was customary, with a small sum to attend to his most pressing needs. With this money, he was able to enroll in the Guildhall School of Music where he began learning the violin. A short time later, he was awarded a grant to study composition and, in view of his excellent results, he was granted a second to study orchestral conducting.

He worked to a phenomenal rhythm of seventeen or eighteen hours a day. His only contact with the outside world was limited to his professors. He studied composition with Berthold Goldschmidt, a great composer, a former student of Paul Hindemith's, who had succeeded in fleeing Germany shortly before the war. As he was Jewish, all his music had been destroyed by the Nazis and he retained a deep bitterness regarding this. He had tried to begin composing again in England, but, there too, because he wasn't English, he had encountered latent opposition. He struggled on giving lessons here and there and, subsequently, earned his living as the conductor of an orchestra.

Salim then studied with Matyas Seiber, a Hungarian composer of great talent, who had been Zoltan Kodaly's student. For the violin, he

Salim 1948

received his instruction from Max Rostal. The term "music studies" might falsely give the impression that Salim buried his nose in books and became an erudite. In fact, his professors taught him verbally, and corrected his work without him having to read anything other than music scores. His ultra-sensitive ears were his best master.

Musical composition (such as "Le chant d'Espérance" (the Song of Hope), a symphonic piece, a version of which for cello and piano still exists) required such concentration in the present that the past, and the painful feelings associated with it, gradually lost their hold over him. His entire being was mobilized to ensure that the music flowed, that there were no lapses or faults, and this left a trace in him, the value of which he would later understand, when he engaged in a spiritual practice.

Naturally, he had moved back into the family home, but the conditions his family were living in were not the surroundings he needed to pursue intensive music studies. Eager for his mother to stop working as soon as possible, he did his utmost to find work as a performer. His brother Victor who had, before the war, acquired some technical knowledge during his apprenticeship, had been assigned to military communications when he had been mobilized three years after Salim. The position of radio operator, which he had succeeded in obtaining, had provided him with the opportunity to acquire training; therefore, he was able to find work quickly once peace was re-established. Through the combined efforts of the two brothers, their mother could, at last, stop working. The arguments between her and her husband were more bitter than ever, prompting the latter to avoid their home; as soon as he came into possession of a little money, he would immediately go and gamble it at the greyhound races.

After the lack of privacy that he had had to endure during his military service, Salim felt an intense need to be alone. The atmosphere at his parents' home was unbearable and he yearned to leave the tiny apartment where they were all living on top of each other. His mother, possessive, as Eastern women often are, was distraught when he told her of his intention to leave the bosom of his family. She fiercely opposed the idea of his departure and even threw herself at his feet pleading with him not to leave. This was a heart-rending moment for him, but he felt that he absolutely could not continue to live with his parents and that it was vital for him to obtain his independence. Through an unexpected stroke of luck, he was able to find a room in the same street, just two doors away, which reassured his mother. When he saw that she was becoming accustomed to this new state of affairs, he moved to a more distant neighborhood. He had found a small room in a run-down house. The upstairs tenant was an extremely absent-minded man. One day, while Salim was out doing his shopping, he began running a bath, then, forgetting the water that was filling his bathtub, he went out. When Salim returned, he came face to face with the fire department who had broken down the neighbor's door to stop the flooding. Unfortunately, an abundance of water had flowed through ceiling onto his music scores, his possessions, and his bed; it was all in a very sorry state. A few days later, the damp that had accumulated between the two stories would cause a catastrophe. One evening, Salim returned home to discover that almost the entire ceiling had come down, strewing the room with rubble. Had he been there at the wrong moment, undoubtedly he would have been seriously injured or perhaps even killed.

He moved into another small room and had to face the—legitimate— exasperation of his neighbors as he practiced his violin exercises for eight to ten hours a day (the rest of his work, composition and study, did not disturb anyone). Fortunately, he attained, with lightening speed, such a level that he began to give concerts and to acquire, as a solo violinist, a certain renown in musical circles.

Solo violinist.

Salim remembered with acute clarity these concerts, and the challenge they represented for him as for any other soloist. The rehearsal with the orchestra would generally take place the day before the concert; after having prepared as much as he could, he would feel, in spite of everything, extremely nervous. All sorts of thoughts would whirl around in his head: "don't forget this, be careful of that problem, don't forget to play this passage like this, etc." Then he would arrive on the stage, smiling slightly and, apparently, very sure of himself, without the audience who were applauding him suspecting what he was feeling. He would bow to his audience, whose sudden tension he had felt as he entered the room.

From that moment, he thought only of the challenge awaiting him and his nervousness immediately left him. He would tune his violin and then give the conductor the sign that he was ready. Generally, a concerto (like Beethoven's or Brahms's) begins, before the entry of the soloist, with a short introduction of three or four minutes, during which he would stand very straight, his regard turned towards the floor, violin in hand. Then, it would be his turn; at that moment, only the music counted.

He always experienced a great deal of success, even when he felt he had not been at the height of his potential and he was not satisfied with himself. He knew, however, that the artist must never let anything show; he must welcome the applause with a smile, even if he is tired, dissatisfied, or ill.

A promising future declared itself to him; he could have had a brilliant career, but his health represented a major obstacle. He was living in perpetual dread of an intestinal crisis occurring in the middle of a concert and would abstain from all food during the preceding day.

His experience as a soloist would later give Salim a very particular understanding of the spiritual dimension of a performance when this concerned great music. He would explain the important symbol constituted by the audience, this great spectator who, although silent, gives meaning to the performance. Indeed, however outstanding the music and the performers may be, if there are no spectators to witness it, the performance will, from every perspective, be a disappointing event; it will serve no purpose and will have no meaning if it is presented to an empty room.

"It is of vital importance to the artists, wrote Salim, that the public come to see them perform. The audience, this huge and silent witness quietly seated in the hall watching the action on the stage without being involved in it, is an essential element in the life of artists. For the presence of the public creates the atmosphere necessary to stimulate the performers and incite them to be "placed" in themselves very differently from the manner in which they normally are. From this unusual state of their being, they are able to demonstrate the outstanding qualities of their art through their particular talents, talents that would otherwise remain unused and become gradually dormant— and an opportunity for inner growth would thus be lost to them.

"An audience invariably makes great demands on an artist's attention. These demands create in the artist a certain tension that brings a special inner state with a very particular kind of force and energy that are not customary to him but which (apart from being the requisite "fire" giving life to his talents) help make him intensely vigilant and conscious of what he is doing. All this goes largely to free him from his habitual way of sensing himself and allows another aspect of his nature to rise to the surface of his being, elevating him and giving him the different taste and feeling of himself he needs—and which he intuitively values deeply. Later, he is mysteriously impelled to want to find this heightened inner state and feeling of himself—the true source of which he is ignorant—again and again. It seems to him that he can only get it through repeatedly seeking and accepting the challenge of confronting this gigantic outer witness, the spectators in the auditorium, for the sake of the sensation it evokes in him each time he has the opportunity to perform in front of them."

Improvised orchestral conduction. Film music. Musical prodigies.

In 1947, Salim won a first prize for orchestral conducting. While he was pursuing his musical studies, he was often called upon to conduct an orchestra because the programmed conductor had pulled out at the last minute. He remembered one evening where the audience was already there and the musicians were anxiously awaiting a conductor who never came. A replacement had to be found with the utmost urgency. A runner was sent to Salim's apartment to beg him to come to their rescue at this critical moment. He dressed quickly, went immediately to the concert hall and discovered to his horror that, among the works he was going to have to conduct, some were unknown to him. These were pieces by Vaughan Williams. However, he had no choice. The audience was there, not suspecting what was happening. He would have to perform come what may. So, he accomplished the extremely skilful feat of conducting at the same time as sight-reading the score. The audience noticed nothing and the concert was a success.

During this period he wrote the music for two short film dramas produced by a Polish company. These were followed by a proposition for a much longer film, but Salim realized, if he allowed himself to be tempted, he risked being labeled as a film music composer which might cause him difficulties in getting his symphonic works played in the future. This is what happened to great composers such as Georges Auric and Miklos Rosza. The numerous and very beautiful pieces of music they wrote for cinema would disappear sooner or later along with the films, and their other works are performed rarely, if ever.

Salim would talk about how tempting it is for a composer to agree to write music for films. He knows that he will have the satisfaction of hearing it played immediately, that he will probably get a very good orchestra for its execution, and, furthermore, that he will be generously paid. The contrary is true when trying to get a more serious work played; he will have to fight constantly; not only will he not be paid, but he will sometimes have to remunerate the musicians himself.

However, works that a composer writes in response to an inspiration are generally of a level superior to those that are written to order, particularly if it is simply illustrative music. When, subsequently, Salim had to resolve himself to accepting this kind of compromise to put food on the table, he always suffered from the constraints that were imposed on him because he felt, as he put it, that his true vocation was to bring into existential manifestation secret messages coming from another world within him.

Salim possessed a phenomenal memory for everything relating to music. When he left England, in early 1950, his repertoire of violin solos included more than thirty-five concertos, some fifty sonatas, and more than two hundred other pieces.

On several occasions, musicians, performers, and composers couldn't bring themselves to believe that he had begun composing and playing the violin so late and yet arrived so quickly at such an advanced level. To have done so bordered on prodigy, and, in fact, Salim had abilities that were prodigious in everything relating to the artistic field; he would always say that it was as though he had already done such things in an elusive past.

Similar phenomena have been observed in other artists, for which the only explanation is that their incomprehensible abilities were developed in other lives.

Thus, a Venetian professor, Anton Door, wrote, in 1902, of Clara Haskil, a very talented pianist of Romanian origins, who was a child prodigy—she was then seven years old :

"Anything that is played to her, she is able to play it back from memory, without a single fault, and, what is more, in no matter what key. I presented her with one of Beethoven's sonatas; she sight-read it perfectly without a single hitch. We find ourselves before an enigma; such maturity in the brain of a child is truly alarming."

This prodigy is also manifested, in a different way, in some mystics, who show from a very young age an uncommon interest in spiritual questions and show evidence of astonishing determination, such as Thérèse d'Avila or Ayu Khadru, a great yogini, who began practicing Tibetan Buddhism at the age of seven. This is a very encouraging phenomenon, as it means that no sincere effort, whether it be in the artistic or spiritual field, is ever wasted.

A love, a heartbreak.

His passion for music compelled Salim to work relentlessly as though he was trying, through his creations, to tear down an invisible veil that separated him from another dimension, an intangible dimension, where would be revealed to him the hidden mystery behind existence, life, and death. Furthermore, the music helped him, to a certain extent, to forget all the tribulations he had suffered in the past and the emotional solitude in which he was living.

Life sometimes plays strange tricks. One day, a young woman, originally from Malta, saved Salim's life in dramatic circumstances. He fell in love, a love that was reciprocated. He found in her the companion he so needed. Alas, his happiness was not destined to last, as, just a few short months after they met, his love, who was only twenty-eight years old, developed breast cancer. Salim, desperate, cancelled all his concerts to be at her side. He saw her decline rapidly. When the end came, his devastation was beyond anything that words could describe; life seemed crueler and more absurd than ever.

To relieve the pain and despair that gripped him, he threw himself back into his work with even fiercer determination. He resumed his concerts. When a performer arrives on stage and bows, smiling, to the audience who are already rejoicing in anticipation of his performance, they do not suspect the personal difficulties, or even tragedies, that may be affecting the artist. He must, come what may, meet his audience's expectations and this sometimes demands of him extraordinary effort and abnegation. He must forget everything and live in the present.

In addition to music, Salim was always very drawn to painting; during his childhood, he had been limited to tracing ephemeral images in the sand or, sometimes, using a piece of metal, scratching in frustration at a few flat stones. After the war, he was finally able to procure the materials he required and began producing a few canvases for himself. However, he had to choose between painting and music, as he  had neither the time nor the means to pursue two such demanding passions. Music triumphed. Even so, he always regretted not having the opportunity to develop his potential in the pictorial arts. For that matter, a few years later, when he was in France, he took up painting again for a while in order to earn a little money. His paintings, which found buyers quickly, were mysterious; their colors were deep, a striking light always illuminated the canvas, and from the whole emanated a strange and unreal atmosphere.

One of Salim's painting

The Call of Destiny – December 1949.

It was at this time in his life that strange and subtle feelings began to stir within Salim, plunging him into a state of inexplicable unease the nature of which escaped him. He experienced a feeling of incomprehensible unrest, as if the elusive memory of a distant past, too obscure to be discernible, was beginning to wake silently within him, a little like the feeling after a dream that leaves a disturbing impression, but which one cannot remember.

He passed his days in a state of vague dissatisfaction and, without understanding the true reason, being ever more unhappy with his present life, with the feeling that he was missing something indefinable—which made him morose and even drove him to avoid the company of others.

Without him realizing it then, the way in which he vibrated within himself—as well as the unconscious desire that he carried constantly within him to remember something that escaped him would attract to him the favorable conditions, and the people, who, unknown to them, would play a decisive role in allowing this enigmatic memory to secretly manifest itself within him.

Salim wrote many times about the surprising faculty of memory and he always emphasized its importance. He distinguished two types of memory: the memory that relates to ordinary life, which prevents the human being from being new and open to the present; and another type of memory, naked, silent, and free from all visual, verbal, or acoustic aids. The awakening of this memory can be more or less manifest in someone, according to the level of being and evolution that he has attained; this awakening signifies that a deep trace has been engraved in this person's being by intense work accomplished in a previous life, whether it be of spiritual, artistic, or scientific interest.

Salim would give, on occasions, performances of his own music. For these concerts, he would gather other musicians around him, in particular a pianist, Tamara Osborn, with whom he studied the piano a little. Salim spoke to her of his interest in and particular attraction to the finesse of French music (such as that of Saint-Saëns, Fauré, and, particularly, Debussy), telling her how much he would like to go and study in France. To his great delight, she told him that she knew a Russian composer, Thomas de Hartmann, who was living in France and that he was about to spend a few days in England; she added that, during his stay, he would visit a certain Mr George Adie and that, if Salim would like, she could arrange a meeting. Glad of this opportunity, he eagerly accepted.

It was a typical London December evening, glacial and misty. After dinner Salim went to the home of this Mr Adie, who lived a little way outside London, a long journey from Salim's apartment. It was very cold and he was chilled when he arrived. He met the gathering: the host, his wife and their children, Mr de Hartmann and his wife, and a few others. Thomas de Hartmann, a portly and affable man, regarded Salim kindly. Salim told him he had heard much about him from Tamara Osborn and expressed his desire to go to France to study with him. After a period of reflection, Mr de Hartmann asked Salim if he could play for him a representative extract of his music. Salim had brought two recordings, one of a sonata for cello and piano, the other of an orchestral piece that he had composed for a film. Everyone present listened attentively, then, after a moment of silence, Thomas de Hartmann declared: "But you have as much proficiency as me, if not more. And you have such a remarkable mastery of the orchestra that I'm not sure what I could bring to you. Besides, I no longer live in Paris, but in the United States where I must soon return. I advise you to write to Nadia Boulanger who is French and lives in Paris. She is a very great teacher; perhaps she will take you as a student." Salim was struck to hear him mention Nadia Boulanger whom he had heard spoken of on a number of occasions with much praise.

Then, Thomas de Hartmann added with great seriousness: "As for your music, I accuse you Sir, of being a mystic! Have you ever been interested in a spiritual quest?" Salim, surprised and annoyed that the discussion was moving away from the only subject that interested him, that is to say, music, replied quickly: "Not at all, I believe in nothing; I am first and foremost a musician!" During the war years, he had come into contact with such absurdities and suffering that the deeply religious feeling which had inhabited him as a child had been swept away.

Thomas de Hartmann resumed: "Your music categorically belies your words." and, addressing himself to their host, he added: "George, why don't you lend him Ouspensky's "The New Model of the Universe?" Mr Adie, a fairly tall, thin man with penetrating blue eyes, who had been observing Salim throughout the entire conversation, stood up, without a word, and went to find the book.

Salim took his leave a few minutes later, before his host had had time to return with the book in question. It was already late and he went out into the foggy street with the unattractive prospect of a long journey by bus and tube* in a glacial cold which he suffered from enormously, both physically and mentally; physically, because he had come out of the war much diminished, and morally, because such a climate compelled him to regret the blue sky and the heat he had known in the Orient throughout his youth.

He waited, shivering, at his bus stop, congratulating himself, he who had such difficulties reading, on having escaped this chore, when he heard the sound of hurried steps behind him. Turning, he saw Mr Adie who, with no coat in the London winter, was running towards him with the book in his hand. They talked for a few minutes while he waited for the bus.

Mr Adie asked him with undisguised curiosity: "What inspires your music?" After a momentary hesitation, Salim replied: "The sky, space, the stars, the Cosmos... I would like to go to the stars; this world is of no interest to me at all!" When the bus arrived, Mr Adie pushed the book forcefully into his hand. Salim saw that he remained where he was for a moment, continuing to follow him with his eyes, until a turning took him out of sight.

Having arrived home frozen, Salim put the book on the floor thinking to warm himself first with a cup of tea. Then he picked up the book, the thickness of which was, for Salim, who never read, entirely discouraging. He opened it hesitantly at the first page and came across the following sentence:

"So that the first step towards understanding the idea of esotericism is the realisation of the existence of a higher mind, that is, a human mind, but one which differs from the ordinary mind as much as, let us say, the mind of an intelligent and educated grown up man differs from the mind of a child of six."

Immediately, without knowing why, Salim was gripped and intrigued by these few words that he read and reread many times; he then

---

* The tube is the commonly used term for the London Underground, which US readers would call the Subway. (Translator's Note)

leafed through the book here and there and came across a chapter further on entitled: "What is Yoga?" With difficulty, he read a few passages on hatha yoga as a means of reaching a spiritual end the description of which resonated mysteriously within his being.

From this decisive moment, his life would take an entirely new direction.

A statue of Buddha.

Mr Adie contacted him again a few days later and invited him to a family dinner at his home, with his wife (who proved to be an excellent pianist) and his children. He asked Salim what he thought of the book he had lent him. Salim had to reply, with embarrassment, that it was beyond his capacities to read such a work, as he was practically illiterate, and that he had only been able to read a few sentences from it concerning hatha yoga. George Adie, incredulous, needed a little time to understand that, although his guest could easily read the most complex orchestral scores, he never read books.

Nevertheless, Salim mentioned the few paragraphs that had caught his attention. His host, who sensed an exceptional receptivity in him, developed a strong paternal affection towards him. He invited him back on several occasions and one day, showed him into a small room where stood a magnificent statue of the Buddha in the meditation posture, which was over a meter tall. The cleverly positioned lighting fell on his head, inlaid in the Indian style with small, sparkling, colored stones, which seemed to be swathed in a mysterious glow. The face with closed eyes radiated unutterable serenity and peace.

This vision impressed Salim to the greatest extent imaginable; he remained transfixed in front of the statue for a long moment, while Mr. Adie, who had not failed to notice Salim's deep emotion, stayed silently by his side. On returning home, Salim felt the irresistible need to put himself into the same posture as this Buddha, a posture he adopted without difficulty, and, with his eyes closed, he began to focus on a sound he heard inside his ears and head, without even knowing that what he was doing was called meditation.

He sensed that another world had just opened up to him. Since his childhood in Baghdad, he had carried within himself a burning inner questioning which, until that time, had remained unanswered.

Years later, when recalling the power of the impact this statue had upon him, Salim would say: "There is no doubt that a silent memory without words or images, coming from a spiritual practice already undertaken in a previous life, awoke within me, irresistibly impelling me to sit, and it guided me, particularly in that I took, as an aid to concentration, an inner sound that I discovered much later to be known in India by the name of Nada (Nada-Yoga)."

In his books, Salim described this sound as resembling "the gentle murmuring of the wind or the constant noise of the ocean waves." The value of this inner sound and the reason that it has been used since the distant past as a concentration aid in India arises from the fact that, unlike the ever changing internal and external conditions which one is accustomed to, this mystic sound possesses a strange continuity that is not of this world.

Furthermore, the more one concentrates on the sound, the louder it becomes. This strange celestial sound becomes a sort of measuring tool for the meditator; as, as soon as his inner absorption fluctuates, becoming stronger or weaker, this benevolent, crystalline sound also varies in intensity in his ears, making itself more shrill or finer.

Afterwards, despite a very full schedule, Salim dedicated long hours to meditation. Instinctively, he felt the importance of intense concentration. In less than a month, he began to experience beatific states.

The Gurdjieff groups.

George Adie was a remarkable man and his way of being was, for Salim, both teaching and example. He invited him to attend some meetings of a small group he led based on the teachings of G. I. Gurdjieff. Salim immediately sensed the crucial importance of the ideas presented. The concepts discussed created an echo within him, waking in his being a passionate longing to find the meaning of phenomenal existence.

The fundamental concept of Gurdjieff's teaching was "self-remembering," in other words, consciously recalling one's own existence in the present. The human being ordinarily lives in a sort of dream, lost in his projections and his conditioning, and acting simply by automatism. Yet coming out of this dream state is possible; to do so, it is necessary to come back to one's self to the present, to come back to the reality that escapes us as long as we are lost in our mental world and our imaginations. This "self-remembering" requires specific efforts and it is necessary to be confronted with the difficulty of putting it into practice in order to realize the power of the inner sleep one is plunged into without knowing it.

Gurdjieff's teachings included other, more theoretical, aspects that

George Adie 85 years

Salim did not succeed in understanding. As he did not read books, it was impossible for him to read Gurdjieff's writings or the work of reference on his teachings written by Ouspensky, his best-known disciple, entitled, *"In Search of the Miraculous."*

Salim felt intuitively all the importance of this "self-remembering"; he would develop his own spiritual work based on this essential component, with such intensity that it would allow him to have powerful spiritual experiences.

His interest, until then, had been directed entirely towards music. He felt that the existential questions he had carried within him since childhood could find their answers through this spiritual work. He had already experienced, while composing his music, unusual states of consciousness, so he immediately understood the crucial importance of consciously maintaining his attention on an object, and not allowing it to wander without restraint.

On one hand, he strove in his active life to maintain a state of "self-remembering" and, on the other hand, devoted himself regularly to intense meditation practice, during which he would concentrate on the Nada, the sound that can be heard within the ears and head.

Regarding meditation, Salim was wholly without a guide and could only rely on his intuition, as, at that time, the Gurdjieff groups did not practice meditation. Moreover, in 1949, both in England and France, meditation was far from common and no-one around Salim practiced it.

In the meantime, he had procured the address of Nadia Boulanger in Paris. With difficulty, he wrote her a few words of fairly unconventional English, enclosing the score of his first symphony for orchestra, as well as the recording and score of a sonata for cello and piano. She replied immediately, inviting him to come and see her.

Chapter 3

France : 1950-1967.

A difficult decision.

Salim suddenly found himself faced with a dilemma and a decision implying a sacrifice that would not be easy for him. He realized that if he left for Paris, he would lose contact with his musician friends in London, thereby breaking ties that were of great importance to his musical work. In addition, he would have to abandon the fruits of several years of hard labor, through which he had been able to acquire a certain renown, in England and start a new struggle to make his name as a solo violinist, composer, and conductor in a country where he did not speak the language.

However, he knew deep down that in spite of the sacrifices he would have to make and the difficulties he would inevitably encounter, this leap into the unknown had to be made, because an imperious and incomprehensible attraction was pulling him towards France.

He was going to have to turn his back on everything he had accomplished in Great Britain so far, and look resolutely forward, without knowing what the future held for him by way of successes or by way of failures.

As much as he enjoyed travelling and being, thanks to the experience of his childhood, accustomed to adapting quickly to a new environment, Salim had always had to confront a strong sense of apprehension when he needed to cope alone in external life. In addition to his extremely introverted artistic temperament, his childhood spent in the Middle East, where the rules of life were very different from those that prevailed in the West, had not allowed him to acquire a faculty for coping in a world that remained incomprehensible to him. He was always surprised by the ease with which people knew where to go to find what they wanted whether to meet their everyday needs, undertake some administrative procedure, to find a job or somewhere to live, etc.

Moreover, when he was a child, he had always travelled with his family. His father spoke with ease the different languages and dialects of the countries they visited and possessed the knowledge of the rules governing the external world that Salim always lacked.

In this year, 1950, despite the handicap constituted by his lack of ability in responding to the demands of external life, it was alone that he had to leave for France and learn the language and the customs of a country that he did not know at all. He finally left England, equipped with Nadia Boulanger's address, his baggage, mostly made up of the scores of his own musical works, his repertoire for violin, and a few canvases that he had painted in London.

Solitary arrival at the Gare du Nord.

His stay in France did not get off to a particularly auspicious start. Some English friends had written at the last minute to acquaintances in Paris, asking if they would meet Salim and, if possible, accommodate him for a few days during which they would help him to find somewhere to live. They were supposed to meet him at the Gare du Nord, identifying him by the violin that he was carrying. Alas, when he got off the train, no one was there to meet him. He waited for an hour, alone on the platform, extremely worried, not knowing what to do. His friends in London had, unfortunately, not given him the address of these people who appeared to have forgotten him. Besides, even if he had had their telephone number, he probably would not have called them, because, apart from the fact that he didn't speak a word of French, the telephone, at that time, petrified him; not being accustomed to using it, he didn't understand what was being said to him and was thrown into a panic as soon as he was asked a question.

At a loss to know what to do, he finally decided to go into a hotel opposite the station, which did not seem too expensive, which, for that time, is as much as to say it was a pitiful establishment with squalid rooms. He had to be very frugal because he had little money and knew that he would not be able to earn a living straightaway; he possessed only few savings made from his concerts. Fortunately, Dr

Padel, whom he had met through Padre Strover, had generously offered to send him a small sum from London every month to help with his living costs—he did this regularly for the entire two years that Salim spent studying with Nadia Boulanger.

The day after his arrival, asking his way several times in English, Salim became acquainted with the Parisian metro[*] and arrived at the home of Nadia Boulanger, who lived in Rue Ballu, near the Place de Clichy.

Nadia Boulanger.

Of Russian origin on her mother's side, Nadia Boulanger was born into a family comprising four generations of musicians. Encouraged by her father Ernest, himself a composer, conductor, and singing teacher, she began learning to play the organ and studying composition at the age of nine. She won her first prizes for organ, accompaniment, and

composition at the age of sixteen. She studied under Gabriel Fauré, who was himself one of Saint-Saëns's students. She was, for a period of time, Igor Stravinsky's teacher.

When her sister, Lili, a winner of the Prix de Rome, died in 1918 at the age of 24, Nadia declared that she would never compose again and began to devote herself to conducting, the distribution of her sister's work, and, above all, education. She would continue her impressive career as a teacher until her death at the age of 92. For

Nadia Boulanger

more than 70 years, she would be one of the most influential teachers of composition of the twentieth century. Over the course of her long career, the thousands of students who came from abroad to attend her classes were captivated by her talent and knowledge.

---

[*] The Parisian subway. (TN)

One of her students, Igor Markevitch, the composer and renowned conductor, had this to say about her:

"In the first year I was there (at the beginning of the 1930s), every week we worked on one of Bach's cantatas; it was just extraordinary the way Nadia Boulanger revealed these works to us; that is to say, we immediately had the feeling that, until then, we had remained on the surface of things while listening to them and that, suddenly,

Igor Markevitch

we were entering into them, that the whole organism was laid bare before us. I remember, once, my fellow student, Igor Stravinsky's son, said: "One has the feeling that a work suddenly becomes as deep as the ocean", and that is really what we all felt; that all these works took on an additional dimension, a further depth, and revealed to us a great deal which we might have overlooked all our lives if she hadn't played them to us. It was to the point where, if we brought her a score that we had composed, while she sight-read it, she would be able to correct a mistake, something that we had missed ourselves... this extraordinary eye; this eye assisting the ear in an absolutely remarkable way."

Nadia Boulanger was a very noble, sensitive, profoundly religious woman of the Catholic faith. She welcomed Salim with great kindness and, for two years, not only did she have him attend her class in musical composition and analysis free of charge, but she also gave him private lessons, never accepting the smallest payment from him. On the contrary, knowing the material difficulties with which he was struggling, she did her utmost to help him and sometimes recommended him to interesting people among her acquaintance.

Finding Accommodation in Paris.

The day after he arrived, Salim moved to another hotel located near the Ecole Militaire, recommended to him by one of Nadia Boulanger's American students. Being naturally ingenuous, he was easy prey for dishonest people; so it happened that a short while after moving into this place, he had all his clothes stolen—apart from those he was wearing that day.

When he told Nadia Boulanger about the misadventure that had just befallen him, she sympathized and, to his great surprise, at the next lesson, she presented him with a large parcel of clothing which she had obtained for him. Despite the fact that the clothes were not quite his size, he was nonetheless profoundly grateful to her and very pleased to have them.

Speaking barely a word of French, it was difficult for Salim to sort out any petty annoyances which might arise. For example, as he had, before leaving London, shipped some of his baggage, containing records and scores, he went to the customs service to pick them up. Seeing that they were dealing with a defenseless foreigner, the customs officers first started to laugh and joke amongst themselves, then they made gestures that were explicitly designed to ask him for money. As he did not understand how much was being requested of him, Salim ingenuously pulled out all the money he had on him, which the unscrupulous state employees immediately took. What was an unexpected tip for them represented a not insignificant sum of money for Salim and he had to go without food for several days.

Through some of Nadia Boulanger's American students, he was able to make friends with a French singer of around fifty years old who had a fairly good grasp of English. When he told her about the money he had had to give to the customs officers to get back his belongings, she was indignant at this manifest abuse of office. So, to help him, she found the time to come and see the hotel manager to talk to him about the theft which Salim had fallen victim to in his establishment. After a lengthy, animated discussion, of which Salim

did not understand a word, the hotelier finally recognized his responsibility in this matter and agreed to accommodate him free of charge
for a certain time as compensation for the loss incurred. However, the
room was infested with bugs, so after two or three months, Salim
wanted to find alternative accommodation compatible with his meager
financial resources.

After a long search, he finally found a room to rent by the month
in an extremely modest hotel. He had hoped to give concerts in Paris,
which would have enabled him to earn a living, but he was not known
there. Furthermore, it was difficult for him to undertake his violin
practice in the hotel building. So, he moved once again, into a small
room, also rented on a monthly basis, on the top floor of a hotel near
Montparnasse railroad station, where playing the violin was more or
less tolerated.

To feed himself, every day Salim bought a few provisions in the
first shop he had found nearby. Taking the money out of his pocket,
he always left it to the sales clerk to deduct the amount he owed for
his purchases. It took him some time to realize, after he had bought
the same products in another local grocery store, that the man was
stealing a great deal from him, sometimes taking twice the amount
due.

The Gurdjieff Groups in Paris, The Shroud of Turin.

Mr Adie, who came to France from time to time, did not fail to
visit him and, noting his solitude and spiritual needs, suggested putting
him in touch with the Gurdjieff groups in Paris. These constituted,
along with Nadia Boulanger, two spheres through which Salim came
to know almost all the people he would associate with until his departure for India at the beginning of 1968.

On a number of occasions during his various moves, he had to
carry heavy suitcases containing his orchestral scores. Because of the
frailty of his health, these physical efforts contributed to causing him
a strangulated hernia which had to be operated on urgently. As he had

no money or social security cover, he went to explain his situation to the British Consulate which kindly found him a small clinic where he could have the operation free of charge. A few days later, when, barely recovered, he came out of hospital wanting to take up his hotel room again, it had been re-let.

An elderly lady, Madame Régnier, whom he had met in the Gurdjieff groups and who was highly musical herself, felt great kindness towards him. When she learned that he was looking for a place to live, she immediately found a room for him at the house of some friends, at a modest price, where at last he could enjoy full freedom to play the violin.

One day when Madame Régnier, who was a great admirer of his music, invited him to lunch at her house, she showed him a photo of the Shroud of Turin (the linen cloth which is alleged to have wrapped Christ's body after the crucifixion).

Salim felt such a shock when he saw the majestic face, marked by a noble severity and displaying an entirely exceptional internalization, that he remained motionless in front of the photo for a long time. Whether the Shroud of Turin is genuine or not does not alter in any way the striking impression that emanates from it, and which moved Salim so deeply that he always kept a photo of it on him thereafter.

The Shroud of Turin

The forty-eight exercises of counterpoint.

From their very first conversation, Salim realized that Nadia Boulanger was an outstanding teacher. She knew how to explain and emphasize the structure of a musical work in a most astonishing way. Moreover, she proved to be extremely demanding and difficult to please. When she discovered that Salim was already very good at orchestration, she focused instead on musical structure and form, thereby assisting him enormously in refining his symphonic works. She brought him to a better understanding of the relationship between music and spirituality and caused him to make such progress in two years that he would be eternally grateful to her.

Nadia Boulanger had more students than she could take, chiefly Americans, some of whom were extremely rich and would fly in every week from the United States to take classes in music analysis, which she gave in English and which Salim attended for two years.

During these classes, she sight-read, at the piano, scores by Bach, Mozart, Stravinsky, etc., with remarkable ease, and would ask of her students, for instance: "Which is the important note enabling harmonic modulation in this place?" Salim would immediately raise his hand to answer. To begin with she would ask him, but, very quickly, she began to say: "No, not you. I know you know." She would only let him speak if nobody else in the class had found the answer; then, addressing the other students, she would exclaim: "He has an extraordinary ear!"

She was always overwhelmed with work; sometimes, when she received Salim for a private lesson, she showed him a pile of counterpoint exercises that Stravinsky had sent her to correct for him, and she would sigh as she said: "But I don't have the time; I just don't have the time…"

She gave Salim many musical exercises for him to do at home. In addition to the important harmony and compositional homework, which he had to hand in to her every week, she asked him to do counterpoint exercises based on a cantus firmus in major and minor modes, first with four voices, then, increasing the difficulty, with eight voices—in other words, music for two choirs. The main difficulty with this type of work resides in the fact that the use of consecutive fifths and octaves is not allowed.

The first time Salim handed in eight counterpoint exercises, Nadia Boulanger received it with a dissatisfied, "Is that all?" The following week, he worked very hard and came back with more exercises, but she did not seem pleased for all that and said to him again with apparent severity: "Is that all?" He went home, depressed, unable to understand such strictness. He applied himself with increasing determination and succeeded in completing yet more exercises, but, merciless, she still asked him: "Is that all?"

Weeks passed in this way. Salim worked to the utmost limits of his strength. After five or six months, he was managing to provide between forty and fifty counterpoint exercises from one lesson to the next. However, when Nadia Boulanger greeted him yet again with her inevitable "Is that all?" he broke down in tears, protesting that it was impossible for him to do more! She seemed suddenly so moved by his distress that she put her hand affectionately on his shoulder, explaining to him that there was another student waiting in the corridor who had won first prize in counterpoint at the Conservatoire. She called him in and asked: "How many eight-voice counterpoint exercises can you do in one week?" The young man replied: "Seven or eight in each mode; that's a maximum."

This episode marked Salim forever. He felt boundless gratitude towards Nadia Boulanger for having pushed him beyond his limits in this way. She was the instrument through which he understood that if one strives with tenacious sincerity, one can always do more than one thinks possible. Thus, she intensified his natural liking for effort, which subsequently, had a crucial influence on his spiritual practices.

She asked her students to demonstrate honesty in their musical work and swiftly recognized in Salim this integrity which she valued above everything. Sometimes, she asked him to leave her with some of his counterpoint exercises that she particularly appreciated, so that she could show them to her students at the Conservatoire, where they must have remained to this day.

His meeting with Nadia Boulanger was a decisive event in Salim's life. She was a woman of great kindness and an extraordinary teacher who, without even expressing it in words, inculcated in her students the crucial necessity for effort and accuracy in any musical creation. Her astonishing capacity for concentration and her constant search for a truth of being had made her into an extraordinary woman. These qualities, which she embodied in exemplary fashion, resonated profoundly within him.

Nadia Boulanger: The faculty of attention.

During an interview on the occasion of her ninetieth birthday, Nadia Boulanger stated:

"What appears to me to be most frequently lacking is attention; that is to say, really a type of character. You have people who have such concentration that everything takes on importance and then, in other people, it passes them by, they have forgotten, so, they will do again tomorrow what they did today; no progress is possible because the phenomenon which occurred, immediately disappears."

"So, before encouraging someone, one needs to ask whether he has a love within him, whether he can show an interest in what he does, whatever that may be, because devoting oneself to something is of interest in itself; that is the difference between people, between beings, and which gives some individuals an extraordinary margin for sensational activity, and others, who are what I call 'the sleepers'…

"I was fortunate enough to be raised by an unbelievably intelligent mother who knew exactly what a child's education should be. She adored me; she had lost a child before I was born, so I was the miracle arriving in the home; she loved me enough to be merciless in her judgments. There was one thing she could not allow and that was a lack of attention. And I grew up from a baby not accepting that one could not pay attention."

Spiritual work in Paris.

While devoting himself passionately to his music studies, Salim continued the spiritual practices embarked upon in England. Without his being conscious of it in the beginning, he found himself sustained by a naturally devotional disposition.

Being a composer turned out to be a true blessing. Later, he liked to say that it was music which had been his master. A composer of symphonic music works on scores comprising up to thirty-two staves; he must hear all the instruments at once, which requires from him a particular division of attention in order to follow the different melodic lines which overlap and intertwine, the harmonies which constantly metamorphose, as well as the varied rhythms which unfold simultaneously throughout the work. Thus, Salim exercised his attention in a manner which would prove to be of invaluable help for his practice and which, furthermore, explains the results he obtained in this sphere from the beginning of his quest in 1949.

During meetings of the Gurdjieff groups in Paris, which he attended from time to time, Salim would hear people reporting their difficulty in practicing "self-remembering" in the present. He saw for himself that any stimulation from the outside or the slightest thought sufficed for him to forget to be conscious of himself. However, as he had worked on his attention both as a solo violinist and as a composer, he did not become discouraged; he knew that it was possible to maintain concentration without fluctuation for long periods, if one is disposed to do so by a strong interest. For the artist, it is the feeling of elevation brought about by the music; for a spiritual seeker, he needs to cultivate

Example of a 32 stave score. The instruments are shown from top to bottom:
Actual size of the score: 43.3 cm x 30.7 cm.

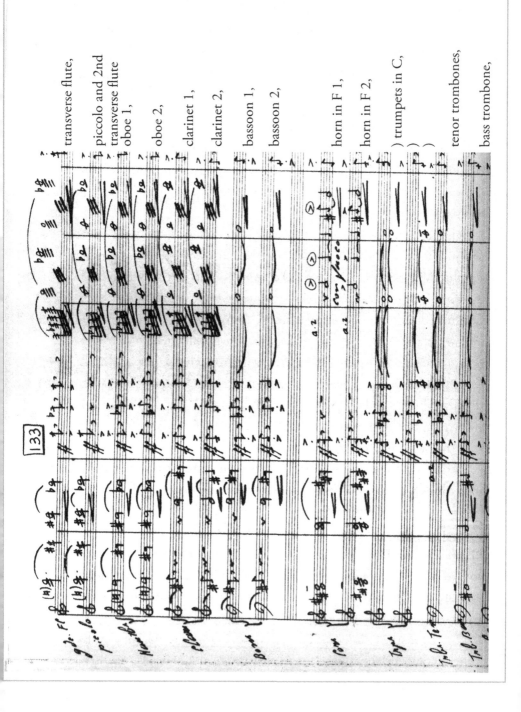

Detail of percussion instruments (3 staves): cymbals, triangle, glockenspiel, large bass, tom tom, bass drum, tambourine, military drum.

timpani,

percussion instruments (see détail)

harp

piano,

first violins,

second violins,

violas,

cellos,

double basses.

his interest deliberately through understanding the importance of what he is trying to accomplish within himself.

Salim had immediately grasped the full importance of returning to the present. Already, after having left the air force, when the memory of the painful events he had lived through in the war came into his mind, he would say to himself: "Return to the present." However, holding himself in the present required him to renounce, from moment to moment, the thoughts, images, and associations of ideas that would constantly arise in his mind in response to the stimulations of the outside world; to achieve this, concentrating on the sound he heard inside his ears and head proved to be very valuable and effective.

He had practiced many exercises with passion for long hours in order to master his art as a solo violinist, so he viewed as evident the necessity, in his spiritual practice, to practice his concentration in exercises which came to his mind, according to his needs—as if he was remembering them—so as increasingly to prolong a state of inner vigilance in active life.

He chose exact times, for a set duration: for example, when he had to go somewhere on foot, he would decide that for the entire duration of the walk, he would concentrate on the sensation of the soles of his feet as they touched the ground so as to remain conscious of himself from one step to the next, striving from second to second to retain the memory of his own existence.

In the beginning, he discovered that hardly had he taken a few steps than, abruptly, and in an unaccountable manner, he became absent and dispersed again, completely forgetting about this important spiritual work and his intention to remain concentrated. Two, or even five, minutes later or longer, he was just as surprised when, suddenly, as in a flash, there was a strange, inexplicable and very rapid inward movement that took place in him and he had come back to an awareness of himself again. At that very instant, he realized that, not only had he altogether forgotten about this exercise, but that—what was even more curious—in an incomprehensible way, the knowledge and feeling of his existence had been strangely obliterated at the same time. He was mysteriously swallowed up and—so to speak—"died" in this state of self-forgetfulness.

So, he would start again patiently and resolutely to focus his attention on the soles of his feet and feeling them as they touched the ground in order to succeed in remaining conscious of himself over longer periods, which demanded renewed determination of him.

Salim would always say to his students that he was tragically human, that he was no different from other seekers, and that he had had to be tenacious to put into practice and maintain the quality of the spiritual exercises that he imposed on himself. He never made these efforts through blind constraint, but because he wanted to make them, just like an artist who voluntarily imposes a discipline upon himself because he fervently wants to succeed in mastering his art.

Knowing oneself.

An important part of this spiritual work consisted of studying oneself in order to discover what was causing the loss of this "self-remembering." It was in this way that Salim saw in himself states of being which proved to be serious obstacles on his path. As soon as he stopped focusing on music, the fear in which he had lived throughout his childhood, as well as the tragedies he had experienced during the war, occupied his inner world. He perceived the need to fight against these states and thoughts which constantly returned and which had become habitual for him. Therefore, he applied himself to replacing them with their opposite every time he noticed their presence within him. For example, if he felt anxiety, he strove to arouse a feeling of confidence; or if he felt sadness, he deliberately evoked joy.

Aside from these states of fear, anxiety, or sadness, he saw that he also had within himself a tendency to speed up when he was doing something, as if to rid himself of it and go on to the next thing, which he did just as fast, in a state of tension, all the more so as he always had lots of things to do between trying to earn a little money, his music, and meditation.

He noticed that in fact this is a very widespread attitude, this wanting to be rid of what one is doing, to be able to go on to the next occupation, which will be carried out with the same feverishness, and so on, with the result that one does not live and one is never in the present.

So, he set himself the task of deliberately slowing down, even by a very little, to use everything he was doing as a practice to remain more conscious of himself in the present. This deliberate slowing down, however infinitesimal it might be, provided him with the necessary opportunity to no longer identify with what he was doing, in which he was lost, and he could start to observe himself impartially. This particular work immediately revealed to him all the needless agitation, inner tension, and useless irritations, which, as soon as they were perceived by his mental gaze, slackened and subsided of their own accord, or, at least, his perception of them would give him the ability to control them to a certain extent. This required a particular kind of calm willpower which proved to be a beneficial aid and a protective friend.

In a few months of subtle but steadfast efforts, he managed to establish a state of relaxation and a subtle slowing down within himself which would assist him enormously in his future practices.

Obstacles to meditation – the fateful week.

Despite the spiritual sweetness he had already tasted, Salim had to fight, like any seeker, against resistances within himself. He recounts the following sequence of events in the final chapter of his book, La Quête Suprême (The Supreme Quest):

"On the first day of that week, he was very ill and, on that day, he neglected his meditation sessions and the various concentration exercises he had invented for himself, telling himself: 'tomorrow'…

"On the second day, he awoke with the beginnings of toothache and anxiously wondered where he would find the money to pay a dentist if it got worse; once again he neglected his meditation and other concentration practices, telling himself: 'tomorrow'…

"On the morning of the third day, the dental pain had eased, but he had headaches and, again, he did neither meditation nor any concentration exercises on that day, still telling himself: 'tomorrow'…

"On the fourth day, he received a letter which troubled him for the rest of the day and, once again, he neglected his meditation sessions, telling himself: 'tomorrow'…

"On the fifth day, he found himself without food or money, and worried enormously, wondering how he would find the means to subsist over the next few days, and he neglected once again his meditation sessions, telling himself: 'tomorrow'…

"On the sixth day, it was still night when he rose and he twisted his ankle in the darkness, which caused him much pain; as he could not adopt the Lotus position to meditate, he again found an excuse to say: 'tomorrow'…

"The seventh day was a very fine spring day; the sky was of a deep blue that brought delight to the heart; the sun shone with a radiant glow and gave off a delicious warmth. But, His Majesty, the author, had no wish to apply himself to meditating on that day! And, suddenly, he broke down, sobbing, realizing that, for him (just as for any other aspirant), the right moment, the favorable moment to accomplish his spiritual practices would never come—he had to create it."

The change of direction in his interest. Meditation on thoughts.

Notwithstanding his desire to remain present to and conscious of himself, Salim was, despite himself, carried away by all sorts of worries and preoccupations. He saw that if he was too troubled by the day's events, his meditation suffered.

As it was not in his nature to remain passive in the face of this challenge, he plunged into a profound inner questioning on the reasons for his failure, despite his will, to succeed in maintaining the remembering of himself over a long period. Why did he lapse yet again into this strange forgetting of oneself in which people habitually spend their lives without being conscious of it? Hardly had he taken the decision to remain present to himself than, mysteriously, he forgot it, and sank back into being, so to speak, "asleep within himself".

He realized then that the primary factor in his fall was the change of direction in his interest; his interest was changing in response to external or internal stimulations. He needed to cultivate such a burning desire to remain conscious of himself in the present that this aspiration would become stronger than all the manifestations of the external world.

When he happened to encounter too great a resistance within himself to be able to meditate, he discovered that vigilantly watching his thoughts became a means of freeing himself from them, while at the same time taking the utmost care not to become identified and entangled with them. The exceptional inner presence, sharp attention, and strength of will that this called forth from him was at first practically impossible to maintain for more than a few moments.

He turned part of his attention to the movement of his lower abdomen without interfering with its normal breathing rhythm and, at the same time tried to watch every thought and image that passed across the screen of his consciousness with the utmost vigilance. He tried not to let even one thought or image slip by without being fully aware of it, without allowing himself to be carried away by it and lose himself in it.

As he said later, it is precisely what makes the difficulty of this particular form of meditation, because there is no other support for the aspirant in his efforts to free himself from his customary state of being other than the thoughts themselves, which keep coming and going across the sky of his consciousness.

He found little by little that each thought that arose in him had a definite beginning, climax, and an end; and hardly had one thought vanished than another arose suddenly to take its place and that when he remained truly inwardly distant and unentangled with his thoughts, then they quieted down considerably of their own accord, becoming less and less frequent.

Reminders in life.

By assiduously practicing the study of himself to see more clearly the habits and tendencies that were causing his fall, Salim saw that he had a tendency to put off until later that which should be done immediately, especially when it was something difficult that he did not like or dreaded doing. He decided to transform this tendency, perceiving the importance of doing so for his practice; indeed, he would later say to his pupils, that if one puts off until later that which should be done immediately, one will do the same when it comes to meditation and to obeying the inner memory, the "self-remembering" when it manifests itself within one.

He understood that he who gives the order within himself and he who must obey are, mysteriously, one and the same person, and it is from this that the difficulty arises. He would say to himself inwardly: "Salim, you are going to obey me." In the beginning, Salim balked at obeying, but, as he was highly motivated, he obeyed. Later, because he had already obeyed, when he gave himself an order again, it was easier and, in a few weeks, he no longer needed to give himself an order—he obeyed immediately.

He also set as a regular discipline over himself to do something every day that he did not want to do and not do something he wanted to do, so as to develop a particular willpower which proves necessary on a spiritual path.

As a consequence of the efforts he had made during his meditation and other spiritual practices, Salim began to receive an unhoped for assistance in his life, which would not have been possible for him previously. He observed that, at the most unexpected moments, he was, without having sought it, suddenly called back to himself and, for a very brief instant, he became intensely conscious in a way which was not common to him in his active life previously. For no apparent reason, an exceedingly subtle, swift inner movement occurred within him, bringing a deep global consciousness of himself. At the same time, he felt a strange sensation, as if an invisible force within him was trying to convey secret knowledge to make him see something about himself which had hitherto remained concealed from him. At that moment, he was also conscious of the presence of that enigmatic sound, the Nada, vibrating mysteriously in his ears with a supernatural radiance and strident intensity.

He learned that, whatever his occupation, whether internal or external, he had to be immediately available to the call of this divine visitor every time it appeared at the door of his being. Nothing else must count in that privileged instant. He must always be inwardly ready to answer this call and so he tried, with tranquility and without force, to prolong these invaluable moments in their duration and their depth.

Contemporary music and the music of Bach.

From time to time, Nadia Boulanger would give Salim tickets for contemporary music concerts. Once, she procured an invitation for him to attend the premiere of a work by a now forgotten composer and she asked the day after the concert what he thought of the music. After a moment of hesitation, Salim gathered his courage in both hands and responded frankly: "If someone tells you that a burning boat has sunk and that a thousand atrociously burned people drowned while emitting heart-rending screams, he will undoubtedly make a temporary impression on you; he doesn't need to be a great musician to attract your attention by recounting such horrors—all he need do is engage in a profusion of trumpets, percussion, orchestral caterwauling, and so on. On the other hand, elevating the listener and maintaining his interest without pointless exaggeration, through beauty alone, is quite another thing!..." Nadia Boulanger remained silent for a moment, then, putting her hand on Salim's, she said, with her pronounced French accent: "You are right!"

She loved Johann Sebastian Bach's music, which she played on a small organ located in a corner of the room she taught in. Salim greatly surprised her on the day that he declared: "It is true, this music is, mathematically speaking, the most perfect, but it has a weakness: the rhythms are too repetitive and monotonous and the pieces always end abruptly, leaving the person listening unsatisfied; there is a lack of the rhythmic surprises necessary to sustain the interest of a demanding listener." Nadia Boulanger looked at him, disconcerted, then, after a minute or two of silence that worried Salim, to his astonishment, she nevertheless recognized, with her rigorous honesty: "It is true— Bach's rhythms have always been his weakness."

Salim worked with her regularly for two years, then his visits spontaneously became less frequent. He continued to see her from time to time to show her his new musical creations. She never stopped encouraging him and showing, as was her wont, great kindness towards him.

Financial worries and dental problems.

After these two years of studying with Nadia Boulanger during which he had lived parsimoniously on his savings and on Dr Padel's small subsidies, Salim found himself in a most precarious financial situation. He needed, at all costs, to find a way of supporting his needs which, although minimal, nevertheless preoccupied too much of his attention. On one hand, he was solicited by an abundance of inspirations which, no matter what, had to be put down on music paper and, on the other hand, he felt an intense need to devote himself to his spiritual practices. However, he had to waste a lot of time trying to earn a little money, and this necessity remained a constant source of worry for him which incessantly interfered with his other more elevated and, for him, infinitely more important preoccupations.

Through connections, he found work giving a few music theory lessons, here and there, to children, or work as a copyist, consisting of copying out separately the individual parts for the various instruments in an orchestral score. However, these few financial resources still proved uncertain and he constantly had to try to procure new ones.

For lack of money, he began to skip meals more and more often, to the point where, his continual intestinal attacks adding to his money problems, he came to a state of chronic weakness which no longer allowed his body to fight efficiently against infection; so, one day, he finally found himself afflicted by five abscesses in five different teeth at the same time.

At the time, he was visiting London; as he did not have the money to pay a dentist, he went to a hospital to take advantage of free care; his treatment was carried out by students, as part of their practical training, and they managed to break every one of the five teeth, leaving the roots in the jaw. A surgeon at the hospital had to repair the damage. He found himself without teeth on the whole of one side of his upper jaw.

A decisive spiritual turning point.

As a soloist, Salim gave his all, as much when he was preparing for his concerts as when he was on stage. Similarly, when he was composing, he was one hundred percent absorbed in his compositional work which required from him concentration beyond the reach of most people. He quite naturally carried this same inner attitude into his spiritual practices.

Encouraged by some first spiritual experiences of a phenomenal character, he worked relentlessly on himself. Yet, he knew intuitively that the experiences he had had since the beginning of his practice were not yet the true experience that would allow him to cross an irreversible threshold.

It was after having meditated intensively for several hours a day and having tried to remain as concentrated as possible over the course of his activities in external life for a little more than five years that he had the following decisive experience.

The day after his return from England, while he was still suffering enormously with his jaw, without being able, for lack of money, to buy painkillers, Salim sat on his bed to meditate, determined not to let his physical problems alter the quality of his concentration.

While he was becoming more and more absorbed within himself, he was finally rewarded for his assiduous efforts through an experience of an entirely different nature than those he had previously had, in which he experienced the strange feeling of being dead and having returned to his Source of Origin.

Twenty-five years later, he attempted to communicate the incommunicable nature of this enlightenment in his first book, The Way of Inner Vigilance[*]:

"One day, as he was meditating, and as he kept plunging ever more deeply into himself, stubbornly holding onto the subject of his meditation with growing but quiet determination while at the same time constantly increasing the intensity and strength of his concentration without at any moment letting it falter or fluctuate, abruptly, as the sensation of his body became ever finer and more rarefied, this sacred Nada inside his ears started to vibrate in a most unusual way, thundering in his head with an incredible power and shrillness he had not known before. Suddenly, with a formidable force and astonishing rapidity, he was sucked up to the top of his skull. At the same time, he felt that his forehead had ripped open from inside, and the vision of his two eyes had inwardly merged into the center of his forehead. Simultaneously, he had the strong and strange feeling of having died and gone back to his Source of Origin. He was also seized with the inexpressible sensation that he was immersed in and united with the Great Whole, and that he had discovered and understood the mysterious secret behind life, the stars, and the Universe. He was equally pervaded with an extraordinary sense of immense "cosmic aloneness." An eternal vast silence reigned.

Afterward, and for many days, his body seemed incredibly light and free, as if transmuted into ether. Something of this sensation remained with him ever after. He also experienced a strange and indefinable state of well-being, bathed in an ineffable inner stillness, contentment, and indescribable feeling of love hitherto unknown to him, a profound melting tenderness in the solar plexus.

---

[*] Chapter 40.

Later, as he tried to formulate into words the strange secret he had discovered concerning life, the stars, and the Universe, he found himself utterly unable to do so, although the reality of this mysterious comprehension stayed always with him from that day onward.

Moreover, through this unusual spiritual experience, he received, without having fully understood it at first, a foretaste and subtle knowledge of the after-death state, a subtle knowledge and higher understanding that kept silently growing in him, becoming ever clearer, deeper, and more affirmative each time he sat and meditated again.

From that momentous day onward, his existence took an entirely different meaning for him. His thoughts and feelings flowed in a new direction, and his aims in life changed drastically. He looked upon everything from another perspective and in a totally new light. Except music, all the things that used to interest him in the past and that had seemed so important before, suddenly meant nothing to him anymore.

After this crucial event for him, he felt a great need to confide in someone and, in his extreme solitude, he spoke of this experience to some of the leaders of the Gurdjieff groups. Never having had an experience of this nature themselves, they were perturbed by Salim's account. They decided that he was embarking on a dangerous path and advised him against pursuing his meditations and the type of exercises he was practicing. He was extremely surprised and hurt by their reaction.

As these people displayed disconcerting certainty, he found himself nonetheless shaken by their advice; he started to doubt himself and ended up following their advice. For a while, therefore, he ceased some of his spiritual practices, but, feeling an imperious need to return to them, he finally decided to resume his meditation, determined, from that time on, not to confide in or ask the opinion of anyone concerning his spiritual experiences.

The Gospels. Christic experiences.

In our cultural environment, one hardly imagines that someone might not know the Gospels. Yet, Salim only discovered them at the age of thirty-three, when he had just had the above-described spiritual experience. It was Padre Strover who, having learned with astonishment that he knew nothing at all about this sacred text, had given it to him in the form of four small separate booklets. Salim had kept these opuscules for more than ten years without reading them. One day, not knowing what prompted him so to do, he began to look at them.

Because of his lack of formal education, he always experienced the greatest difficulties in reading. Therefore, on that day, he set about discovering the Gospels, going back over the same sentences several times in an attempt to grasp the content. When he came across Christ's words: "I and the Father are One", he felt suddenly moved and, without understanding the reason, he even began to weep. The tragedy of the crucifixion made a particular impression on him and, subsequently, he could not help thinking of it incessantly.

A few days later, seated in his meditation posture, he was deeply concentrated and inwardly absorbed when, suddenly, he completely lost his individuality such as he knew it before, to be transformed into an inexpressible state of being, which he later qualified as a mysterious formless state. Suddenly, Christ appeared to him in the form of a luminous figure which "entered" within him. It was as if, by losing his individuality, he had, astonishingly, become Christ.

It is impossible, Salim recognized, to describe experiences which have nothing in common with the reference system of the tangible world. When, a few moments later, he returned to his habitual state of being, he was moved to the extreme. Nonetheless, he could not help but wonder if he had been the object of a hallucination and if he had not imagined what had happened. He spent several days in an indescribable state of well-being which progressively faded. He then found himself extremely depressed.

After around ten days, while he was still wondering, albeit without understanding the meaning of this mystical experience, as if to dissipate his doubts and assure him of the reality of what had happened to him, the same phenomenal experience suddenly recurred during his meditation with even greater force, leaving him completely overwhelmed. From that moment, for almost three months, Salim became totally insomniac. He could no longer sleep, without, for all that, feeling fatigue, and made the most of this in order to meditate virtually day and night.

Through this astonishing experience, he realized that it is only when the human being succeeds, in a moment of intense concentration, in losing his ordinary individuality, that he may discover within him his True Self, in other words his Divine Nature, Christic or Buddhist. He also understood that art has an important role to play in kindling an elevated aspiration in humanity which, otherwise, would remain shrouded in its customary ignorance.

However, art can only fulfill this function insofar as the artist himself touches something of this Supreme Truth during his creations. In this way, certain statues of Buddha, which emanate an impersonal bliss of a spiritual nature, attempt to awaken in those who gaze upon them an echo and desire to feel for themselves an ineffable peace which is not of this world.

In retrospect, Salim realized that every one of the extraordinary experiences he had been able to have throughout his life had allowed him to acquire yet more spiritual understanding, but once this understanding was acquired, it was no longer necessary for him to experience them again in the same way. "That is the reason" he would say, "that, in general, these powerful experiences never, or at least rarely, recur in exactly the same manner."

Although he had decided to remain silent regarding his spiritual experiences, as he felt so alone at that time, he made the mistake of speaking about this Christic apparition to some Christian friends, who told him that in no way could Christ manifest himself to a non-Christian! He was deeply saddened by their remarks.

Spiritual work on another level.

After having had the revelation of his True Identity, of his Buddha-Nature, Salim felt that the various means he had employed until that point were no longer appropriate. From this time forward, his principal occupation had to be trying to remain conscious of himself and connected with his Inner Source. He had clearly known the sublime aspect of his being to which he had to surrender himself, and perceived what was the side of his nature that must move out of the way and be repeatedly renounced to permit this divine light in him to continue to shine forth.

He felt guided by a higher intuition, feeling that the effort which was then required of him would have to be of an entirely different character. It was the beginning of spiritual work on an entirely different level.

He needed to go in two directions at the same time: upwards, towards the Light which he had found within himself, and, if he wanted a transmutation to be able to occur in his being, downwards, into the dark depths of his ordinary self. He had understood that the discovery of the Sublime within him should not be used to escape himself, but as a means of seeing oneself as one is, in the purity of this dazzling light.

Indeed, he perceived that, when he was inwardly present to this Superior Aspect of his being, he could no longer, under its intransigeant gaze, behave in the same way as he did when he found himself in his habitual state of being. All the things that he thought, said, and did when he was engulfed in his habitual condition of waking sleep became inconceivable in a state of remembering and of presence to himself.

He perceived that, as long as he was aware of himself, inwardly connected to his Supreme Being, he was not able to do other than act in conformity to this Hallowed Witness. His thoughts, speech, and actions were inevitably influenced and governed by a higher knowledge and very particular understanding proceeding from it, rendering him compassionate in his contact with the outer world and conscious of the feelings, problems, and sufferings of others. But, as soon as he forgot himself again, becoming inwardly disconnected from his True Source, he started once more to behave, like everyone else, through his ordinary lower self, with its fears and desires.

Indeed, however powerful this irreversible experience had been for Salim, he discovered how very hard indeed it was to stay present to this ineffable aspect of his nature and maintain it in active life in its purest state for more than a short moment, before it was engulfed and smothered again by the exacting demands and pressures of the conditions of earthly existence which will blindly keep claiming priority over all else.

Madame Seu.

Salim lived in an extremely precarious fashion. His health, already failing since the trials of the years he had spent in the air force, continued deteriorating. In Paris, he made the acquaintance of a doctor who showed great kindness towards him, although he remained as perplexed in the face of Salim's case as his colleagues in London had been. He told Salim that, as his body was obviously trying to eliminate something that it could not tolerate, perhaps it would be possible to go along with it and artificially trigger these repeated attacks of diarrhea with drugs. Not knowing what to do to relieve his condition, Salim agreed and, for around nine months, he followed this drastic treatment daily, unfortunately to no effect. Quite the contrary, he weakened considerably and, as a result of water retention, his knees started to swell to the point that he could no longer bend them. He reached the point of not being able to walk and foresaw, with dread, the time when he might become disabled. He who already encountered so many difficulties in surviving, what would he do if he became disabled?

This doctor, who was an extremely decent man and never asked Salim for payment, told him, in order to reassure him, that the water would eventually be eliminated following several months of rest, but he advised him all the same to find a place where he could be looked after.

Salim felt completely alone and distraught; he did not know what to do to get into a nursing home; in any case, he could not have borne the expense. In the Gurdjieff groups, he had met a musician, Nelly Caron, and, fortunately, she knew an extremely religious woman of mature years, Madame Seu, who came to see him and generously agreed at once to offer him hospitality in her apartment on Rue Saint Dominique.

Because he was a composer, Salim often met people along his way who loved music and quite naturally took an interest in him and provided him with providential assistance.

He could not leave his bed for around nine months during which he wrote, as will be seen in detail later, the musical work that he considered to be his most important: a mass for mixed choirs, two string orchestras, celesta, harp, glockenspiel, and percussion. He dedicated it to the doctor who, during this difficult period, came devotedly to visit him on a regular basis, to give him injections and medicines. He extended his generosity to the point of subsequently continuing his care free of charge, and Salim always expressed heartfelt gratitude towards him.

Throughout all the time that this ordeal lasted, Salim looked for ways to earn a little money so as not to be a burden to Madame Seu. Through Nelly Caron, he eventually found a few people wishing to improve their English. As his knowledge of this language, although far from being perfect, was nevertheless better than theirs and, furthermore, his accent was excellent, they were happy to come and converse with him. They met up once or twice a week around his bed and, recalling the Baghdad street storytellers, he told them stories of Mullah Nasreddin and tales from the "Arabian Nights."

He felt deep gratitude towards Madame Seu who welcomed him with such generosity into her apartment. He did everything in his power to avoid disturbing her. As the doctor had promised him, the swelling in his knees progressively reduced and, little by little, he was able to regain his mobility. As soon as he was in a position to get up, he prepared his meals himself, taking great care to leave the kitchen in impeccable condition. He also made sure that his room was never untidy and endeavored to adapt his rhythm of life in such a way that his hostess was troubled as little as possible by his presence.

As the apartment was quite large and his room was far enough away from Madame Seu's room, who, in any case went out to work during the day, he could play the violin without disturbing her. He was able to stay for several years with his generous benefactress, until she decided to sell her apartment to enter a convent.

A tender relationship. Some friends in solitude.

Since the death of his sweetheart in London, Salim had been living in great emotional solitude, from which he suffered enormously. Around 1955, he met a young woman towards whom he felt great tenderness. She loved classical music, but, to Salim's deep regret, was not interested in any spiritual quest. She came to see him regularly in Rue Saint Dominique. Two years after they met, she lost her job in Paris and had to go back to her family in the South of France. Their relationship came to an end at that point and Salim, who had become attached to her, was very saddened by this separation.

He resumed his solitary life and, despite strong emotional needs, he remained alone for many years, because he knew that, from that time on, it was no longer possible for him to form an attachment to someone who did not have any spiritual aspirations.

A well-meaning friend, aware of the difficulties Salim was struggling with, invited him to spend a few days' vacation with him, arranging for a young musician who was attracted by spirituality to join them. Due to the possessions and property this young woman had inherited from her parents, she enjoyed a certain degree of financial security and could have helped Salim with his day-to-day difficulties. However, he could not envisage the idea of forming a relationship with a woman out of self-interest. Later, other friends also tried to persuade him to make an advantageous marriage, but he always refused.

Too occupied by his artistic creations and spiritual practices, Salim had few friends. Mr Adie, whom he had met in London and who had been the providential instrument awakening within him the desire for a spiritual quest, never missed an opportunity to pay him a visit when he came to Paris. Mr Adie had considerable appreciation for Salim's music and was a great moral support to him. Shortly after they met in England, George Adie had suffered cancer in his right lung; he had to undergo surgery, during which the lung had been removed. To compensate for his weakened condition, he had learned to slow down all his movements and be sparing with his words in a way that greatly impressed Salim. He guessed, without Salim saying anything about it, the financial difficulties Salim was struggling with. He would sometimes arrive unannounced at Salim's lodgings and, carrying him off to a good restaurant, insisted that he eat heartily. One day, he gave him a small radio, on which, when he had enough money to buy batteries, Salim could listen to music—this was his only entertainment. However, as the batteries never lasted very long and were expensive, Mr Adie some-times brought him a big bag of them, and he felt filled with gratitude towards this man who understood so well what was important to him.

From time to time, George Adie, who had become like a father to Salim, seeing him too thin and tired, would decide to take him on vacation for three or four weeks, either in the South of France or in London, with his family, where he would oblige him to eat to regain his strength. Salim would enjoy playing sonatas for the violin and piano with Mrs Adie, who was an excellent musician. Once, she even organized a public concert, during which they presented one of

Salim's sonatas, together with another composed by Mr de Hartmann, which met with great success.

During these stays in London, Salim's host often suffered pain and slept badly. If he saw a light on in Salim's room, he would occasionally come in the middle of the night to talk with him in order to take his mind off things; indeed, Salim would sometimes spend long periods meditating during the night. It was on one of these occasions, when they were both in the kitchen, each with a cup of tea in front of him, that Salim gave him an account of the spiritual experience that, unhappily, he had previously spoken of to other people. But George Adie knew how to listen; he let it be seen that Salim's account was making an impression on him, nodding his head from time to time or simply remaining silent, communicating spiritually with his companion through his attentive presence alone, which was a great comfort to Salim.

Nelly Caron admired Salim's music enormously and helped him several times to have some of his works for small ensembles or his sonatas performed. She herself played the piano, as well as a recent instrument called the "Martenot Waves", taken from the name of its inventor, Maurice Martenot. At her request, Salim wrote some pieces for this new instrument which she had the opportunity of performing successfully on a number of occasions.

Through this friend, he made the acquaintance of Manfred Kelkel, a very sensitive composer from the Saarland, who had suffered a great deal in his adolescence during the war. The two swiftly developed a close friendship.

Salim immediately considered Manfred Kelkel to be a composer of great talent and, for his part, Kelkel saw in Salim an orchestrator of great finesse. Being a manager in a music publishing company, Éditions Heugel, and in contact with other publishers, Manfred Kelkel was thinking of writing a treatise on orchestration in collaboration with

Salim (who still wrote his music under his first name, Edward).
However, Salim did not feel capable of undertaking a project of such
scope, which would have demanded a literary technique he did not
possess. Therefore, the project was abandoned.

Salim's major musical work: his Mass - 1956

The unexpected spiritual experience he had had of the vision of
Christ awoke in Salim an intense need to express in music, not only
something of the devotional state he felt, but also the sense of wonder
he had felt for this Invisible Universe, which was infinitely more real
than the tangible universe and which radically eclipsed the limited
knowledge ordinarily conveyed by the senses.

Thus he was driven, he knew not by what force that surpassed
him, to want to write a Mass. As he did not understand Latin and
knew nothing of its pronunciation, he asked Madame Seu to help
him find a priest who would agree to explain to him the procedure of
the Catholic liturgy. The cleric who came to see him asked him with
curiosity the reason he wanted to write a mass given that he was not
even a Christian! Quite unguardedly, Salim then spoke to him about
his spiritual experiences, as well as the holy vision of Christ he had
had and which had moved him so deeply. Just like his Christian friends,
this priest declared, bluntly, that it was quite impossible and even
unthinkable for a non-Christian to experience such grace. Once again,
Salim was deeply shocked by such a reaction—especially coming from
someone who was supposed to be a man of God.

On a number of occasions throughout his life, Salim had to face
the incomprehension and intolerance of people of various religious
beliefs and denominations. It was as a result of these experiences, of
which only a few among many others are mentioned in this biography,
that he came to speak, in his books, of the damage that blind faith
can cause throughout the world.

Work on writing his Mass commenced. Inspiration came to him in
an uninterrupted flow; however, as he would say himself, following

the inspiration, the long labor to bring his work into the world began. He had to fight to try to remain as faithful as possible to his initial inspirations.

Nine months later, the Mass was finished and, as ever, Salim was eager to show his new creation to Nadia Boulanger. So, as soon as his knees allowed him to walk again, he arranged a meeting with her. Feeling great respect for her, he took seriously anything she might express, in terms of an opinion in the field of music or even reflections on life in general.

Nadia Boulanger examined the score he presented to her very attentively, reading it page by page, while exclaiming from time to time: "But, it's so honest, it's so honest!" Finally, to Salim's surprise, she asked him to leave it with her for a while. A month or two later, she contacted him to explain that she had shown his Mass to Henri Barraud (the Director General of Radio France at the time) strongly recommending it to him and that, accordingly, the orchestra scores now had to be provided with all urgency, as his work was going to be broadcast over the airwaves.

The preparation of the orchestra scores represented quite a considerable amount of work—as many as required of each instrumental and choral part having to be copied out separately—all the more so as photocopying and computers did not yet exist. Not having the means to pay a copyist, Salim immediately took the task upon himself, working day and night to be ready in time.

On September 26, 1956, he was overjoyed to hear his Mass performed by the Orchestra of Radio France (which has since become France Musique) and conducted by Eugène Bigot.

As he was not a known composer, the work was only accorded a minimum of rehearsals (three in all, including one for the choirs alone and two with the orchestra). Furthermore, a strike affecting the electricity supply disrupted one of the work sessions with the orchestra. So, in the end, only two and a half hours of rehearsal time with the choristers and other musicians were possible.

Eugène Bigot had brought his students from the Conservatoire with him to this single dress rehearsal. While continuing to conduct the orchestra, he explained to them from time to time, with unbridled enthusiasm, what the composer had done to produce this or that orchestral color, this effect, or that blend of unusual harmonies. Sometimes turning to Salim, he shouted to him in his head voice : "Not only a great musician, but a poet!"

The Mass was extremely well received, as much by critics as listeners. Through Nelly Caron, who knew people in high places in radio, Salim had access to a "listeners' report", which was intended for internal use at Radio France. In this type of document, as anonymity had to be respected, the writers, who were all renowned musicians and music critics, were required to sign using initials which were not their own, but related to an administrative designation. This report stated:

"The inclusion for the first time in the radio symphony orchestra's program of a work by Edward Michael prompted a brief presentation (CC). This sincere, lively work exhibits charm through the freshness of its inspiration and a happy blend of archaism and modernism (CF); the style is simple, direct, and original, without excess (DF); extremely fine colors of orchestration (CC, DF). The choirs are well arranged, with a good tessitura (CF). The Sanctus and Agnus Dei, lack nothing in grandeur, depth, or character (CC, DF), and comprise moments of authentic mysticism (CC, DF) and communicative emotion (DF). All of it is musical—very apt (CC)."

Nelly Caron, who had informed André Cadou, conductor of the Musique de la Comédie Française, of the time Salim's work was being broadcast, received the following letter from him:

"Thank you for having told me about Edward Michael's Mass, broadcast at lunchtime. I listened to it so attentively that I didn't notice I'd forgotten to enjoy the excellent dish that I had been served... Don't take this as a criticism, or even a regret, but as evidence that this mass is curiously charming in its sincerity. And one can sense in it what you call 'elevation of the mind'. So, thank you."

This same performance was rebroadcast a second time some months later.

As a conductor, Eugène Bigot lamented what is known as "contemporary" music, which he was sometimes obliged to conduct; he confided to Salim that just like the instrumentalists in the orchestra, he did not like this cacophony, but, needing to earn a living, musicians were obliged to bow to the radio's demands and play what was imposed upon them. As they had spent years mastering the technique of their instruments, it saddened them to have to, for example, turn around their violin or cello and tap on its body to satisfy the inspiration of certain modern composers...

Over all these years, Salim could not help observing that modern art, whether music, architecture, or painting, was no longer able to produce beauty, because, he said, "The very process of creation is now based on erroneous concepts. Indeed, in order for an artist to succeed in conveying a feeling of an elevated nature, he must, without even consciously realizing it, manage to efface himself, at least partially, as a limited individual, so that the superior aspect of his nature, which is impersonal and complete perfection, may use it as a channel. Moreover, the artist needs to master the techniques and laws of his art to allow this inspiration to manifest itself in the phenomenal world. Yet, the contemporary artist absolutely does not seek to efface himself before something higher than himself, the existence of which he does not even suspect. On the contrary, he does his utmost to express what he calls "his personality", in other words, the inferior and imperfect aspect of his nature, which can only result in something incapable of elevating those for whom it is theoretically intended."

On this matter, Nadia Boulanger warned her students against the desire to "express oneself", saying to them:
"You are going to be teachers; you are going to be performers. If you are performers, you are going to play with complete honesty, not to express yourselves, but to express the work; not to try to say

my Beethoven sonata, my Chopin scherzo, but the scherzo, not even Chopin's scherzo. This scherzo was given to Chopin to write; a piece that no longer needs Chopin to be a masterpiece; it is so beautiful, it no longer needs the performer, it no longer needs the listener, it no longer needs anything, it is in the air, as though resplendent with light, and then, either you look at it or you do not. "

Knowing that Salim was trying to have his Mass, which he felt so strongly about, performed, some friends recommended that he speak to a priest from Saint Eustache Church, who was himself a composer, was in charge of performances of religious music, and had at his disposal the necessary choirs and orchestra. So, Salim went to see him and played him the private tape he had in his possession of his liturgical work, which had been recorded during the radio performance. The cleric, undoubtedly thinking that Salim did not appear very European, gave him a reserved welcome. Nevertheless, he listened to his recording with interest, then asked him: "You're a Catholic, of course?" Embarrassed by such an unexpected question, Salim had to admit that he was not. The man resumed: "But you are a Christian at least?" When Salim answered him once more in the negative, the priest then retorted that it was impossible for him to have a mass performed in his church written by a non-Catholic, and still less by a non-Christian.

The "Nocturne". The Lili Boulanger Prize.

Following the performance of his Mass, Salim wrote a Nocturne for solo flute and orchestra which was performed for the first time at the end of 1957, thanks to Manfred Kelkel. On this occasion, Nadia Boulanger wrote him:

"My Dear Michael,

You can't imagine how happy I am to have heard this moving and beautiful Nocturne. So true and refined in the best sense of the word. Regret to say it so hastily—am really overworked—but, you hear, and so you will know how really I feel happy.

Have always known you are "a musician", but here is a new aspect
of your personality. The orchestra sounds so well; and it reminds
me a score of you I cannot locate in my memory. In the sadness of
not seeing you is the joy also to see a new turn, I do hope, of your
life—the first steps are the hardest. If Mr Barraud has heard the
Nocturne, he must have been pleased to have shown his confidence
in the Mass.

I really congratulate you and am really not surprised but very happy;
and with my wishes, I send the wish very strong to see you soon.

As ever,

Nadia Boulanger 15 Dec 1957."

In addition to the few music theory lessons which he gave to children
at home (walking to their homes more often than not, for lack of
money to pay for the metro), Salim had found, through contacts, some
engineers whose office was next to the Bourse and whom he went to
see every Friday at lunchtime to converse with them in English.

One Friday, when he had not eaten for several days and had only
three metro tickets left, he went to give his English lesson anxiously
wondering: "What shall I do if they don't pay me today?" This is
exactly what happened; at the end of the class, one of them blithely
asked him: "It won't put you out if we pay you next Friday?" Too
timid to argue, Salim agreed, nodding his head, then got back on the
Metro to go back home.

He knew that, short of a miracle, he could not hope to find the
money to procure himself a little food for perhaps as much as a week.
Strangely resigned, he placed himself in the hands of Providence.

When he returned home, the corner of an envelope sticking out a
little from under the door caught his attention. Surprised to see that
it came from the United States, where he knew no one, he opened it
and read:

Dear Mr. Michael,

The Board of Trustees voted yesterday, at the Annual Meeting of
the Fund, to make an additional "Award of Merit," for this year

36. RUE BALLU. 9ᵉ
TÉLÉPH : TRINITE 57-91

My dear Friend

You can't imagine how happy I am to
have heard this moving + beautiful nocturne
So true and refined in the best sense of the
word. Regret to say it so hastily - am really overworked - but, you hear — + so you will know how
really I feel happy.

Have always known you are "a musician" -
but here is a new aspect of your personality -
the orchestra sounds so well — + it reminds
me a score of you I cannot locate in my memory.

In the sadness of not seeing you is the joy
also to see a new turn, I do hope, of your
life — The first steps are the hardest. If
Mr Barraud has heard the nocturne he must
have been pleased to have shown his confidence
in the Mass —

I really congratulate you + am really,
not surprised but very happy — + with
my wishes, I send the wish very strong
to see you soon

As ever
Nadia Boulanger

15 Dec 1957

only, and I have great pleasure in informing you that you are one of the two composers chosen to share this prize. Each one will receive the sum of one hundred and fifty dollars, - $150. - and the Treasurer will forward you this amount as soon as I hear from you in what form it would be best to send it to you.

The Board of Judges consists of Nadia Boulanger, Aaron Copland, Alexei Haleff, Walter Piston and Igor Stravinsky, who recommended the prize-winning scores.

With my personal congratulations and all best wishes.

Sincerely yours,

Winifred H. Johnstone Secretary Lili Boulanger Memorial Fund.

Contrary to what the letter said regarding a future payment of the money, a check for one hundred and fifty dollars was enclosed with it... Deeply moved and delighted to have won this prize for his Nocturne for flute and orchestra, Salim used his last metro ticket to go quickly to the bank to cash his check, just before the counters closed. That evening he treated himself to a feast which, several hours later, made him very ill. The first thing he did the next morning was to go out and buy a large quantity of thirty-two stave music paper to be able to write down one of his orchestral works which, for lack of the appropriate paper, had remained in draft version.

This manna from heaven, together with a few music theory lessons, would help him to survive for several months without too much difficulty. It was not only a financial blessing, but also a moral support for him to be awarded this prize from such a large number of participants. As with his Mass, Nadia Boulanger had asked to hold onto the score without revealing her reasons. He discovered, therefore, upon receiving this unexpected letter, that she had taken the initiative of entering his work into this competition. In 1952, thanks to a friend who had informed him of the existence of the Vercelli competition, he had already won a prize with his musical adaptation of an Old Testament psalm for male choir.

Without this support from Nadia Boulanger, Salim would never have succeeded in having his work performed. Since the end of the

```
              Lili Boulanger Memorial Fund, Inc.
                     122 Bay State Road
                     Boston 15, Mass.

                                    March 19th. 1958.


      Mr. Edward Michael
      117 rue Saint Dominique
      Paris 7.

      Dear Mr. Michael:

      The Board of Trustees voted yesterday, at the
      Annual Meeting of the Fund, to make an additional
      "Award of Merit", for this year only, and I have
      great pleasure in informing you that you are one
      of the two composers chosen to share this prize.
      Each one will receive the sum of one hundred and
      fifty dollars, - $150. - and the Treasurer will
      forward you this amount as soon as I hear from
      you in what form it would be best to send it to
      you.

      The Board of Judges consists of Nadia Boulanger,
      Aaron Copland, Alexei Haieff, Walter Piston and
      Igor Stravinsky, who recommended the prize-winning
      scores.

              With my personal congratulations and all
      best wishes.


                          Sincerely yours,

                          Winifred H. Johnstone
                          Winifred H. Johnstone
                          Secretary L.B.M.F.
```

war, the winds of modernism were blowing through music and it was becoming increasingly atonal and arrhythmic. Among those having influence in the music world, from the radio selection committees to publishers and critics, almost all were partisans of serial music.[*]

---

[*] See note on serialism and twelve-tone music p.149

Salim therefore encountered strong opposition from these people who criticized his music for still being tonal. This antagonism only increased with time as so-called contemporary music swept away any creation conserving a traditional form and it became increasingly rare for an author to even write notes.

When a composer wished to make one of his new works known, custom demanded he submit it to the radio selection committee. If it was accepted, he would then have to find a conductor willing to program the piece into one of his concerts. And, if the critics gave it a favorable review, the music publishers might agree to print the score and, in principle, also then work on its promotion.

Salim's compositions were systematically refused by the selection committee. In 1958 however, when he presented his "Nocturne for flute solo, celesta, harp, and orchestra", which had just received the Lili Boulanger prize, as the work had been awarded first place in a competition whose jury included Igor Stravinsky himself, it would have been difficult for the committee not to accept it, despite it not corresponding to their tastes.

After this broadcast, he used subterfuge to have some of his other orchestral works played, temporarily re-baptizing them "Nocturne" for the duration of the performance. However, he could not use this process indefinitely and he continued to encounter great difficulties in getting his music known, even though it was extremely well received by the public every time he succeeded in having it performed.

In 1954, before the performance of his Mass and the awarding of the Lili Boulanger prize for his Nocturne, Salim had, through the doctor who had treated him with such devotion and who had, for the occasion, made his immense waiting room available, organized a private concert to present some of his chamber music, including a trio for violin, alto and cello in which Salim undertook himself the part for violin. Among the guests was the music critic Jean Hamon from the "Combat" newspaper, who wrote the following review:

"... I also wanted to mention a young English composer of Eastern
origin on his mother's side: Mr Edward Michael.

He is hardly a day over 35, and I was hearing his chamber music
for the first time. We were maybe a hundred or so in the audience,
who were to experience the revelation of a musician! This was a
remarkable attempt to integrate oriental tones into Western music,
with all that might bring by way of suppleness, color, and new
expression; but beyond what might have been nothing but cunning
exoticism, Mr Michael translates the deep movements of a soul
yearning particularly towards the heights of philosophical and
religious meditation, a soul on a quest for purity, for infinite tenderness, and for living peace. This does not exclude the melancholy,
or even the despair of a creature fighting for its ideal and suffering
from its failures, imploring God to come to its aid and trusting
gently in him, buoyed by hope.

"Contained within 'Elégie', and 'Prière' for Martenot Waves and
'Trois Rituels' for two Waves and tambourine, or the Trio for
violin, alto, and cello, is inspiration which seizes you violently,
this strange emotion that one experiences is a revelation of beauty.

"There are many young instrumentalists and others, illustrious,
who are looking for quality works for their repertoires: they will
find better than that in the work of Edward Michael. When can
we expect a public concert where everyone will be able to judge
for themselves?"

However, a good review and favorable reactions from the public
did not constitute, for all that, elements likely to invert the balance of
power that was irresistibly establishing itself in favor of modern music.

"Kamaal."

After his Mass, Salim felt a pressing desire to translate a glimpse of
a mystical quest into music, by way of a tale he had invented and
entitled "Kamaal"—named for his young hero who faces many tribulations before discovering the flower of immortality. Mr Adie helped

him to write the text in English and Nelly Caron, assisted by a friend, Madame Villequez, translated it into French. Later on, Manfred Kelkel's brother produced a German version and a lady he knew translated it into Italian. The tale was, in fact, destined to become a symphonic work with narration.

As soon as the text was finished, Salim began composing the music. Given the length of the piece, however, he often found himself short of paper. Therefore, every time he was able to earn a little money giving a music theory or piano lesson to a child, he found himself facing a painful dilemma: should he eat or buy music paper? As inspiration called to him with imperious insistence, most of the time, music paper would triumph over food. Indeed, whenever he began a work, inspiration would take hold of him and the same process would recur: it was no longer possible for him to think about himself, about feeding himself, or about anything else at all, until the moment the work finally saw the light of day.

Once the music for "Kamaal" was finished, he went to see Nelly Caron and played her a few passages on the piano. Greatly moved by the beauty of his new creation, she asked him whether it would be possible for him to create a reduction for Martenot Waves, flute, string quartet, and piano; if he was able to do this, she would undertake to find performers and have the piece included in the program of a public concert. Salim was hesitant about the idea of reducing, for a small ensemble, a piece composed for orchestra, but this was an opportunity he could not afford to miss of having his music heard. He therefore rapidly completed the reduction, having planned to destroy the score for this simplified version immediately after the performance (which he duly did). Thus, "Kamaal", in this reduced version, was performed in 1958, conducted by its author. This was a great moment for Salim; his work was very well received by the public and was the object of an extremely favorable review in the magazine "Musique" which said:

"The word revelation, so frequently over-used, resumes all its truth and its purity when listening to the work of Edward Michael whose musical "presence" is indisputable.

"This likeable artist must have meditated on Plato's words: "In Art, the artist must always have the ideal of Beauty present." The Parisian press has already spoken very highly of this composer whose Mass, played on the radio, received warm approval from music lovers who were listening. This year, Mr Michael presented "Kamaal", an enchanting tale, to a large and enthusiastic audience. A very charming work, full of personal discoveries; the author has been able to create a skilled and subtle atmosphere of intense poetry. This is music written from the heart and which touches the heart of the listener. The career of Mr Michael, who was recently awarded the Lili Boulanger prize in America, is one to watch; it will certainly have some wonderful surprises in store."

Music for the Gurdjieff groups.

After the broadcast of his Mass in 1956, the Gurdjieff group leaders became interested in Salim's compositions. So, when Thomas de Hartmann (whom Salim had met in London and who wrote music for the groups) died, they suggested to Salim that he replace him.

Over the years, he composed more than seventy pieces of piano music for them. These were intended to accompany complex movements called "sacred dances", the aim of which was to help the performer to work on his attention and remain concentrated. To avoid these movements being forgotten, the groups produced private films. The music from fourteen of them was essentially composed by Salim and played on the piano by him during filming; several commercial records were made from these recordings. This work brought Salim very valuable financial support during times when he badly needed it.

In 1957, he was also asked to write a descriptive piece of music for choirs and orchestra for a radio program being produced based on the book by Georges Ivanovitch Gurdjieff: "Beelzebub's Tales to his Grandson." Being, unfortunately, greatly misunderstood at that time, Gurdjieff's work provoked passionate opposition from the clergy and Salim did not escape this intolerance. After the broadcast, he even received threatening letters from some fifty people who reproached him for having agreed to collaborate in this production, which they qualified as "diabolic"! Despite the problems this episode caused him in his subsequent dealings with radio, Salim absolutely did not regret having lent his support to the production.

Regarding the Gurdjieff groups—whose extreme seriousness and sincerity he never failed to emphasize—although Salim had always felt a deep gratitude towards them for the help he received from them, he could not, because of his oriental temperament and his deeply devotional nature, integrate into their way of thinking or adopt their approach to spiritual practice. He was unable to approach a spiritual quest intellectually and encountered difficulties communicating with people in the groups who saw his lack of formal education and his problems coping in external life as failings in his practice.

The call of India.

For a mysterious reason that went far beyond the fact that he had an Indian grandmother, India always attracted Salim in a very particular way. It was around 1947, in London, shortly after the end of the war, that he had had, for the first time, the opportunity of attending a performance of Indian dance. He never forgot the indescribable feeling that this performance, given by the great Indian dancer Ram Gopal, had awakened deep in his being—a feeling which, at the time, represented an enigma to him. It was as if this evocation of India awoke in him elusive memories that troubled him strangely.

After having met Mr Adie and learned of hatha yoga in Ouspensky's "The New Model of the Universe", he began alone, from the illustrations in a book, to execute a few postures. He continued his practice after his arrival in Paris and, in 1955, through Nelly Caron, he met someone who had spent many years in India, particularly in Madras, and who gave lessons in hatha yoga. With him, Salim learned some new asanas as well as some pranayama exercises (controlled breathing). This man showed great benevolence towards Salim and, rapidly perceiving his financial difficulties, no longer asked him to pay for his lessons. He would even invite him to lunch at his home from time to time and Salim thereby had the opportunity of sampling some Indian cuisine, which he loved.

One of his hatha yoga teacher's two daughters practiced the very same type of dance from the South of India as Ram Gopal: Bharata Natyam. Seeing how much Salim was interested in everything relating to this part of the world, and particularly in dance and music, she offered to dance for him one day. On this occasion, Salim felt once again flooded with inexplicable emotions, as if he was receiving a strange call, whose meaning he was unable to grasp. He returned home troubled; the sacred nature of these dances aroused enigmatic feelings within him which seemed, nevertheless, strangely familiar, but left him disconcerted. It was as though, in an incomprehensible way, he knew them already or had already experienced them in a distant past; but when, where, and in what circumstances...?

India was now coming more and more frequently into his mind, arousing within him the insistent desire to go there. However, he did not have enough money to live from day to day, so how could he consider such a journey? He was going to have to wait for many years before the deep aspiration he felt for this country would finally be satisfied.

His health again.

After the difficulties that had led him to the home of Madame Seu, Salim had, little by little, recovered the use of his legs, but his health remained extremely precarious and his intestinal problems became so acute that he had to go to England several times to be admitted to hospital for one or two months, sometimes even longer.

These stays were very difficult for Salim, because he would find himself in communal wards, with sometimes fifteen to twenty patients groaning or talking constantly throughout the day and snoring at night— not to mention the radio that broadcast cheap music all the time. He found himself in conditions that made his meditation particularly difficult. Furthermore, his spiritual work having developed his already naturally exceptional sensitivity even further, he suffered enormously from this lack of privacy, which brought back all the bad memories connected with the war.

During these hospitalizations, the doctors tried, always in vain, to discover the origin of his crises of diarrhea and intestinal spasms. At least he ate a little more and, despite his various problems, he regained some strength. On his return to France, he would begin writing music again and looking for ways to have it performed.

Hatha yoga as a practice.

Salim tried to practice his hatha yoga postures (asanas) as regularly as possible, which undoubtedly helped his body considerably, perhaps even enabling him to survive. He realized that mastering the technical aspect of the hatha yoga postures with a view to improving his health was certainly interesting, but it was missing the essential point. For most important was the inner state in which he practiced his postures. In other words, he felt the imperious need to be intensely present to himself when he was working on his asanas.

His entire practice was based on the clear distinction between his ordinary state of consciousness (in which the inner space of his being was generally occupied with music, but also, as it is for everybody, all sorts of images, thoughts, and automatic associations concerning the past and the future) and a superior state of pure consciousness, accessible through concentration in the present, and which is beyond form, time, and space. Salim later explained to his pupils that to recognize even the beginnings of this state within oneself was the start of the path for the aspirant, and that he would then know in which direction his attention and efforts should be directed.

He understood that one of the major obstacles preventing an aspirant from maintaining this inner presence to oneself continually is a lack of unity between the three components of one's being, in other words, mind, body, and feeling. Without realizing it, one is constantly in a state of disunity, the body goes in one direction with its constant needs, the mind wanders among all sorts of preoccupations or internal chatter, and feeling is absent most of the time. In order for a spiritual practice to have the greatest chances of success, it is a great help to bring these three aspects of oneself together to make them work in unison. The body should contribute through sensation and relaxation, the mind by focusing its attention on a support, and the feeling through a state of respect and devotion towards that which one is seeking to attain within oneself.

This unification of the three aspects of his being was something Salim had already practiced as a soloist: while his body had to master the technical aspect of the instrument, his mind had to remember the thousands of notes in the work being played without allowing himself at any moment to think of anything else, and his feeling was exalted by the music, maintaining his interest over time. He knew from experience what it is to be whole in what one does and to what extent one then finds resources within oneself; it is this that allows great artists to accomplish marvels.

Thus, when he was suddenly brought back to himself, realizing that once more, he had fallen back to sleep within himself, he would wonder about the aspect of himself that had caused his fall. Was it his body that had laid claim to his attention with its constant demands? Was it his mind that had carried him far away from himself, into the past or the future? Or was it his feeling that had weakened? He would then tirelessly renew the effort to reunify himself again in order to re-establish himself in a state of being and of consciousness different from his ordinary state.

Slow walking.

The fact of finding himself alone, without a master, without books, as he did not read, represented a great trial for Salim. Of course, he had friends in the Gurdjieff groups, but they were unable to help him, because his meditation practices, the means he employed, the inner sound in particular, but also all the exercises that he invented for himself, and the experiences that he had through the intensity of his concentration were unrelated to the work of Gurdjieff. Thus, he felt entirely alone, without external help.

During his daily meditation sessions, when he was concentrating on the Nada, the inner sound that he heard inside his ears and head, to which he added corporeal sensation and breathing, he descended deeply within himself; a most fine and ethereal energy would delicately permeate his whole being, miraculously transforming his feeling of himself and his consciousness. This extraordinary sensation of transparency of being and of consciousness brought with it an unparalleled felicity and delicious peace beyond any words. The Nada would sing its mysterious song inside his head, and his head seemed to become strangely translucent, with his consciousness extending out in all directions around him. This sublime Nada sang in his ears with such supernal beauty and intensity that the entire Cosmos appeared to be vibrating with it. Nothing else seemed to exist but this enigmatic song of the Divine, composed of all the subtle harmonies and ultrasounds in the mystical world, ever vibrating through space far into infinity.

However, even if he reached very high states of consciousness at certain privileged moments during his meditation, he had to admit that, as soon as he rejoined the outer world and entered into contact with other people, he almost immediately lost a large part of the positive effects.

He had been able to observe that, the further he succeeded in being conscious of himself in a way that was not habitual to him in his active life, the further he would go in his meditation. Conversely, the more his meditation deepened, allowing him to experience ever more subtle and ethereal states, the more he was able to come back to himself in his active life; one affected the other. It had always seemed evident to him that if one reduced one's practice to a few moments of meditation in the morning and in the evening, one would somehow begin from the "bottom" each time, without being able to truly tear away from oneself to experience and prolong the taste of another state of being and of consciousness.

To put this superior state of consciousness of himself to the challenge of movement and to succeed in re-evoking it during his everyday activities as well, he began to practice slow walking between two meditations, rediscovering, without knowing it, a classic Buddhist practice. This walking had a particularly calming effect, on both the physical and the mental planes and later became a prelude to his seated meditation. He would keep his attention fixed firmly on the movement of his feet, fully aware at each fraction of a second where the foot that had just left the ground was, attentively following it throughout the whole period it was moving in the air until it finally came down and touched the ground again. Then his attention turned straightaway to the other foot and, in a likewise manner, he was vigilantly conscious of its every movement from the moment it left the ground to the moment it came down again.

When his concentration became very sharp and sustained, he was astonished to perceive how shrill and strong the inner mystical sound vibrated inside his ears, like a divine token benignly assisting him and inspiring in him the desire to make yet further efforts.

Work in life – Listening to the sound of his voice.

In addition to the few music theory lessons he gave to children, Salim found work from time to time as a copyist, which involved separately copying out, as many times as necessary, the different instrumental parts required for the execution of a work for orchestra or chorus. At that time, when photocopying did not yet exist, it was a meticulous task, demanding sustained concentration if errors were to be avoided. The task could represent several hours work a day for weeks, or even as much as a month. In order not to lose himself in what he was doing and to use this work for his practice, Salim applied himself to retaining constantly the sensation of both his left leg and his hand while he was writing. This allowed him to work without useless tension or fatigue; he was happy to do this work, not considering it a chore and without wanting to be rid of it, as one generally has a tendency to do with everything.

By always seeking to consolidate and increase his state of presence during his active life, Salim gave himself a demanding spiritual exercise which brought him the greatest benefit; to listen constantly to the sound of his voice when speaking to people. It involved listening to the actual sound of the voice itself and not merely the voice in general. He took care not to interfere in any way with the tone of his voice, or purposely attempt to change it, but continue, patiently and dispassionately, to listen.

This particular and unusual way of working brought to his attention the side of himself—or rather, the who in him—who usually spoke, and with what aspect of himself he was habitually identified. He was at times surprised, and even shocked, to hear in the sound of his voice the changes of pitch, intonations, and accentuations that were all so revealing of the feelings that he was secretly harboring in him at that moment.

Each time he was abruptly called back to himself from this unhappy state of self-forgetfulness, he saw immediately and better understood into what aspect of himself he had fallen asleep again, and which side of his nature had once more taken over, speaking in his name and acting to his cost, without his having been aware of it.

One day, he found that his voice, of its own accord, took on another tone, a special tone, one that felt astonishingly true, tranquil, and natural. There was no mistake or any doubt whatsoever when this took place. For, at that moment, he felt curiously separate and distant from his voice, which had a new and genuine ring in it; it seemed to rise from another part of his being, vibrating from the depths of his solar plexus.

Truly divided – Concentration exercises as a prelude to meditation.

Despite the transcendent states he reached, Salim still observed within himself some resistance in the face of the constant renouncement that was asked of him. While he was meditating, the most wonderful of inspirations would come to him, the music was calling him, he had to write it! In other words, he was divided and, as he later said to his pupils: "truly divided!"

How to remain in the present, empty and available to that which called to him from within? Salim had understood that it is always "now" that the effort must be made rather than waiting for the internal or external circumstances to change, that it is in the very instant that the transformation of oneself occurs and never later on or tomorrow. He needed means. He invented—or remembered from an inaccessible past—specific concentration exercises that mobilized simultaneously the body, the mind, and the feeling (he described several of these in his books), which he would practice in his room, with all the intensity he was capable of and for a sufficiently long period of time, before devoting himself to his meditation so as to be able to re-establish a purity of consciousness and an inner silence that he had recognized within himself as belonging to the Sacred.

He would then feel inhabited by an unusual presence that would transport him to another plane, beyond time and space, where reigned the absolute immobility of the Infinite Being. The Nada resonated within him so spectacularly that, not only did it give him the impression of hearing the song of the Universe within his being, but this mysterious sound also gave him the indescribable feeling of perceiving the vibration of a vast eternal silence.

Meditation while observing one's thoughts.

At other times, when he was encountering too many difficulties to meditate, he would come back to the observation of the thoughts and images that arose in his mind, without allowing himself to identify with them.

Each time he turned his attention inward to look at his thoughts and try to seize them, he found only phantoms and nothing tangible for him to get hold of. His thoughts had vanished instantly into the void, leaving in their place only a mysterious vacuum.

He realized he had found a subtle, highly effective, and astonishingly simple weapon with which, through patient and repeated practice, he could eventually free himself from the tangles and tyranny of his ordinary thinking and rise to higher spheres of the mind.

As he plunged deeper into himself in as tranquil and simple a manner as possible, while continuing to watch his thoughts, they quieted to such a great extent that the gap between each succeeding thought became much wider and more evident. As he fixed his attention on this gap, or void between every individual thought and managed to increase its duration, he would begin to feel in him a most extraordinary inner silence and sublime peace beyond anything that anyone can ordinarily know. It appeared to him as a divine cosmic balm, sweetly filling his whole being with an indescribable sense of sacred serenity. What at first seemed to him to be a mere emptiness was in fact filled with an infinite expanse of a highly subtle and impersonal Consciousness, a mysterious invisible "Spectator" silently witnessing.

As he described it later, this unusual state of consciousness can in some way be compared to a translucent sky without a here or a there, an up or a down, a front or a back—a clear, translucent, and immeasurable sky where there are no clouds, birds, or any other object passing across it. Without having known it, he owed to its benign grace his existence, his intelligence, and the continual animation and sustenance of his life.

In addition to the elevated states he attained through this form of meditation, he understood, little by little, that this practice enabled him to be increasingly conscious of the thoughts and associations of ideas that unfolded within him throughout the day.

Spiritual dreams. The different categories of dreams.

It was at this time that Salim had several distinctive dreams which were, for him, incontestably spiritual in nature, and which brought him precious guidance at moments in his life when he was in the greatest need of help. These dreams would normally come to him very early in the morning, when he was on the point of waking.

Those related below are given by way of example only, as he had many others.

In the first dream, he found himself in a vast room, illuminated on his left by high windows. In a corner, in front of him, was a bed. A fairly old spiritual master was lying on this bed. The master was the size of a child. He was crucified like Christ, and was agonizing on his cross. An atmosphere of intense suffering reigned in this place. It was Salim's duty to take care of this dying man and he felt deep sorrow for him. Through the large door that opened behind him he could hear a sizeable crowd which, unconcerned by the pain of the man being crucified, chattered incessantly. Little by little, this crowd entered into the room until, finally, it entirely filled it. Salim tried in vain to interrupt this futile and pointless prattling. He was saddened by his powerlessness to make this mass of people understand the gravity of the drama that was unfolding.

The dream ended there; distraught by the impression that it left within him, Salim remained preoccupied by its meaning for a long time. He realized that, in fact, the man being crucified was him, or, rather, the superior aspect of his nature, and that the noisy crowd was composed of the different characters who, within him as within every human being, invaded his mind and represented a source of continual distraction. All this inner chatter and all these futile thoughts were preventing him from remaining centered on his goal, in other words, preventing him from connecting with the Divine Aspect of his nature which would remain crucified within him until he discovered the means to silence these interferences.

At another time, he had a dream that made a strong impression on him. He found himself in a deep well, dark and frightening. Far above him, he could see a bright light while all around him there was nothing but mud and darkness. He felt lost and terrified. He called for help in order to be able to get out of this well. Instantly two arms, without a body, descended; one was holding a large hammer and the other enormous nails. The two hands quickly set to work, hammering a nail into the wall of the well around every fifty centimeters until they reached top, then the arms vanished.

Salim awoke very troubled, anxious to decipher the meaning of this dream. It took a little time for him to understand the message: help would be given him, but only up to a certain point. It would then be up to him to accomplish his share of the effort required to climb the ladder and reach the inner Light he aspired so ardently to reach.

In the third dream that came to him at this time, he found himself in a cathedral. A faint bluish glimmer fell from the stained glass windows; a strange atmosphere reigned. Many tombs lay side by side in the nave and a tall priest dressed in a long dark robe addressed him with solemnity; he was speaking to him directly in his mind, without the medium of words. As Salim was not able to grasp what the priest was trying to communicate to him in a severe manner, the priest then raised his arm to order him to look to his right. Salim turned apprehensively and saw, just behind him, a naked figure, neither man nor woman, standing on a tombstone. What struck him was that in the place of its head, was a white marble cross. While the asexual being descended slowly into the burial vault until it had completely disappeared, the marble cross was confirming, with an uninterrupted affirmative nod, that in fact, what the priest was trying to communicate was right and just, and that he must accept it.

It was only later that Salim understood the meaning of this mysterious dream. At an unexpected moment, he abruptly realized that, if he wanted to progress in his spiritual approach, he would have to die to himself. The marble cross in the place of the head symbolized that which must be continually sacrificed, in other words the mind and the idea that one has of oneself.

Following the various experiences he had in this domain, Salim classified the dreams in three categories.

The first included all the ordinary dreams that one might have, which result from the influence of events experienced during the day, during the preceding days, or even in a more distant past. These dreams can reveal certain aspects of oneself, and it may prove interesting to study them. It is principally this category of dream that is the object of interpretation in contemporary psychology.

The dreams described above belong to a second category and are extremely important for an aspirant engaged upon a spiritual path. Their purpose is to help the aspirant overcome certain difficulties encountered in his quest or to understand which direction he should take, which he is unable to fathom in his diurnal state due to his identification with the demands of the external world. These dreams come from the superior aspect of his nature and always leave him with an impression of profound mystery which insistently incites him to question their meaning.

Finally, there is a third category of dream which Salim subdivided into two. It includes, on one hand, telepathic dreams. This type of dream results from receiving thoughts or intentions that another person has just emitted about the author of the dream. It testifies to a particularly receptive state that can occur during nocturnal sleep. For example, a person receives a letter whose content has already been revealed during a dream; or an acquaintance or even a stranger may come to visit, and the dreamer had encountered this very same person recently in a dream.

And there are, on the other hand, premonitory dreams, whereby one is forewarned several days before a person dies, or of a danger to be avoided. One can even dream, as is the case in the example that will be mentioned below, of an event that will only happen many years later. One finds oneself then, with amazement, in the same places, making the same gestures, and feeling the same feelings that one experienced in a dream a long time before.

While Salim was still living in Paris, he had a very curious dream which unfolded in three sequences and which left him, subsequently, feeling very troubled. Initially he was walking beside a young blond woman on a high mountain plateau and, on arriving at a clump of three trees that stood out against the sky, he raised his hand to wave goodbye as she moved away from him to his right. He then found himself walking alone along a cliff top beside the ocean; he looked down towards the foot of this cliff where three huge smooth rocks rose up and were being battered by the waves. A strange atmosphere permeated the scene. He lifted his head quickly but the sun was so dazzling that he had to raise his arm to protect his eyes. The scenery changed once more, and he was now walking in a western street which was becoming ever foggier, colder, and more sinister; he felt so frozen that he cried out vehemently: "But, I don't want to go this way, I want to go where there is some sun!"

The years passed and, when he found himself in India, in Darjeeling, he was walking on a high mountain plateau, alongside a young woman who had become his wife, when he suddenly realized that she was the very same woman who had appeared in the dream he had had in Paris three months before even meeting her for the first time, more than nine years previously. Then, the same three huge trees that he had seen in his dream came into view on the horizon.

Three weeks later, when he was in Pondicherry, tormented by a decision he was facing concerning his marriage, he was walking along a cliff top, in deep thought, letting his gaze drop down to the shore where there were three huge blocks of smooth stone; surprised to recognize the scenery from the second part of his dream, he raised his eyes suddenly, but the sun was so strong he had to protect his eyes with his arm, and the whole scene came flooding back to his memory with astonishing clarity.

Lastly, several months later, he had gone back to his family in London for a few weeks; he had been heartbroken at having left India. He decided one day to go out and walk a little. It was a glacial month of December; he found himself plunged into the thick London fog when, suddenly, he remembered, with his amazement, the final part of his dream, while saying to himself in despair: "But I don't want to stay here, I want to go back to India, where there is some sun!" It was as if, mysteriously, he had been warned, nine years earlier, of the ordeal that he was currently going through.

Salim often spoke in his books of the state into which a human being is plunged during his nocturnal sleep, and which is an indication, both of the state one will experience after death (although that will be on an entirely different scale), as well as of another dimension in which time no longer exists for the sleeper.

When one dreams, the psychic world in which one is immersed no longer obeys the rules of time and space of the familiar universe that one experiences in the diurnal state. Premonitory and telepathic dreams illustrate the unsuspected possibilities of the mind and its mysterious capacity to transcend, on occasions, the spatio-temporal dimensions in which one is ordinarily imprisoned.

Rue du Cherche-Midi.

In 1958, Madame Seu, who had just lost a very dear friend, suddenly decided to enter a convent, to which she also donated her apartment. Salim was therefore confronted with the necessity of finding somewhere else to live.

He told Nelly Caron of his problem who, in turn, explained his situation to her friend Madame Villequez (with whom she had trans-lated the text for "Kamaal", Salim's symphonic tale, into French). During the ensuing conversation, Madame Villequez, learning that he was practically without financial resources and did not know how to overcome this stroke of bad luck, told Nelly Caron of a tiny box room she owned on the sixth floor of the building she lived in on the Rue du Cherche-Midi; she explained that, if Salim would be willing to live there temporarily, she would be happy to make it available to him free of charge, and would even provide a bed with sheets and blankets. Salim quickly accepted this offer, coming, as it did, like a blessing from heaven.

The cubbyhole measured about 2.70 meters long by 1.50 meters wide. There was just enough room for a small chair at the end of the

Salim rue du Cherche-Midi

bed and, in a corner against the wall, stood the imposing pile of orchestral music scores that Salim had composed, a pile which would, over the years, become taller than he was. The only suitcase he owned, containing his few spare clothes, was stored under the bed. A small window allowing him to see the sky opened onto the courtyard. There was neither water, nor heating, nor electricity. The toilets and a tap were located on the landing. Despite the fact that the conditions proved to be very different from the comfort he had known at Madame Seu's apartment, Salim was happy to have a roof over his head that allowed him to stay in Paris; without it, he would have had no choice but to return to England, something he wished to avoid at all costs, as he could no longer bear either the climate or the atmosphere of London.

Although Madame Villequez had offered him this cramped cell on a temporary basis, because she envisaged, sooner or later, knocking through into the adjoining bedroom to create a studio, he would stay there for nearly ten years, practically until his departure for India, constantly aware, nevertheless, of the precariousness of this shelter which he knew to be temporary.

He got into the habit of sitting on his bed to write his music, placing before him, by way of a small table, a plank with two foldable supports, which he would fold away afterwards and store against the wall. When he practiced his hatha yoga, he would perform certain postures on the bed and, for others, he would slide underneath it, placing his suitcase on the chair. He went once a week to the public baths, which were then still in existence, near the Rue de Rennes.

As he often worked until very late and did not always have the money to buy candles, he would sometimes write his music by nothing more than the light of the moon which, on certain nights, weakly lit his window. As it was impossible for him to cook, he had to content himself with a few pieces of fruit, cheese, eggs, and raw vegetables, together with some bread. He was later able to procure a small camping stove on which he would make a cup of tea when he had money to pay for the gas cartridges.

In addition to the chronic lack of substantial food that added to his health problems, every year, when the leaves on the trees began to turn, they announced another ordeal to be faced and one that would prove to be not insignificant. In effect, as his miniscule room had no means of heating, he suffered enormously in the winter. He had to write his music muffled up inside his coat and wrapped in blankets, but, despite this, he could not avoid feeling frozen on the coldest days of the winter.

His financial resources were so minimal that, each time he managed to give a music theory lesson to a child or copy a few scores in order to earn a little money, he found himself confronted again with the same dilemma: would he use this sum to feed himself or to buy music paper. Inspirations would sometimes shout in his ears with such insistence that they gave him no respite until he granted them the right of being brought into the manifest world.

It was, therefore, the music that most often prevailed and, instead of buying something to eat, he would visit the specialist stationer, where he had become a regular customer. He was always in need of this precious paper, as he wrote an enormous amount; in fact, despite his difficult life, he was very inspired. He was badly dressed and his friends, who often thought he looked haggard, did not suspect that the reason for this was lack of sufficient food.

The precarious existence that he was leading and his lack of formal education continually caused him difficulties, particularly when it came to defending himself in a western society which remained incomprehensible to him and to which he never succeeded in adapting. Every time he found himself facing a situation that required a certain degree of education, he was confronted by his incapacity to resolve it. So when,

ÉCOLE D'ART MARTENOT
NEUILLY · 23, Rue Saint-Pierre · MAL 34-08
AUTOBUS : 43 · 73 · 82 · 174   MÉTRO : SABLONS
PARIS · 11, Rue Daubigny · WAGRAM 99-24
AUTOBUS : 30-31-53-84-94 · MÉTRO : MALESHERBES

Je soussigné, Maurice MARTENOT, Directeur de l'ECOLE d'ART
MARTENOT, Professeur au CONSERVATOIRE NATIONAL SUPERIEUR
de MUSIQUE de PARIS, Chevalier de la LEGION d'HONNEUR, au
titre du Ministère de l'EDUCATION NATIONALE,

Certifie connaître, depuis plus de dix ans, Monsieur
Edward MICHAEL, demeurant 21, rue du Cherche-Midi à PARIS .

Indépendamment de la grande estime que je lui porte.pour
ses qualités humaines exceptionnelles, j'ai la plus grande
admiration pour son oeuvre de compositeur .

Sans se laisser influencer par les diverses tendances
contemporaines, on trouve chez Monsieur Edward MICHAEL,les
marques d'une sincérité totale, mettant toujours son Art
au service de la spiritualité .

Fait à NEUILLY, le 8 février 1965 .

Maurice Martenot

Declaration from Monsieur Martenot for the renewal of Salim's residence permit.

I, the undersigned, Maurice Martenot, director of the ECOLE D'ART MARTENOT, Professor at the CONSERVATOIRE NATIONAL SUPERIEUR de MUSIQUE de PARIS, Knight of the LEGION OF HONOR, under the Ministry of NATIONAL EDUCATION, Certify that I have known, for more than ten years, Mr Edward MICHAEL, residing at 21, Rue du Cherche-Midi in PARIS. Independently of the great esteem in which I hold him for his exceptional human qualities, I have the greatest admiration for his work as a composer.

Without allowing himself to be influenced by various contemporary tendencies, Mr Edward MICHAEL displays the traits of total sincerity, always placing his Art at the service of spirituality.

NEUILLY, February 8, 1965

for example, he had to renew his residence permit every year and he had to prove he had the financial means to meet his living costs, he found himself faced with a veritable headache. Fortunately, he received help from his friends, in this case, Maurice Martenot and Nelly Caron, the latter having never ceased to provide him, throughout all these years, with precious help writing letters for him that he would not have been able to write alone and always striving to promote his music.

Unexpected kind assistance.

Near the building where Salim lived was a grocery store run by two young women and their mother; driven by his lack of money, Salim had the idea, one day, to go and ask them if they might agree to sell him any damaged fruit or vegetables or any other expired products that they might have left over. Looking at him with an air of surprise, they nevertheless acquiesced to his timidly formulated request with kindness and asked him to return at the end of the day. That evening, when he returned, they had prepared a carton full of fruit, carrots, and wilted lettuces for him. To his surprise, they wanted no payment at all, even proposing that he come back to see them two or three times a week. His heart brimming with gratitude, he returned home.

From this moment, they ensured he was supplied regularly with blemished fruit and vegetables. Just a few days later, to Salim's great surprise, they put into his hands a box covered in aluminum foil which he felt was warm, then they pushed him gently towards the door without saying a word; he guessed that they had put aside a hot dish for him. His throat tightened with emotion and he could not help letting a few tears run down his cheeks; one of them put her arm around his shoulder accompanying him kindly to the door.

Throughout the years that he lived in this place, they showed remarkable generosity towards him, supplying him two or three times a week with a hot meal, not to mention the spoiled groceries. He discovered that they liked music and, when one of his works was broadcast on the radio, he would make sure he told them. They were delighted to hear his compositions and never failed to tell him how much they enjoyed them.

Everything is ritual.

However difficult the conditions in which he found himself might be, Salim did not, for all that, neglect his spiritual practices. Every time he had a free moment, he would sit on his bed in the lotus position, facing the window, then he would close his eyes and begin to meditate. And, when he was outside, in the street or on the metro, he never wasted his time; he would undertake the diverse exercises for concentration in active life that he was continually discovering—or rediscovering from an undetermined past.

He felt that he must invent what he needed for himself, his experience as a musician constituting for him an invaluable support.

He noticed the extent to which, over the course of the day, the repetition of familiar gestures, become automatic habits, proved to be an obstacle to the state of inner vigilance that he wished to consolidate within himself. He therefore did his utmost to transform this routine into a practice of awakening. He would say to himself: everything is ritual.

Each morning, instead of getting up, washing, dressing, and eating automatically, without interest, in a state of inner oblivion, he focused on the Nada and followed his different physical movements through his mind's eye. At first, this required certain inner preparations that had to be renewed daily. When he was rightly centered in himself during his various activities, he was surprised to see how different the same gestures—washing, dressing, eating, and so on—could be made to be each day. He began to discover hidden meanings and even unusual beauties in ordinary things or situations where he least expected them, and which had always escaped his attention before. What is more, he started receiving subtle understandings as well as flashes of spiritual insights into himself and things that were of incalculable value for his inner quest. Apart from opening the doors to other new experiences, this enabled him to read, behind the veil of outer appearances, the secret mysteries of other living creatures, plants, and what seem to be inanimate objects.

The act of eating.

Salim realized that the act of eating represented an important moment for his spiritual practice. He took his meals alone in his bedroom. He observed that a strange phenomenon occurred within him at this precise moment: often the harm that others had done to him would suddenly resurface, and he would find himself brooding over what he would have liked to say to these people who had wounded him, in other words, he was "eating" them while he ate his food. He therefore undertook a specific practice to invert this tendency. With every mouthful, he took care to send them a benevolent thought.

At other times, he noticed that mealtimes were occasions during which sadness might rise up within him. He would eat with a sort of heaviness, without appetite. He saw that this also needed to be transmuted, as the food that he was eating was living and he had a responsibility towards it.

Like all human beings, he was placed in the situation of having no choice in that he had to eat to survive; but he saw that he could, at least, consume his food with a different inner approach and disposition of mind than one ordinarily does. It was not for him a mere sentimentality. Thanks to his spiritual experiences, he knew that life is not what it appears on the surface. Its outer aspect is certainly not all there is to it, for, as he later said, behind the visible world lies a far greater and more important Universe that can be known by a seeker through the efforts he makes to know himself.

Several times, during intense moments of inner presence in active life, he entered into direct contact with the living element that he was eating.

A tomato, for example, actually felt pain when he cut and ate it. And he realized that being sensitive to the kind of suffering the tomato underwent at such a time contributed to alleviating at least some of its anguish, as well as to prepare it to accede to its impending death in a quieter state than it would otherwise do.

The tomato felt that the person cutting it knew its fears and through his sincerity of feelings and silent understanding, it was helped to sense that the imminent loss of its individuality as a tomato would not be in vain and that only in this way could it be transformed into something finer for its evolution to a higher form of life.

While remaining truly present and conscious of himself while eating his food, without being identified with the act of eating and his association of thoughts, as one generally is, Salim began to get very subtle glimpses of his ordinary self engaged in eating.

As he persisted in making efforts to maintain a state of intense inner presence while eating, these momentary glimpses not only came to him more frequently, but they became also deeper and more prolonged, until in the end they revealed clearly to him the way his ordinary self received each morsel in his mouth, the way in which he ate it, the sort of pleasure he derived from absorbing it, including even the secret fears he had in him should he perhaps not have enough of it for his enjoyment or survival.

The arising of this particular consciousness rendered it possible for him to distinguish this individual in him, while remaining distant, in the background, silently watching the person who was occupied in eating, thus showing the latter to be different and separate from itself.

In this way, it merely bore impartial witness both to the individual in him consuming his food, as well as to the act of eating, without itself being involved in either of them.

Time stops.

As Salim succeeded in remaining ever more present to and conscious of himself, in terms of both depth and duration, it became increasingly clear to him that his perception of time differed according to the level of consciousness on which he found himself.

The deeper he went in meditation, and the loftier the spiritual states he touched, the more the motion and feeling of time altered and took on an entirely different aspect. The greater the merger into a higher state of consciousness, the slower and less perceptible time became until, in the still more exalted mystical states, it felt as if it stopped altogether.

In this state, there was nothing but the sense of an "Eternal Nowness", accompanied by an indescribable tranquility. When he reached this deep state, Salim began to feel and to understand what was meant by true adoration. In fact, without having intended it, he was in a state of reverential adoration.

This alteration of the movement of time also occurred during certain concentration exercises in his active life. One day while he was concentrating both on the sky above his head and on the earth beneath his feet and on himself between earth and sky, (an exercise that he explains in detail in "La Quête Suprême" [The Supreme Quest]), while he was walking on the Pont de l'Alma in Paris, time stopped completely. Just as with a movie where one pauses on an image, the world came to a complete standstill; the people walking, the cars driving, all activity in the city froze in absolute silence, then movement resumed its habitual course.

Many years later, he found the description of a similar experience in a book about time that a friend had given us; it was "Living Time" by Maurice Nicoll; Salim discovered in it some comprehension and descriptions of experiences he had had and which he had not been able to speak of, being unable to express them. The experience was related as follows:

"Now, I Joseph, was walking, and I walked not. And I looked up in the air and saw the air in amazement. And I looked up unto the pole of the heaven and saw it standing still, and the fowls of heaven without motion. And I looked upon the earth and saw a dish set, and workmen lying by it, and their hands were in the dish; and they that were chewing chewed not, and they that were lifting the food lifted it not and they that put it to their mouth put it not thereto, but the faces of all of them were looking upward. And behold there were sheep being driven, and they went not forward but stood still; and the shepherd lifted his hand to smite them with his staff, and his hand remained up. And I looked upon the stream of the river and saw the mouths of the kids upon the water and they drank not. And of a sudden, all things moved onward in their course." (The Apocryphal New Testament)

The various experiences Salim had were both an encouragement to him and the sign that he was moving in the right direction. This was even more necessary as, sometimes, because of the solitude in which he found himself and the lack of direction from a master, he experienced moments of veritable despair.

New morning exercise. The power of thought.

Although, thanks to the generosity of Madame Villequez, Salim was not paying rent, he still had to feed and clothe himself. "How?" was the question that haunted him much of the time. How was he to feed himself, to procure music paper, to have his work performed, to find more time for his meditation... ; he was overwhelmed by too much "how?"

It was in this context that he understood that the moment he opened his eyes in the morning was particularly important, for the very first thoughts that arose in his mind had a significant effect on his being and his feelings and determined, any unforeseen events in external life notwithstanding, what the rest of the day would be for him. All the imaginings, the inner chatter, and, particularly, the type of repetitive thoughts that crossed his mind at this moment would continue to color his being and his feelings throughout the day, for better or for worse. By their incessant repetition, these thoughts would plow their furrow ever more deeply into his being. Consequently, he realized the importance of a practice at this moment of waking in order to impress a determined direction in his mind, so as not to be submersed in anxiety over what external life might be reserving for him by way of surprises on that day.

This practice would be based on a spiritual law, whose great importance Salim had come to realize, that two thoughts cannot coexist. Consequently, it is in this that resides the human being's hope of succeeding in controlling his mind.

Salim invented a series of words and syllables—without any particular meaning in order to avoid any association of ideas—forming a sequence that he would repeat, changing the order of it in such a way as to demand from him an effort of vigilance if he wanted to avoid making mistakes; this demanded of him a mental renouncement that was not easy to achieve, but he quickly saw its benefits. (He explained all the details of this exercise in his book "Pratique spirituelle et éveil intérieur" [Spiritual Practice and Inner Awakening]).

He also accorded great importance to preparing his day, using imagination in a positive way to visualize himself in the various circumstances of this day as he wished to be, that is to say, always more vigilant and present to himself.

At other moments of the day, he would, while inhaling consciously, repeat sequences of words within himself such as "strength, courage, confidence," or, to renew his effort by drawing on a devotional feeling, short prayers, such as: "Immaculate Source, Grant me Thy Grace, give me the strength to remain actively conscious of myself."

He would also use the power of thought to help his body, repeating "from instant to instant, by the Divine Grace, I am becoming better and better."

A very dear friendship.

Not long after his arrival in this neighborhood, Salim met René Zuber, a man of around fifty-five years old, who was a member of the Gurdjieff groups. He was a filmmaker by profession and, when the groups wanted to produce a private film of their sacred dances, it was always who organized and supervised the filming. Every year or two,

René Zuber

the groups released a new film, presenting ten to fourteen of the dances, for which Salim wrote the music. As he did not have a telephone, and René Zuber lived about half an hour's walk from the Rue du Cherche-Midi, every time a new project was determined upon, the filmmaker would go to Salim's lodgings to ask him if he could come to watch the dances (also called "movements" by the groups) so as to be able to compose the music for them.

His meeting with René Zuber and his wife was providential for Salim who was living in great solitude. A very strong friendship was formed between them. Sometimes, he would receive a surprise visit from one or the other inviting him to come and share their meal. When they left Paris for an apartment located in a south-western suburb, in a very pleasant, verdant area, they had the generosity, having observed the conditions Salim was living in, to let him have the use of their apartment whenever they went on vacation.

René Zuber regularly travelled to North Africa to visit the Sufis. He mentioned one day, in Salim's presence, the striking lesson that one of them had given him in just a few words. When he asked if there were other masters in the area, the Sufi had answered him: "There are millions of masters, but not a single disciple!"

Salim explained later to his pupils that this Sufi had wanted to emphasize the extent to which each of life's circumstances can become a means to spiritual growth and, therefore, is somehow a "master", but that, generally, one does not know how to learn from it.

Whenever Salim spoke of the Zubers, it was always with deep gratitude. When, in 1974, on his return from India, he was confronted with undertaking the procedures to settle his divorce, it was René Zuber who came to his aid and found him the lawyer he needed. When

René Zuber died a few years later, Salim knew he had just lost an invaluable friend and one of the rare people with whom he was able to have a deep personal exchange.

Salim abandons the violin.

During the eight years that had passed since his arrival in France, Salim had always battled to preserve his soloist's technique; it was difficult for him to practice his violin, because of the neighbors who could not tolerate hearing him working for hours on end. He had also played for free here and there in private, simply to experience the pleasure of giving a real concert.

A young playwright suggested one day that Salim write the music for the play he was planning to produce. He had contacted a flutist, a violinist, a viola player, and a cellist, and asked Salim if he could compose for this ensemble. Salim immediately agreed to help him for free and, to expand the group a little, added a piano part, which he proposed to play himself, while conducting the other musicians with the hand that would be free from time to time. Unfortunately, for the whole of the play's run, he was in agony due to his health problems, which gave him no respite.

Following this painful experience, he realized that giving concerts would henceforth be impossible for him. So, when he moved to the Rue du Cherche-Midi, he decided to stop playing the violin altogether and to devote his energies entirely to his spiritual practices and his musical creations.

Throughout this time, India never stopped calling silently to him. Manfred Kelkel, who had married, invited Salim to his house from time to time and, sometimes, Salim would share with his friend his desire to travel one day to this country that fascinated him so; it was a keen nostalgia that arose within him at the most unexpected moments and held his attention with insistence.

Having his music played.

Manfred Kelkel, whose style was more modern than Salim's and who, through his senior position at Éditions Heugel, had had a good introduction into the world of music, had, little by little, acquired a certain renown. Making use of the friendships that he had been able to form with certain conductors, he succeeded from time to time in having some of Salim's creations performed. In fact, it could be said that, for Salim, their meeting was a blessing. The Saarlandish composer greatly admired the mysterious orchestral colors of Salim's music; he always proved to be of precious assistance and was, for Salim, a constant source of encouragement. Throughout these years leading up to Salim's departure for India, despite the hostility with which the contemporary artistic lobby opposed all music that was still tonal, Manfred Kelkel always strove to have his friend's symphonic works performed.

Through Nelly Caron, Salim one day had the opportunity of meeting a famous soprano, Noémie Perugia. After having listened to the recording of his Mass, the singer was so moved by the music that she asked him if he might have a composition for voice and small orchestra. She added that she would be happy to organize a public concert followed by a broadcast of the work on the radio. It so happened that, scarcely one or two years earlier, Salim had composed just such a piece for mezzo soprano, two flutes, piano, and string orchestra, entitled "Les Soirées de Tedjlah." As Noémie Perugia was very well known, she was able to have the project broadcast on the radio without going through the selection committee.

The concert took place at the "Ecole Normale de Musique", before a very exclusive audience. The orchestra that Noémie Perugia had succeeded in putting together was conducted by Salim himself and the work met with unequivocal success, as far as the public was concerned, and great enthusiasm from the performers. The evening was recorded by a team from the radio and aired several days later.

When she gave concerts playing the Martenot Waves, Nelly Caron always tried to have Salim's compositions included in the program. She even succeeded in releasing a record featuring a compilation of several works for Martenot Waves by different composers, including the "Elégie" for Waves and piano composed by Salim. On this occasion, Jean Hamon, who had already shown interest in Salim's musical creations, wrote a laudatory review in his newspaper "Combat".

Having one's music played was a difficult enough task, but having it printed proved to be even more problematic. Nevertheless, Manfred Kelkel succeeded in interesting Éditions Ricordi in Salim's Mass. Later, again as a result of his recommendation, Éditions Transatlantiques and Éditions Choudens agreed to publish more of his orchestral works.

Musique et Radio.

Towards the end of 1961, an article appeared in the review "Musique et Radio" entitled "The composers of today" which said:

"The attention of the musical world has been drawn particularly towards Edward Michael after the two performances of his Mass by the French Radio diffusion (Mass for choir, two string orchestras, celesta, harp, glockenspiel and percussion). We declare at once that this work of lofty inspiration cannot leave one indifferent and emphasize that it cannot leave the veritable public indifferent— which is rather exceptional with a contemporary work—for on the whole modern music is not made to please music critics only.

"One guesses in this composer a real power of expression, a surprising originality which shows an authentic creative personality, a strongly developed craft.

"However, the case of this musician enables us to state once more that it is not necessary to use those so-called vanguard processes to create a new language or a way of expression that does not borrow the current formulas of writing. Without counting that the use of the twelve-note system deprives of all definite entity music based on this system and of all personality the composers who naively believe to be original.

"This authentic creative mind, Edward Michael, was born in England by oriental parents. He lived in several regions of the Orient (among which Baghdad) until the age of 19. He then

Les compositeurs d'aujourd'hui

EDWARD MICHAEL

EDWARD MICHAEL

L'ATTENTION du monde musical a été particulièrement attirée sur Edward Michael depuis les deux exécutions de sa *Messe* à la radio française (Messe pour chœur, deux orchestres à cordes, célesta, harpe, glockenspiel et percussion). Disons tout de suite que cette œuvre de haute inspiration ne peut pas laisser indifférent. Et j'insiste en soulignant d'un trait rouge que cette *Messe* ne peut pas laisser indifférent *le véritable public* — ce qui est assez rare pour une œuvre contemporaine — car en somme la musique nouvelle n'est pas faite pour plaire *seulement* aux critiques musicaux !

On devine chez ce compositeur une réelle puissance d'expression, une originalité assez étonnante qui situe une authentique personnalité de créateur et enfin un métier très poussé.

Mais le cas de ce musicien nous permet de constater une fois encore qu'il n'est pas besoin de faire appel à ces procédés dits d'avant-garde pour créer un langage neuf ou une façon de s'exprimer, qui n'emprunte pas les formules courantes de l'écriture. Sans compter que l'emploi du dodécaphonisme par exemple enlève toute entité définie à la musique basée sur ce système et toute personnalité aux compositeurs qui croient naïvement faire de l'original !

Cet authentique créateur, Edward Michael, est né en Angleterre de parents orientaux et vécut dans plusieurs contrées d'Orient (dont Bagdad) jusqu'à l'âge de 19 ans. Il vint ensuite poursuivre ses études de violon et de composition à Londres. Ses professeurs furent Berthold Goldsmith, Matyas Sciber et, à Paris, Nadia Boulanger.

LISTE DES ŒUVRES

Les œuvres suivies d'une croix sont éditées chez *Ricordi, Paris*. Toutes les autres œuvres en administration chez le même éditeur.

LIST OF WORKS

The works followed by a cross are published by Ricordy, Paris. All other works are in administration with the same publisher.

Symphonie pour grand orchestre.

Deux Symphonies pour orchestre à cordes (dont une a été exécutée à Paris il y a deux ans).

La Vision de Lamis Helacim, poème symphonique pour orchestre (exécuté à Londres deux fois).

Rhapsodie concertante, pour violon deux orchestres à cordes, célesta et percussion (une exécution à Londres).

Quatre Quatuors à cordes, dont deux exécutés à Londres et un à Paris, plusieurs fois.

Sonate pour violoncelle et piano (nombreuses exécutions à Paris, notamment à l'École Normale il y a deux ans).

Cinq Nocturnes (Vocalises), pour mezzo-soprano, deux flûtes, quatuor à cordes et piano) (exécutés à Paris il y a six mois par Noémie PERUGIA).

Images d'Orient, pour orchestre.

Fata Morgana, poème pour orchestre.

Nocturne, pour flûte solo, célesta, harpe et orchestre à cordes (Prix Lili Boulanger), exécuté trois fois par la R.T.F. Paris.

Le Jardin de Tinajatana, suite exotique pour orchestre (plusieurs exécutions) (+).

Élégie, pour orchestre (plusieurs exécutions ; il existe un enregistrement-réduction pour ondes et piano chez Teppaz) (+).

Messe, pour chœur, deux orchestres à cordes, célesta, harpe glockenpiel et percussion (exécutée à la R.T.F., dir. Eugène BIGOT) (+).

Psaume, pour chœur d'hommes a cappella (Diplôme Vercelli).

Trois Incantations, pour chœur de femmes.

The attention of the musical world has been drawn particularly towards Edward Michael after the two performances of his Mass by the French Radiodiffusion (*Mass for choir, two string orchestras, celesta, harp, glockenspiel and percussion*). We declare at once that this work of lofty inspiration cannot leave one indifferent and emphasize that it cannot leave the veritable public *indifferent*—which is rather exceptional with a contemporary work—for on the whole modern music is not made to please music critics only.

One guesses in this composer a real power of expression, a surprising originality which shows an authentic creative personality, a strongly developed metier.

However, the case of this musician enables us to state once more that it is not necessary to use those so-called vanguard processes to create a new language or a way of expression that does not borrow the current formulas of writing. Without counting that the use of the twelve-note system deprives of all definite entity music based on this system and of all personality the composers who naively believe to be original.

This authentic creative mind, Edward Michael, was born in England by oriental parents. He lived in several regions of the Orient (among which Baghdad) until the age of 19 He then continued his violin and composition studies in London. His teachers were Bertold Goldsmith, Matyas Seiber and, in Paris, Nadia Boulanger.

continued his violin and composition studies in London. His teachers were Bertold Goldsmith, Matyas Seiber and, in Paris, Nadia Boulanger."

Despite his difficulties, Salim could begin to believe that, in spite of the omnipresent influence of modern composers, he would, finally, one day, become known, but, at the beginning of 1962, a terrible event occurred that would crush his career as a musician and leave an indelible trauma within him.

Salim and contemporary music.

Not long before, Madame Janot, whom Salim had met when he was writing music for the Gurdjieff groups and whose husband had just been appointed managing director of Radio France, thinking to help Salim, pressured him into becoming the student of a dodecaphonist composer who was very much in vogue at the time. This teacher showed great kindness to him and, having learned that his financial situation was difficult, had the generosity to give him free lessons for six months.

Salim had tried to interest himself in the work, but really he knew within himself that all these so-called avant-garde creations—to describe which the critics were quick to use, with overflowing enthusiasm, adjectives such as: great, interesting, new, etc.—would be forgotten, while the music of composers such as Debussy, Mahler, César Franck, and Richard Strauss would remain. Furthermore, the critics themselves, when speaking of this music, could not prevent themselves qualifying it as "beautiful"!

In contact with these contemporary composers, Salim felt keenly that music that does not fulfill its true role—to move the listener and evoke in him a presentiment of the existence of other dimensions of a spiritual nature—cannot be called great music. As he had said to Nadia Boulanger: "It is so easy to suggest, in music, horror, ugliness, and brutality, which are already sufficiently present in everyday life; it is not necessary to be a great artist to evoke these aspects of existence. But to create beauty, to elevate the listener to unaccustomed heights—which should be the purpose of art—demands that the artist himself has an exceptional quality of being, as one can sense looking upon the faces of Beethoven, Gustav Mahler, or César Franck."

Salim often passionately affirmed: "No matter what one is drawn to accomplish in life, whether it be musical creation or something else, a particular type of effort has to be made to be honest towards oneself. Lying does not require effort, it comes about by itself; but honesty cannot manifest itself automatically, it demands uncommon sincerity and force from the artist. Before daring to call himself a composer, if he is concerned about being true in that which he wishes to offer to the world, a musician must first accept the necessity of passing many years in hard work to succeed in mastering the incontrovertible mathematical laws of music theory."

And he would add: "Perhaps this is the reason that, when one hears a symphony by Beethoven or one of the monumental works of Gustav Mahler, or Richard Strauss's "An Alpine Symphony", one senses that the melodic lines, the harmonies and the different modulations that they contain go exactly where they are supposed to go, without possible error, and that it could not be otherwise. In other words, the development of the melodic lines and the harmonies constitutes something inevitable meaning that, when the listener hears these musical creations, even if he has never heard them before, he has the inexplicable impression of knowing, in advance, where each note and each harmony is going to go, thereby procuring in him the feeling of an intangible truth, which finds its echo within his being—a truth that contemporary "music" cannot, in any way, attain. It is for this reason that atonal, abstract, serial*, music is nothing more than an appalling lie."

---

* Dodecaphony is a technique of musical composition devised by Arnold Schoenberg. This technique gives comparable importance to the twelve notes of the chromatic scale and, thereby, avoids all tonality. The dodecaphonic series is conceived as a succession that allows each of the twelve sounds to be heard, but without repetition of any of them.
The order thus established forms an immutable series of intervals, which the whole development of the work is based upon. This principle, and this was one of the aims

Still on the subject of this fundamental question of honesty in the artistic domain—which is also applicable to the spiritual realm—Salim explained that every time someone tries to be honest towards himself, this endeavor forces him to become more internally present and awakened.

Leonard Bernstein: the "Boulangerie".

On the occasion of Nadia Boulanger's ninetieth birthday in 1977, Leonard Bernstein, the famous American composer and orchestra conductor, mentioned in an interview the evolution of music in the 1950s and 1960s and the situation of Nadia Boulanger's students who wanted to continue composing tonal music:

Leonard Bernstein 1977

"I am not a member of the 'Boulangerie' as it is called in the United States, and this term 'Boulangerie' is very interesting,

---

of its inventor, removes all hierarchy in the pitch, each having the same importance in the melodic flow. Because of this, it goes against the principles of tonal harmony and creates (a term that Schoenberg denied) atonality.

Dodecaphony led to serial music, theorized and then developed by Arnold Schoenberg from 1923. Many musicians adopted Schoenberg's concept in their compositions: Alban Berg, AntonWebern, Milton Babbitt, Olivier Messiaen, Stockhausen and Pierre Boulez.

because this slightly ironic* word began to circulate during the 1950s, when serial music had gained much influence. There were new 'guides', new 'führers', like Stockhausen and Pierre Boulez, and that changed everything in the musical environment. All Nadia's students were suddenly labeled 'La Boulangerie' and found themselves relegated to behind the scenes, somewhat belittled."

In other words, anyone who wished to continue writing tonal compositions found themselves outcast, with no chance at all of having their music performed, which is what happened to Berthold Goldschmidt, conductor and composer, who was Salim's composition professor in England. He had escaped the Nazis in 1935 with an already successful career behind him; nevertheless, he encountered such opposition on the part of modern composers that he eventually stopped composing.

Berthold Goldschmidt: Surviving the dictatorship of dodecaphony.

In 1992, when he was eighty-nine years of age, after an eclipse of sixty years, the public and the critics developed a renewed interest in Goldschmidt's work, particularly in Germany. Here is what he said at this time:

"The two world wars that struck this century had a terrible influence on the natural development of the arts and music. The radical fracture occurred when the young generation decreed that it wanted nothing to do with the influential cultural currents of the pre-war period. They did not want harmonious sound. They wanted to create new methods of music, of music production. It was then that Boulez, Stockhausen, Berio, Nono appeared, they were radicals. They declared, 'we want no more to do with the harmonious sound of the past'.

"These very talented musicians, Stockhausen, Berio, Boulez, and

---

* Nadia Boulanger's surname means baker and a 'boulangerie' is the French word for a bakery. (TN)

others, exercised an intellectual dictatorship, that was encouraged by the European radio stations. The more moderate composers lost the opportunity of expressing themselves. I remember one day asking an influential man in radio in Cologne whether, given the significant harm I had suffered in terms of time and opportunity (during the war), I might be able to have my concerto for cello aired once more. He retorted: 'Don't even send me your score! We're carefully filtering the music'. I burst out laughing. Is this really how it works? Music must be written in such a manner that it no longer bears any resemblance to the last century's art of transcription!

"Many people became turncoats. I never did that. In fact, I wanted to preserve my own guidelines, not because of moral reasons or snobbery, but because I did not believe it was right.

"I found the severe, almost military, dictatorial discipline[*] of the dodecaphonic school taxing. They had, in a manner of speaking, donned a straight-jacket, which they wore with pleasure; I would not have been able to bear it. What I write is the emotional expression of my personality.

"I realized that I could not be a part of this new conception of music. I first had to try to understand it. I must have spent an enormous amount of time dedicating myself to this music and listening to it. I was trying to discover something in it that would be able to move me. I did not succeed and that completely disarmed me.

"As this tendency reigned supreme during the 1950s and 1960s, I considered that it no longer made sense to continue composing. I could not break with my old methods, and then one finds oneself excluded, sinking little by little into a bottomless abyss. I never hoped I would one day be able to emerge from it.

---

[*] Schoenberg had made it a rule that none of the twelve chromatic sounds could be repeated within a series.

"From 1960 to 1980, I wrote nothing at all. My self-esteem as a composer had been wounded, because it was being said that everything that had been done before was absurd. When one hears that, one feels truly morally discouraged and one's musical consciousness is destroyed. I felt more or less ridiculous when I wrote something in 'conventional language'.

"I was not wanted, I was not in demand, I no longer had a future. I believe this pause did me good. It allowed me to put my ideas in order and strengthened my power of concentration. After around fifteen years, one feels more optimistic.

"This horrible pressure was lifted in the 1980s. One could breathe freely once more. I still stand by what I had written up until that moment, in terms of both quality and quantity. I told myself that I might perhaps have a second chance. This chance presented itself after thirty years, it was simply a question of surviving those years!"

Schoenberg and the standardization of notes. Ansermet and atonality. A few "popular" concerts.

Salim was hit by the full force of this dictatorship of serial music, which he could not subscribe to because, as he would say: "This music accords the same value to all the twelve notes, which is, musically, a lie. The fourth, the fifth, and the eighth, considered in India and in Ancient Greece to be sacred intervals, occupy a much more important place than the second, the third, and the sixth.

"Everything that becomes uniform dies. There are no two like individuals in the world and, if one attempts to make them so, it will always be at the cost of what is best in them. They will inevitably be diminished and reduced to the condition of depersonalized puppets, as can be observed in the misleading advertising that, today, besets us on all sides. To be arbitrarily new, incontrovertible mathematical rules based on thousands of years of experience are being broken. When one decides, intellectually, to assign the same value to all the notes, in other words, to standardize them, this results in ugliness, just like certain political regimes which sought to annihilate the individual and everything that had some value, thus managing to deprive the human being of his taste for life.

"The standardization of the modern world is destroying all the factors of psychic and spiritual growth. Architecture, once so varied from one country to another, is giving way to identical blocks of concrete. From one end of the planet to the other, people today dress in the same manner and receive the same stimuli from advertisements, cinema, and television. Pop 'music' is always the same, to the point that one could not say who has authored it! It is quite the contrary when one listens to the work of a great composer, from Mozart to Debussy and Mahler, one can, without ever having listened to it before, affirm: 'This music can only be that of Mozart, of Debussy, of Mahler, or of Beethoven…'"

In the books that he later wrote, Salim explains that the tonic constitutes the original hearth, the center whence musical creation radiates and to which it must return at the end of its journey, just as a spiritual seeker endeavors to rediscover the Original Source whence he came and into which he will be reabsorbed at the end of his terrestrial peregrinations. The vital symbol of the center has been abandoned today, he would say, not only in the artistic domain, but also in ordinary existence. Modern music is set adrift and this aimless drifting provokes serious disturbances in the human being without him realizing their origin.

In his work, "Les Fondements de la Musique dans la Conscience Humaine" (The Fundamentals of Music in the Human Consciousness) published in 1961, the great musicologist and conductor Ernest Ansermet shows that the evident sense of music—in other words, what causes its direct address to the listener's sentiment and not his/her thought—occurs because it obeys a certain tonal law. For him, the very root of the musical act consists in linking the intervals into a system. From this, he concludes that atonality is entirely mistaken concerning the perception of music by auditory consciousness, inasmuch as it treats each interval in isolation and not as one element of an overall structure. Therefore, strictly atonal works cannot, according to him, claim to be music, but only successions of sounds, as they no longer have that internal coherence, that "evident sense" that differentiates music from mere noise.

Ernest Ansermet created, not without struggle, part of the masterpieces of Bartok, Honegger, and Stravinsky; few of his contemporary conductors could boast that they had supported modern music as much as he. Therefore, it cannot be said that he was stuck in the past; on the contrary, he was an exceptionally modern mind, but he would nonetheless refuse musical, and even historical, legitimacy to Arnold Schönberg and his disciples who, he wrote, had "questioned the tonal foundation of musical structures, without realizing that they were thereby questioning the very foundation of the sense of music and all its human meanings." Two generations later, he regretfully wrote, "There is no longer any normative law; tonal law seems to be a convention of the past; there is no longer any law at all; all is permitted: God is dead."

To quote only a few examples of the heights of absurdity that could be reached, at the time when Salim was struggling, with so much difficulty, to have his works played, he attended the première of a symphony for "electric kettles" that the so-called composer was "conducting"; the noise produced by the steam escaping from the spouts was supposed to constitute the melody!

He was also invited to a concert given by a modern Swiss "creator" who performed his masterpiece on a piano that he had had specially brought over from his country for the occasion, and whose strings had been intentionally cut. The "artist" hammered furiously on his mute instrument before a disconcerted public. Then, seized by a "creative" fury, he began to smash the keyboard using an axe prepared for this purpose. Finally, he concluded his performance before the dumbfounded audience by blowing up what remained of the piano with a small stick of dynamite. The work was loudly applauded! Its author even received an injury to his leg in the explosion and had to be taken to hospital.

Also worthy of being described here was the demonstration indulged in by a very well-known American modern composer in 1952 who, on the evening he was presenting his work entitled "Four and a half minute symphony" for the first time, crossed the room to the applause of the audience and sat down at the piano where he remained motionless and silent for exactly the duration of time announced in the title. The "music" amounted to the noise made by the astounded public as they whispered to each other...

The drama of January 1962; the critics assassinate a composer.

An event with decisive consequences for Salim's career took place on January 9, 1962. One of his orchestral compositions, "La Vision de Lamis Helacim" (Lamis Helamcim's Vision), was, by chance, going to be played at the Théâtre des Champs-Élysées. It was an important and decisive concert for him, because the evening was going to be broadcast on Radio France two days later. His publishers and a very influential public were present. The music column of the French newspaper the "Figaro" announced his work in the following terms:

"Conducted by Manuel Rosenthal, the National Orchestra will, next Tuesday at the Théâtre des Champs-Élysées, give the first hearing of a new work by Edward Michael: "La Vision de Lamis Helacim". The young composer, a student of Berthold Goldsmith in London and of Nadia Boulanger in Paris, is originally from the Orient, and most of his works display influences from the ambience of oriental music. He has notably composed several symphonies: a symphonic poem, "Fata Morgana" and a suite for orchestra, "Le Jardin de Tinajatama". Many of Edward Michael's works have already been played in London."

Two other contemporary composers featured in the program, André Jolivet and Jean Rivier, who both occupied influential positions both at the Conservatory and in radio.

Salim's work was extremely well received by the public who applauded it at length. The next morning, a review of the evening appeared in the "Figaro":

"Before a full house, the National Orchestra last night presented three new works at the Théâtre des Champs-Élysées.

"Firstly, La Vision de Lamis Helacim, a short symbolic piece by Mr Edward Michael, marked by a sober orientalism, which received much applause. Born in England, but with oriental ancestry, Edward Michael is already known to the Parisian public for a Mass—broadcast twice on the radio—for a symphony for strings, and several pieces of chamber music.

"Jean Rivier's Seventh Symphony, which followed, exhibits a desire for rhythmic renewal.

"The third creation of the evening was Jolivet's Symphony for strings. Two movements frame a piece that is long and slow, but of incontestable lyrical inspiration.

"Before the interval, Michèle Boegner lent her very personal melodic style to Mozart's Piano Concerto in B flat K.595."

When Salim returned home after the concert, he felt transported and imagined the future with great hope. He believed he might finally be able to move beyond a certain point, after which things would begin to become easier for him.

The following afternoon, the team from the radio was producing a public recording at the Théâtre Récamier of the reactions of three very well-known critics: Antoine Goléa, Claude Samuel, and a third whose name Salim had forgotten. Their discussion was to be broadcast immediately after the retransmission of the concert and, as with the previous evening, his publishers had all come to learn of the reception these famous critics had in store for his music.

Antoine Goléa, who was very influential, was known for his intransigent opinions and his passionate defense of serial music, which he considered to be the only contemporary music worthy of interest.

(When asked what Richard Strauss would have meant for the evolution of music in our time, his response was astonishing: "Nothing, to be exact!")

Until then, on the rare occasions that he had succeeded in having his works played, Salim had, from certain critics who still appreciated tonal music, encountered a favorable reception. On this day, however, he was dealing with critics who were entirely oriented towards avant-garde music. Salim might perhaps have been able to obtain benevolent neutrality from them, but he had not followed the obligatory custom of going to meet these "authorities", of flattering them and even of making them a gift. In his almost total destitution, how would he have been able to find anything to offer them? Perhaps he should have at least come to show allegiance, to praise them, and to receive forgiveness for still being tonal. On several occasions, he had been advised to develop relationships with these critics, to invite them out and to tell them how magnificent they were. Where would he have been able to receive them? In his box room on the sixth floor? As for inviting them to a restaurant, he did not even have the money to feed himself adequately...

The history of music should lead critics to be prudent in their judgments, because one is struck by the regularity with which many of them were mistaken. Most honor that which is in vogue for a certain "intelligentsia" around which they gravitate. Certain great musicians who, during their lifetimes, were massacred by the critics, are now adulated. The most spectacular case is that of Bizet, whose première of "Carmen" was a catastrophe, whereas this opera is currently the most played lyrical work in the world.

Is the profession of critic not, by definition, a negative one? Antoine Goléa published an autobiographical work whose title speaks volumes: "Je suis un violiniste raté" (I am a failed violinist).

As Salim later wrote in one of his books: "It is so easy to destroy but so difficult to create".

When the trio of professional critics who, from the outset were prejudiced against Salim, began discussing his work, it was a by the

book execution. They did not pronounce a single word even to acknowledge the finesse of the orchestration. The fact that the audience had
dared to like the work and had shown its enthusiasm bore absolutely
no weight on their evaluation, they who were there precisely to tell
this public who to adulate and who to execrate. They could not find
language hard enough and one of them even concluded with this
"definitive" sentence: "He even finished his work on a perfect chord!"
while another went even further: "And it wasn't just the end!" as
though it were a veritable crime to use consonant chords. They were
so odious that a man in the room, whom Salim did not know, stood
up and became vehemently indignant about the virulence of their
words. Whereas the piece under discussion had lasted around ten
minutes, the desire to totally destroy both the music and its creator
was so imperative for these denigrators that they continued the
massacre for more than an hour. As for the praise for the two other
composers, it was delivered in less than ten minutes for each.

Salim, stunned, heard them pronounce his death sentence in
musical circles. The criticism was, moreover, so exaggerated that the
producers of the program, nauseated by this blind demolition, had
the most venomous part cut out of the retransmission. Furthermore,
the public absolutely did not share the opinion of these "experts" and,
in the days that followed, Salim received, to the surprise of the
personnel at Radio France who forwarded the letters to him, several
dozen letters from listeners expressing their appreciation of his work.

But the harm had been done with regard to his publishers and
those who could have offered him the opportunity of having his
compositions played. Salim returned home in a state of total despair,
sat down on his bed and contemplated the pile of not yet printed
scores that represented all that he possessed in this world, music that
he had written at the price of so much self-sacrifice, work, and hardship.

The power of these famous critics was such that, from the
following day, his publishers informed him that they were going to
stop the printing of all his works, including his Mass, and that it

would be of no use for him to offer anything else to them in the future. Salim was already experiencing difficulties in his relationship with his publishers. When he visited them, as he was poorly dressed, they showed him little respect. Instead of considering the value of the artist, they saw only a man who did not know how to assert his worth in the closed circle of the Parisian music scene, a milieu that had become infatuated with novelties and only wanted to hear so-called "contemporary" music.

Following this event with its catastrophic consequences, Salim was labeled as someone the critics did not like. And his few friends in the musical field, frightened by the idea of being seen in his company, avoided him; he had become pestilent. Only his loyal friend Manfred Kelkel remained by his side and continued to battle to find him opportunities, rare though they might be, to have his music played.

Salim was so demoralized that he went to see Nadia Boulanger to play her the private recording that he had of the work that had unleashed such an outburst of hatred towards him. She listened to it and said to him honestly: "It's of no use sending work to the radio selection committee; the so-called 'contemporary' music composers who form this committee no longer know how to read a score and, consequently, they lack the means to evaluate them."

When, a few months later, Salim met Henri Barraud, the former radio director, he expressed his sympathy and acknowledged that Salim's work was full of sensitivity and that his orchestration showed great finesse. But what could he do? Part of the murderous critique had been cut; it had not been possible for him to do any more.

Completing the publication of scores already in progress, at the author's expense.

This drama was, after the trauma of the air force and the death of the woman he loved, the third great tragic blow in Salim's life, an existence which had already been more than filled with difficulties. He would often spend hours lying on his bed, staring at the ceiling, and asking himself anxiously what his future held in store and how he would survive when he reached old age. He became extremely ill and remained plunged in this despondent state for several weeks.

In addition to this, he had to find the money required to complete, at the author's cost, the printing of seven of his major works, particularly his Mass, which had been halted by his publishers.

Despite the fact that he no longer played the violin, he had continued to take great care of his instrument. When he still gave concerts, a sort of very special communication would establish itself between him and his violin. It was an excellent violin which was also extremely valuable. Salim, who was in dire straits, decided, with a heavy heart, to make some money from it. He was so lacking in practical sense that he did not realize that he could have approached a specialist store where he would have been given a good price for it.

He simply let some acquaintances know of his intention and finally found an amateur violinist who offered him much less than its real value. When he returned home that evening with the money in his pocket, he felt heartbroken at having had to separate from a faithful companion who had served him so well in the past.

However, this sacrifice was far from proving sufficient. During a stay in London to see his family, acquaintances put him in touch with a billionaire and his wife, so rich that they could sometimes afford to gamble away in a single night sums as staggering as one hundred thousand pounds sterling, which they did not refrain from bragging about in Salim's presence, in a semi-drunken state. On this occasion, he asked them for a little financial assistance in order to be able to finish publishing his music. They responded with indignation: "But you only have to work!" Salim, who was toiling as much as was humanly possible, wearily replied that he was working, and very hard too, and added: "If it were Beethoven who had come to see you to request your assistance, what would you have done?" They coldly replied: "You are not Beethoven!" Recalling this painful incident, Salim confessed that he returned home full of bitterness.

Following this pointless humiliation, having also turned in vain to several other people, he resolved to sell some of his unpublished works to a talentless, but extremely rich, American composer, who had them performed under his own name and whom Salim promised never to reveal his identity. On several occasions, he yielded some of his creations to him, including several symphonies and other orchestral works to which he was very attached, so that at least the scores that remained in his publisher's hands might finally be published.

All these painful processes took months. In the meantime, as shall be seen later, Salim was able to enjoy a short respite when he had the opportunity of leaving for a few weeks on a journey to the East.

Finally, he succeeded in assembling the required sum to finish the printing of his seven works. When he gave this money to his publishers, he did not obtain any kind of receipt and was only entitled to a standard contract, as if it were they who had paid all of the costs of publication themselves. One of them even refused to correct the engraver's mistakes when it was Salim who was bearing the cost, and irritably fired at him: "But these mistakes will not be noticed; nobody hears the difference in modern music!" Salim, horrified, tried to explain to him that, in the kind of music he wrote, these errors would cause unacceptable dissonance, but it was in vain, and the scores were printed as they were.

Voyage to the Orient, 1962.

Following this terrible event, which put an end to Salim's hopes as a composer, and while he was desperately seeking money for his publishers, an important and, for him, very necessary distraction presented itself in his life.

His thoughts often turned to the East with a painful nostalgia. Life in the West seemed false to him; everything appeared untrue, fabricated, and empty. The modern arts and contemporary music illustrated well for him the gloomy and aimless existence of the materialist world that most people live in.

He sorely missed the colorful atmosphere of the East, the warmth of feeling, and the climate. Yet, he knew that his financial situation prohibited any possibility of returning there. Furthermore, he felt deep down that he would now be culturally disoriented everywhere he went, because, now, he was, so to speak, neither Eastern, nor Western.

Was it because the memory of the landscapes of his youth came back to him at times, tinged with nostalgia, or was it by mere chance that one night he woke up several times after having, to his surprise, dreamed each time that he was in the East. Although these dreams were bathed in a somewhat unreal atmosphere, they contained nothing disquieting. Nevertheless, these dreams, made up of successive sequences unfolding in various places and with various people, were of such intensity that he retained a tenacious impression of them which remained with him for several days. Then, with time and his daily preoccupations with survival, he forgot this agitated night and its strange oneiric content.

It was only around six months later that some people from the Gurdjieff groups, who were interested in the Sufi masters of Central Asia and wanted to take on a seventh companion accustomed to the East for a trip they had planned, suggested to Salim that he join them. As he had no money, they offered to pay all his traveling costs; in return, he would be of some use to them, because, due to his youth spent in the Middle East, he had experience of this type of country and the mentality of its inhabitants. It is needless to say how pleased Salim was with this unexpected opportunity of being able to return to the sun and atmosphere of Eastern life. He gratefully accepted, in spite of the difficulties he knew he would have to face because of his state of health.

Their small group comprised two women and five men, including Salim. Apart from Madame L., an overbearing woman who was leading the expedition and was quite interested in a spiritual quest, the other people, although kind, did not appear, in Salim's eyes, really to be spiritually motivated; it seemed to him that they considered this journey rather as a tourist adventure.

Iran.

Their journey, which stretched over four weeks, led them first to Iran. After interminable formalities, when Salim came out of the airport, his attention was drawn to an old man sitting on a donkey, coming from the street opposite, and heading towards them. He was suddenly filled with astonishment, because this scene with the old man and his mount had figured among the dreams he had had six months previously when he had dreamed of the East. During the days that followed, while he was staying in Tehran, he remained very troubled by the memory of this incident.

A short while afterwards, the group travelled by car to a small village, not far from the capital, by the name of Pir-Bahram, where stood the tomb of a holy man. Among the numerous visitors who flocked there, friendly pilgrims offered to share with them the food they had brought. Salim constantly felt the strange sensation that this place had something mysteriously familiar about it, which he could not define. When he entered the monument, he stumbled on the staircase and his head hit the inscription written in Arabic script which was on the wall facing him. Suddenly, he was overcome with a sense of disbelief, because he remembered having experienced this same incident in one of the successive dreams he had had in the course of that agitated night six months earlier. He was conscious of perceiving the details around him much more clearly, which, in the dream, had appeared somewhat blurred and unreal; nevertheless, he could only acknowledge, beyond any possible doubt, that it was the same place. He could not understand by what mysterious means it had been possible for him to see in a dream, several months earlier, events that had not yet taken place and he could only remain perplexed and at a loss.

Back in Tehran, the small group went to visit a large closed market, a sort of souk, whose picturesque appeal had been extolled to them. There they found stalls laden with fruit, pastries and oriental confectionary (such as baklavas and Turkish delight), heaps of vegetables, and all sorts of other foodstuffs. They also saw young children, little boys and girls of around eight years old, working like slaves, busy weaving carpets with surprising skill.

It was still the reign of the Shah of Iran; the country was fairly stable politically. The Sufis, who are the mystics of Islam, were persecuted, as is still the case in many Muslim countries.

While Salim was busy admiring the dexterity of these children, he suddenly began to feel a curious uneasiness and became aware that a man selling art objects on the neighboring stall was staring at him with extraordinary intensity. At the same time, the memory suddenly came back to him of one of his dreams of six months before in which the same scene had appeared to him.

Questions without answers. A Sufi master.

Disconcerted by these repeated disturbing incidents, Salim began to wonder about the abilities of the human mind which, for an unknown reason, may, at times, touch other ordinarily incomprehensible dimensions and mysteriously see, in the course of a nocturnal dream (or even in the diurnal state, at very specific moments), situations and places, far from the place one actually is, and that one only discovers much later. The question of why such phenomena occur remained an enigma for Salim, or rather, he did not accept giving an arbitrary and subjective answer to it.

In this Persian market, the merchant, who had been staring at Salim for quite some time, finally approached him and murmured to him in English: "Do you want to come and see my master?" Very surprised, Salim hesitated for a moment and then asked him who his master was and where he lived. After a few words of explanation from the stranger, Salim indicated to him that he willingly accepted and, at the same time, enquired whether it was possible for them to take Madame L., who was haggling a short distance away, with them, adding that she too would be most interested by this meeting. The man looked at her for a moment before responding, then nodded his head in the affirmative. So, they fixed an appointment for the following afternoon at the hotel where their guide arrived at the scheduled time to pick them up in an old car. He took a somewhat winding route, perhaps to ensure that he was not being followed, and took them outside the city, to a bare, arid place where stood a single, rather pretty house, surrounded by some trees. He led the two visitors inside, into a large room, at the end of which stood a venerable and impressive old man with a long white beard. Peacefully seated, his ten sons, all already adults, surrounded him; it was evident to Salim that they adored their father. The latter spoke neither English nor French, but their guide served as their interpreter.

The master showed himself to be very amiable and interested by all the questions Salim put to him. He offered them tea (Salim declared that, in his life, he had never drunk any so delicious), while speaking about his spiritual work which consisted principally in respecting strict moral rules, spending long hours in prayer, and performing dervish movements. After around two hours, as it was starting to get late, Salim and Madame L. took leave of their host and his sons who, for the entire duration of their visit, had followed the conversation with great interest. Finally, their guide took them back to their hotel and, with a typically oriental warmth of feeling which greatly touched Salim, bade them farewell as he knew that his guests were planning to leave Tehran the next day and that they would undoubtedly never see each other again.

Persepolis. Dangers avoided. A tokroul.

One evening, they arrived near the ruins of Persepolis. Walking among the remains of the buildings, Salim felt overcome by strange feelings. It seemed to him as if he could almost see women clad in the ancient style, ambling by, bearing water pitchers on their heads. He felt intensely that something from an extremely remote past was still present in these vestiges of a vanished greatness. Over the following days, he came back on a number of occasions to walk around this mysterious place. His companions did not understand what, in these apparently silent stones, attracted him so strongly. Later, he learned that Darius III, King of the Persians, who had been defeated by Alexander the Great, had begged his victor to spare Persepolis, but, as so often happens in the tragic history of humanity, the thirst for destruction triumphed and the city was laid waste. It was as if Salim had, in some inexplicable way, picked up the lamentations of a departed people.

After this singular encounter with a far-off past, he wrote a symphonic work which he entitled "Au Seuil de Persépolis" (At the Threshold of Persepolis).

Some days later, following a rather long journey by car, the group arrived in a small town where they went to the only acceptable hotel. Salim, who still suffered from car-sickness and had just suffered an intestinal crisis on the way there, reached his room exhausted, without being able to eat anything, as often happened to him. After dinner, the two women decided to go for a stroll in the neighborhood before going to bed. Salim intervened to tell them that it was not prudent for them to go out at this late hour, all the more so as they were not covered, but, due to the heat, were lightly dressed in the Western style. As they persisted, he then suggested that all seven of them go out together. As soon as they moved away from the hotel, men suddenly appeared from everywhere and started to follow them. Within a few minutes, an incredible crowd of men uttering remarks they did not understand, but which they guessed to be lewd, had gathered behind them. Salim insisted to the others in a firm tone that they return immediately, as the situation was becoming too dangerous! Without any further argument and feeling ill at ease, they all turned back, but had to clear a passage through this gathering of men who moved aside, as though regretfully, to let them go back to their hotel. After this incident which could have ended very badly, evening walks were over with.

The following day, they went to visit an old mosque which the hotel manager had described as remarkable. After having asked, with gestures, permission to enter of the man who seemed to be the attendant, they took off their shoes and went into a magnificent, imposing edifice. The walls were covered in verses of sacred writings and decorations of astonishing beauty, which it was strictly forbidden to photograph. Madame L., having, despite everything, insisted on taking a few souvenir snapshots, the worst was narrowly avoided.

In effect, as soon as one of the faithful who was praying saw her using her camera, he rushed towards her, his knife raised; Salim leapt between them and, by some incredible reflex, shouted out the only words that came into his mind and which begin the Muslim prayer: "Bismillah el Rahman el Rahim..." (In the name of Allah, the all-compassionate..."). Surprised, the man hesitated an instant, then lowered his arm, while another, ripping the camera away from the woman, threw it angrily to the ground. As though regretfully, the wrathful man put away his dagger and, before leaving them, addressed a few words to Salim, which he did not understand. In fact, the language of Iran is Persian, but, as in all Islam, prayers are recited in Arabic, in the same way that in former times, Latin was the liturgical language of all Christendom. Madame L., whose recklessness had actually endangered the entire group, was furious at having her equipment damaged.

During another excursion, the group stopped near a "tokroul", a kind of tower at the top of which corpses were placed to be devoured by vultures. The people assigned to this funeral rite lived permanently in these edifices, from which they were only allowed to go out to obtain fresh supplies; they were considered as a sort of untouchable. Their task, which consisted of cutting the bodies into pieces, before carrying them onto the platform, was renewed from generation to generation in these same towers where these poor people were born, grew up, and died.

Pakistan. The Khyber Pass.

Throughout this four-week journey, Salim continued to be preoccupied by the question of finding the money necessary for printing his music. Despite the change of scene and his joy at returning to the East, this major concern remained ever present at the back of his mind and did not leave him throughout the voyage.

After Iran, the small group went to Pakistan. Upon his arrival in Karachi, Salim was struck by the strange feeling of having returned home.* Inexplicable emotions were awakening within him and making the insistent desire to go, one day, to India increasingly rise to the surface of his being. Why India?... he neither understood nor was able to explain it to himself. Furthermore, regarding this part of the journey, apart from a few silent, fierce looking sadhus, whom the group encountered in various places, but from whom he did not glean a great deal, Salim found nothing capable of interesting him in terms of his spiritual research.

To go by road to Afghanistan, which constituted the last stage of their journey, they had to take the Khyber Pass which protects the Indian sub-continent from invaders coming from the West. At the time that the British Empire reigned over the Indies, young English officers would here pursue the fierce Pathan rebels, indomitable warriors who, in the secret caves of their mountains, expertly made rifles which they brandished against the colonial rulers.

When the group embarked upon the famous Pass, where numerous soldiers had met their deaths, discovering the commemorative inscriptions serving as reminders that this or that regiment of the British Army had been entirely massacred in that location, Salim once again had the inexplicable experience of remembering having already seen them in a dream six months earlier. He ceased to be surprised when this phenomenon recurred, but nonetheless remained troubled over it.

The group stopped at a "chaikhana" (a sort of oriental café) to quench their thirst and shelter from the intense heat for a while. Salim

---

* Pakistan was part of India until the Partition in 1947, at the time of Independence.

knew to what extent the kind of heat that holds sway in the East can become unbearable for Westerners who are not accustomed to it. He knew that when one is very thirsty, one has to drink slowly and, if possible, only water, unsweetened soda, or tea. One of the properties of the latter is that it cools the drinker shortly after it has been drunk; this is undoubtedly the reason that it became the staple drink of the desert Bedouins. Despite his advice, the other members of the group rushed to take the sweetened drinks, which they drank ice cold and in great haste, which had the unpleasant consequence of making them perspire profusely.

While his companions were chatting in the chaikhana, Salim, who had remained outside, exchanged a few words with some Pathans who were there. They immediately began laughing and joking with him with such natural and touching simplicity that this only increased his fervent desire to return and live in the East. They had, so to speak, adopted him and treated him like one of their own, presenting him with sweetmeats and offering him a delicious coffee. They put a turban on his head and dressed him in a sort of long robe, while one of them placed his own rifle on Salim's shoulder for some photos to be taken. And Salim felt, during their friendly embraces, a poignant nostalgia for this part of the world where people are still in touch with their feelings. When the other members of the group came out of the chaikhana, he had to say farewell, with regret, to his new friends before setting off again towards Afghanistan.

Afghanistan, the Buddhas of Bamiyan.

Their journey then led them through the country to Bamiyan, a most impressive place where two enormous statues of Buddha stood out against the arid cliffs, the tallest being 53 meters in height and the second, 38 meters tall.

These statues were sculpted in haut-relief, that is to say, they stood out from within a niche set into the sandstone cliff. It is believed that the upper parts of the faces were made from large wooden or metal

masks. There emanated, from these two gigantic statues, an incredible beauty and an unutterable inner nobility. As the group was leaving the site and Salim was turning his head to admire them one last time, he suddenly had the memory of having already experienced this same situation in a dream in which, as in this instant, he turned to contemplate the two Buddhas standing out from the cliff pierced by caves in which anchorites had practiced meditation in days gone by, before religious persecution had driven Buddhism from these lands.

The great statue of the Buddha of Bamiyan

The statues no longer exist, they were completely destroyed by the Taliban in 2001.

A strange premonition. Unresolved questions.

In Kabul, the group rented two jeeps to continue their excursions. Salim travelled in front, next to the local driver. Within a short time, he made friends with him as well as with his brother, the other driver. Swiftly, they came to telling him about their lives. They were married and each of them was the father of two children, sons, of whom they were very proud, declaring that they were glad not to have daughters, which Salim found totally absurd and unfair, but, so as not offend them, he kept his thoughts to himself.

One morning, when everyone was about to leave, Salim suddenly adopted a disconcerting attitude, energetically refusing, for a reason that was quite incomprehensible to him, to take his place in the jeep. He heard himself say to his companions that they would have an accident on that day. They were most skeptical, not sparing him their jibes, and eventually left without him. After their departure, he felt furious with himself; he could not understand why he had made such an assertion. The words had come out of his mouth as if it were someone else and not he who had spoken them. He felt ashamed of his behavior for a long time and could not manage to forgive himself for his impulse, which he even considered to be absurd. What he had said to his fellow travelers kept coming back into his mind and unsettling him. To take his mind off things, he decided to make conversation with one of the hotel guests who, to his surprise, turned out to be strongly interested in a spiritual quest and was receiving teaching given by a Sufi master.

The return of the two jeeps was scheduled for the late afternoon, at around six o'clock; but the evening came and no car appeared on the horizon. Finally, with the hours passing, Salim went to see the hotel manager to express his concern to him. The manager, used to the vagaries of tourists, promised Salim, all the same, that if his companions had not returned by midnight, he would inform the police with a view to carrying out searches. At last, the two vehicles arrived, late in the night, one towing the other. The one Salim would normally have been in had, indeed, had a serious accident; a truck had hit it with force and, if Salim had been sitting in his usual place next to the driver, he would have been, judging by the state of the jeep, seriously injured, if not killed.

The landscapes of Afghanistan are mainly made up of rocky, arid mountains devoid of vegetation. One only finds more hospitable areas near water. One day, when the jeeps had just traveled alongside a river, bordered by some trees, and were leaving this to ascend once again onto the desert slopes, Salim, looking towards the foot of a mountain foothill, felt a shock on seeing, some twenty meters below, a group of around fifty chained prisoners working, watched by armed men dressed in khaki... just as they had appeared to him in a dream six months earlier. More perplexed than ever, he felt defenseless in the face of the silent questions which whirled about his mind.

In addition to this strange phenomenon. consisting of rediscovering certain places and events previously seen in dreams, he also frequently had the experience, when he found himself in a place or meeting someone for the first time, or was doing or saying something that he had never done or said before in his present life, of finding himself in an inexplicable state for a fraction of a second with the strange certainty that these actions, events, and meetings had already occurred! But where, when, and how he could not specify. These types of phenomena, which were beyond him, began to manifest themselves within him shortly after he left the air force and never ceased until the end of his life. Every time this happened to him, he felt troubled and disoriented before an enigma which was beyond him and which remained unanswered for him.

End of the journey. Brother Lawrence of the Resurrection.

It was paradoxical, to say the least, that Salim, who so loved traveling, quickly became sick on all trips, whatever the means of transport. Since his youth, he had always been confronted with this problem, which became particularly tiresome for him during the war when he found himself obliged to make long trips by truck. From necessity, the doctors of the time had to examine this issue, which arose when soldiers had to be transported in landing barges. Indeed, the state of some of them, who became extremely sick in choppy seas, risked compromising the success of a surprise attack. The doctors who were seeking a remedy to sea sickness discovered that these disorders were caused by a malformation of the inner ear and so it was to this that Salim owed the nausea that afflicted him as soon as he got into a car, onto a plane or, worse still, onto a boat; even a train journey quickly caused him to feel unwell.

Nevertheless, he felt much joy at making this unexpected long journey, which he felt was like an window opening to provide him with new impressions and a change of atmosphere; a breath of air which he greatly needed after so many years spent in what was, and would remain for him, a materialist and too intellectual West.

On his return, he went back to his miniscule cell, as well as the distressing problem he had temporarily put aside: finding money to pay his publishers in order to finish printing his scores.

In his solitude, Salim would draw unexpected support from a small book that he had discovered in London during a visit to his family; it was "Practice of the Presence of God", by Brother Lawrence of the Resurrection, which comprises only a few letters and short maxims. These texts, originally written in French in the seventeenth century, enjoyed a certain celebrity, making them worthy of a translation into English.

When there was any question of an intellectual elaboration, however brilliant it might be, Salim could not enter into the author's thoughts and abandoned the book within the first pages, whereas Brother Lawrence was obviously speaking from a direct mystic experience in which Salim recognized himself:

"I know that for the right practice of the presence of God, the heart must be empty of all other things because God will possess the heart alone. As He cannot possess it alone without emptying it of all besides, so, neither can He act there and do in it what He pleases, unless it be left vacant to Him.

"There is not in the world a kind of life more sweet and delightful than that of a continual conversation with God. Only those can comprehend it who practice and experience it.

"One way to recollect the mind easily in the time of prayer, and preserve it more in tranquillity, is not to let it wander too far at other times."

Aix-en-Provence. A new performance of the Mass.

A short time after his return from the East, Salim was given the opportunity of attending the contemporary music festival, taking place over a whole month in the summer, in Aix-en-Provence, in the Centre d'Humanisme Musical (Center of Musical Humanism), whose director was an influential modern composer.

He had been invited there by the organizers who expected support for this modernist trend from him, which undoubtedly would have made life easier for him on many fronts. However, he could not pretend to like something which he perceived as a betrayal of the artist's mission, which must consist of creating beauty and expressing, through the laws of harmony themselves, irrefutable truths. No longer being able to bear hearing dissonance all day long, he returned home two days before the end of the event, which greatly displeased the festival directors and did little to improve his relationship with the contemporary music world.

At the same time, thanks to the intervention of Raymond Janot, recently appointed Director General of Radio France, Salim's Mass was performed again and broadcast on the radio. Eugène Bigot, who appreciated Salim's music, was happy to be able to conduct it a second time. On the day of the broadcast, there was a storm which considerably marred the broadcast quality.

Nadia Boulanger, whom Salim had informed of this new performance of his Mass, had also listened to the program with great interest and wrote him the following short note of appreciation:

"In spite of the storm, was able to hear your Messe, dear Edouard Michael, and was very impressed by the emotion it transmits. The authenticity of its expression, really moving. Sorry to say it so badly, but this little message is better than silence. So, very affectionately," Nadia Boulanger, 23 Jul 1963."

Prediction of Salim's books.

During one of Salim's visits to his family in London, his brother insistently suggested going to see a man renowned for his remarkable

PALAIS DE FONTAINEBLEAU

LE DIRECTEUR

ÉCOLES D'ART AMÉRICAINE
FONDATION RECONNUE D'UTILITÉ PUBLIQUE

Bureau New-York : Fontainebleau Schools, 122 East 58 St. N. Y. 22

CONSERVATOIRE DE MUSIQUE

ADRESSE PERSONNELLE : 36, RUE BALLU, PARIS (IXe)

In spite of the storm - was able to
hear your Mass, Dear E.M - + was
very impressed by the emotion it
transmits - the authenticity of its
expression, really moving
    Sorry to say it do badly - but
this little message is better then
silence . So very affectionately
        Lydia Boulanger
            23 Juillet 1963

gift of clairvoyance, who was offering a demonstration of his talents that evening. Salim, who was never interested in divination sessions, clairvoyance, mediumship, etc., only agreed in order to please his brother and to take his own mind off things. The room was filled with curious spectators; Salim and his brother sat discreetly in one of the back rows. This clairvoyant was a humble person, very religious, who asked only for a token donation. He did not make a marketable commodity of his extraordinary abilities, which he considered as a divine gift.

He began to divine, in a troubling way, events concerning members of the audience. Thus, he said to a woman: "I see a plane in flames which is falling, falling, falling... The young injured pilot wants to jump; he can't pull himself out of the cockpit!" And he imitated a plane going into a spiral dive and crashing to the ground. The woman suddenly began to sob inconsolably; it was her son; a pilot who had disappeared on a mission during the Second World War. She said, in tears: "If only I knew where he was buried; we have never been able to find his grave". The clairvoyant then put his head into his hands.

He made a terrific effort of concentration; his face flushed with the tension in such a way that one might have thought he was going to have an apoplectic fit. Finally, the gathering heard his hesitant voice: "I see... a church... a cemetery... France... you will find him..." and he then gave the name of a village which sounded French. Afterwards, it was learned that the woman had indeed found her son's grave in the location indicated.

Then, to Salim's horror, as he did not want to be the center of the audience's attention, the man targeted him and, pointing him out, said: "I hear wonderful music coming from this man, saintly music". After a moment of silence, he added: "He's a composer, a wonderful composer". Salim was very surprised, because it was the first time he had met this astonishing character who knew nothing about him. But the clairvoyant continued: "He's also a yogi, a real yogi". At these words, Salim said to himself inwardly that he did not at all like being called a yogi, especially in public. The man finally resumed: "He will write wonderful books one day to help the world".

Although impressed by the clairvoyant's previous assertions, Salim found this last prediction concerning him highly improbable and, turning to his brother, he said: "It's impossible, how could I write a book when I can't even write a simple letter?" And he completely forgot about this incident, only remembering it many years later, when, precisely, the improbable had become reality!

Spiritual work walking in the street.

Salim always showed absolute sincerity and did not hide from his students the difficulties he had encountered in his practices; he thus demonstrated that he knew, through experience, the problems seekers encounter and he explained how he had approached and finally overcome them.

All the circumstances of the day were, for him, so many opportunities to return to himself in the present. Thus, to put to good use the times when he was walking in the street to go from one place to another, he gave himself various exercises, among others that of using the color red as a reminder.

Whether it was a passerby's clothing, a car, or the traffic lights, every time he saw something red, it was a reminder to him to recollect himself and become conscious of himself again in a way which was not habitual to him.

One day, when he was coming out of his humble cell on the Rue du Cherche-Midi to go to Rue du Bac, which is not very far away, he set himself this practice: using the color red as a reminder, he arrived at the end of the road and was surprised not to have encountered the color red once; was this possible? He decided to turn round and go back in the other direction, and there, he saw that he was constantly coming across the color red; there were people wearing red scarves, red jackets, the rear lights of cars braking and displaying red all the time; he understood that there was an aspect of himself that did not want to make the effort of letting go; the habitual aspect of his being, which wanted to continue thinking about his music or his preoccupations, rather than coming back, moment by moment, to the present. When Salim later recounted this to his students, he added that by understanding what had occurred within him, he had visualized himself, and mentally given himself a good boot in the backside—a detail that amused them greatly....

At another time, still with the color red exercise, when he had just recollected himself, another color red appeared, and he recollected himself again, and so on, four or five times in a row, when, all of a sudden, he realized that there was someone within him saying: "But I've just done it...", in other words, it is too much, I have had enough. Salim said to himself then: "But what do I really want?"

Still in the street, he practiced listening to the inner sound on the busiest roads, such as Boulevard Raspail, not far from Montparnasse Railroad Station. He fought with tranquil determination to hear the Nada, in spite of all the bustle that surrounded him and the permanent blaring of horns (in those days, drivers were still allowed to use their horns). He succeeded in this way, no matter what the external racket rumbling around him, in hearing the Nada vibrating within him with such clarity that it absolutely could not be muffled by anything external.

In the beginning, when he was trying to hear it while walking outside, he would take a tree or an object in front of him as a landmark and aim for it continually (looking at it as though out of the corner of his eye), using the distance separating him from it as a temporary aid to remain conscious of himself. When he reached this landmark, he immediately aimed at another, always in front of him, all the time listening within himself to this sacred sound. He noticed that, in this way, he began to be protected from a pernicious identification with external conditions, as well as from harmful influences coming from without.

One day, he was walking faster than usual, as he had many things to do, and, while he was hurrying, he projected himself into what awaited him. Arriving at the bottom of his apartment block, he suddenly realized that he had lost himself in this acceleration and asked himself: "but ultimately, how much time have I really saved by rushing?" He turned back on himself and retraced the route, walking normally, while remaining present to himself; he then noticed, with his musician's precision, that he had not even gained a few minutes, and that, for these few minutes, he had let go of that which was most precious to him: this presence to himself in a continual nowness. He saw the extent to which rapidity is a trap, particularly in our time, when one is always racing and where one has less time than ever, and how essential it is to slow down, be it ever so little, to fight against the external agitation and not to hurry needlessly, out of mere habit.

Salim also realized the importance of using the contact of the senses with the external world as a means of practice. Whenever he was walking along the street, he would practice another exercise in relation to the act of seeing.

He looked into the far distance at whatever object, tree, or building happened to meet his gaze, and as he looked, he kept slowly repeating to himself "seeing . . . seeing . . . seeing . . . seeing . . . " At the same time, he strove with all his being, for about ten seconds or so, to really see this object, tree, or building. Then, without losing this highly alert inner state, he turned his gaze elsewhere and looked intently at another object while he performed the same conscious act of seeing.

Not to yield to distraction, he constantly reminded himself what was at stake for him in this mysterious inner combat. He struggled continuously to renew the intensity of his attention even as it had started to degenerate, and immediately strove to regain the purity of this "highly awake" manner of seeing. He drew force from the word itself—which he was quietly repeating—to become fully conscious with the whole of himself of this alert way of seeing, without at any time allowing himself to name the object he was looking at, describe it, or mentally express any opinion whatsoever concerning it. His attention was absorbed solely in the act of seeing the object in view. As a result of all this work, he gradually came to see in what sense one generally looks at life and things without really seeing them.

He put this particular spiritual work into the act of hearing as well. He chose a particular sound from among all those that happened to be there at the time and fixed his attention on it for a few moments, before exchanging it for another one. And, while he was quietly repeating to himself the word "hearing . . . hearing . . . hearing . . . ," he exerted himself with the whole of his being to be fully aware of the act of hearing without the interferences that generally go on within oneself when one listens.

He discovered that, as with the act of seeing, in this domain also, one listens but one never really hears. These exercises are very similar to certain practices that the Buddha taught in the famous Satipatthana Sutta, on establishing attention.

Salim realized that it is only through conscious concentration of this kind that a seeker can succeed in tearing away from himself in order to begin really to look at what he sees and really to listen to what he hears. It is only in this way, he would later say to his pupils, that he can, in an ordinarily inexplicable way, possess what he has really seen or really heard and which, thereby, becomes for him internal wealth, which cannot, in any way, be compared to the material wealth of the external world.

An experience of mystical love.

One day, as Salim quietly descended into himself during his meditation, remaining inwardly ever so still and silent in a state of continual self-abandonment, a moment came when he was stirred by a most unusual feeling of love, filling him with a sublime and tender melting sensation spreading all around from his solar plexus, a sensation so unusual and strong that he found himself afterward weeping violently without fully understanding why. This out-of-the-ordinary sentiment gave him the strange sensation of experiencing extreme sadness and happiness simultaneously.

The experience of this uncommon love deeply affected and marked him. He recognized that what had taken place in him was an out-of-the-ordinary sentiment of mystical love, a most tender and strange love that could not be compared to anything one normally knows in life. For in this case, this particular love was not stimulated by nor directed to anyone or anything external. There was simply an inexplicable state of love, a most unusual melting sentiment of profound mystical love that he had become immersed in and one with.

He was so deeply moved that his whole body shook with the weeping that this strange and ecstatic love had provoked in him. As he understood it later, this intense weeping with which he was so suddenly seized was mainly due to an aspect of his being that was not ready to support such an uncommon and powerful experience.

He became attached to this ecstatic emotional state, which devoured him, rendering him tense, withdrawn and melancholic, unable to work and only wanting to retire ever further into himself and brood on this experience.

He thought again and again about these intense moments with the avid desire to relive them. It became an obsession, constantly gnawing at him, and drawing him away from what his true aim should be. He went through much torment and suffering before he realized his mistake.

He realized, little by little, that he should not become attached to out-of-the-ordinary states and to mystical phenomena that he might experience. He should never at any time, either consciously or unconsciously, seek to recreate such moments, no matter how fascinating and wonderful they might have been. He understood that experiences of such an extraordinary nature could not come again at one's command, in exactly the same manner, bringing with them exactly the same states that one has had before.

He had to learn to cultivate in himself the attitude and subtle art of always starting his meditation with the utmost sincerity and inner stillness as if it were for the first time, forgetting all that took place on previous occasions.

Although, during his meditation, he sometimes experienced very strange mystical phenomena and was given foretastes of transcendent emotional states, he understood that they might come as an encouragement and subtle indication, silently showing the way, according to the particular need of the moment, before being partially withdrawn from him for a certain time. He could afterward have to pass again through moments of difficulties until he succeeded in making the right efforts to rise to yet greater heights in himself. At that time, other experiences would come unexpectedly to help him advance still further in his spiritual journey.

The three appointments with himself.

To prolong even more another state of being and of consciousness of himself in the present, Salim decided to fix three appointments with himself at various points in the day. After his morning meditation, he visualized in advance, with all the intensity of his being, the three times fifteen minutes of intense spiritual work he wanted to accomplish on that day within the movement of the existential world itself. He made three appointments with himself—their frequency and duration being subsequently increased—at different times of the day and, during these fifteen minutes, he would try, with his entire being, to hear the Nada in his ears as an aid to remaining conscious of himself in a way that was not habitual to him, while continuing to do what was required of him in active life, whether talking, writing, washing, eating, etc.

He changed the timetable for this spiritual work every day, so as to put his practice to the test in all of the possible situations. When he forgot this first appointment with himself, he would not allow himself to execute this exercise later, because, in this way, he observed that each missed opportunity was lost forever. He would wait for the time of the second appointment with himself. And, if he also forgot the second, he would wait for the third.

He forced himself to cease this work at the very moment when he had decided to stop, in order to understand what was happening within him at that moment. What was his internal reaction when he realized that he was no longer allowed to continue? Did he not find himself facing the fact that his bodily existence was not permanent and that, just as he was losing the opportunity to work on himself at the scheduled time, he would also lose, when his earthly existence reached its term, along with the precious gift of his life, the opportunity of accomplishing something crucial to his evolution?

In the beginning, he was disconcerted to observe that he often forgot these very important appointments. It was as if, somewhere within him, he wanted to forget them so as to avoid the effort required of him to remain intensely conscious of himself. And, even if he remembered to begin this work on himself at the scheduled time, he experienced great difficulty maintaining this intense state of awakening within himself in the agitation of existential life; he perceived with sadness how fragile this particular consciousness of himself was, how it was almost impossible to preserve in the movement of everyday life, and that, in very little time, it would alter and would be mingled with his habitual state of being, until the moment when he would entirely lose it and become once more, so to speak, absent to himself.

Sometimes, even if he remembered to execute this spiritual exercise at the scheduled time and he succeeded, more or less, in maintaining this unusual state of consciousness for fifteen minutes, he did so somewhat half-heartedly.

It was by facing the difficulties that he encountered within himself in this way that he realized in what way he was still attached to what he was habitually and he understood ever more what he was required to renounce, in order that a sufficiently significant change might take place within him in order to enable him to be inhabited permanently by a very particular presence: this mysterious presence which fulfilled him and gave him the plenitude that he had sought to obtain from the moment he had embarked upon this mysterious quest.

New spiritual understandings.

One day, while walking outside, Salim was busy carrying out a concentration task consisting of fixing a distant point situated in front of him and trying to be constantly aware of all the objects to the right and to the left of this point in order to create within himself a particular expansion of consciousness, when he was struck by the very peculiar realization that, as he was moving forward, the objects were continually moving further away from the point he was focusing on. There was apparently nothing spectacular or new in such an observation; yet he suddenly grasped, through a mysterious intuitive insight, that the truths people passively accept as being immutable—and for which they are ready to fight—take on quite another meaning according to the perspective from which they are contemplated.

Seen from a higher state of consciousness, a truth will take on an entirely different magnitude, an entirely different value and an entirely different strength than if it is considered from the customary state of being in which one ordinarily lives. Moreover, even within the context of ordinary life, someone can repeat a truth word for word; it will nevertheless lose something of its rightness and its power if it is not connected to the reality of the moment.

During his meditation practices, on another occasion, he came to understand something which proved to be of the greatest importance, not only for all the concentration exercises he undertook in the turbulence of active life, but also to better comprehend the ultimate goal of his quest and of all this work on himself. He discovered that as his meditation was deepening and he was becoming more absorbed within himself, there would occur within him a clear shift in position, slight or significant, according to the degree to which he succeeded in distancing himself from his customary individuality.

This shift of position within oneself is perceptible when one contemplates a statue of Buddha. His eyes are symbolically closed to the external world and focused towards the interior, towards another aspect of his being into which he seems so mysteriously to have metamorphosed. The enigmatic smile which adorns his face displays the inexpressible silence and the internal peace in which he is immersed.

Moreover, Salim realized that this important shift in position within himself that he had noticed, during his meditation practices, during his exercises in concentration, and also when a strong recollection of consciousness suddenly occurred during his day-to-day activities, also happens, albeit to a lesser extent, in a receptive person who listens to a great musical work, without the latter recognizing what is happening within him in order to be able to appreciate the crucial value of it. The fact that he feels moved and elevated when hearing the music of a great composer actually creates, within his being, a subtle shift in position that he does not perceive.

This understanding merely confirmed for Salim the importance that great music—if it is authentic—can exercise in existence to help human beings begin to be placed within themselves somewhere that they never ordinarily find themselves.

Another fundamental understanding that Salim acquired as a result of his tenacious concentration practices and which he later conveyed to his pupils, is that, when a seeker begins to awaken internally and to become conscious of himself in a way that is not habitual to him, he cannot not know it; and, by contrast, when he sleeps again internally and becomes engulfed once more in his customary state of absence to himself, he does not know it, until the moment when a recollection of consciousness occurs suddenly within him and he begins again to awaken internally.

Through all the spiritual practices he undertook with determination and understanding, Salim was able, at certain privileged moments, to suddenly touch a superior dimension and mysteriously see what seemed to be all the different aspects and all the diverse possibilities of a being, a thing, or a situation simultaneously.

Divine Providence - August 1964.

In August, Paris became a desert. During all those difficult years, this period of the summer always posed a particularly acute problem for Salim. The few pupils that he had generally all went on holiday, as did his friends; even the providential grocery store near his home was closed.

At the beginning of August 1964, when he anxiously counted what little money remained to him, he decided, after long reflection, to buy a packet of crispbreads, a few raisins, some almonds, a few dates and dried bananas, a little sugar, a packet of powdered milk, a bar of chocolate, and a box containing sixteen portions of soft cheese, having been told that, wrapped in aluminum foil, as it was, it would not go moldy (Salim did not, of course, possess a refrigerator).

He carefully divided his meager provisions into thirty-one portions, giving him, for each day of the month: a piece of crispbread, six raisins, two almonds, half a date, a quarter of a dried banana, a half-portion of cheese, a minuscule piece of chocolate, a teaspoon of sugar, and a teaspoon of powdered milk which he mixed with cold water. Once he had reduced his food to this ultra-frugal diet, Salim weakened very rapidly. From the third day, the hunger became almost unbearable. It was a genuinely testing renunciation to have to restrict himself to his ration for the day while he had the rest of the food in front of him and his stomach demanded it without respite. After a short time, it became impossible for him to continue his hatha-yoga practices, as he became out of breath immediately. However he continued his pranayama exercises, but gently and without holding his breath for too long.

It was a magnificent summer; the weather was very fine and, to forget his hunger, Salim would go out very early in the morning to the Jardin du Luxembourg in order to be there when the gates opened. There was nobody there at that time and he could enjoy the beauty of nature in peace. He loved watching the sunrise and admiring the sparkling of the luminous rays through the foliage of the trees. He spent long moments in the garden, occupying himself in a positive way by undertaking spiritual concentration exercises. Sometimes, when he felt too weak to continue walking, he would stay seated on a bench. He always had music paper on him to jot down his flashes of inspiration in pencil. When it was too hot, he would go home and only return to the park when the sun had lost its heat.

He realized that it was preferable to eat his meager meal at the end of the day, as he discovered that, if he ate in the morning, the hunger proved harder to bear. He drank a lot of water to at least put something in his stomach to calm it a little. Once he returned to his room, he would meditate for a long time or compose.

When he talked about this month, which seemed to him so long and so difficult, Salim admitted having been constantly astonished in observing that, when he was occupied with his meditation or when he was writing his music, he would come to be so absorbed that he hardly felt his hunger. But, as soon as he ceased to be so concentrated, an intolerable feeling of hunger would seize him with such violence that he would be overcome with dizziness, forcing him to lie down for a few moments.

Sometimes, when he was sitting in the park, he would look at the sparrows and the pigeons, which came very close to his bench, and he would marvel at seeing them pecking at a scrap of food that they alone managed to see. He was astonished by the way in which these little creatures managed to find subsistence there where he could distinguish nothing.

At the same time, he felt more than ever the extent to which he did not belong in the West, where he always remained a foreigner. He thought of his "Elegie" and his "Jardin de Tinajatama" the orientalism of which some modern composers had criticized, whereas, on the contrary, the musicians of the orchestra were charmed by what they termed "the Arabian Nights atmosphere" of his music. In addition, the thought that he was incapable of coping in this very materialistic world always came back to his mind. He remembered the impression that he had had during his journey in the East two years previously, when, arriving in Pakistan, he had said to himself: "At last, here I am at home!"

As one day succeeded another, curiously, despite the fact that he felt increasingly weakened and light, he experienced, at times, during his meditation, spiritual experiences that astonished him and constituted a much-needed support. It was during these out of the ordinary moments that he realized more than ever that meditation, when it is really intense and profound, constitutes, in reality, a kind of initiation into death—but dying in order to find, within oneself, the True Life, which is beyond time and space. The month passed in this way, sometimes with moments of exceptional elevation and sometimes with moments of despair. After four weeks, exactly three days before the end of the month, Salim was seized with such anguish and such a feeling of uncontrollable hunger that he could no longer restrain himself and, throwing himself on the little food he had left, devoured it in one go! But, strangely, instead of relieving his hunger, he felt hungrier than ever.

Despite the state of torment and solitude that oppressed him, he put himself back into the hands of Divine Providence for the time separating him from the return of his first pupil at the beginning of September.

He remained lying on his bed for a while, then decided to go outside and walk a little. It was the beginning of the afternoon; he was plunged into himself, practicing a spiritual exercise, when he seemed to hear, as if through a fog, a voice calling to him: "Salim, Salim!" As his weakness was making him dizzy, he turned slowly in the direction this call seemed to be coming from and saw Madame Janot, the wife of the managing director of the radio, who had been obliged to come back to Paris for a reason which she explained to him, but which he did not really understand. She was in her car and while she was talking to him, he saw her as if in a dream. She said to him: "But what's happened to you? You're so thin!" Then she added: "We haven't seen you for such a long time! What's become of you?" She continued: "This evening, we have a few friends coming for dinner; among them will be a person who would be so glad to hear your Mass; would you bring your recording and come to eat with us?" Lowering his head to conceal the tears that came to his eyes, he accepted immediately, experiencing a feeling of overwhelming gratitude towards Providence which had come to his aid in this way.

As he had no money to buy a metro ticket, he set off immediately after collecting the recording of his mass. As Madame Janot lived a long way from the Rue du Cherche-Midi, it took him all afternoon to reach her home, stopping on every bench that he found on the way to rest a little. Finally, he arrived, exhausted. Madame Janot's mother, who opened the door to him, greeted him by exclaiming in surprise: "But you look so tired! And what have you been doing to get so thin?"

Salim avoided answering by asking her for her news. She led him into the living room where several people were standing, all unknown to him.

After the usual introductions, he found a chair in a corner where he sat down, listening to the exchanges of conversation, the sound of which seemed strangely distant to him. He understood nothing of what was being said. The people were talking of politics, with what seemed to him to be such assurance that he felt even more lost in a world that remained always foreign to him. All these people seemed to him so brilliant and so intelligent that he felt even more ignorant. The curls of smoke that bathed the room bothered him a great deal, especially on this evening when he felt so exhausted.

At last, Madame Janot asked the guests to follow her into the dining room. Sitting at the table, Salim said to himself that he would have to be very careful not to eat quickly. However, once the soup was served, he no longer perceived anything except the sound of his breath and the soup going down his throat. He was suddenly surprised by hearing the voice of Madame Janot's mother, who, ladle in hand, was offering him some more, serving him without waiting for an answer. At the same moment, he met the eyes of a guest and of one of the children who were staring at him, with an air of astonishment. Realizing that he must have behaved in a way incomprehensible to the others, he was ashamed of himself. He scolded himself inwardly, reminding himself once more to eat the following dishes more slowly, especially the solid food, as he knew he risked becoming unwell. Without saying anything, Madame Janot's mother, who threw him a look now and again, both penetrating and full of kindness, discreetly made sure, throughout the meal, that he was served copiously.

Once the dinner was over, Madame Janot invited everyone into the living-room to listen to Salim's Mass, its composer remaining peacefully seated and unassuming while it played. He hardly heard the music; he was plunged into a state of euphoria that he could not explain. When the music came to an end, there reigned a moment of silence during which he became aware that all eyes were fixed on him. He sensed that the audience was sincerely moved by his music and each person came to congratulate him.

One of the people present, a man of around fifty years of age, confessed to him with a great deal of emotion how much he had been touched by the finesse of his orchestral colors and by the feeling of authentic mysticism that emanated from the work. He added that he greatly regretted that his wife was not there, because, as she herself was a musician, she would have been delighted to discover this music. After a moment of hesitation, he asked Salim: "Would you give us the pleasure of coming to dine at our home tomorrow evening, bringing your Mass with you? We are expecting some guests, who are all musicians, performers, who would, I'm sure, be as interested in hearing your work as I am in hearing it again. Come at the end of the afternoon, we'll listen to your Mass before dinner." Salim, extremely moved by this unexpected invitation which guaranteed him another meal for the following day, accepted, thanking the man for his kindness. He was, in any case, always happy for his Mass to be discovered, especially by people in whom he perceived a sincere interest.

Later in the evening, when Salim, feeling extreme fatigue, was leaving, Madame Janot's mother accompanied him kindly to the door. When she shook his hand, he felt her discreetly slide something into his palm. Once outside, he discovered with emotion that it was a banknote thanks to which he would be able to buy a book of metro tickets and, consequently, would not have to walk home nor walk to his dinner the next day... and there would even be a little change left over!

That evening, when he reached his room, at the moment he went through the door, he was seized by a strange certainty that he was, inexplicably seen, or rather observed, by something invisible—as if to reassure him. At that very moment, he remembered the park sparrows who always managed to survive by pecking here and there for food invisible to his eyes, and he started to sob. The words of Christ in the

Gospel of Saint Luke* came back to him with a feeling of profound reverence and, in spite of the physical discomfort that he felt shortly afterwards, he went to sleep in a state of unutterable tranquility and elevation.

When he woke up the next morning, it was still dark. The hardships he had undergone during this month of August whirled ceaselessly about his mind and he was flooded with uncontrollable anguish. The torment of these four weeks, which had been so hard to bear, could be repeated in the future and might perhaps be even worse. He felt a sensation of overwhelming solitude and was once more unable to distance himself from the painful thought that he felt like a foreigner in the West, that he did not belong in this part of the globe. He thought of his old age and what the future might hold for him with apprehension. For the nearly fifteen years he had been in France, his life had been becoming ever more precarious and the difficulties encountered in having his music played more and more insurmountable. How would he manage to survive in this society devoid of elevated aspirations and which only concerned itself with the materiel aspect of existence?

His eyes fell on the enormous pile of music which stood at the foot of his bed, a pile that had not ceased to grow over the years. At that moment, a fleeting thought, which, subsequently, would return with insistence more and more frequently, crossed his mind: what weight this pile represented, in reality, for him, what a burden for him to feel chained to! As long as nobody heard what these thousands of sheets contained, it was only paper, paper that weighed on him and kept him prisoner. As long as this mountain of scores remained before him, he would never be able to give himself to his spiritual practice in the way he was realizing he should do. He felt, as he had many times

---

* "Do not worry about your life, what you will eat; or about your body, what you will wear.
Life is more than food, and the body more than clothes. Consider the ravens: They do not sow or reap, they have no storeroom or barn; yet God feeds them. And how much more valuable you are than birds!" (Luke, 12,22-24)

before, torn between music and his sadhana*—which, over the years, had continued to take an increasingly important place in his life. And India returned to his mind, calling him with such insistence that he felt more frustrated than ever.

The prospect of the evening awaiting him and the meeting with interesting musicians pushed him to get up. He completed his morning ablutions, then, sitting on his bed in the lotus position, he plunged into his meditation. When he opened his eyes, the day was well advanced; it was a beautiful summer's day and he decided to join his friends the sparrows and the pigeons in the Jardin du Luxembourg. He spent a few hours there, sometimes undertaking spiritual exercises, sometimes rapidly noting on music paper the inspirations that came to him.

When the time came, he returned home to collect the recording of his Mass, as well as two or three orchestral works, then left for his meeting with his new acquaintances. They lived in a beautiful house located on the higher slopes of Saint-Cloud, a suburban town to the west of Paris. Salim was very warmly welcomed by his hostess who introduced him to the other guests. Among them was a young singer who was both proud and happy because a record of the opera by Maurice Ravel "L'Enfant et les Sortilèges" (The Child and the Spells), in which she was singing the principal role, had just been released. In contrast to the previous day, Salim felt at ease among these young performers. The conversation focused mainly on music; they told interesting anecdotes about their experiences with conductors and contemporary composers.

Salim spoke to them of symbols in relation to the Cosmos and the spirituality that he had discovered in music, and the reason that tonality, which represents the centre to which all Creation is connected and around which only can it be expressed in the right way, must not be abandoned. Everyone showed a keen interest in his explanations, which he illustrated on the piano. He explained to them, furthermore, that,

---

* A sanskrit word signifying a method of spiritual realization.

without this tonal centre, music can only result in an abstraction devoid of meaning, as can be verified in all contemporary art, the works of which, whether music, painting, or sculpture, are born of an intellectual idea and no longer of an aesthetic sentiment.

Salim deplored indeed the fact that feeling no longer plays its role in the art of today and that it is intellect which predominates. He observed that this intellectual approach had also infiltrated the different spiritual paths that he had the opportunity of encountering in the West and was beginning to spread in the East as well.

After listening to his Mass, everyone expressed their appreciation for his music with such enthusiasm that he felt moved to tears. This work represented, for these musicians, proof that it was still possible to create something beautiful and new without rejecting tonality.

After long exchanges on art and modern life, Salim, who was hungry, was happy when his host suggested they move to the table. The decision he had made to eat well that day, with a view to being able to hold out the following day, was, in the end, not necessary, because, as all the guests expressed their desire to receive a copy of his Mass, as well as the other pieces that he had brought, one of them, who had professional reproduction equipment, suggested taking care of this for everyone, if they agreed to come to lunch at his home the next day.

Salim subsequently kept in contact with these kind people and did not forget to inform them of any rare performances of his works that he succeeded in obtaining, always thanks to Manfred Kelkel. Thus, in that summer of 1964, Salim, this human "sparrow," was able, thanks to Providence, to hold on until the appointment he had at the beginning of September, at Porte Maillot, to give a piano lesson to a ten-year-old boy.

A piano lesson. I like going there. Babysitting.

When he began teaching this child the piano, the latter had great difficulty sight-reading the music. He had worked with other teachers previously, but without success. As soon as he had played more than three or four notes, he would panic and make mistakes. He could,

however, read the notes and find them on the keyboard. So, Salim tried
to understand where his problem lay. By observing him attentively, he
noticed that, every time the young boy played, he was quite attentive
at the beginning and clearly understood the score, but, after only a
few notes, his gaze became vague and he would slip into a kind of
absence; no longer seeing the notes that followed, he immediately
made mistakes. Salim gently explained to him the phenomenon that
was occurring within him and told him that he would temporarily
stop him after the first four notes, but that it would be up to him to
remain attentive and clearly see just these notes while he was playing
them.

When the boy regained a little confidence in himself, seeing that
he could correctly recognize these first four notes, Salim then asked
him to move on to five notes, during which it would be up to him to
remain attentive. In this way, he gradually increased the number of
notes until the moment that the child understood for himself that, if
he wanted to sight-read the music without making mistakes, he would
have to, during the whole time he was playing, remain as attentive
and as present as possible.

Salim would later say to his pupils that humanity is like this child.
People do not understand that their principal problem in life resides
in the fact that they do not succeed in remaining attentive and present
internally during contact with their fellow humans.

Going to see another pupil one day, Salim realized that he wanted
to be rid of this lesson, which he considered a chore. He was going to
waste a lot of time, because, to save the cost of a metro ticket, he
walked to the pupil's home, which was some distance away. It would
take him two hours to walk there and another two hours to walk
back. He would have preferred to stay at home and write music or
meditate. He realized then that life was inflicting a sort of enforced
yoga on him and that, if he did not do with love those things he was
obliged to do, if he went to see this pupil saying to himself: "Oh, I

don't like doing this", this attitude could only harm him spiritually and would even become more marked over time. So he decided that, throughout the journey time, he would repeat inwardly: "Oh how I love working with this child, oh yes, I love it, love it, love it, love it…". Very soon, he no longer needed to repeat this "mantra" within himself, he arrived at the home of this pupil not wishing to be elsewhere or doing something else, which would prove to be a spiritual gain of great importance for him.

Again to earn a little money, he occasionally babysat for a neighbor who had two little girls, aged six or seven years, to whom he would tell little stories to entertain them. As they were twins, he remembered, one evening, an oriental tale narrating the adventures of a pair of twins, one of whom was born already an accomplished saint, while the other one had to battle hard over the years to become one. When he finished his tale, one of the two children, looking at him wide-eyed, declared with touching simplicity: "You know, Salim, out of these two brothers, I prefer the one who struggled to become a saint, rather than the one who already was one when he was born." And her sister added: "Me too!" Salim remained dumbfounded before these two little girls and said to himself with emotion that, sometimes, children intuitively understand important things about life, which, all too often, escape adults. Subsequently, he could not prevent himself from thinking with gratitude of the impromptu lesson that these little girls had given him and which had an effect on his spiritual efforts.

Once one has thought, said, or done something.
By assiduously pursuing the study of himself, of others, and of the world in general, Salim noticed a law whose implications were fundamental to spiritual practice, namely that once one has said, thought, or done something, one can no longer prevent oneself from re-saying it, re-thinking it, or re-doing it.

He observed for example that if someone, during an encounter with another person, says to himself inwardly, "I don't like this person", every time he happens to see that person again, this same negative impression will be repeated in him. Unless he deliberately works on himself to free himself from his conditioning and strives to be new in the present, he will imprison the other person and himself in what he thought the first time and he will no longer be able to prevent himself from repeating it; and this applies to everything around us, to the music one listens to, the food one eats, the places one finds oneself in, etc.

Salim understood how this law of repetition was preventing him from seeing or understanding something or someone in a new way.

To free himself of this hindrance, he put into practice an exercise consisting of looking at what was happening in front of him from far behind his eyes, from inside his head. The shift in position that was occurring within his being rendered possible a particular withdrawal, enabling him to experience the act of seeing, in its nakedness, without being involved in what presented itself to his gaze; there was, within him, no more "for" or "against", and this freed him from the blind reactions of his ordinary self, resulting from what he commonly liked or disliked. He experienced a certain inner freedom, giving him the clear feeling of being "apart" from what he was observing. Following this change of perspective within his being, everything seemed new to him, richer and more intensely alive.

A destitute taxpayer.

In our civilization, a lack of formal education renders the slightest administrative process problematic and filling in a simple form becomes a headache. This is the painful experience of many immigrants, but the latter are often able to rely on their community. Salim was living as an artist, with an intense inner life, but in extreme materiel destitution and great solitude.

One day, he was summoned to the tax office and was asked to declare his means of existence. When he listed his meager resources, the person behind the counter retorted, incredulous: "But one can't live on that! You eat meat, you drink wine, you go to the cinema, and you buy clothes! How do you manage to pay for all that?... Not to mention electricity, telephone, heating, and rent for your apartment!" When Salim tried to explain to her that he did not eat meat, did not drink wine, and only went to the cinema when he was invited, that all his clothes had been given to him by friends, that he had no electricity, telephone, heating, or apartment, but just a small room lent to him by a friend, it was in vain. So, a little later, he received a visit from a tax official who began, without saying anything, to take notes. Worried, Salim told him that the bed on which he was sitting, together with the chair that completed the furniture, did not belong to him and that the only things he actually owned were the pile of music at the foot of his bed and the suitcase. The man looked at Salim for a moment in silence, then his physiognomy became more affable, he reassured him and left.

This did not prevent the tax authorities from asking him all the same for a little tax on his "income"; not knowing how to defend himself, Salim struggled to put aside, coin by coin, the amount demanded which, although very low, represented once again the sacrifice of a certain number of meals.

Hospitalization for malnutrition. The ordeal of winter.

The difficulties Salim had so long been encountering in managing to nourish his body would finally get the better of him. He was introduced by a friend to a doctor at the Bichat hospital who, noticing his swollen belly and his legs swollen with edema, and observing his extreme state of fatigue and weakness, had him hospitalized. After a number of unpleasant examinations, the doctors, still not understanding the cause of his intestinal troubles and not suspecting his financial situation, told him: "You're quite simply presenting all the symptoms of malnutrition; you have to feed yourself better!" They fed him up for a month and gave him a bill on his discharge, which, not being covered by social security, he was quite incapable of paying. The mother of two children to whom he gave piano lessons came to his aid. He did not know how she managed it, but she succeeded, to his great relief, in cancelling his debt.

A few months later, when he was in Great Britain, he was again hospitalized for malnutrition. They kept him for two weeks, during which they administered high doses of tonics to him.

Finally, even later, he once more had to stay in hospital in Saint-Cloud, again for dietary deficiencies; a doctor friend took care of the payment formalities.

As an Oriental, Salim was already extremely sensitive to the cold by nature. So, during that same period, he had to face several particularly hard winters. Washing himself in cold water was very unpleasant and, in his state of weakness, he was constantly catching colds and flu. Only having an old raincoat to protect him, he suffered enormously from the cold, the rain, and the snow which, sometimes falling heavily, got into his shoes. Moreover, these shoes had finally become so worn and broken that he constantly had to cut to his size makeshift soles out of bits of cardboard taken from garbage bins. He always carried these in his pockets so as to be able, if the ones he had put in before putting his shoes on became too wet, to pretend an urgent need on arriving at someone's house and discreetly change them. As for his socks, they enabled him, more or less, to decorate his ankles so that it could not be seen that he was actually barefoot in what remained of his shoes.

Some unexpected resources.

A young composer whom Salim had introduced to the work of the Gurdjieff groups, one day came, for the first time, to see him at home. When he saw the conditions Salim was living in and the difficulties he was encountering in managing to subsist, he spoke to him of some friends who took care of illustrative music for television and who could, perhaps, use his compositions as background music to accompany the news—as was still the practice at that time—which should bring him some royalties. So the young man took him to the television center's technical premises where he introduced him to three or four people who proved to be very benevolent towards him; they advised him to make some non-commercial recordings of his most descriptive orchestral works, which they undertook, as far as possible, to use during news broadcasts. They warned him to expect, however, a certain delay before the Sacem (Société des Auteurs, Compositeurs et Editeurs de Musique— [Society of Music Authors, Composers, and Publishers]) collected the money and paid the sums that would be due to him.

After a number of new tribulations, he finally found the necessary means to record four or five non-commercial discs from private recordings of his orchestral works, which he gave to his new television friends. While waiting to receive his first royalties, he continued to give music theory and piano lessons to his few young pupils.

In order to help him further, one of these illustrators told him that, if he agreed to write lighter music, he would put him in touch with a British company which would automatically take responsibility for the costs of performances and recording. This company would then take care of distribution of the records intended to be used as background music for documentaries and films in different countries. Needless to say, Salim accepted this proposal without hesitation.

During a trip to London to see his family, he made contact with the publishing house he had been told about. Being naturally ingenuous, he always had a tendency to trust people, so he immediately signed a contract for several works. When he naively asked the manager whom he had dealt with how the Sacem was going to become aware of the broadcast of his music, the latter looked at him in an embarrassed way, then, after a moment of silence, told him quite simply: "You know, you'll never be a rich man..."

As a matter of fact, he received very little by way of royalties from Britain. His friend Manfred Kelkel made inquiries for him at the Sacem which replied that the organization in question was known and that it had, in various countries in Europe and America, satellites intended to collect funds under false names, that it was nearly impossible for the Sacem to find any trace of these, and that these practices were, unfortunately, common. And what was even more scandalous, was that the music thus filed under contract could no longer be used by the composer himself.

It took nearly a year for Salim to begin receiving some payments, mainly from French television; the amount of these royalties, low to begin with, increased gradually, until they became a real blessing for him when he had just arrived in India. Although insufficient for living in Europe, the amounts that the Sacem paid him enabled him, nevertheless, to meet his needs when he was in Poona and Madras, as well as covering the costs of his various trips across India and Nepal.

Destruction of his music. 1965.

Despite the intense spiritual experiences he was privileged to know, Salim passed through moments of despair and solitude that he never revealed to his friends. Seeing how the people around him lived, their way of thinking and their principal preoccupations, he could not help feeling the extent to which they lacked even any knowledge that there existed an infinitely higher goal than the motivations that ordinarily animated them. He had grasped directly that short of accomplishing the effort to raise himself to another level of being and of consciousness and to establish himself there, the human being can only continue to live very partially and feel, through his limited sensory perceptions, an infinitesimal part of the whole of possible existence.

He had always been absolutely convinced that spiritual and artistic treasures are the only valid goals in existence. Unfortunately, he said to himself, such aspirations are absent from the lives of the majority of people, who, to fill this lack, are, despite themselves, pushed by forces beyond them to run in every direction and to give themselves over to all sorts of feverish activities, more often than not without any specific goal and without even a genuine interest in what they are doing.

Salim continued to think about his own life in the West, the way it had unfolded until that point, as well as apprehension concerning the future and what it might hold for him in this part of the world when he became old. The desire to leave everything and go to India became more and more imperious. Perhaps he would find what he was looking for there, but how could he leave? With what money? And then, he had this enormous pile of music which his gaze continually encountered and which was piled up in front of him like a temptation and a burden that would never leave him in peace; music which was a part of himself, or rather, as he said, which represented "the best part" of himself.

After the disastrous reviews of January 1962, despite all of his efforts combined with those of Manfred Kelkel and other friends, it had become clear to him that it would never be his lot to one day see his music recognized in musical circles where only dry intellectual manipulations now prevailed.

It might be thought that true talent always triumphs in the end. Yet experience shows that a composer must be appreciated at least a little during his lifetime, if only to encourage him to pursue his work despite the financial or other difficulties he cannot avoid encountering along his way. The National Conservatory of Music keeps musical works which are unknown and have never been played. How many masterpieces lie dormant in dusty closets? Some museums house scores for unknown operas that are more beautiful than the celebrated works of Verdi and Puccini, which, nevertheless, attain great heights in this area. By chance, Salim once heard on the radio an absolutely remarkable unappreciated opera entitled "La Samaritaine" (The Samaritan), written by Max d'Ollone, a French composer who remains to this day in obscurity. He also heard of a contemporary of Debussy, recognized by the latter as having a very great talent, who was so thoroughly torn to pieces by the critics that he finally burned all of his music; he is now entirely forgotten. It must also be considered that, even having acquired a certain degree of renown, a composer is never shielded from the quirks of fate. Arnold Bax, an English composer, greater than the majority of those who are famous in the United Kingdom, whose music, influenced by Debussy, is imbued with mystery and great beauty, is practically never played; many composers of immense talent disappeared in the turmoil of the Nazi regime. Miraculously, Walter Braunfels, Alexandre Zemlinsky, and Berthold Goldschmidt have been pulled from entirely unmerited obscurity and, after fifty years of silence, are played once again; finally, Johann Sebastian Bach, who is today praised to the skies, had fallen almost into obscurity when he was rediscovered by Mendelssohn who republished his work at his own expense. As for Monteverdi, it is barely a few decades since he too was pulled from obscurity.

Aside from his financial difficulties and the fact that there was little hope he would ever have his music played or published, Salim felt that while this enormous pile of scores, which continued to climb towards the ceiling, remained before him, he would forever be its prisoner. The works of a musician are like children; they demand all the attention of their creator, who must, after having brought them into the world, engage in combat in order to achieve the goal for which they were conceived, namely to be heard by an audience.

Assessing the uselessness of pursuing this unequal struggle against a world that had become insensitive to beauty, Salim reached the depths of despair. Finally, in his despondency, he felt that there was only one solution left to him: to destroy this mountain of music so as not to be crushed by it.

The terrible decision made, he divided the enormous pile of scores into small parcels which he tied with string and, very early one morning, he made several trips down from the sixth floor to put them next to the garbage bins. With every descent, he experienced the grievous feeling of undergoing a repeated death.

In the evening, when, heartbroken, he walked past the spot, everything had disappeared. This music, which had demanded so much work from him, so much effort and self-denial, for which he had starved for long years, had ended up in the hands of garbage collectors...

From that most painful of all days, he banned himself from writing any more music. There only remained the works already printed and a few scores still in London (around thirty pieces).

During the months that followed, when inspirations came to him, he repressed them firmly, because he knew that, as soon as he began to jot them down, he became, in his own words, "like an intoxicated man" or even "like a woman about to give birth", unable to stop himself as long as the work remained unfinished. Throughout the process of creation, he no longer lived, not eating, not sleeping, not noticing if it was day or night, consumed by an ardent fire over which he had no hold. It is for this reason that he later wrote that great artists are beings sacrificed to bring some light to the world. Over the following years, as he needed money, he composed, on the advice of his friends from television, some new descriptive orchestral works ("Nathan le Prophète" [Nathan the Prophet], "Quatorze Esquisses Pittoresques" [Fourteen Picturesque Sketches], "Quatre Rituels" [Four Rituals], etc.) intended to be used as background music for documentaries and which he placed with specialist publishers.

With the exception of this music, which was his bread and butter, he kept to his decision to no longer compose and no longer allowed himself to yield to his inspirations. The forces that he had put to the service of his musical creations, he henceforth turned entirely towards his spiritual quest.

It was in reference to his own unimaginably painful experience at the time that he resolved to destroy his own music that Salim wrote in his first book, "The Way of Inner Vigilance":

"If it be his fate that all the perfection he so painfully struggled to achieve throughout his existence should one day suddenly crumble and come to nothing, even bringing disaster in its trail, yet in the very midst of this situation, no matter how hopeless it may seem, he must, in the depths of himself, somehow learn to be as quiet and unruffled as possible. He should strive to find in himself the courage and fortitude not to let this situation submerge him to the point of interfering with his spiritual work and his other duties and obligations in life."

Meeting his companion, a common attraction to India.

Salim had by this point reached the age of forty-five. The desire to go to India continued to plague him, but, at the same time, he knew his limits when it came to coping with external life and, besides, he still lacked money.

Mr Adie, who had been so good and so understanding to him during all these years, no longer able to tolerate the cold and damp climate of England, decided to go and live in Australia. After the removal of one of his lungs, which he had undergone several years earlier, he needed a drier and more clement climate. His departure only strengthened in Salim the desire to also leave Europe.

In the course of 1966, he got to know a young woman who wanted to go to India just as much as he did. This common attraction to this country immediately made them close. Soon, a more tender feeling arose between them. She was brilliant and Salim admired her great literary abilities. The ardent desire that she had to learn Sanskrit met with such strong opposition on the part of her parents that the latter finally threw her out of the family home.

Salim did everything in his power to encourage her and help her in these difficult times, by way of the modest royalties that he was beginning to receive. During a stay in London, in order to pay for some expensive dental treatment that she urgently needed, he managed to sell some of the remaining works of his youth to the American composer to whom he had already sold other pieces of his symphonic music.

Premonitory dreams.

One morning, very early, while Salim was half awake, he had a premonitory dream which forewarned him that the relationship he was in the process of forming would be among the most difficult for him; he woke up, troubled, then went back to sleep and had a second dream which confirmed the first in a striking manner. The meaning of these two dreams not being open to error and the warning making a great impression on him, he decided to cancel the ceremony planned to bind him to his companion. However, he had been alone for so long, the tender sentiment that he felt towards her and their common attraction to India caused him to relent and finally, despite this disquieting premonition, they were married.

His companion obtained a grant to study Sanskrit and left for India towards the end of 1967, hoping that Salim would find the resources to join her there soon.

Before she left, Salim had suddenly to leave the cubbyhole in which he had managed to survive for nearly ten years, as Monsieur and Madame Villequez were at last going to undertake the transformations they had been planning for a long time, consisting of connecting his box room to the adjoining bedroom to make a studio. He did not know where to go or what to do. Finally, after several enquiries, he was offered, through friends, a small room on the seventh floor of a building located on Rue Ledru-Rollin, in exchange for piano lessons for the daughter of the owner, who occupied an apartment three floors down. The building was at the intersection of a number of streets and the traffic noise was infernal day and night.

During the few months he spent in that room, to earn a little money, he composed an illustrative piece of music entitled "Sept Préludes Symphoniques" (Seven Symphonic Preludes).

Later, when he was in India, in three months he wrote, for the same reasons, "La Tragédie de Masada" (The Tragedy of Masada) an enormous descriptive work for large orchestra, characterized by its dramatic power and orchestral colors

La Tragédie de Masada.

Salim heard Masada spoken of for the first time by a friend in London. This tragedy made a very strong impression on him.

The story unfolded in the former Palestine in the year 69 AD. The last bastion of Jewish resistance to Roman domination took refuge in an impregnable fortress situated at the summit of Mount Masada, where the soldiers, their families, wives, and children made up a total of 960 people. There, they held the Roman legions of Titus in check for three years. The Romans had to construct four large towers and an access ramp to reach the level of the fortress. Finally, helped by unexpected winds, they succeeded in burning the great wooden gates. When the defenders of the city saw that their defeat was inevitable, anticipating the exemplary punishment awaiting them for having dared defy the might of Rome, rather than surrender, they chose to commit suicide collectively. Each soldier executed all the members of his family with their consent, then all the soldiers together drew lots to choose ten among them who would put the others to death. In the same way, from the ten survivors, one soldier was designated to kill the nine others, and lastly sacrificed himself. The following day, when the Romans entered Masada, they found only the silence of death, until the moment they discovered with amazement the tragic spectacle spread before them. So extraordinary was the courage of the Jewish rebels that it earned the admiration of the Romans themselves, who avowed that they would not take any joy in their conquest and gave a victor's funeral to the rebels' remains.

The music was intended for a film project that, unfortunately, was not realized. Salim had, however, the pleasure of hearing his composition broadcast on the radio, as a friend, who was conducting the performance of a contemporary symphonic piece, managed to slip it into the same program without the radio selection committee knowing anything about it. Although only descriptive music, it made a strong impression and the radio's secretariat informed Salim that over two hundred enthusiastic listeners had taken the trouble to write to congratulate them and ask the channel to broadcast this composer's music more often. Despite the fact that such praise, coming from so great a number, proved extremely rare, the opposition Salim met with from the contemporary music lobby did not diminish for all that.

The work was released as a vinyl record by Montparnasse 2000. Salim wrote these few words for the record cover:

"While I was composing this music, I imagined what it must have been like for this small handful of a few hundred rebels to be surrounded by an innumerable army of Roman soldiers, determined to save face before such defiance. (...) I admit that when I wrote this music, I experienced it in the depths of my being and I was even surprised sometimes to find myself crying as I was composing it."

The desire to go to India becomes a reality.

By one of those mysterious chances, which sometimes accompanied him and allowed him to keep going in the most difficult moments of his life, Salim met a doctor who had just returned from a trip to India where he had gone in search of a master. Recognizing Salim's strong desire to go there himself and seeing his financial difficulties, this man had the astonishing generosity not only to offer him a plane ticket on an Arab Air Line charter flight, but also to provide him with various essential items: a suitcase, a sleeping bag, medicine, etc...

The limitations of a story.

Salim, seeing his ardent aspiration to visit India fulfilled, turned with hope towards this new life that was awaiting him, but he could not forget the constant struggle that the eighteen years he had spent in Paris had represented for him.

Throughout all those years, he had seen the hopes he had based on music crumble one by one. His health problems had proved to be such a handicap that he had been obliged to give up not only his career as a solo violinist, which he had begun in England, but also conducting, which he had studied with passion. He had had to face other trials when, one day in January 1962, a cabal of critics had sounded the death knell for his hopes of making his music known. Yet, he had found the necessary inner reserves to pursue, for three more years, his work of musical creation before finally resolving, in 1965, to destroy by his own hand most of the compositions that had cost him so many sacrifices. Finally, instead of seeing his situation improve over the years, he had seen his material condition become ever more precarious without glimpsing a way out of this impasse.

When one peruses the story of an entire life, one skims through, in a few moments, the unfolding of long years that it is, in fact, impossible to grasp in their true duration. The ten years Salim spent in his cell on the Rue du Cherche-Midi signified, for him, that many times three hundred and sixty-five days where he had to find, every morning, the strength to fight for survival while still pursuing his musical composition.

More than twenty-five years later, when he told me this tale, he retained so vivid and painful a memory of those ten years that it seemed impossible for him to communicate what he had really experienced.

It was thanks to his spiritual practice and to the powerful experiences he had that he could find the necessary strength to come through this ordeal. It was sometimes his lot to live through such phenomenal experiences that he dared not open up to anyone, not even his friend Mr Adie. He keenly felt, at such times, the impossibility of being able to rely on someone capable of guiding him. And so he hoped that India would give him the master his wishes called for.

London miracle.

Before leaving Europe, Salim visited London to see his family and settle some final details regarding his illustration music with his English publisher. He did not suspect that this would be the last time he saw his father alive.

His parents lived in a fairly quiet spot, not far from a crematorium surrounded by a very beautiful garden, where Salim, during his London stays, liked to walk from time to time. He went there one Sunday morning dreaming of what India had in store for him. Arriving at a place where he had to cross the street, he looked, as was his custom, to the left and seeing no car coming towards him, he stepped into the road. Suddenly, he had the horrible sensation that a dark wind was blowing over him and death had brushed past him. At the same time, he heard the sharp screech of brakes followed by the sound of a collision. He turned and saw that, behind him, a car had mounted the pavement, ending its mad trajectory against a streetlight.

The driver, unhurt, had just got out of his vehicle. He was both furious at Salim and distraught, constantly repeating: "I don't understand, I don't understand! Something took my hand and turned the steering wheel with force; I just don't understand it!" Despite his anger, he was visibly extremely shaken. Salim realized that, accustomed to French traffic, he had forgotten that, in England, the cars drive on the other side of the road, and he had therefore looked the wrong way when crossing. Without this providential and inexplicable manifestation, which had turned the car aside, he would have been knocked down and, in all likelihood, killed, because, as the streets were almost deserted at that early hour, the driver was traveling at high speed.

Salim could not help thinking how many times, since he had come into the world, an ordinarily incomprehensible event had saved his life, whether during his childhood, during the war, during his trip to Afghanistan, and again this time.

No longer falling into self-forgetfulness.

Throughout those years spent in Paris, due to a deep understanding of the vital importance of this work on himself, Salim had succeeded in finding within himself the necessary resources to use the situations he found himself in as springboards to attain higher levels of consciousness and of being.

He had understood that the fate of every seeker is to begin again, always beginning again to make the effort to recollect himself until the interval between the moments where he is conscious of himself gradually decreases, and some degree of continuity of being can be established within him.

The state of awakening that he was trying to consolidate within his being was not at all easy to render permanent, but he showed an unwavering determination, as he keenly felt the tragedy of the customary state of absence to oneself in which one habitually passes one's life and which is, in fact, a form of inner death. He came to realize that it was only when he was occupied in maintaining himself in that state of presence to himself that he began to experience a subtle felicity and a feeling of strange inner security and peace that was not of this world; as soon as his efforts faltered, the torments and concerns of external life regained the upper hand and overwhelmed him.

Little by little, the times he was conscious of himself in a continual nowness were increasingly prolonged, until the day that something was established within him: he was no longer falling into self-forgetfulness, a threshold had been crossed.

He would, henceforth, pursue his efforts at another level. However, he was entirely lucid and honest with himself and he knew that he was not yet free of all attachment to the tangible world: he had not yet succeeded in permanently surpassing the separate individual self, which is so difficult to achieve as evidenced by the lives of the great mystics.

Early 1968 – India at last!

Back in Paris, Salim began to prepare for his departure. The day finally came where he found himself on a plane to Bombay: his most cherished dream was coming true.

After several hours in the air, his charter plane stopped in Cairo and, to his dismay, all the passengers had to disembark. For some reason, which remained incomprehensible to him, the authorities took his passport and only returned it after a seemingly interminable wait, then admonishing him to hurry up and join the other passengers. To his horror, he discovered that the aircraft that was to carry the passengers to Bombay could not even hold a quarter of those who were waiting. A crowd of various nationalities gathered around the plane. Salim thought anxiously of his companion who had gone to India ahead of him, and who would be coming to meet him at the airport. Thus, contrary to his temperament, he found himself busily jostling with fierce energy to make himself a path through the sea of people and finally succeed in boarding the plane. It was only once on board that he worried about the fate of his baggage, which had been checked onto the previous flight and which he nevertheless found without difficulty on arrival. He later learned that the surplus passengers had had to wait for a week in Cairo for a new flight.

Once safely installed and, above all, relieved to be able to continue his journey, he began to consider with interest the other passengers, who, like him, were going to Bombay. There were no Westerners, just Pakistanis, Indians, a few Asians, and, especially, many Arabs dressed in traditional djellabas. The flight seemed very long; finally, six hours late, at around midday local time, the plane reached its destination.

On leaving the aircraft, he saw from afar, with a sense of relief and joy, his companion who had come to meet him. Throughout the long rickshaw ride to get to the station, where they were going to take the train to Poona the same day, he experienced the indescribable feeling of having come home. Yes, he finally felt at home!

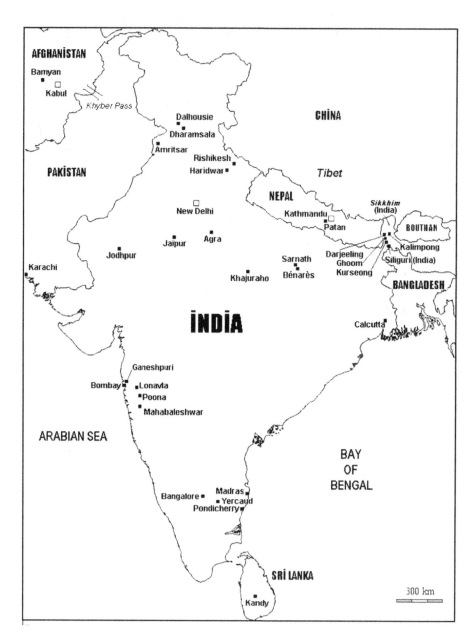

Edward Salim Michael's journeys in India.

Chapter 4

India : 1968-1974.

Poona* 1968-1970

The first morning.
They waited for the train to Poona in a sort of small waiting room
with a bed, located in the station itself and called a "rest room". The jet
lag added to the fatigue of the journey and the emotions experienced
in Cairo made Salim sink into a deep sleep from which he did not
emerge until shortly before the departure of the train.

It was still light when the train set off and Salim, who, with joy in
his heart, was gazing out of the window at the landscape streaming
past and becoming gradually more mountainous, had the inexplicable
feeling that everything seemed strangely familiar to him. He could not
help repeating: "I'm home... I'm home at last!"

Dusk fell very quickly, creating a mysterious atmosphere, he
remained fascinated by the landscape, which the darkness was flooding,
and by the mountains standing out against the sky.

It was dark when they arrived in Poona, the very place where his
grandmother had been born, and Salim felt strong emotion rising
within him. The official porters in their red uniforms, each one
identified by a number, rushed towards them to take their baggage,
hoping to make a few rupees to feed their families. In India, Salim
rediscovered, both the vivid smell and dirtiness of the East and the
warmth and atmosphere he loved so much. Furthermore, and what
was most important to him, he found there a respect for the Sacred, a
respect quite specific to that country which was and still is the spiritual
centre of the world.

---

* Poona was re-baptized Pune in 1976, Benares is also known as Varanasi, Pondicherry
became Puducherry in 2006, Calcutta became Kolkata in 2001, and Madras became
Chennai in 1996.

As Deccan College, where they were to spend the first few days, was a little outside the town, Salim and his companion went there by taxi. The place was so dimly lit that his companion, after a long and fruitless search, had to resolve to wake up the other occupants of the building to find the room that had been reserved for them. Overcome by fatigue, Salim lay down on his bed, pulled down his mosquito net and lost all sense of the world until sunrise. He was pulled from sleep by the voice of a man who, not far from there, was singing a bhajan to the accompaniment of rhythms he tapped out on a mridangam*. Salim listened in wonder asking himself if he was not dreaming. Everything seemed so unreal to him and yet so mysteriously familiar. The melodic line of the bhajan, which he heard only once, on his first awakening in India, remained forever etched in his memory.

After having carried out his ablutions, he went out to familiarize himself with his new environment. Deccan College, which was fairly large and imposing, had been built by the British in colonial times to house convalescing soldiers, as, due to the altitude of about 600 meters, Poona was considered a sanitarium. The town stands on a kind of plateau surrounded by hills and small mountains. At the top of one of these hills, located not far from Deccan College, rose an imposing white temple, which Salim contemplated as if in a dream. At the foot of the hill, he also saw a squalid encampment of poor people whom he later learned were Namalis, considered as outcastes.

Deccan College included, surrounding the main building, several bungalows, mainly occupied by staff. Salim and his companion would move into one of these a few months later and would live there for nearly two years. It was a very beautiful place, well-maintained, with landscaped flowerbeds here and there.

Indira Devi.

After those first days at Deccan College, Salim and his companion were graciously accommodated for a while by an Indian woman who

---

* Indian percussion instrument.

lived on the other side of Poona, a little outside the town. Not far from this temporary home, was a temple and a small ashram inhabited by a woman named Indira Devi, who was considered a saint. Despite the fact that she was not very well known in India, she nevertheless enjoyed a certain renown in Poona. A venerable old man named Dilip Kumar Roy, who was a former disciple of Shri Aurobindo and whom she regarded as her master, also lived there. The place was also home to quite an elderly man, Shri Kanta, who acted as a general handyman, and a dozen women who took care of household chores and gardening.

As soon as he saw the temple nearby, Salim went there. Dusk had already fallen when he opened the gate into a small garden brimming with flowers. Removing his sandals, he went into the sacred place where some people, sitting in silence, were gathered before a statue of the god Krishna. A faint glow lit the room, which was fragrant with incense. A man of around fifty, surprised to see a stranger, got up and went towards Salim. After exchanging a few words in lowered voices, he told him of the presence of this saint to whom Salim asked to be

Indira Devi

introduced. He was immediately invited to cross the courtyard, climb the stairs, and enter, at the end of a short corridor, a room inside which several people were sitting on the floor round a woman dressed in ocher, aged about forty-five, extremely beautiful and radiant: Mataji Indira Devi.

She regarded him tenderly and, with a charming smile, said in English: "Here comes a friend". Then, she added: "He is so kind, he is so noble". Surprised, Salim said to himself that he knew he was hyper-sensitive and could not bear to see anyone suffer, whether it was a human being, an animal, or even a plant, but the idea that he was noble had never crossed his mind. On the contrary, he was quite poor and destitute, in search of someone who might help him go further in his spiritual quest. He did not feel comfortable hearing such words. She considered him at length, with a delicate smile, and motioned to him to sit down.

Everyone one was gazing at her with respect and the greatest veneration. During the long silence that followed, Salim guessed that most of these visitors had come there simply to receive what is called in India her "darshan", that is to say the gift of the regard and the presence of this saint. Occasionally, one of them would respectfully address a few words to her in English or Hindi (which Salim did not understand) calling her Ma—which means "Mother". She would reply in a sweet voice, full of love, which greatly struck Salim. The group was mainly composed of distinguished Indians belonging to wealthy families. The venerable Dilip Kumar Roy, who was sitting with Indira Devi and who was addressed as "Dadadji" spoke little. Furthermore, despite his imposing appearance and his kindness, his speech was a little unclear, so Salim preferred to turn his attention to Indira Devi.

After some time, the visitors began to withdraw quietly after performing "Pranam"—the traditional greeting where one bows to the ground, not before a person, but before the Divine Principle which inhabits the yogi or the holy person to whom this homage is addressed. Indira Devi motioned Salim to stay, then, when they were alone, asked him where he came from and the reason for his journey to India. During the ensuing conversation, Salim saw that she was deeply religious and realized that hers was the Bhakti-yoga way, the path of devotion—which did not leave him unmoved, as he himself was of a religious temperament.

Nevertheless, after leaving her that evening, and despite the fact that he felt spiritually intoxicated, he realized that she could not really help him in his quest. In fact, some mystics sometimes have an innate ability—resulting from a practice in another existence—to maintain in almost all circumstances, a devotional attitude, but they do not know how to transmit it. Moreover, in this little ashram, Salim saw no one devote himself to meditation or take any interest in the study of himself. However, as he very much liked the atmosphere of this temple, he regularly visited this saint during the two years he spent in Poona, and without helping him directly, she nevertheless played a significant role in his sadhana.

Natco House. Adopting a puppy.

Shortly after his arrival, Salim became seriously ill, suffering from his customary intestinal problems. The person with whom he was lodging temporarily introduced him to Dr Patki, a very kind man who quickly became a friend and treated Salim throughout his stay in Poona. After a series of examinations, some of which proved very painful, the Indian doctor, like his Western colleagues, had to confess his ignorance in the face of this problem from which Salim suffered so much and for so long.

Some time later, Salim and his companion left to live on the first floor of a house known as "Natco House", in a small apartment owned by a French woman who worked at Deccan College and who had to go back to France suddenly to undergo surgery. They lived there for two or three months while she was absent. Although this apartment was located far from Indira Devi's ashram, Salim visited her from time to time and, on some mornings, attended pujas (religious ceremonies accompanied by singing) during which Dadadji would sing bhajans.

One day, leaving the house, he saw a poor puppy, which must have been hit by some vehicle or other, as it was painfully dragging its broken hind legs, and its tail, which was broken and bloody, was covered with flies.

At the sight of this pitiful animal, Salim, who could not bear to see it suffer in such a way, immediately made enquiries to find a veterinarian. In India, veterinarians tend to livestock, but never dogs, which, more often than not, live in a feral state. The one he went to was very difficult, but, in the end, agreed to keep the poor creature for a few days, to operate on and treat it. After two weeks of treatment, Salim settled the bill and retrieved the little animal, which he kept.

Hatha Yoga with Iyengar. Moving into Deccan College.

Natco House was situated at an intersection of noisy streets; added to the incessant racket made by the traffic were the honking of rickshaw and car horns and even the nearby whistling of steam locomotives whose mechanics rhythmically released the pressure, as though to amuse themselves. Beside the house, there was a Christian convent inhabited by Indian nuns. Salim would occasionally seek a little silence in their garden; sitting on a bench, he would immerse himself in his reflections. "India," he said to himself, "is an immense country, how can I find, without any guidance, the spiritual help I have come to seek?"

The only person he had heard of while he was still in Paris was a renowned hatha yogi called Iyengar, who actually lived in Poona. As Salim was passionate about hatha yoga, he lost no time becoming his pupil and regularly took private lessons with him.

Iyengar 1968

Iyengar possessed an astonishing mastery over his body and taught the various asanas and pranayama exercises with undeniable skill, but Salim did not find in him what he was looking for, as this famous hatha yoga master did not teach or advocate any meditation techniques or self-study, aspects of the practice whose importance Salim had experienced. Iyengar focused his attention solely on the physical results of this path.

Salim, nevertheless, took advantage of the opportunity offered by his great technical expertise to perfect his own knowledge in this field.

He heard about a hatha yoga center in Lonavla, about forty kilometers from Poona; he went there one day, full of hope, only to be disappointed, the master was dead, he saw only a Westerner and a few Indians who were living there on subsidies which were probably still being paid to them as a posthumous homage to the dead master.

A few weeks later, Salim moved again, settling with his companion in a bungalow in Deccan College for the rest of his stay in Poona.

The small house, which was slightly raised to avoid flooding during the monsoon, was set out lengthways, with two fairly dark bedrooms and the kitchen as well as the shower room opening onto a long corridor. By Western standards, comfort was somewhat perfunctory: the bathroom, which had no water supply, consisted of a drain for the shower and squat toilets. The water ran only sparsely, for about two hours a day, early in the morning, from the single tap located in the kitchen. Every day, therefore, Salim ensured that two large buckets and several pans were filled to make adequate provision for cooking, washing, and drinking during the day. Sometimes, the precious liquid ran a little more freely and for longer, but this was the exception. He had to share the accommodation with red cockroaches, mosquitoes, lizards, and two or three bats, who remained obstinately attached to the corridor ceiling during the day and flew off silently at nightfall.

The laughing villagers. Salim organizes himself.

Some five hundred meters from the bungalow was a small village inhabited by very poor people. When they learned that the new occupants of the accommodation were foreigners, they timidly came to ask Salim if it would be possible for them to come for some water every morning after he had taken his own supply. As they were considered outcastes by other Indians, they knew in advance that they would have met with refusal from someone of their own religion. Of course, Salim saw no inconvenience in sharing water with them. Therefore, every morning, he was able to witness a long procession of women carrying large pitchers which they patiently filled. They were constantly laughing and joking while waiting their turn. Salim was greatly struck by the fact that he had never met in Europe people more cheerful than they were, and this, despite their extreme poverty. In trying to understand the reason for their joy, he came to the conclusion that, unlike Westerners who always live in their own heads, these penniless women were still in touch with their feelings and lived very much in the present.

As for the quality of the water, which often came out muddy from the tap, it inspired so little confidence in Salim that he boiled it for a long time and carefully filtered it before drinking it. In a country like India, it was necessary to disinfect the water and protect oneself from mosquitoes, flies, scorpions, the innumerable red cockroaches that ran around everywhere, mice, and even rats, which managed to get into the bedrooms.

Gradually, he learned to organize himself. He even found a place nearby to buy fresh milk. As Deccan College was located outside Poona, he had to take a rickshaw to go into town where he had to haggle at length for every purchase, no matter how small.

Indeed, when traders saw they were dealing with a foreigner, they tripled or quadrupled prices, which turned any small transaction into an exhausting debate.

Within the grounds of Deccan College lived, with his family, an employee who was responsible for handling supplies and who traveled about on a bicycle lent to him by the

1969 - Salim in front
of his bungalow.

Institute. Salim thought he might agree, for reasonable remuneration, to do his shopping for him. The man was only too happy to accept and, for his part, Salim could only be delighted with this arrangement, as his emissary proved to be very honest.

The death of his father.

Shortly after his arrival in Poona, Salim learned of his father's death. He had been suffering from a serious lung condition. During his visits to London, Salim had seen him coughing all day long, unable to catch his breath. Yet, despite the fact he was continually spitting blood, he did not want to go to hospital for treatment; he was afraid of hospitals.

It was still early one Sunday morning, when Salim received a phone call from his brother. He knew immediately that it was to announce the death of his father. He was greatly affected by this news when he learned later, in a detailed letter, how he had died.

He had been taken to hospital. When Salim's mother and brother went to visit him, he suddenly stopped breathing, putting an end to his suffering. But Salim was saddened to learn from his brother that the hospital team immediately took action to revive him.

A few minutes later, he stopped breathing again, but the doctors, who had no mystical knowledge in a field as serious as that of life and death, strove again to revive this crippled old man of eighty-nine, forcing him once more to return and occupy his ravaged body. Finally, it was only on the third occasion that the poor man obtained the right to leave the prison of his corporeal envelope, which had become useless to him.

Salim knew, through his repeated mystical experiences, that to hold back a human being in this way, by not allowing him to leave his body when the time had come for him to be released from his suffering, could only be compared to what would happen if one prevented a child from being born when his moment of delivery arrives.

The funeral took place just ten or twelve hours after his father's death. Salim knew that such a short delay causes much suffering to the deceased, as he remains connected to his body for around three or four days. The deceased is not afflicted in the same way if he is cremated instead of buried, which may explain the burial customs of India.

Following this phone call, thoughts of his father stayed with Salim all day. When evening came, he lit a candle with his mind intensely occupied in thinking of him. He found himself, all at once, plunged into a strange state during which, suddenly, his father appeared to him. He was smaller than his actual size but seemed surprisingly strong and healthy. Overwhelmed with grief, Salim drew him to his breast to tell him how much he loved him. His father replied, with a kind of impatience, that he too loved him very much, then, abruptly, he disappeared. Finding himself suddenly alone, Salim came out of this curious trance. He realized in a flash that his father had come to tell him that his grief disturbed him, that he had to let him go and not hold onto him through his thoughts—all the more so, given that, with all the spiritual work he had undertaken, his ability to concentrate had significantly strengthened.

Subsequently, whenever the image of his father came into his head, immediately, he visualized him happy, smiling, and bathed in divine light. He never allowed himself to let his thoughts stray to the deterioration of his father's body, which rested beneath the earth.

Improvement in Salim's health.

Throughout his time in India, Salim prepared his meals himself, returning to the cuisine of his childhood, based on rice, vegetables, and fruit. Although his health still remained very fragile, it nevertheless improved quite quickly. He attributed this fact to the atmosphere of India, which was doing him good, as well as to the freedom he enjoyed to be able to devote himself to his spiritual practices. He could begin to have some confidence in going out more freely. He noticed, however, that his intestinal crises would recur every time he was invited to eat with friends.

Salim, who was always very much a morning person, loved to watch the sunrise while carrying out his spiritual exercises walking outdoors. Sunset was another time that particularly fascinated him, as, in the tropics, night falls quickly and creates an enchanting atmosphere.

He began to meditate a great deal and made the most of those times in the day when he was not attending to his daily chores to undertake all sorts of concentration exercises—of his own invention—while taking long walks on the plain which stretched behind the college grounds. He felt himself borne up in his efforts by the spiritual climate that is quite specific to India. At various times of the day and night, bhajans rising from the temples could be heard in the distance. Even in the big cities, small decorated altars served as ubiquitous reminders of the preeminence of the spiritual.

India's hundreds of millions of inhabitants are deeply religious and communicate to the entire country a particular vibration which, in turn, arouses in many of them an aspiration towards the ultimate quest. Without counting the wandering monks, hermits, and ascetics of all kinds who gather in their millions during Kumbha Mela, the huge religious event that takes place every three years.

Imaginary India.

How could Westerners, coming from a world where the principal preoccupations are money and material goods, not be dazzled by this universe where other values still reign? Indians are principally attracted to the spiritual, while in the West, it is sport that draws the crowds. However, not all yogis are necessarily exceptional beings. Paul Brunton, a disciple of Ramana Maharshi, who lived in India for several years, mentioned in his book "A Search in Secret India" that his work summarized the result of his travels—"summarized", because, he said:

"The exigencies of space and time required me to write of one yogi where I had met more. Therefore I have selected a few who interested me most, and who seemed likely to interest the Western world. One heard much of certain so-called holy men who possessed repute of having acquired deep wisdom and strange powers; so one travelled through scorching days and sleepless nights to find them— only to find well-intentioned fools, scriptural slaves, venerable know-nothings, money-seeking conjurers, jugglers with a few tricks and pious fraud. To fill my pages with the record of such people would be worthless to the reader...

"I come now to the realization that India's holy men are an extremely mixed lot. Many are good inoffensive people for the most part, even though they seem anaemic from the angle of power or wisdom. Others are either failures in worldly life or just men looking for an easy living..."

Paul Brunton himself searched determinedly for someone truly worthy from a spiritual point of view, and he was about to give up, discouraged and sick, when he was guided to Ramana Maharshi. On the subject of Ramana Maharshi, he wrote:

"There remains a cultured remnant of holy men who condemn themselves to long years of undistracted search, to periods of painful self-denial and to ostracism from the conventional world of organized society because they have gone forth in search of truth."

Alexandra David-Neel, who also lived for several years in India and was familiar with Hinduism, had likewise noticed—as she recounts in her book "L'Inde où j'ai vécu" (The India where I lived), that, as one of her Indian friends had told her:

"There are in India over five million professional saints. The term may seem strange, but there is no better to define the people alluded to by my friend. A professional saint is a man whose sole profession, his livelihood, is to be either an ascetic, a contemplative mystic, a cynic philosopher, a perpetual pilgrim, or to give the appearance of being such... My friend added: 'ninety percent of these "saints" are real rogues, imposters or slackers who have chosen this kind of "profession" in order to be fed without working. To these must be added the individuals in love with vagabonding, for whom dressing like an ascetic permits them to wander about the country without it costing them anything, sleeping in temples and receiving alms from good people'."

Indeed, in India, when someone decides to devote himself to spiritual life, he immediately receives respect and support; in addition to this, he is no longer subject to the oppressive straitjacket of caste. It is inevitable that some will seek in this an escape from difficult situations without having a real desire for inner realization.

People thirsting for the spiritual come to this country ingenuously expecting to find, in any ashram, masters of wisdom or even "Jivan mukta"[*]. This was not the case for Salim; the call of India was not the fruit of appealing reading or of imagination, it was something very profound that drew him irresistibly to that country, which he nevertheless regarded with love and lucidity.

While he could easily be abused in external life—and he had been robbed and exploited by unscrupulous people more than once—with regard to his inner life and spiritual realizations, he always showed discrimination. In contrast, he saw many Westerners, both men and women, who knew how to cope in external life and who were not easily fooled, swallow any fable as long as it was uttered by an Indian with a sufficient gift for acting. In this vein, he had the opportunity of witnessing a conversation between a Westerner and a postal worker in Madras. The man behind the counter, attracted by the beauty of the woman, told her in a confidential tone: "I'm the pupil of a tantric master[**] and I also now practice tantric initiation. I work here in the Post Office, but that's because I do not want to reveal to everyone that I've become a tantric master". The woman, immediately intrigued,

---

[*] a Jivan mukta (from the Sanskrit words jiva and mukti) is someone who has attained, while living in a human body, the ultimate goal of Hinduism which is liberation from the cycles of re-birth.

[**] In Hinduism, the path called "Tantric" uses sexual energy to attain the Absolute. This is a path that Salim considered full of traps and particularly dangerous.

asked him about his master; but no, she could not meet him, he was dead; no, he couldn't tell her his name, it was secret; no, he could not reveal the place where he had been initiated, it was somewhere in the Himalayas. What was tragicomical was that the woman believed him!

In Poona, among other picturesque figures, Salim met a young Swami of about twenty years of age (a Swami is a man dressed in the ocher robes of the monks) who had developed quite an effective little act, as he was already surrounded by credulous Indians full of veneration. He demonstrated his high level of spiritual realization in a rather surprising fashion. While he was walking tranquilly with his "disciples", he would suddenly stand still for one or two minutes, transfixed, staring. The first time it happened in his presence, Salim, surprised, asked the pupils what was happening to their Swami and was told with a gentle reproach: "Shhh, the samadhi* has seized him". After a few moments of immobility, the man suddenly resumed his walk as if nothing had happened, then, abruptly, a few steps further, the tetany took hold of him again. This also happened to him when he was eating, and everyone would wait to take his next mouthful until the master came out of his "samadhi"!

This young Swami was ambitious: this act, which worked so well with the Indians, must surely work even better with the Americans. His dream was therefore to go to the United States and he would come to see Salim occasionally to get a few "tips" on this mirific land. Although cunning, he was, despite everything, very naïve and thought that all Westerners (Salim who, in Europe, was taken for an Oriental, in Asia, was taken for a Westerner) knew America; he did not therefore understand why he could not get from Salim recommendations for success in this fabulous country of wealth and luxury. It should be noted that, during these visits, in the absence of his audience, he forgot or did not think it worthwhile to enter "samadhi"!

---

* Samadhi: state of beatitude for the one connected to the Divine.

Mr Dady.

When Salim moved into his bungalow at Deccan College, he brought with him the young dog he had taken in. It did not take him long to realize that his company was going to cause problems. Indeed, the occupants of the neighboring bungalows, who were mainly Indians, did not look kindly on this animal; when his protector was not at his side, children and adults alike often threw stones at him. As Salim continued to care for and feed him, the dog had become attached to him to the point where he would not stop whimpering whenever his adopted master went away. Salim saw with sadness that it would be impossible to consider traveling for his spiritual quest while he was responsible for this animal; he therefore decided to find him another master.

But, when he began to look for a new home for him, he had the unpleasant surprise of discovering that the majority of Indians did not like dogs at all. He recalled his poor canine friend mercilessly killed in Baghdad by a policeman, and he found in India the same indifference to the suffering of animals. Since his arrival in this country, he had been continually struck by the manner in which buffalo and cows were treated, constantly being beaten while they dragged heavy carts loaded with enormous burdens. They were all frightfully thin, receiving practically nothing to eat, despite the services they rendered their owners— who had no hesitation in abandoning them without compassion, if they became blind or too old to be useful.

While Salim continued to look around for a kind soul who might give a home to his dog, someone told him about a rich Parsi named Dady who owned an office in town and who was renowned for his goodness. Maybe he could, through this person, find a family who would agree to take his animal, who, moreover, thanks to the care that Salim had lavished on him, had become superb to look at.

Salim made haste to meet this man. The latter was so surprised to receive a visit from someone who cared about the future of a dog that he immediately established with his visitor deep bonds of friendship that lasted until his departure from this world. He found someone fairly quickly to accommodate Salim's pet and Salim was surprised by the sorrow he felt at separating from this animal to which he had become, without realizing it, strongly attached.

He had occasion to appeal to the kindness of Mr Dady again when, one day, as he was walking in the city, he saw a blind horse wandering miserably in search of food and bumping into vehicles on the road. The drivers did not even try to avoid it, grazing and tearing the skin of this unfortunate beast in passing with an astonishing insensitivity to its suffering. The kind Parsi, whom he telephoned to describe the tragic plight of the animal, arrived within a short time to end its ordeal with an injection.

Mr Dady was a man of around forty-five years old, tall and thin, very interested in questions of a spiritual nature. He was unmarried and lived, with some members of his family and many servants, outside of the city, in a sumptuous white villa guarded by six or seven huge dogs which barked ferociously at anyone approaching the house.

He devoted all his time to relieving the suffering of the most wretched of all human beings: lepers. He had converted a large estate that he owned into a center where they were treated by two or three doctors who lived there permanently. The infrastructure even included a plastic surgery department to repair, as much as possible, the horrific ravages that the disease had inflicted on the faces and bodies of these unfortunates. Mr Dady showed Salim photos of some patients before they underwent surgery; the sores on their horribly disfigured faces laying bare the bones. One could not but be moved and understand his pride in seeing the result of grafts, which, although imperfect, had, all the same, restored to these poor beings a more acceptable appearance and existence.

This benefactor would, from time to time, scour the streets of Poona in search of other lepers. As he often had difficulty convincing those he encountered to come for treatment at his home (as these poor wretches were afraid that they might be treated in a radical, permanent way and fled at full speed—if they could still walk), he would ensure he was accompanied by one or two residents of the colony to reassure them.

Sometimes, Mr Dady would come to find Salim by car to invite him to have tea with him and discuss his activities and his interests in the spiritual realm. He showed a particular interest in the books of Paul Brunton. One day, he invited Salim to visit the leper hospital. The community, which numbered three to four hundred lepers, was practically self-sufficient. The buildings were surrounded by fields belonging to the estate, which supplied wheat, vegetables, and fruits of all kinds, the surplus of which was sold, bringing in a little money for these poor people. They ran the colony themselves with efficiency, as some of them were highly educated. Salim marveled at their organization. They had their own herds of cows and goats for dairy products, as well as chickens whose eggs they sold; they even harvested honey, spun their own clothes, and made oil lamps, candles, and other basic necessities. They were no longer contagious, but they preferred to stay there as they had been rejected by their communities because of the disease's indelible consequences on their bodies. In addition, they needed to continue to be medically supervised and undergo treatment every six months.

Salim was welcomed with surprising warmth by these former sufferers who surrounded him, expressing their joy, laughing merrily, and talking incessantly to him in their own language, which he did not understand. When they began to sing bhajans, he noticed with amazement that some of them possessed voices of extraordinary beauty. They were quite obviously as happy as possible and well protected in that place.

What would have been their fate without the kindness and extraordinary generosity of Mr Dady? Salim subsequently had the opportunity to see in Benares, and especially Calcutta, lepers dragging along the pavements what remained of their poor bodies, deformed to an unimaginable point, without anyone caring what became of them.

He was so touched by his visit to this center that, a few years later, when he was obliged to leave Madras and return to France, he envisaged returning to live in Poona and help Mr Dady care for the lepers. But destiny was to decide otherwise.

Gurus and castes.

Over the following years, Salim traveled in various parts of India, visiting a number of ashrams and meeting several gurus. He did not find the master he was seeking. The teachings he encountered did not apparently ever envisage the transformation of undesirable tendencies. As he himself had already understood it is precisely the inclinations and conditioning of the human being that block the road to his Celestial Being; he remained always dissatisfied with what he saw.

Although the gurus he met knew very well how to talk about spirituality and although some of them were very sincere and, moreover, had some powers* (which inspire such fascination), Salim could not content himself, as did their disciples, with worshipping them, receiving their blessing and taking refuge in the tranquility of their ashrams. How many times had he found himself facing a man considered a spiritual master, who, while looking him straight in the eye, with the intense gaze of the Indians, exclaimed emphatically:

"I was waiting for you! Where have you been?" Salim immediately thought, "Well, well, once again someone waiting for me! Really, I should cut myself up into little pieces to satisfy all these demands!"

And he said to himself: "A true master would never welcome someone like that, so as not inflate his ego. The very act of declaiming this same sentence, with the same intonations, is enough for me to know where I stand on the subject of these pseudo-masters. It is so easy to trick credulous Westerners with these kinds of flattering declarations."

In addition, Salim could not help noticing that certain gurus were still prisoners of the blind beliefs in which they had been raised.

---

*By powers is meant supranormal faculties, whether developed through various yogas (such as being able to stay without breathing in a state of trance for days or even months), or manifesting themselves spontaneously as the result of previous lives (such as materializing objects, etc.). Of course, this refers to real powers, duly verified, not the deceptions that exist in abundance in India.

Thus, he happened to see a guru, or the devotees around him, taking care not to let a Westerner—regarded by orthodox Brahmins as an untouchable— look at their food, for fear it would become "defiled".

This "defilement" to be avoided is the basis of orthodox Hindu practices. It is enough for a person considered by them as being from an "inferior" caste to look at their meals in passing or even accidently let his shadow brush against the food meant for them to render these foods "unclean" in their eyes.

Should not someone supposed to have attained a high degree of spiritual elevation, Salim thought, wonder what is the nature of this "purity" which is so fragile that a shadow or simple glance may jeopardize it?

It should also be said that this exclusively external issue of purity is not peculiar to Hinduism and is also found in other religions. It was in response to these kinds of practices that Christ declared:

"What goes into a man's mouth does not make him 'unclean', but what comes out of his mouth, that is what makes him 'unclean'."
(Mat. 15,11).

Some cultivated Indians strove to convince their countrymen that in ancient India, the four castes—which consist of Brahmans or Brahmins (priests), Kshatriyas (warriors), Vaishyas (merchants) and Shudras (peasants)—corresponded to occupations and skills and were not determined by birth. As for the outcastes, they were from indigenous tribes, living apart from Hindu society and who, coming into contact with it, found means of subsistence by taking responsibility for humble or unpleasant tasks that were willingly given over to them. However, the antiquity to which they refer goes back so far that only scholars have knowledge of it. It even happens sometimes that Westerners, enamored of Hinduism, seek to defend the current caste system using, as a support for their arguments, the antiquity of this tradition, which from all points of view, is unjustifiable.

It has already been 2500 years, since the Buddha rose against this arbitrary division based on birth and not on merit:

"Not by matted locks, nor by lineage, nor by caste is one a Brahmin; he is the Brahmin in whom are truth and righteousness and purity." (Dhammapada, 393).

And again, to the Brahmins, who reproached him for accepting a Chandala (low caste) as a disciple:

"There is a marked difference between ash and gold, but nothing similar separates a Brahmin from a Chandala. A Brahmin is not born like the sacrificial fire, he does not miraculously descend from heaven, he does not arrive carried by the wind, he does not rise up from the half-open earth. The Brahmin leaves the womb of a woman just as the Chandala does. All human beings possess the same organs; there is no difference between them. How can one consider them as being possessed of a different essence from each other? Nature recognizes no such distinction".

Karma. Doctrine and abuse.

The doctrine of karma pervades all Hindu philosophy. It is an impersonal law of causality, taken up by the Buddha, and which has nothing to do with any moral retribution.

Throughout the world, human beings have always sought to know the reason for the injustice and suffering they undergo and that they see around them. The West has responded to this troubling question by attributing them to the will of God, a will that is incomprehensible to human beings, but which they must accept. Mystical India, meanwhile, recognized the law of the chain of cause and effect, an indefinite chain, too impersonal to be able to satisfy the popular thirst for justice; thus, the original doctrine was distorted into a notion of fault and merit. It is precisely this idea which, at present, is circulated in the West, with its dangerous corollary of condemnation and severity with respect to others.

While it is true, as Salim explained in his books, that every human being is and can only be the result of what he has made of himself in a recent or distant past (that is to say the way in which he behaved and what his principal interests in life were) and that he sometimes finds himself placed in situations that seem to him to be unduly harsh, but which, without him realizing it, he has drawn to himself by the manner in which he vibrates within himself; this does not mean, however, that everything that happens to him by way of tragedies or difficulties is the consequence of wrongful actions committed in the past. It should, indeed, not be forgotten that every human being undergoes, from childhood (when he is still very vulnerable), the conditioning of his environment and his era as well as the destiny of the country he is born in—a sometimes terrible destiny, as seen in Rwanda, Bosnia, Cambodia, Tibet, or during the Second World War—and this, without any "karmic fault" to be expiated.

There are certainly causes for all these tragedies and these causes have produced effects (which is the strict definition of the law of karma proclaimed by the Buddha, namely: "There is no effect without a cause"), but the cause is not necessarily attributable to the person who is subject to the effect. It is this constant confusion between the cause of suffering and the responsibility of the person who is subjected to it, which results in the word "karma" being thrown, without thinking, in the face of the unfortunate, in a way that can only be described as intolerable—as is the case with the untouchables in India.

Throughout all the years he lived there, Salim could not fail to feel an infinite compassion towards these poor people who were constantly treated with contempt, because the popular Hindu belief attributes the fact of being born untouchable to faults committed in other existences.

One day, while he was walking in the street, he saw a Brahmin who needed to have his damaged sandals repaired. As handling leather— the skin of a dead animal—would have meant defiling himself, the Brahmin addressed himself to an untouchable. He remained at a certain distance from him, so as not to be defiled, and threw his shoes at him, which the cobbler humbly picked up and hastened to repair. Once the work was done, it would have been disrespectful for him to throw the shoes back at their owner, so, he placed them on the ground, then distanced himself sufficiently for the Brahmin to be able to reclaim them; the Brahmin left on the ground a derisory sum, which was, according to him, all that this man deserved—given his bad karma, because of his birth as an outcaste!

Salim said to himself: Does that Brahmin ever wonder what might be the feeling of this unfortunate man, always treated with such contempt? Does he imagine for a moment that terrible mental prison in which this pariah is shut away, a mental prison which is worse than a physical prison, from which it is sometimes possible to escape?

Indira Devi told Salim: "Indians are so cruel!" But if one is brought up in the belief that everything painful that happens to us is "our fault", that all the ordeals that others are subjected to are "their fault", one might logically become completely insensitive to the suffering of others.

The notion of karma is currently very popular in the West. One uses it readily, just as in India, to explain the inexplicable. Salim, invited one day to the home of a very devout Christian, mentioned that terrible tragedy, the horror of which surpasses our capacity of imagination, the methodical extermination of six million Jews and of hundreds of thousands of Romany gypsies (men, women, and children) during the Second World War, genocide planned with cruelty cold enough to turn one's blood to ice; his conversation partner, surrounded by her family and her guests, declared, with a kind of contempt and an indifference that left him speechless: 'It was their karma!'

One throws the term 'karma' around in this manner, without understanding what it really means, and, in this way, one rids oneself of all collective responsibility by letting it be understood that it is the victims who are to blame. What irony!

From this absurd perspective, should it be inferred that Christ was crucified because of wrongful deeds that He may have committed in a previous life? In other words, because He was subject to "bad karma"? Salim could not help wondering how it was possible to be so devout and yet to show such insensitivity in the face of others' suffering?

When someone has continually heard it repeated, from his earliest infancy, that he is an inferior being, that he is to blame for his misfortune, he comes to believe in this negative image of himself and this leaves a deep mark on his psyche, from which it becomes impossible to liberate himself. This is why, even though many untouchables have embraced Buddhism which gives them back their human dignity, the majority, heavily influenced by a belief in retributive karma, remain shackled to their fate, with bitterness and a crippling sense of guilt, which keeps them locked inside a mental prison with no way out, unless those who throw the word "karma" in their faces realize the harm they are doing and desist from using this term whose real meaning escapes them.

In the Samyutta Nikaya, the Buddha clearly protests against this popular belief in "punitive" karma.

Is suffering brought about by myself alone, good Buddha?" asked Kassapa.

"No, Kassapa."

"Then by another?"

"No, Kassapa."

"Then both together, myself and another?"

"No, Kassapa."

"Then is it brought about by chance?"

"No, Kassapa."

"Then is there no suffering?"

"No, Kassapa, it is not that there is no suffering. For there is suffering."

"Well then, perhaps you neither know nor see it, Buddha."

"It is not that I don't know suffering or don't see it. I know it well and see it."

"But to all my questions, good Buddha, you have answered no—and yet you say you know suffering and see it. Please teach me about it."

"Kassapa, there are two wrong views. One says that oneself is the

entire author of a deed and all consequent suffering one brings
upon oneself and this is so from the beginning of time.

The other says that it is deeds by other people that bring about
one's own suffering.

"You should avoid both these views, Kassapa. Here we teach another
way. All deeds, whether your own or another's, are conditioned by
ignorance and that is the origin of this whole mass of suffering. By
ending that ignorance in yourself, and by way of yourself in others,
wisdom comes into being and the suffering ceases."

Despite the texts and teachings of the Buddha, many Buddhists,
throughout Asia, also use this word karma with the same punitive
connotation. Thus, in the various Buddhist traditions, women are given
to understand by the monks that they were born women because of
"bad karma" which they brought upon themselves in previous lives
and that, consequently, they cannot aspire to as high a level of spiritual
accomplishment as a man; on the other hand, they add, if the women
accumulate merit during their present lives, they "will create good
karma for themselves", which will perhaps allow them to be reborn as
men in a future existence. In this way, women are conditioned to
doubt their spiritual potential and this represents a major obstacle to
their commitment to the Path. Consequently, unlike Christianity
with its strong feminine monastic tradition and its great female mystics
who are acknowledged and venerated, there are far fewer Buddhist
nuns and they are less respected than the monks.

As they do not benefit from the same conditions for their spiritual
practices nor the same support from the laity, it is not surprising that
women's spiritual accomplishments are rarer in Asia and, very often,
not recognized and not broadcast, which reinforces in the women
themselves, as well as in the monks who maintain this discourse, a
belief in their lesser capacity to attain the ultimate accomplishment.
Thus, belief creates the obstacle which justifies the belief…

Salim later emphasized to his pupils that this constant misuse of
the term "karma" to justify all the tragedies and all the evils that weigh

down this world allows very easily avoidance of one's duty to help one's fellow beings.

Acknowledging that the suffering to which one is subject in life—and which cannot, in any way, be avoided—is often innocent and is the incontrovertible consequence of manifestation in the tangible, with all that this entails in terms of dangers, tragedies, catastrophes, etc, should one not, Salim would say, be aware of the necessity to cultivate compassion towards all those beings caught in the net of samsara? Furthermore, he would add, if an aspirant wishes to attain his spiritual goal, he will need to achieve a state of being whereby compassion emanates from him as naturally as light emanates from the Sun.

Muktananda.

Fortunately, not all gurus are prisoners to caste prejudice. Those who have really attained a high level of spiritual accomplishment—such as Ramana Maharshi or Swami Ramdas[*]—no longer adhere to such external distinctions.

When he had the opportunity to visit Muktananda at his Ganeshpuri center, not far from Bombay, Salim was able to see that he also did not care about the "taint" of caste, but rather concerned himself with the conduct of those who were living in his ashram.

Salim went to spend two or three days there. On his arrival, he found himself warmly welcomed by the mother[**] of the ashram who spoke English. Some sacred texts intoned by Muktananda himself had been recorded and were broadcast throughout the day by loudspeakers, so as, he said, to create a devotional atmosphere in the interior of the ashram. He knew that the vibratory power of sounds is extremely important and may constitute an aid or an impediment to spiritual

---

[*] A Bhakti yogi who left his teachings ("In quest of God, in the vision of God"), in which he protests against the caste system, to his disciples.

[**] The mother of the ashram is the female disciple who assists the master, generally taking responsibility for material tasks and often acting as an intermediary between the master and the external world.

Muktananda

practice. It is precisely for this reason that it is such a tragedy that, in the West, one is constantly bombarded with music that is not spiritually favorable. Even without switching on the radio or the television, this music is in the air, subtly influencing beings who, without knowing it, are like antennae, at every moment receiving and emitting all sorts of vibrations so few of which turn out to be beneficial to inner quest.

Muktananda was shouldering a heavy burden; he had to constantly find funds, not just for the upkeep of the center, but also for the daily meal of around a thousand children from the surrounding villages whom he was supporting. He personally ensured that neither money nor food was wasted or misappropriated.

The permanent residents had to participate in the agricultural work on the vast neighboring tracts of land which belonged to the community and supplied fruits, vegetables, and cereals. Muktananda had to admonish some Westerners who had supposedly come on a spiritual quest and behaved as though they were on vacation, preferring to calmly laze around the ashram rather than to work up a sweat in the fields.

Salim found Muktananda rather sad and solitary. No-one asked him questions of a spiritual nature. Most of those who were there did not even know what they were looking for and were not prepared to make the slightest effort. One afternoon, Salim sat near him with the ashramites. He took the liberty of breaking the silence and asked Muktananda questions concerning the spiritual approach practiced in the ashram. As Muktananda did not speak English, he had to turn to the mother to translate. Muktananda immediately came to life and responded with a great deal of interest; his eyes, which had previously been melancholy and distant, began to shine as he expressed himself.

The conversation which ensued between them in the presence of the group, who listened with surprise, lasted for around two hours.

Muktananda was known for unleashing a particular force which ordinarily remains latent in human beings and can normally be awoken only after long practice leading to powerful spiritual experiences. This force, or Shakti (as it is called in India), which constitutes an aid to the aspirant, does not, for all that, spare him from having to later make the efforts of concentration indispensible to attaining illumination (which, moreover, is not synonymous with liberation). What is more, the range of action of this energy depends on the levels of being and of consciousness of the person in whom it has been awoken. A vast literature having been written on this subject, some harbor the illusion that it is enough for them to receive this initiation in order to be illuminated and liberated forever.

Muktananda saw straight away that this Shakti had already been awoken in Salim who was, himself, capable of awakening it in others. He commented on this to the mother of the ashram who immediately translated his words for Salim.

Muktananda then told him that there were some people in whom he had not succeeded in unleashing this force and he asked Salim to do it. As soon as he saw that Salim had succeeded, he wanted him to stay at the ashram. He took him aside and, through his interpreter, insisted at length, offering him a room as well as facilities to prepare his own meals, and even promised to grant him anything else he could wish for if he would agree to stay by him. However, this was not possible for Salim, he was not alone. Nevertheless, he retained from this visit the memory of a simple and sincere man.

He had the opportunity, at the end of 1974, to see Muktananda again while the latter was passing through London. Muktananda remembered Salim well and, still desiring his company, reiterated his invitation. However, he had just moved to the United States and Salim preferred to stay in France.

Satya Saï Baba.

Satya Saï Baba

Salim had the opportunity one day to go to Satya Saï Baba's tiny ashram in Poona while the latter was there on a visit. Salim found a man whose age was difficult to determine, of small stature, with an astonishing head of curly hair. A great crowd was hurrying to receive his "darshan", while, being fanned respectfully by a disciple, he was sitting on a sort of small raised armchair. He was simply venerated by his followers who sang him beautiful bhajans. After around two hours, the famous guru, known for his power of materialization, left for another part of India where other worshippers were awaiting him. It was not this kind of spiritual approach that Salim was looking for. Everything that he had seen until then had sometimes proved to be beautiful and moving, but insufficient for his needs.

A surprising holy man. Know that you are the Sublime!

In Poona Salim also had the opportunity to go to the ashram of a holy man whose behavior was disconcerting to say the least. He was present one morning when the holy man entered the room where his disciples were respectfully awaiting him. With his foot, he knocked one of them over, declaring emphatically: "Do you believe in God? Do you believe in God? I don't", then he knocked another off his balance and then a third, all the while repeating the same phrase. And, while everyone was watching him, dumbfounded, he began to jump and dance crying: "I got it, I got it, I got it!" Apparently, the same scene was repeated every morning. Some took him for a madman, but Salim understood that this solitary man wanted to show that blind belief in God is without worth and that only direct knowledge matters. Unfortunately for his disciples, this holy man offered no means of attaining such an experience!

After having visited several ashrams, Salim could not help but notice that, often, the person that his disciples took, without discernment, for an infallible guru had perhaps only had a minor spiritual experience which he had taken for a great realization; he believed himself to have already reached the end of the path, whereas he had only taken his first step in an immense Inner Universe. It is so easy in India to pass oneself off as a master, the Indians being always ready to venerate someone who speaks of spirituality.

The fact that these gurus are honored and supported materially prevents them, Salim said, from knowing the ordeals of life. They may delude themselves, thinking that they are liberated from the bonds of their ordinary self, which has not passed through the fire necessary to a true transformation and, with the slightest stimulation, a manifestation of self-esteem or vanity, which is not proper in a true master, may re-emerge.

Anagarika Munindra.

On the other hand, Salim had the opportunity, at this time, of meeting a Theravada Buddhist master, Anagarika Munindra, around 50 years old, who, although ill, was kind enough to receive him in the hospital where he was being cared for, some eighteen kilometers from Poona.

On that morning, very interested by the prospect of meeting this master, Salim arrived at Poona station well ahead of time. Despite the fact that it was called an express, his train was nevertheless extremely late. Shortly after its departure, the engine began to produce a deafening racket, undoubtedly to impress the passengers and to make them think that the train was advancing at a phenomenal speed; however, when Salim looked out of the window, he saw, to his surprise, a frail withered tree pass before his eyes at a snail's pace. This "express" completed the eighteen kilometer trip in the record time of nearly two hours—which means at a vertiginous average speed of nine kilometers an hour! In consequence of this, Salim arrived at the hospital much later than expected, around midday, at the time that the Buddhist master was eating the only meal that Theravadian monks take during the day.

According to his explanations, his teachings were based on strict meditation, undertaken with eyes half-closed, while concentrating intensely on a point located between the nose and the upper lip. He said to Salim that, in order to test the concentration of the monks in his monastery, he pricked their hands with a needle or even burned them with a stick lit for this purpose. They should be able to remain impervious to the pain and not to feel it until some time later, in other words when coming out of their meditation.

Although their meeting had been brief, Salim was impressed by the rigor of this Buddhist master. After having taken his leave of him, Salim left for the station, just in time, he thought, to catch the 2.30 pm train to Poona. The "express" was finally announced at ten o'clock in the evening, after an interminable wait on the platform, in the stifling heat of the afternoon, having to bear the thirst and the bites of hundreds of mosquitoes who treated themselves to a banquet as soon as night fell at around six pm.

A liberating understanding.

At the same time as consecrating himself to his spiritual practices, Salim had to confront an obstacle that many seekers have to face sooner or later: that of one's sexual needs. He realized that, until he had understood and resolved this issue, which sometimes robbed him of too much of his attention, he would not be able to consecrate himself wholly, as he wished to do, to his quest and to meditation. He had always felt certain that it was not in continually and blindly giving in to this physical need that a man might one day attain the mental tranquility and inner liberty necessary to remain open to a higher calling. He was convinced, deep down, that it was unrealistic to hope to put out a burning log by continually throwing oil on it and that, on the contrary, by behaving in this way, it was the man himself who would end up being consumed by this desire for a satiety impossible to attain.

While working on himself, during the course of the long walks that he took every day in the area around his bungalow, one morning he saw a bird's nest in which the female was busy sitting on her eggs. He felt with compassion the severe constraint to which she was subjected in remaining thus immobile day and night, without being able to leave the nest and depending on her partner for food. He could not help thinking of her fate if ever her partner were to accidentally die. Then, passing by the same spot a few days later, he saw that the brood had hatched and the parents were busying themselves with filling the insatiable beaks of their little ones.

On another occasion, the unusual commotion of a flight of crows unexpectedly caught his attention. He immediately left his bungalow to discover some thirty of these birds flying in frenetic circles above one of their chicks which must have fallen from the nest and was crying on the ground. Salim was surprised by the solidarity of these crows who were ready to sacrifice themselves to protect the tiny injured creature— which, incidentally, succumbed to its injuries shortly afterwards—from any predators.

Salim could only remark with astonishment what a considerable sum of attention and energy was to be found thus constantly mobilized to protect the young and the continuation of the species. And it was in reflecting on the behavior of these birds and the manner in which they found themselves bound to their progeny that he suddenly understood that, if Great Nature had to count only on the good will of the various creatures peopling this planet in order to assure the perpetuation of species, they would never agree to make the enormous efforts and the continual sacrifices that such an achievement demands of them.

He realized with a sentiment of reverential awe that Great Nature, who has no other concern than the continuation of species, had been forced to find a ruse to oblige all creatures to submit to her will. She had, therefore, implanted in them an irresistible and insatiable urge for sexual pleasure, whatever the consequences of that might be. He then understood, with great lucidity, that, when he felt a sexual need, it was, in fact, Nature herself who was pushing him to want to satisfy it. This understanding had a determining effect in helping him to control this demanding aspect of his nature and to no longer be a slave to its blind demands.

Later, Salim asked of his pupils how many men would feel what they called "love" for the woman they desired if she had lost her sexual attractions, if she was ill, emaciated, aged, toothless? He emphasized that man, because it is principally man who is programmed to feel physical attraction, should always remember that woman is a human being like him, fragile, vulnerable, and destined to age and to die.

The anger of Indira Devi.

From time to time Salim went to visit Mataji Indira Devi; he liked the atmosphere that emanated from the ashram very much. As Indira Devi was asthmatic and very much affected by this, she stayed in the ashram practically all the time, without going anywhere. Sitting tranquilly in her chair, she would always welcome him with the kind smile that was characteristic of her, saying of him: "He is so kind, he feels things much too deeply." At other times, she would add: "He is so dependent, he will suffer terribly in life."

The holy woman gave him the name of Amal, which means "pure". When Salim tried to explain to her that, in French, this name sounded like "one who is hurt" and that he would prefer another, she nevertheless insisted on calling him this. When she discovered that he did not know The Bhagavad Gita, she offered him a copy in English, translated by Shri Aurobindo whom she had known personally.

Salim discovered this text with the greatest of interest. He found it extremely inspiring and he even went as far as to say that, of all the great spiritual texts, this was the one that contained the highest spiritual truths.

Often, while he was sitting at her feet in the company of other visitors, Indira Devi would give him a knowing look, then, turning towards the others, she would declare: "He remembers..." He, disconcerted, would ask himself: "But what am I supposed to remember? I don't understand; what is she talking about?" At other times, still throwing him those looks, full of mischief, with which he was becoming familiar, she would mention a particular kind of Indian deer which exudes a sweet odor and exhausts itself by continually chasing after the source of this smell, without understanding that it comes from itself. And Salim, more and more troubled, would wonder: "Why is she saying that? She said it before, the last time that I came, as well as the time before, and the time before that too. Why is she always repeating the same story?" He would go home unsettled to the point of not wanting to go back and see her again. However, the devotional atmosphere and the beauty of the temple had such a strong attraction for him that he could not help but go there again.

Since his arrival in England before the war, Salim had always remained very aware of the gaps in his formal education and of his difficulties in expressing himself. He had often had to endure the contempt of his music publishers, as well as of people around him. On one of his visits to Indira Devi, the person accompanying him, who was in a very bad mood that day, mocked him, in a very contemptuous manner, in front of others, for his lack of formal education.

To the surprise of everyone around him, the holy woman entered, in a state of such anger towards the person who had just uttered this disagreeable remark that the walls of the ashram trembled, and she vehemently declared: "My child, my child, if you cross the whole of India, you will not find anyone who knows what this man knows." And Salim who had been left stupefied by the strength of Indira Devi's reaction, said to himself: "But what do I know? I don't know anything, the very reason I came to India was to seek this knowledge!" After this incident, which seemed incomprehensible to him, he decided to stop, temporarily at least, his visits to the ashram.

The eagle's flight – initial efforts.

Not long after his last visit to Indira Devi, as he was coming out of his bungalow one day to walk and to practice his daily concentration exercises, Salim saw on the ground, not far from him, an enormous eagle holding something in its talons. With his beak the eagle tore off a morsel of the prey that he was perching on, then he lifted his head and, with extraordinary dignity and at an impressively leisurely pace, he looked right and left before dropping his head back to his prey.

Salim stayed still, fascinated by the formidable size of the bird of prey, and he wondered, in amazement, how a bird so large and heavy would be able to take off. He waited curiously, not daring to make a noise, when, suddenly, he saw the eagle pushing hard against the earth with his feet while unfurling his enormous wings which he beat so strongly that, very quickly, he rose into the air. He had climbed just a few meters when he slowed his wing beats considerably until, finally, he was able to hold himself completely immobile, his wings wide open, gliding and still climbing ever higher into the incandescent skies of India.

An astounding silence suddenly pervaded Salim who stood transfixed and filled with wonder. He had just realized something vital to his spiritual practices. This remarkable bird had, effectively, just taught him that it is the quality and the intensity of one's initial efforts that prove decisive in allowing a seeker to detach from himself in order to be able to ascend to higher and higher states in the sky of his being. He needs to learn the delicate art of knowing when and how to relinquish his effort in order to be able to, so to speak, "glide" like an eagle.

While he was still contemplating the bird, who was now no more than a distant dot, in a fraction of a second, all the important events of his life, all the spiritual experiences he had known until that moment, and all the enigmatic words spoken by Indira Devi came to him at once in a strange and fantastic panoramic vision. Suddenly, he grasped, in a moment of fleeting intuition, all that she had wanted to make him understand when she said: "he remembers..." or when she spoke of the deer who chased after a scent without knowing that it came from itself, as well as other allusions that, at the time, had left him confused and puzzled.

He realized suddenly, and not without apprehension, that what Indira Devi had tried to tell him was that he should not lose any more time looking for someone to guide him, but that he should continue alone, following the direction he had already taken, without waiting for outside help.

It was certainly not easy for him to accept that he had only himself to count on to find his path through those inner territories that do not belong to the visible world and which prove so enigmatic. Nevertheless, Salim felt that he had no other choice but to proceed alone, however difficult that might be for him.

After he had taken this decision, when he returned to see Indira Devi, she welcomed him with a look full of mischief and kindness and even began laughing silently, as though to let him know that she knew all that had happened to him. Afterwards, she never again made any allusion in his presence to the fact that he "remembered" nor did she speak again of the deer chasing after a scent that came from itself.

He therefore pursued the meditation practices and concentration exercises that he was continually finding for himself—as though he remembered them from some unfathomable past—without speaking to anyone about the strange experience that he had had or the ensuing decision.

More than anything else.

Following the understanding that he had gained concerning the kind of efforts that would henceforth be required of him, Salim learned, through a very specific relinquishment of himself, to allow himself to be seized, during his meditation, by the most subtle transparency of being and of consciousness which arose gently within him, to the point of being metamorphosed into this ethereal state. This immaculate state made its presence felt in his active life as well so that he constantly carried out the necessary inner steps to reanimate it whenever it began to weaken in him.

He understood yet more deeply that it was to the extent that he succeeded in being intensely present to himself, in terms of duration and depth, that his ordinary individuality could begin to, so to speak, dissolve by itself, thus leaving space within him so that the Impersonal Aspect of his double nature could replace it and bring him the tranquillity of soul and the beatitude that he aspired to. The more he managed to remain internally present to himself, the more this sanctified state remained within him—provided that he wanted it more than anything else.

Every moment counted for him, he worked on himself while walking alone out of doors, while doing his shopping, while talking to someone, as well as while cooking. The spiritual practices that he undertook during the following months proved decisive for him; he was transported by a devotional fervor, accompanied by a subtle bliss. Afterwards, he never again considered the world or existential life in the same way as in the past.

The month of May in Mahabaleshwar. The precarity of life in India.

As the month of May approached, the Indian heat became scorching. Animals, plants, and human beings were plunged into a state of apathy and constant fatigue, all waiting for the first monsoon rains to come and relieve them from the intensity of the heat.

Mr Dady told Salim that the monsoon generally arrived in Poona regularly on about June 4 or 5, but that, before it broke, the heat of May was hard to bear. He offered to drive him to the mountains to a place called Mahabaleshwar, some sixty-five kilometers from Poona, to spend this difficult month there. He had already spoken of the exceptional beauty of this place where he owned a farm. Salim was happy to accept; his friend found him a bungalow to rent there, not far from his farm, where Salim could buy milk and other foodstuffs during his stay.

Before Mr Dady went back to Poona, where his good works required his presence, he took Salim to the summit of a mountain where stood a very ancient temple, nearly two thousand years old, which, although it had been uninhabited for a very long time and invaded by vegetation, remained, nevertheless, in very good condition. The building was made up of huge blocks of stone, meticulously fitted together, with no mortar. Salim, admiring the extraordinary panorama that could be seen from that spot, thought longingly that the place seemed to him particularly favorable to spending his life there in meditation. But how could the water and food necessary to survival be procured in this isolated place? He wondered how the yogis of times past had managed to solve this problem.

To the left of the dwelling occupied by Salim, a poor shack sheltered an Indian family whose work consisted of maintaining the neighboring house, a fine residence belonging to a well-off Indian who spent his vacations there. One afternoon when Salim had gone out as usual to undertake concentration exercises while walking outdoors, he saw the wife surrounded by her children, standing still in front of their hut. When he greeted her with the traditional "Namaste", she did not respond, but remained as though transfixed, with an anxious look that left Salim perplexed. Suddenly, her husband came out of their home, carrying before him a large stick on the end of which was suspended an enormous snake which he had just killed. The reptile had slithered inside via the thatched roof. Salim, who had sensed their anxiety, felt a great deal of compassion for these people when he thought of the precarity in which they lived.

As Mr Dady had left some time before, arrangements had been made for a local taxi to take Salim back to Poona at the end of his stay. Two or three days before his departure, he was suddenly seized by a strange intuition. He went to the taxi rank to remind the driver, whose name he knew, of their appointment. He learned that this man had died of a heart attack some days previously. He thought sadly of the family of the poor man and wondered how they would be able to manage in a country where there was no state aid. He booked another car which took him back to Poona on the scheduled day to rediscover the extreme heat preceding the monsoon's arrival.

The monsoon.

When he first moved into Deccan College, Salim had remarked, not far from the bungalow, that there were some withered shrubs whose thick branches resembled whitened bones and were apparently lifeless. He said to himself that these plants were certainly dead and that they were only good for burning. However, in early June, as soon as the first drops of the monsoon began to fall, a miracle occurred. He couldn't believe his eyes when, after four or five days of rain, the white stalks seemed to have greened slightly. Regarding them at length with disbelief, he thought that perhaps he was imagining this change; indeed, it seemed impossible that this vegetation, which had been so long without water, could come back to life. Nevertheless, after a few days of further showers, he had to accept the evidence: tiny buds were appearing on the branches which had become entirely green!

Barely two weeks later, these shrubs were covered in incredible exotic dark green foliage which was a delight to behold. The surrounding countryside had also been miraculously transformed; the dry hot earth, covered with stones and dust, had changed into a marvelous carpet of small herbs which had sprung from nowhere.

What a lesson! Filled with wonder, Salim contemplated nature's metamorphosis and thought that human beings were the same as this withered vegetation. They also need to be watered in order for life to be given to them—but watered spiritually, and, albeit, on the condition that, like this land and these shrubs, they are sufficiently receptive. It is necessary, he said to himself, for this kind of spiritual water to fall on fertile earth in order that a special kind of growth might transform a person's being.

Bahout pani he!

Not long after the start of the monsoon, the cow belonging to the old man from whom Salim got his supplies and who lived close to Salim's bungalow stopped giving milk. He found, at some distance from his residence, a young man able to supply him. Salim made arrangements with the young man who agreed to bring him fresh milk every day. Everything went well for the first few days, but, as time passed, Salim began to find the milk paler and paler, thin and tasteless. So, one morning, when his milkman arrived, Salim spoke to him severely in Hindi: "Pani hé!" ("There is water!"). The man gave him an innocent look and responded in a mixture of English and Hindi: "No, no pani hé." ("No, there is no water."). Then, seized by sudden inspiration, Salim quickly went to find a simple medical thermometer which he had brought with him from Paris and which was much larger than those found in India. He plunged it into the liquid in front of the young man who, suddenly, appeared worried. After waiting few moments, Salim withdrew the instrument, pretended to examine it attentively and, showing it to his supplier, firmly declared (laughing to himself all the while): "Bahout pani he!" ("There is a lot of water!"). The young man began to look all around him, then, after a few final wild eye movements, not knowing where to look, he said sheepishly to Salim: "Tomorrow, no pani." Salim answered severely: "Sure?" Shaking his head from right to left in the Indian manner, the young man assured him: "Sure, sure."

Indeed, from that day forward, Salim never had any more problems with the quality of the milk, because, how would anyone dare to cheat and to argue with that amazing device, that infallible and formidable water detector owned by Salim!

The Namalis.

Deccan College's land bordered a road which, a little further on, some ten minutes walk away, ran alongside a river on whose banks lived a colony of Namalis, homeless untouchables, trying to survive in conditions of extreme poverty. They used the water of this river to bathe in, to wash their clothes, to cook with, to quench their thirst, and so on. When swollen by the monsoon, the river flowed freely, assuring the relative cleanliness of its waters, but, when the dry season came, its level fell considerably until nothing was left but a stagnant pool. During this time, an unimaginable odor, perceptible from more than a quarter of a kilometer away, would emanate from this foul water. Ingesting a single drop of this nauseating water would have killed a Westerner within twenty-four hours; however, the Namalis stayed where they were, continuing to use it for all their needs.

When Salim had the chance to talk to Doctor Patki about these poor people, he learned from him that, every woman having an average of ten to fourteen children, infant mortality was very high, but once past the age of sixteen or seventeen, they became immune. Doctor Patki told Salim the incredible story of one of these Namali women who had just been gored in the abdomen by a raging bull. She arrived at his surgery, clutching her intestines to her, after having walked a good kilometer. The doctor operated on her immediately, putting her entrails back in their proper place and closing up her stomach. A few hours later, she went home. This woman survived the ordeal and came back to have her stitches out a fortnight later.

Salim could not understand how this woman could have been able to overcome the pain of her injury, as well as the shock of seeing her intestines coming out of her body, to manage to walk, carrying them in her own hands, to the doctor's surgery. The pain threshold of these poor people who were so destitute and used to suffering in a thousand different ways was certainly not the same as that of Westerners. Their way of life developed in them a sort of endurance for pain that would be unthinkable for a European.

One sometimes hears tell of exotic spiritual disciplines which demand extraordinary physical resistance. The grueling conditions sometimes found in the East and which the inhabitants of these countries are subjected to from their childhood undoubtedly prepare some of them to bear the bodily suffering involved in such practices—such as, for example, a fakir whom Salim managed to see in Benares and who, for many years, had held one of his arms in the air until this limb became completely withered.

Meditation: is Consciousness condensed in matter?

Salim knew that meditation, in the most authentic meaning of the word, demanded his complete vigilance and the greatest sincerity. But he had also understood that he would have to take care never to force it.

The effort of remaining present to himself, although firm, must, at the same time, be quiet and full of gentleness. The intensity of this effort had to be just right, neither too much nor too little. He learned, little by little, the subtle art of recognizing when he was approaching the right and delicate moment to begin cautiously relinquishing his effort, to abandon himself to that which was superior within himself, and to what extent he could do this without risking falling back into his habitual state.

As he deepened his meditation and prolonged its duration, he felt the liberation and the expansion of his consciousness more and more. His consciousness seemed to grow infinitely and to become more and more luminous, fine, and ethereal. Furthermore, instead of the dense and weighty matter of his bodily form that he was used to feeling, he felt the indescribable sensation of a very subtle and ineffable ethereal transparency of being.

An intense longing arose from deep within him, encouraging him to want to give himself over forever to this unaccustomed state of being, but, at the same time, he realized the impossibility for him of such an accomplishment at this stage of his spiritual evolution.

Every time that he came out of his meditation, he felt the disconcerting sense of his consciousness retracting and becoming matter once more, thus returning to his dense and habitual bodily form. While he was reaching ever higher levels of being, he experienced, when coming out of his meditation, the feeling that there occurred effectively an expansion of his consciousness, every time that it was no longer condensed in a material form, and a retraction when it condensed itself once more and returned to its dense material form.

A mysterious thought then began to grow and to take form in his being: perhaps the final liberation of consciousness for a human being consisted in permanently losing the need (ingrained by force of habit) to descend once more into matter and to take some kind of form— which was ordinarily necessary to him in order to experience the feeling and the knowledge of his existence.

Furthermore, and on a much wider scale, a dizzying question arose in his mind and would not stop troubling him: was it possible that these myriads and myriads of celestial bodies inhabiting this immense Universe were, themselves, only consciousness condensed in matter and that the whole Cosmos had, itself, a secret need to liberate itself from its imprisonment in its material manifestation?

The Nada, an invaluable aid.

From the beginning of his spiritual quest, Salim had used, as a concentration aid, the mysterious sound, resembling the continual murmur of ocean waves, which he perceived in his ears and inside his head. His extreme sensitivity, along with his natural interest as a composer, had allowed him to develop various kinds of spiritual practices linked to this sound, which became particularly strident during his stay in Poona. In India, he would find confirmation of the accuracy of his intuition. While he was travelling in Rajasthan, he came one day, not far from Jaipur, to a small temple whose interior was strikingly decorated with murals. He had just arrived when he learned that, for some incomprehensible and insane reason, the people responsible for the building's maintenance had decided to repaint the walls and thus to cover over these ancient and very beautiful frescos. They represented various hatha yoga asanas accompanied by Sanscrit text. Salim's companion, who was studying this very language, was able to photograph them before they disappeared. Once the inscriptions had been reproduced on paper, while translating one of them written alongside a drawing illustrating the Lotus position, she said to him: "It's strange, these notes mention a sound, the sound that you hear in your ears; this writing shows that this is a particular type of yoga, Nada Yoga."

This incident confirmed to Salim the importance of this sound and the fact that this path had previously been known in India. Nevertheless, during the years that he lived there, he never found anyone who practiced it. He later learned that there is a reference to the Nada in the yoga treaty entitled Hatha Yoga Pradipika.[*]

The awareness that it was a known type of yoga from India's past encouraged Salim to rely even more on this aid. From the beginning of his Sadhana in Paris, he had noticed that the intensity of this sound was in proportion to the intensity of his concentration; in other words, the deeper his concentration, the louder and clearer the sound would become. He realized the value of it in his meditation as well as in the various concentration exercises that he practiced in his active life. In the beginning, he couldn't keep his attention fixed on it without interruption. However, following his initial efforts, it commenced to appear to him suddenly at most unexpected moments of the day. Like a divine emissary, it knocked at the gate of his soul, calling him to

---

[*] Many years later, we discovered that, in his book "A Search in Secret India", Paul Brunton mentions his meeting with the Radhasoamis, who followed teachings in which listening to this inner sound was very important. The Radhasoami faith, also called Sant Mat (the Path of the Saints) is, in fact, still practiced in India. And in the Shurangama Sutra, essential to Chinese Mahayana Buddhism, Avalokitesvara claims that he achieved illumination through concentration on this subtle inner sound. The Buddha congratulates Avalokitesvara and declares that this way is the supreme path to Awakening.

himself; as soon as he became aware of its presence within his being, Salim said inwardly: "It is here! It is here again, singing inside my ears, calling me!" for he felt that this was the way in which the Absolute called to him.

Salim later explained to his pupils that the Absolute has no form and nor does it have "vocal chords", the call is internal, it might be a thought which comes to mind or the Nada making its presence felt, and the manner in which one welcomes it will determine the frequency of the future visits of this heavenly messenger.

Whenever he realized that he had stopped listening to this sound, he endeavored to retrace his mental path, trying to find the moment of the fall, was it when someone had spoken to him? Or when a thought, an image or an association of ideas had crossed his mind? And he would start again, without blaming himself or feeling guilty, fixing his attention on the Nada with yet greater determination.

He had understood that it is the most difficult of things to fix one's attention permanently on an aid and he saw the futility and the obstacle even that blame or guilt would constitute.

He had seen how fruitful this listening to the Nada, even partially, was to his practice. After having had to resolve himself to pursuing his Sadhana alone, he felt the necessity of trying to remain attentive to this sacred sound at every moment. Nevertheless, he met with resistance in himself and, sometimes, he no longer wished to make this effort, at those times he said to himself: "What do I want?" At other moments, it was as though a voice within him was saying: "What is the point of all these efforts?"

So, even though he had already had very unusual mystic experiences, there was still this resistance within him that would spring up and manifest itself in this "What's the point?" However, he would not allow himself to listen to the voice of temptation and returned to his endeavor.

To sustain his feeling, he repeated to himself what became for him a sort of prayer: "Immaculate Source, You must be my final and ultimate end, and the whole of my life, as all that I think and all that I do—meditation, spiritual exercises, and every day activities—relates to You alone, the unique aim of my incarnation, now and forever."

He saw that it was not enough to hear the Nada resonate within him and that there was an essential difference between consciously listening to it and simply noticing its presence.

The more he listened to it, the more he felt himself in an inexplicable state of inner security which bore no relation to the tangible world, a mysterious inner security in which he felt that death was an illusion. This mysterious inner security was independent of all problems that he might encounter in the tangible world, including illness.

He decided to listen to it, without interruption, for one hour each day. Then one day each week. He prepared himself mentally all week long, and finally, he was able to listen to it seven days out of seven, from morning to evening, without losing it even for a fraction of a second. He even managed to be aware of it during his sleep. This primordial sound was there, in him, and in all things at all times. He could hear it vibrating mysteriously in the Cosmos and in all the heavenly stars, just as it was also vibrating in the Sun in a most spectacular way.

As a result of all his efforts, a moment finally arrived when he became strangely distant from himself, and he started viewing everything around him from another perspective altogether. He felt that his vision seemed to have inexplicably receded to the outside top part of the back of his head, from where he silently and impartially began to witness all that was taking place around him. Everything would then be seen to be in a constant state of flux. From this uninvolved position, he perceived that there was absolutely nothing permanent in any animate or inanimate object that met his gaze. The whole panorama of outer existence appeared to unfurl in front of him as a sort of strange and fantastic dream. And behind it all, he saw mysteriously through his mind's eye, so to speak, the unity of all things—"That" which was pervading him and everything else at the same time.

Metta, Karuna, Mudita, Upekka.

When a Buddhist monk spoke to Salim of the Brahmavihara, the sublime abodes of Brahma, he immediately intuitively understood how important this was to his practice. The Brahmavihara comprise, in fact, meditative practices common to Hinduism, Jainism, and Buddhism. In striving continually and developing feelings of benevolence, compassion, joy, and equanimity, the meditator is thought to raise his meditative consciousness to the state of the god Brahma.

These four feelings are (in the Pali language):

Metta: loving kindness,

Karuna: compassion,

Mudita: sympathetic joy,

Upekka: equanimity.

Salim began to work with these words, repeating them in Pali because of the particular vibrations attached to these words which had been used in India since long distant times. Turning himself towards the four points of the compass in succession, he awoke in himself the feeling corresponding to the word that he was saying and he sent this feeling out to the whole world. He also used these four words as a mantra. Breathing in, he would say Metta, at the same time kindling within himself a feeling of benevolent love, then on the following inbreath, he would say Karuna, still evoking within himself the corresponding feeling, then Mudita, then Upekka. He practiced this while cooking, while cleaning his room, or doing anything else. To avoid his practice becoming mechanical, he would change the order of the words for each series, starting the first series with Metta and finishing with Upekka, then starting the second with Karuna and finishing with Metta, starting the third with Mudita and finishing with Karuna, etc.

Living in two worlds at the same time.

The concentration required for spiritual practice is not of an intellectual order; it is a question of establishing within oneself another state of being and of consciousness, while, at the same time, because one has no choice, responding to the demands of external life; this requires a specific division of attention which must be exerted. Through his practice, Salim succeeded in living in two worlds at the same time: on one hand, the manifest and crude world, perceptible via his sensory organs, and, on the other hand, a translucent and ethereal world which he carried in the depths of his being. Thus, in a very particular way, his gaze remained turned towards the outer world, but, at the same time, his mind was directed towards the interior of himself.

This division of attention mysteriously created in him an expansion of his consciousness and a certain balance was established between the exterior world and the interior world. As he later said to his pupils, paraphrasing the Gospel according to Matthew (22, 21), in this way he gave unto Caesar what belonged to Caesar and unto God what belonged to God.

A new canine adoption. The law of Nature.

Salim always felt a particular affection for dogs, perhaps because of their ability to show unswerving loyalty, which humans are rarely capable of.

One afternoon, leaving his bungalow, he saw in the distance a black bitch, unimaginably thin, staggering with hunger. Overcome with pity for the poor beast, he quickly went back into the kitchen and grabbed whatever he could find by way of food (rice, vegetables, milk, etc.), then, calling the animal, he put everything down on the ground, picking it up and putting it back down several times so that she could clearly see what he was doing. He then backed away by about fifteen meters. The dog, suspicious, moved very slowly towards the food, which she sniffed before beginning to eat ravenously, wagging her tail all the while and lifting her head from time to time to look at

Salim who didn't move so as not to alarm her. In India, most dogs are wild; not only are they never fed, but, as soon as people see them, they throw stones at them—as Salim had seen done in Baghdad as a child.

The following day, to his astonishment, he saw that the dog had come back at the same time and was sitting not far from the bungalow, hoping to receive more food. He again went to look for some leftovers to give her and placed them on the ground, as he had the day before, but this time not backing quite so far away. The day after that, expecting to see her again, he prepared something for her. He did indeed see her reappear, watching him from a distance and wagging her tail. After a fortnight, when he was only backing away by about two or three meters while she ate, to Salim's horror, she arrived accompanied by six pups, all terribly thin. He found himself suddenly, without having sought it, face to face with seven dogs needing to be fed.

The pups were not yet weaned, but, as the mother didn't have enough milk, they were so hungry that they quickly began to eat whatever Salim prepared for them. Even so, they were trying to suckle their mother, whose patience never ceased to astonish Salim. As soon as she came close to them, her little ones threw themselves on her teats which were almost empty, jostling each other and fighting, while she remained immobile and stoical, only reacting when they caused her too much pain.

Although the food that she received was exclusively vegetarian, the dog's flanks became steadily less hollow and her coat shiny; the pups also began to change in appearance. Two of them suddenly fell seriously ill and, despite Salim's attentive care, taking them to the vet daily for a month, they died. A third pup contracted a contagious illness and it was necessary to put the poor animal down to save the others. Although reduced, the family still had three pups and their mother, who weaned them without further delay. So Salim had to feed his four dogs, which he did twice a day.

The dog, from then on, would allow Salim to approach her, but she remained wild and fled at the approach of anybody else. He was probably the only human being to have ever shown her any gesture of affection or of kindness. As he might have expected, he met with the same problems with his Indian neighbors as when he had welcomed his first four-legged companion. The dog slept outside, close to the bungalow, and she was normally quiet, but she had a strange habit of howling loudly on nights when the moon was full, which did nothing to help Salim's relations with the neighborhood. So, in these circumstances, he took the precaution of bringing her inside.

Although she was used to eating rice and vegetables, the dog one day joined with two other wild dogs to attack a lamb. When Salim saw the attack from a distance, he ran as fast as he could to intervene, but the poor beast had already received a fatal injury to its throat and died soon afterwards. He showed the dog, in no uncertain terms, that he was not happy with her. For two or three days, unable to forget the scene, he gave her nothing to eat and showed her no sign of friendship. During this time, she remained, day and night, at a slight distance, not moving and not even trying to quench her thirst. Every time she saw him coming out of the bungalow, she whimpered, wagging her tail, to show her joy in seeing him. Touched by the loyalty that she continued to show him, Salim eventually gave in, forgave her and began to feed her once again.

As he knew that his stay in Poona was temporary, there was no question of him adopting these animals. He had to turn to Mr Dady again for help who without hesitation, took one of the pups himself and found a master for the other two. As for the mother, Salim continued to take care of her.

Having just regained a little tranquility, he was surprised one day to hear the racket of a pack of dogs constantly barking and growling. When he went outside to find out the cause, he saw his dog, who was apparently in heat, frantically running away, chased by a dozen dogs in rut who had mysteriously sprung from nowhere. This relentless pursuit continued all day with no respite. The males, who were only interested in leaping on her while she was trying to get away, would not leave her in peace for a moment to allow her to eat, drink, or rest. She finally chose a white dog from the pack. The chosen one then had to fight incessantly, with courage and obstinacy, to try to beat back the others. Despite the fact that the rivals he had to confront were sometimes bigger than him, he nevertheless succeeded in overcoming them, although not without paying the price in multiple injuries. Salim had to resolve himself to sheltering the couple inside the house for the night in order to get them away from the fury of the pack.

During the hours that followed, Salim constantly heard the other dogs scratching furiously at the front door. The next morning, he discovered to his alarm that they had almost succeeded in making their way through by way of having bitten the door panel.

He thought it necessary to let the dog and her partner out for the day, but, as soon as they were outside, the pack recommenced its relentless pursuit as well as tearing each other apart in their efforts to mate with the female. Salim was in torment, not knowing what to do to protect her, and it was only towards the end of the day that he found a way of separating her from her pursuers and bringing her back inside with the white dog for another restless night followed by a final frenetic day. Finally, everything returned to normal once the dog's fertile period came to an end. The whole pack of dogs, including the white one, vanished into thin air just as mysteriously as they had appeared.

Salim was once again struck by the incredible force with which Nature worked, using her infallible weapon, consisting of prompting all the various living creatures to blindly seek an instant of sexual pleasure, in order to ensure that the perpetuation of the species is never, at any time, interrupted.

He had already realized that it was through a living understanding of the true aim of this irresistible thirst for physical ecstasy that an aspirant might one day succeed in controlling this aspect of his nature so as to be able to better consecrate himself to his spiritual practices.

Not long after this incident, his stay in Poona came to an end. Before leaving, he had the dog sterilized so that she would not have any more pups. Because she was so untamed and timid, it was impossible to find anyone to take care of her. When the time came to leave, he felt very unhappy about having to leave her. He later learned that the poor beast had stayed in front of the bungalow without moving for around a fortnight, in despair at no longer seeing her master. As the people who had moved into the dwelling did not trouble themselves to feed her, she must, undoubtedly, have ended up becoming completely wild again.

First spiritual conversations.

About six or seven weeks before leaving Poona, during an outing, Salim met an Indian who appeared very interested in spiritual research. He saw that the man was truly serious and, after an exchange on the various kinds of Yoga, the man asked Salim if he could see him again.

A few days later, he came back, accompanied by some other people, all wanting to meet Salim. They showed a great deal of interest in him telling them about his spiritual journey, the various problems that he had had to face in this delicate area, the traps lying in wait for the unwary aspirant, and some experiences that he had had as a result of his years of practice.

When they came back the following week, these people brought others with them and, at every meeting, their numbers continued to grow. In the end, he found himself, without having intended it, addressing some twenty Indians, eager to find someone capable of helping them in their spiritual quest.

If he had not had to return to France, without doubt the group would have quickly developed, as with everything, in India, that relates to spirituality, and, perhaps, Salim would have had a place where he would have been able to pursue his own work in more favorable conditions than those that he would later encounter in the West; but it was not possible for him to cancel his journey, he needed to see his television acquaintances again so that they would continue granting him the royalties for the broadcast of his music, which assured his financial independence, and he had committed to write some music for new films of their movements for the Gurdjieff groups, so he had to return to Paris.

Slowing to the extreme.

The two years that Salim spent in Poona were, from every point of view, of major importance for him. The atmosphere of India and the conditions in which he had lived had proved to be so conducive to his spiritual practices that he no longer wished to return to Europe.

Shortly before his departure, his companion having gone to Bombay, he had the opportunity of being alone in his bungalow for about two weeks. He therefore decided to undertake some new work on himself, consisting of greatly slowing down his movements during at least certain times of the day, all the while remaining as internally focused and awakened as he could.

In the beginning, as this practice was new, everything went well; however, after two or three days, when he wanted to push this slowness to the extreme, he began to encounter strong resistance coming from his ordinary self. The more he struggled with himself to maintain this slowness, the more this refusal made itself felt, bringing up to the surface of his being, to reveal it yet more clearly, the aspect of his double nature which was opposed to this spiritual practice. Salim realized more than ever the importance of all that he had understood up to then, especially concerning that aspect of himself with which he had to constantly struggle and which he must eventually conquer if he was to have any hope of one day remaining continually in another Universe within himself, which arose from the Sacred.

The Only Reality.

When, during his meditation, Salim was touched by the radiance of his Supreme Being, of himself, he had, little by little, sensed the worthlessness of the ordinary aspect of himself. He therefore wished, each time he was separated from it, to return to that beatific state of reverential inner silence, a little like someone who always wants to listen to the inspired chords of a sublime piece of music to experience the feelings of beauty and subtle truth that they inexplicably cause to resonate in the depths of his being. As he went ever deeper into himself, knowing ever higher states of inner serenity and tranquil ecstasy, not only did his meditation become less and less difficult, but a desire and an unremitting love for it grew naturally within him.

This immutable beatific state, which he experienced during his meditation, became, for him, the sole reality at the heart of the ever changing conditions of impermanent earthly existence. Every time he lost the felicity of this inner presence, he would feel shipwrecked, washed up on a desert island, harsh and scorched; to him it felt like a cruel inner death. He felt a painful need to return once again to the plenitude of the Celestial Aspect of his double nature, which was, in fact, the only True Life there was and the unique source whence superior wisdom might issue.

Leaving Poona.

The day before his departure, Salim went to pay a final visit to Indira Devi. He never forgot her expression or the seriousness with which she told him: "Don't go back to Paris." It was with a heavy heart that he had resolve himself, the following day, to taking the train to Bombay where he went straight to the airport to take his place on the plane. As destiny would have it, when he returned to India later, it was not possible for him to go back to Poona. A page had been turned in his life.

Paris. A Western sannyasin "on a mission."

Through the help of a friend, Salim was able, as a musician, to find a studio in the "Cité des Arts" where he lived for a few months before going back to India. The "Cité des Arts" was, in fact, a large building, comprising a number of studios meant for artists who didn't have a lot of money, and which even had, at street level, a small concert room, intended for lodgers who could make use of it to try out their talents in front of an audience. However, while waiting for the studio that had been promised him to be free, he was accommodated for a week by a couple of acquaintances whom he had helped out in the past.

One day a very significant incident occurred, reflecting the attitude of some people towards spirituality. He saw a young Canadian, dressed in ocher and carrying a rucksack, whom he had already seen at Muktananda's ashram, arrive at his hosts' home and, without any embarrassment, begin to ask everyone present for money. When it came to Salim's turn to be approached, he politely responded that he worked hard to support his own needs and that he had no money to give to the young man; then, he watched the young man for a long time and, seeing what kind of idler he was dealing with, he asked him firmly whether, as a seeker, he thought it right to be given the hard-earned money of others when he had made no effort to deserve it. The Canadian immediately replied that he was "on a mission". Salim asked to know what this "mission" consisted of and the so-called sannyasin* replied that he had been sent by Muktananda. He saw, however, that this fanciful assertion did not, in any way, impress Salim who was surprised that all the others, without the slightest judgment, believed him straight away. He had no hesitation in performing his little act everywhere he went. As soon as he claimed to have been sent as a delegate by Muktananda, who was very well known, both in India and in the West, he was received with respect, accommodated and fed for free.

A little later in the morning, this unusual pilgrim took a bath and left the bathtub in a state hardly worthy of a "sannyasin on a mission". The hostess, displeased, accused Salim in front of everyone of having left the bathroom in an unacceptable condition; she had not a moment's doubt as to the identity of the guilty party, because, in her eyes, the "holy man" could not be suspected of such a lack of courtesy.

---

* renouncer.

It was only after Salim had succeeded in explaining to her that he had not yet used the bathroom, that the hostess had to accept the evidence that it was the Canadian—who, throughout this misunderstanding, had remained silent, not embarrassed in the slightest to let someone else take the blame for him—who was the perpetrator of this rudeness.

As Salim later repeated insistently to his pupils, it is not enough to aspire to find the Divine in oneself; it is necessary to examine oneself ceaselessly and to have the courage to see oneself as one really is if one is to come to know oneself, "Without this," he would say, "one may wander the Earth, filled with passive longing for the Sublime, but without ever attaining it. One may continue, like this Canadian "sannyasin", boasting of one's spiritual search, without realizing the extent to which such talk is in flagrant contradiction with a dishonest way of living and of behaving, which has become such a habit that it is no longer even questioned".

Furthermore, it should be added that this young Anglo-Saxon was not an isolated case and that Salim often encountered other Westerners who had joined the herds of "professional saints" spoken of by Alexandra David-Neel.

Mysterious incursion into another dimension.

One morning Salim woke earlier than usual, beset by a curious feeling of unease that he could not explain. No sooner had he washed and dressed than he incomprehensibly felt a pressing and indefinable need to go out for a walk. However, it was a dark December morning, very cold, still immersed in night, with a thick fog which created a ghostly atmosphere and made it difficult to get one's bearings.

He arrived at the gates of the Buttes Chaumont park, which happened to be open. He went in. The darkness and the fog persisted. Deceived by the unfavorable conditions, he inadvertently strayed into an area that was closed to the public, because, apparently, excavations were being undertaken there. Displeased with himself for not having paid enough attention to the direction he had taken, he had decided to retrace his steps, when he stumbled and fell into a deep hole that he had been unable to see in the dark. Despite all his efforts, he could not manage to get out.

He then entered into contact, without having sought it, with beings from another world, no longer obeying the laws that govern this material universe.

Finding himself at the exit of the Buttes Chaumont park, he was asking himself anxiously if he had not dreamed it all, when, because of the cold, he plunged his hands into his pockets and he felt in one of them an object that surprised him by its unusual feel. Withdrawing his hand, he discovered, to his astonishment, that it was the mauve flower that had been given to him as a farewell gift by one of these luminous beings. Amazed, he let out a cry and fell to his knees so abruptly that passersby, alarmed, wished to help him. A young woman, who was among them, noticed the flower in his hand and was intrigued by its beauty and dazzling color. She asked him where he had found it, because, she said, she had never seen one like it. He regarded her absently, then, with tears in his eyes, repeated in a voice trembling with emotion: "It wasn't a dream, I know that I wasn't dreaming, I know it, I know it…"

Salim had not in any way sought out this astonishing experience. He later recounted this fantastic experience in the form of a spiritual tale,[*] to make it understood that there may come, in the life of a seeker, moments when he needs to take an important decision in order to progress with his spiritual practice, a decision that implies certain renunciations on his part which he may not be ready to make; he thereby risks letting an opportunity pass which may never represent itself.

The Cité des Arts. First hatha yoga lessons.

As soon as the studio that had been reserved for him in the "Cité des Arts" was free, Salim moved in. It was reasonably spacious, furnished

---

[*] In his last work: "Du fond des Brumes" (From the Depths of Mist).

Salim at the Cité des Arts, copying out
La Tragédie de Masada

and fully equipped, with a small bathroom, and there was even a piano; the price was surprisingly low. Not long after he had moved in, Salim, who was impatient to see his mother and brother again, went to London. His mother had aged a lot. Her knees and hands were swollen and deformed by rheumatic joints which caused her a great deal of pain. She could hardly walk and Victor, Salim's brother, had to look after her and run all her errands.

His father's absence gave him the impression that the house was strangely empty. He remembered, with emotion, his father leaning against the front door, a slight smile on his lips, his gaze turned sadly downwards, when Salim took his leave of him two years previously, before leaving for Poona. He went to reflect at his father's grave, his heart filled with compassion thinking of how his father had suffered with his pulmonary disease. He thought of the pain that afflicted the world, of the strangeness of life and the impermanence of phenomenal existence. This visit to London also allowed him to see Mr Adie again, who showed how struck he was with the spiritual change that had occurred in Salim during those two years of intense inner work in Poona.

Back in Paris, he went to see his television acquaintances to give them some new private recordings of his music that he had just had made, because those he had left with them two years before were worn and practically unusable. He once again had to find money to live on and, as life in France was incomparably more expensive than in India, his material difficulties recommenced. So, he began to give some hatha yoga lessons, also awakening in his pupils a particular force, the Shakti, previously mentioned.

He hoped to return to India as soon as possible, but he was obliged to stay in Paris for longer than anticipated, because, due to the war that had just broken out between India and Pakistan, the borders were closed for some time. As soon as they were reopened, he set off, for Pondicherry this time, where his companion had just obtained a new grant.

Madras 1971-1974

Pondicherry. Shri Aurobindo's Ashram.

This city, which formerly belonged to France, is situated on the coast of the Indian Ocean; a heavy humidity prevails in an air infested with mosquitoes. The majority of Pondicherry's inhabitants speak French. Salim was so used to hearing Indians speak in English all over the country that he could not help being a little surprised at first. The roads of the city run parallel to the beach. Those that run alongside the ocean and where one can go for such beautiful walks are home to the wealthier Indians. The further one goes inland, the poorer the neighborhoods become, albeit remaining picturesque.

Because of its renown, Salim was tempted to visit the ashram of Shri Aurobindo. Shri Aurobindo had been dead for quite some time and there was now only the mother of the ashram, a French woman, more than ninety years old, who would appear on the balcony of her bedroom every morning at sunrise, supported by two people (because she could no longer stand unaided), so that the ashramites and the visitors might receive her darshan.

When Salim asked what kind of work on oneself, what spiritual exercises, and what kind of meditation were practiced in the ashram, he was told, in so many words: "You have nothing to do; simply abandon yourself, the Mother does everything for you." Salim, surprised, said to himself that, as the practice of meditation and the sustained effort of concentration discouraged most people, it must certainly suit a lot of people to hear that they have no effort to make.

During another visit, Salim saw, as he arrived at the ashram, a great crowd of men and women filing past a few disciples who were sitting by the entrance; each of these men and women received a sweetmeat blessed by the Mother and offered as a "prasad" (a gift for the devout). As soon as a person had been given his or her sacred candy, that person was immediately transported to seventh heaven and walked like a somnambulist, in a kind of ecstatic trance. Salim, who had taken his turn to receive the prasad, was obliged to note that, when the candy had dropped into his hand, he had not been privileged to feel, as the others had, such an exalted state. He concluded from this that, without doubt, it was faith that he was lacking...

Madras. Premonitory dreams. The trap of intellect.

In Pondicherry, the mosquitoes were a real curse. However, despite their omnipresence, along with the cockroaches, the scorpions, and the rats, and despite the constraints of the strict hygiene rules concerning water and food, Salim was a thousand times happier to be in India than in Europe, because, in India, he felt the call of the Sacred everywhere.

His stay in Pondicherry lasted for around six weeks, after which he and his companion moved to Madras, into a neighborhood known as Besant Nagar, which was a little way outside the city. They moved into a small apartment, on the first floor of a house located opposite the headquarters of the Theosophical Society, bordering the ocean.

The mission of The Theosophical Society, founded in the late nineteenth century by Helena Petrovna Blavatsky and Annie Besant, is to encourage the comparative study of religions and philosophies. Its main headquarters are located in Madras although it has branches in a number of countries. The theosophists claim to follow the teachings published by Mrs Blavatsky in 1888, under the title of "The Secret Doctrine".

In this region of India, the air is saturated with humidity; washing doesn't dry but remains unpleasantly damp and sticky. Besant Nagar being fortunately located by the ocean, a slight breeze was always blowing there, which made the climate more bearable.

During his first walk on the beach, Salim noticed a flotilla of small boats belonging to poor fishermen. He felt a sudden shock when he saw, not far from the water's edge, around one of these craft, some Indians, practically naked, busying themselves with fishing nets in their hands, whom he remembered having seen during a premonitory

dream that he had had shortly before leaving Paris. He also remembered
having noticed, during the same dream, the presence nearby of an old
Muslim man, whom he could not see among these fishermen. Nevertheless, a short time later, he saw that the first floor of the house was
indeed occupied by a wealthy old Muslim man.

Perplexed, Salim found himself once again confronting an enigma
that was beyond him and he could not help wondering: "What can
these dreams mean? Is it possible that I have lived these situations in
another time and another dimension not ordinarily comprehensible
and that I find myself confronted with them in the present so as to
resolve some enigmatic problem that I cannot, for the moment, grasp?
Or am I moving towards a future that I have myself mapped out by way
of some of my thoughts that remain, for the time being, incomprehensible to me? Or are there, in the life of a human being, predestined
events that he absolutely cannot avoid?"

Following this incident, Salim remained very troubled, especially
when he remembered having had, before leaving France, other dreams
of this kind heralding difficult events that were awaiting him in the
future.

He did not confide what had happened to him on that day or his
perplexity in the face of these enigmas to anyone, but he remained
very pensive, trying to apprehend the true sense of these premonitions
and to understand how it could be possible to discover in advance,
living them in dreams, events that would only happen several weeks,
or months, or even years later.

Spiritual erudition is held in high esteem in India and excites admiration and respect; Salim had the opportunity of meeting people who
believed that acquiring a vast intellectual knowledge of spirituality
was a practice in itself. Although he recognized that the intellect had,
to a certain extent, its place in any spiritual approach, he knew that it
represented a trap. Subsequently, he found this same way of seeing
things in some of his pupils. "It is," he would say to them, "necessary

for a seeker not to found his quest on this faculty alone, forgetting that only direct knowledge of the Divine is of real value. One may know many things intellectually (especially if one is brilliant), but without, for all that, having understood them; there is, between academic knowledge and true understanding, a gulf as vast as that which separates the Earth from the Heavens."

Despite the admiration that he felt for people possessing brilliant intellectual capacities, Salim could not content himself with this kind of approach to something which, for him, had become a question of life or death. He realized in the depths of his being that, at the moment of death, it was impossible for anyone to avoid gravitating, by the inexorable laws of nature, towards a state of being corresponding to his level of consciousness and to what he or she had made of him or herself during life. Furthermore, through his repeated spiritual experiences, Salim knew with certainty that, at this vertiginous moment, it was not possible for a human being to comprehend what he was to find himself absorbed into if he had not experienced and recognized this state while he was still alive.

Salim continued, therefore, to devote himself to his spiritual practices as seriously as he could, without being able to share the fruits of his work with anyone. He put into practice everything that he later wrote about in his works for the use of other seekers. His day was entirely devoted to his spiritual work.

He always rose very early. Following his ablutions (in the course of which, he never failed to silently carry out a concentration exercise), he drank one or two cups of tea, then he would immediately begin to meditate. Once his meditation was over, he tackled his daily hatha-yoga exercises. He would then go out to do some shopping in Besant Nagar where small storekeepers, here and there, offered fruits, vegetables, and eggs. During the whole outing, he would carry out one of the various concentration exercises he had invented, which he later recorded in his books. Upon his return, he would boil the milk and the water for the day, then begin to cook, constantly silently undertaking a practice appropriate to the occupation of the moment. He would pass the rest of the day occupied with various spiritual exercises and a number of meditation sessions, in order to exercise his concentration in an unbroken manner, even when he found himself in the company of other people. For Salim, without spiritual practice, life had no meaning, so he enjoyed making these efforts, subtle efforts to remain in the present and to keep his attention continually fixed on the Sublime Aspect of his being.

Experiences of mystic love.

Through the maturation of his practice, Salim was now finding again, but in a much more tranquil manner, the state of ineffable ecstatic love which had moved him so deeply in Paris on the first occasion that it had flooded his being. Now, a profound cosmic calm flowed through him, he felt a very tranquil but sublime tenderness into which he would quietly merge, and, as always during such out-of-the-ordinary moments, this enigmatic Nada made its presence felt more than ever and, with its eternal jewel-like glitter, sang in his ears its supernal song at the same time as it helped him increase his inner absorption. This, as it deepened, always brought him the strange yet curiously familiar sensation of having returned to the mysterious Source whence he originated, and to which he belonged.

The way this divine flame affected him the first time it illuminated his being with its ineffable love can be compared to that of a fierce fire consuming a log of wood, its flames leaping about wildly in all directions in the wind. And the way it affected him later, when he had acquired deeper spiritual comprehension, more control over his thoughts, and greater inner calm, can be compared to the immobile, soft, and beautiful flame of a candle on a perfectly windless evening

Apart from the moments when he sat alone and meditated, something of this beatific state extended itself afterward of its own accord into his active life, silently stirring him with a melting feeling of quiescent and compassionate love.

Contact with the infinitely small and the infinitely big.

Salim had always intuitively felt that it was of the greatest importance for him to continually carry a sense of mystery in order that his meditation should not, little by little, fall into a banal routine practice.

Every time he sat down to meditate, he strove to be new, open, without seeking to rediscover experiences that he may have had before. Thus, during deep meditation, he could perceive, through an inner vision, the incessant flux and changes of the various cells, molecules, and atoms in his body. And he realized how this flux secretly influenced his thoughts, moods, and feelings, according to the special characteristics of these invisible entities in him. Equally, his tendencies, habits, and way of thinking affected and influenced the being and pattern of behavior of these corpuscles and atoms, rendering them what they were. By struggling with the outer leanings and habits he could see in himself, he was inevitably modifying the inclinations, way of thinking, and inner nature of the imperceptible cells and atoms in his body as well.

He understood that every change that occurred in his level of consciousness must also affect the various constituents of his planetary body. Thus, the birth of another state of being and of consciousness in him had not failed to reverberate through the different cells and molecules composing his corporeal envelope, so that their way of consciousness mysteriously underwent a gradual modification which, in return, assisted him in his attempts to elevate himself further within himself and to access ever more luminous territories within his being.

At other times, through meditation and his various concentration exercises, a new faculty awoke in him, allowing him an intuitive perception of the Universe and the objects that surrounded him—an intuitive and direct perception of the fact that, just as the various cells constituting his planetary body were alive, in the same way, the Earth was also an immense living cell in the enigmatic body of the Cosmos. It possessed its own form of life, of intelligence and of consciousness, as well as its own sort of sensitivity to suffering, which it felt much more sharply than one could imagine.

Salim later emphasized to his pupils that it must never be forgotten that we owe an immense debt to our planet—which provides us constantly with air, with water, with food and all other things necessary to our survival and for which we remain ever in its debt.

Just as we are conscious of the fragility of our bodies and take great care to protect them, in the same way, it should be an integral part of a spiritual quest to become more and more conscious of the fragility of the Earth, to which we owe the very possibility of being able to pursue our spiritual practices and to protect it with extreme care, considering it as a true mother—as the Native Americans did.

Krishnamacharya. Desikachar. Asana and bodily perfection.

Salim continued to dedicate himself assiduously to hatha yoga, hoping, against all hope, to find a master in this discipline who would ally the mastery of asanas with an authentic spiritual approach.

The famous Krishnamacharya, who lived in Madras, was, without doubt, a great teacher of hatha yoga, but Salim felt, when he saw him at his home, shortly after Salim had moved to Besant Nagar, the same impression that he had had with Iyengar and with some other hatha-yogis that he had had the opportunity of meeting briefly during his travels. He indisputably possessed great mastery of his body, but was only interested in physical results, with no spiritual dimension.

Salim nevertheless took private lessons with T.K.V Desikachar, the son of Krishnamacharya, throughout the time he spent in Madras. As in the case of Iyengar, the impressive techniques of Krishnamacharya and his son were not accompanied by any meditation.

Salim was always surprised by the way people would accept, without question, affirmations such as: "If one succeeds in executing an asana perfectly, one achieves liberation". Faced with such declarations, he could not help saying to himself: "Does one really know what liberation is?" He remembered having seen one day an astonishing demonstration given by some Korean trapeze artists, who put their lives in danger at every second by executing, with no safety net and more than fifteen meters above the ground, sequences of the most extraordinary jumps one could imagine. The rapidity and, above all, the perfection of their movements were spectacular to behold

However, despite the astonishing perfection they had attained on the physical level, between which and a simple asana, even perfectly accomplished, there could be absolutely no comparison, these acrobats were not, for all that, "awoken". Furthermore, it must be added that, because of the risks to their lives that they took at every moment, their attention was put to the test in an incommensurably different manner than that of a hatha yogi who practices his postures on the ground with no danger to himself.

A guru conjuror.

Salim was, one day, invited to the inauguration of a spiritual centre in Madras, giving rise to a long ceremony, celebrated by Brahmans and dedicated to the guru—himself a Brahman—who was comfortably sitting on a divan, while some disciples recited sacred texts for him and showered him, from time to time, by way of offerings, with grains of rice, flower petals and holy water. The gestures and recitations of the officiants were carried out with a monotony and a lack of concentration that surprised Salim. Sitting apart, some very poor people were patiently awaiting the ritual distribution of the prasad, which consisted of some kind of small sweetmeat. The contrast between these poverty-stricken people and the plump Brahmans was striking; the latter all had plenty of "meat" on their bones and one of them, whose obesity particularly struck Salim, could easily have sheltered triplets in his stomach.

"One can understand the revolt of the Buddha," Salim thought, "faced with all these practices which are so far from the goal spoken of in sacred texts like the Bhagavad Gita."

When the rite was drawing to a close, a garland of flowers was placed around the neck of the guru, who, throwing a look towards Salim from time to time, must have felt that here was someone who was very little impressed, either by him, or by the supposedly sacred ceremony that had just unfolded.

He suddenly made an abrupt movement with his hand and a candy immediately fell at Salim's feet. The man signaled him to take it; Salim did so, thinking to give it to one of the poor children that he had seen outside. When the guru, annoyed, saw that Salim seemed no more impressed than before, he made another sudden movement of his hand, and, to the astonishment of the assembly who let out a cry of amazement, a large, old, silver rupee rolled towards Salim. But, this time, when he stretched out his arm to pick it up, the so-called master quickly leant forward to take it back!

In addition to this impressive "power of materialization", this guru was said to be capable of turning back the waters of the ocean with a simple movement of his hand—should he so wish, of course! This memory reminded Salim of another yogi, also supposed to be gifted with miraculous powers, who, one day, in Bombay, proclaimed that he would walk on water. The next day, a large crowd gathered on the beach to witness this wonder; however, at the last minute, the man sent someone to say that "he didn't want to do it on that day…"

Journeys in India's interior.

Thanks to the financial independence provided by his royalties, Salim had the opportunity, during his stay in Madras, to undertake some new journeys in the interior of the country, which confirmed more than ever to him the difficulty of finding an authentic master. Every three or four months, he set off with his companion on treks of several weeks, during which they visited different regions with a view to meeting with spiritual masters of all traditions.

These excursions were a source of new and enriching impressions, but proved, nevertheless, to be tiring and, often, after four or five weeks, Salim would return to Madras exhausted. Given the extreme delicacy of his health he strove always, to whatever extent it was possible, to prepare their meals in the hotels himself, using a small electric hotplate that he had bought in Paris for this purpose. However, power cuts, which were frequent, obliged him to sometimes eat out; the local cuisine was so spicy that he generally contented himself with a few chapattis (wholemeal flatbreads) which quickly made him very ill.

After each of these journeys, he would find their apartment covered in dust, with a number of enormous red cockroaches, running around at top speed, and the mosquito nets—which he had fixed to the windows to prevent the clouds of mosquitoes from the Theosophical Society's garden from invading the rooms—torn by the wind. On two or three occasions, he even discovered a rat which had succeeded in getting inside, obliging him to carry out a careful disinfection after getting rid of the creature.

Sarnath.

During one of his journeys, Salim went to Benares and to Sarnath, the place where the Buddha first preached the Dharma. During these pilgrimages in these holy places, many times and at the most unexpected moments, Salim would hear the Nada begin suddenly to vibrate in him in such a strident and unwonted manner that he found himself flooded by a feeling of reverential awe. Simultaneously, an incomprehensible phenomenon would occur within him, lasting only a fraction of a second, during which he was seized by the inexplicable certitude of having already lived these situations beforehand, but where, when, and how, when it was the first time that he had been to these places? These questions, as well as numerous others, troubled him very much and often occupied his mind.

There were many occasions when he lived experiences of this kind, completely unexpected, and always causing a profound desire to understand this enigma to arise within him. At certain moments, in the course of his meditations or when he was carrying out an intense concentration exercise, he had sudden intuitive insights relating to "Time", by way of which he understood that, contrary to what the limited senses of the human being would have him believe, time could unfold according to a curved, rather than a linear, movement; there would, therefore, come a moment where time returned to its departure point to begin again its circular trajectory; and the human being also would begin, despite himself, through a constant repetition of certain habits ingrained in him, to devote himself to the same activities he had already dedicated himself to and to relive the same experiences that he had already lived in the past—which could, perhaps, explain these fleeting impressions of having already been through the same events or of having previously found oneself in identical situations.

Salim was always struck by the singular destiny of beings such as Michelangelo, Mozart, Einstein, or of great mystics who, from their early childhood, had demonstrated an unremitting determination to realize their vocation, as though they remembered in advance the aim of their existence. They were irresistibly driven, each according to his talents and his capacities, towards the accomplishment of their destinies, which, later, proved to be so out of the ordinary that the world remained baffled before the mystery of their lives. For Salim, a genius is not the product of chance, he remembers.

Spiritual insights into time. Correcting the errors of the past.

The discoveries relating to the mystical domain, which Salim made at this time, especially those having to do with time, open an entirely different perspective on life. He came, in effect, to this astonishing understanding: "The movement of time is not as one ordinarily imagines it; past events continue to unfold in other dimensions and in another time which are not ordinarily comprehensible. Constant repetition of any kind generates habit. Now, there exists, in the human being, a strange phenomenon: once he has thought, said, or done something, he can no longer help wanting to rethink it, to resay it, or to redo it. An irresistible impulse takes hold in him, which pushes him, despite himself, to wish to repeat it. And with every repetition, this thought, this word, or this act, becomes a tendency which will prove more and more difficult to change—especially if it subsequently turns out to constitute an obstacle to a spiritual quest".

Following these troubling discoveries and these mysterious under-standings, Salim came to realize to what extent it is necessary for an aspirant to seek to escape these repetitions which pursue him from one moment to the next, or from one life to the next, plowing their furrow ever deeper in his being.

How might a seeker act on his destiny in such a way as to change the unfolding of certain events in his life and of certain encounters so as not to find them again in each cycle of existence, whatever form this latter might take?

In moments of deep meditation and through repeated intuitive insights, Salim had already understood that this change could not only be undertaken in the future, as one is ordinarily tempted to imagine. An entirely different approach is necessary to modify a process so elusive and enigmatic; paradoxically, it is necessary to go back in time and change the past itself!

"Isn't it strange?" Salim would say to himself, "to think that it is necessary to change the past? And in what manner may one change the past?... How is it possible to avoid committing the same errors again, re-establishing connections with people who constitute an obstacle to what one is trying to attain spiritually, being continually trapped in the same activities incompatible with a spiritual quest, and so on...?"

By way of direct intuitive insights, he had come to comprehend that the past had not vanished into total nothingness, as one is used to imagining, it waits, in dimensions not ordinarily comprehensible, for suitable conditions to present themselves, allowing it to become manifest once more.

He realized that the manner in which a human being has comported himself, as well as all that he has thought, said, and done in the past, wait inexorably to live again in him and to pursue their manifestation in the present. And, as the past and the future converge every fraction of a second in the present, the seriousness with which an aspirant accomplishes his spiritual practices and the efforts that he makes to liberate himself from his undesirable inclinations and from the tendency of his mind to be always turned towards the exterior are, not only changing his destiny and preparing for him a different future, but also, and in the most mysterious and ordinarily incomprehensible manner, are changing the past, so that it can never again repeat itself in the same way.

Rajasthan. Jaipur.

During another journey, Salim had the opportunity to go to Rajasthan. The train that he took, which was of some bygone era, crossed immense arid territories where nothing grew except for a few small shrubs and bushes withered by a scorching heat. He spent a few days in Jodhpur where he admired impressive ancient citadels built on high hills. Since the dissolution of the principalities following independence, a great number of these fortresses had, little by little, become occupied by common people. He also went to Agra, where he was dazzled by the extraordinary beauty of the Taj Mahal, and to Khajuraho, famous for its temples which stretch as far as the eye can see; however, it was the city of Jaipur which, above all, remained vivid in his memory.

Shortly after his arrival in the city, while he was looking to buy some supplies, his path led Salim to a picturesque square where he saw several merchants who were offering fruit and vegetables for sale on small carts, passersby some of whom wore beards and turbans, women carrying heavy logs on their backs, and poorly-dressed children playing happily among them. In front of him stood a raised temple, accessed by some fifteen steps, whose exterior wall was decorated here and there with magnificent pale blue designs.

While Salim, fascinated, was contemplating the building, he became suddenly aware of a strange atmosphere pervading the locality, giving him the curious sensation that he was dreaming. Something mysterious enveloped the temple, without him being able to define it in any satisfactory manner.

Everything he saw had suddenly acquired a vivid and dazzling intensity, as though he were in a colorful dream. What was yet more baffling was that he was simultaneously overcome by the certainty of having already lived the scene which was unfolding before him, with the same enturbanned people who were passing by, the same heavily burdened women, the same children enjoying themselves, and the same temple with its sky blue decorations. And, paradoxically, he felt, at the same time, the conviction that he was dreaming as well as that of reliving a situation that he had known before in another time impossible to determine. When he came out of this kind of trance, he realized, with a feeling of incredulity, that this experience, which had seemed to him to last an eternity, had, in fact, only lasted a few seconds.

Whenever he pondered the subject of time, Salim could no longer distance himself from the strange certainty, inexpressible in habitual language, that, alongside the time that one knows, or that one, in the ordinary way of things, believes one knows, there exists another time and other dimensions which remain forever incomprehensible to the human being as long as he remains as he is, with his gaze turned only in the direction of the external world.

Subsequently, Salim strove to make his pupils understand that what one really is does not exist in the time that we usually know—which is in perpetual motion and in a state of becoming and of constant transformation—but in another time which is not in motion, which contains all of Life and is closely bound to "Being" and "Consciousness".

Reflections on the present, the past, and the future.

When, at the end of the afternoon, the sun became less fierce, Salim would often go out to spend an hour or two sitting on a rock by the ocean.

He would think of his practice, of the mystery of life. He was still surprised by the fact that so few people around him seemed preoccupied with the same questioning.

During his reflections, he was sometimes seized by dread at the idea that he could so easily have missed the opportunity of hearing about spiritual paths. At such times, he would say to himself, with retrospective fear: "What would be my life today if I had never met Mr Adie, to whom I am so indebted, and if I had not known the spiritual experiences that I have been privileged to have?

Every time he thought of the passing of human existence, which inevitably ends in death, he could not help feeling overcome by a disturbing feeling at the idea that, if life and time unfolded in a circular movement, there must come a moment when a human being finds himself at the same starting point (just like a planet following its orbit around the Sun) to recommence traveling the same path, thus allowing the habits and tendencies that are peculiar to him to take root ever more deeply within him—unless a sufficiently powerful shock should occur, or, at the very least, an unexpected and fairly important event, to modify the course of his existence already plotted and make him take a new direction.

Salim became more and more preoccupied by the thought that the present could not, in any way, be different from what it was, because it resulted inevitably from the way in which one had lived the preceding instant, the past month, the previous year, etc. He realized more than ever that, if a seeker wished to change the course of his future, he would have to focus all his attention on the present and to try to live it in a different manner than he would ordinarily have done, without forgetting that all serious spiritual practice accomplished in the present will, in the most mysterious way, change his past also so that it can no longer pursue him and determine the unfolding of a destiny capable of conflicting with his spiritual evolution—a past which, unknown to him, is always awaiting him in an undetermined future, because all that he has done, said, and thought, remains forever active somewhere in his being and in his consciousness.

While Salim's gaze was directed into the distance, towards the horizon where the ocean seemed to vanish into the infinite, he was thinking that human beings always commit the same error (whether in the field of science or in a spiritual quest) in believing that the finality of every enterprise is located in time. They cannot understand that Eternity, the realization of all their aspirations, and all the knowledge they seek already exist in the present.

Furthermore, through a direct intuitive insight, Salim had realized that, every time an aspirant succeeded, through concentration, in tearing away from himself (from his ordinary personality) so as to create in his being the silence necessary to allow him to become conscious of himself in a manner that is totally unusual for him, he joins, in the most mysterious manner, the past to the future in an "eternal now".

Story of a gas bottle.

The house Salim was living in, which was called "Chand" (all the buildings on the street had names rather than numbers), belonged to an Indian doctor whose office was located at the other end of the avenue. He only came to Besant Nagar to treat his patients in the evenings, as he doubtless worked elsewhere during the day. His waiting room was always full of ill people who even came from neighboring villages.

Aside from his intestinal problems, in relation to which Salim had renounced seeing anyone, he had to consult this amiable doctor on a number of occasions, despite the fact that he had few illusions about the latter's professional capacities, especially in the case of serious illness. In any case, he had no choice, because, not only was he the only doctor in the neighborhood, but the same problem was encountered everywhere in India.

During all these years, in Poona as well as in Madras, as Salim cooked for himself, he used gas bottles rather like those one uses in France. However, the quality of these was very different. One often heard of these bottles exploding, due to leaks or manufacturing faults. So, whenever he had to light his gas ring, he never failed to feel a certain amount of apprehension.

When the bottle was empty, it was hard work to get a new one. There was no point in telephoning to order another. Salim always had to go all the way to the retail store. The manager would always say: "Tomorrow." . But, as he knew all too well what "Tomorrow" meant in the East, Salim would ask him: "Sure?". And, with that typically Indian shake of the head, the other would respond: "Sure, sure!" Despite this promise, the heralded "Tomorrow" never came. Yet, as one depended on these people to get a new bottle, one had to bear their inertia patiently and even give them baksheesh, until, one fine day, the miracle occurred, and a young man appeared on a delivery rickshaw, carrying the much desired gas bottle.

Precarity of existence. Dalhousie.

From time to time, Salim would watch the fishermen on the beach, who, not far from him, were working in silence, repairing their torn nets or damage to their flimsy craft. Despite their extreme poverty, all these men were muscular and well built. When they took to the sea, one would see in the distance, distinct against the horizon, the single sail of these boats, which were not equipped with engines.

Their existence was full of uncertainty and danger. Given the fragility of their boats, they contented themselves with sailing close to the coastline, because, if the ocean were to become rough and capsize their skiffs, they would have to swim to shore and, because the distance that separated them from the beach was sometimes too great, it was not unusual to hear that some of them had been drowned. Thinking of the precarity of their existence, Salim wondered what became of their families when such a tragedy occurred.

During one of his journeys in the country's interior, he went to Dalhousie, a spot located on a mountain in the north of India. He spent around ten days there, during which he visited some Tibetan monasteries and met a number of Rinpoches[*].

He remembered with wonder having seen there some adolescents sitting on the ground outdoors, extremely concentrated, and who,

---

[*] Rinpoche, which means "Precious One", is an honorific bestowed upon Tibetan masters and emphasizes the value accorded to spiritual development in this culture.

without paying any attention to his presence, executed, with astonishingly steady hands, magnificent tankas. These paintings were, in fact, teachings for those who knew how to decipher them. Salim would have liked to ask them for the meaning, but, unfortunately, these young monks did not understand English.

The Tibetan monasteries were perched on top of impressively steep escarpments, the view from which was utterly spectacular. Their temples, as well as their dwellings, had been judiciously built on the south face of the mountain, so as to receive the maximum amount of sun. On the other hand, for a reason that escaped Salim, the Indians, perhaps because they were accustomed to protecting themselves from fierce heat, had strangely built their dwellings principally on the northern slope, where a glacial cold reigned. This was where he was to stay for the duration of his visit.

The comfort of this lodging was very basic. There were not even any toilets, but a simple bucket placed in a cubbyhole adjoining the bedroom, which an untouchable emptied and cleaned every morning. He entered by an exterior staircase and, unseen, discreetly removed the recipient which he brought back a few minutes later. Salim, desirous of knowing the unfortunate who was condemned to performing this humble chore, positioned himself outside one day, in a spot whence he could see the untouchable without being seen himself, so as not to disturb him. The person he saw arrive, shivering in the morning chill, was a pitiful old man with a body crippled by rheumatism, dressed in a simple, ragged shirt and extremely dirty pants. With a heavy heart, stricken with compassion for this unfortunate, Salim said to himself: "What if that was my father?... !" In the afternoon, when he left his lodgings to do some shopping, he saw the old man again; he was sitting against a tree, a little apart, near a square where a small market was being held. Salim browsed the stalls as quickly as possible, wanting to buy him a pullover and some pants. Unfortunately he could only find a small sweater, but it was better than nothing. When Salim approached him, the poverty stricken man, surprised and frightened, because, undoubtedly, he was unused to anyone paying attention to him, began, immediately, to back away. Salim persisted in advancing to give him the pullover. When, finally, the poor man understood that it was a present, he took it with a trembling hand, attempting a small, emotional smile of gratitude. During all this time, Salim continued to say to himself: "What if this man was my father?... What if it was my father?"

Salim, who bore the cold with difficulty, was anxious to leave Dalhousie to rediscover the heat of the plains. As soon as he had the chance, he went to the tourist office which dealt with rental cars, because he knew that it was always preferable to go through an official body. Once a price had been agreed, he returned to pack ready for the following day. On the road descending the mountain, he constantly marveled at the beauty of the countryside passing before his eyes. Every turn held a surprise for him, revealing magnificent rocky peaks, impressive precipices, and majestic trees. At other moments, waterfalls and small foaming torrents, whose waters were a marvelous blue-green color, caught his attention.

Despite the precaution that he had taken in agreeing in advance the price of the journey in Dalhousie, when the driver stopped at a sort of inn to have a cup of tea and rest, he suddenly demanded double the sum that had been fixed the day before, without which he refused to go any further. After having protested at length and seeing that the other remained obstinate, Salim had to resolve himself to telephoning the reservation office. He had a long and exhausting discussion with the clerk, who finally asked to speak to the recalcitrant driver. In the end, and with very bad grace, the driver agreed to continue the trip. However, on the way, despite Salim's strong disagreement, he picked up another man, in contravention of the arrangements made at the office, which was hardly reassuring.

It should be noted that in India, at this time, in taxis and rental vehicles, for fear of non-payers, the handles allowing the rear doors to be opened from the inside were broken and useless, which left the occupants with no possibility of getting out by their own means. The windows were also often stuck and so the customers found themselves at the driver's mercy. There were also worrying stories going around about travelers being knocked unconscious and left for dead in some deserted spot; this kind of misadventure happened particularly to people who had rented a vehicle without going through an official body.

The trains were not necessarily any safer. While Salim was traveling one day in Rajasthan, with his companion, he reserved what is called, in India, a "coupe", a small compartment for two people, the door of which was secured on the inside. Around ten men who had seen them enter the compartment, tried to break in. They disappeared upon coming into the first station where there were some armed police officers, whom Salim hailed from the window.

Just as with his previous treks, Salim returned to Madras tired and weakened by his customary intestinal problems. However, despite the difficulties encountered during these journeys, he took from them a great deal of stimulation in spiritual terms, because, everywhere, he was able to visit places impregnated with mysticism and to encounter people whose sole interest was the quest for the Absolute—even though their way of approaching it might not correspond to his needs.

Satya Saï Baba in Bangalore.

In Madras, Salim made the acquaintance of a pandit called Sundaram, who was a rather well-known Sanskritist. Sundaram knew Satya Saï Baba personally and suggested that Salim meet the famous guru in his main ashram in Bangalore.

Interested in the idea of seeing more closely this man who, because of his amazing powers of materialization, had acquired an extraordinary reputation throughout the country, Salim, glad of this opportunity, accepted willingly.

After a relatively short train journey, they arrived in Bangalore, a reasonably modern town, enjoying a fairly agreeable climate. With the help of the pandit, Salim obtained from the ashram leaders a small room in which he could, during his stay, cook on his electric hotplate. These precautions proved to be sensible when, the day after his arrival, the doctors at the centre announced over the loudspeaker that the mangoes, prepared by the cook, should not be eaten as several hundred people had suffered dysentery after eating this dish the night before.

The ashram was very spacious; it comprised a vast conference room able to hold several hundred people. As well as a great number of Indians, many Westerners were staying there. During the few days that he spent in Bangalore, Salim noticed that no meditation or yoga exercises were asked of the residents, who simply participated in daily tasks and came to listen to the lectures given by Satya Saï Baba and a few scholars.

Every day, a crowd of people visited the ashram to venerate Satya Saï Baba and receive his darshan. Hundreds, and even, on some occasions, two or three thousand people, had to be fed every day, which necessitated a fairly impressive level of organization. The master of the establishment had permanently by his side several devout people who took care of all the administration. The meals were served in the Indian manner, on banana leaves which were thrown away after use. Apart from what was necessary for the maintenance of the center, Satya Saï Baba used the large donations he received to do good around him, opening schools and hospitals for the most disadvantaged.

In a corner of the property, Salim saw a young elephant chained closely to a tree by one of his hind legs. He was fidgeting ceaselessly, moving his head and his shoulders in all directions, while, with his trunk, he occasionally picked up the food placed in front of him. Salim felt compassion for this poor animal, obliged to remain restrained in this way and confined to a space too restricted for him. From time to time, he was liberated from his chains, when Satya Saï Baba came to bring him a particular sweetmeat, which he seemed to very much appreciate. After a few moments, when his master left him to go back inside the main building, the elephant would follow him; it was touching to see him go continually from one side to the other, turning in front of the entrance, trying to see how to get in through the door which, of course, was too narrow for him.

The evening before his departure, Salim attended a lecture given by a pandit and, as he didn't know any of the Indian languages, he didn't understand a word—which must have been the case for the majority of Westerners who were there. At the end of the lecture, Satya Saï Baba, who was sitting a little apart, suddenly stood up, went towards the orator and, to everyone's surprise, materialized a gold chain which he put around the man's neck.

The next morning, to the surprise of Salim who, at that moment, was meditating, Satya Saï Baba, having learned from the pandit Sundaram that Salim was leaving that day, came to visit him, accompanied by some Indian disciples. Taking into account the number of visitors who flocked daily to the ashram, this personal visit was a privilege. During the ensuing conversation, translated by the pandit Sundaram, (Satya Saï Baba didn't speak English), he learned that Salim was constantly suffering from serious health problems; he then materialized some pills (which Salim took shortly afterwards, but which, he had to admit, had no effect) and presented him with five or six books containing an English translation of his lectures.

Suddenly, Salim became aware of a strange silence which descended upon him and enveloped him, despite the external noise which he continued to hear. It was as though time had suddenly stopped and he found himself plunged into a mysterious "eternal now". He felt then, as had already happened to him several times before, the inexplicable certainty of having already lived, in an enigmatic past, what he was living in the present. He felt himself in an extremely distant and inexpressible state when, suddenly he heard a voice which communicated something to him, directly into his mind, without the habitual recourse to speech. His mind had simultaneously formulated it in words and in English, which was the language that Salim knew best. The voice said to him: "There will come a day when you will be placed in a situation where you will not know what to do; don't worry, don't worry, don't worry, don't worry...".

When Salim became conscious once more of his environment, while still perceiving the voice, which repeated ever more quietly: "don't worry, don't worry...", he was at first convinced that someone had spoken aloud, but he quickly realized that he had heard this voice within himself. He remembered then experiences of the same kind which had already occurred to him while he was living in Paris. Moreover, a year or two later, he lived a similar phenomenon, while he was still in India.

Salim was convinced that these unusual experiences were due to a state of extreme inner openness, in which he found himself at certain moments, and were not attributable to the supernatural powers of someone else, because he was alone on the other occasions that such phenomena occurred.

When, subsequently, he was uprooted from India, which he loved so much, and found himself terribly alone in France, without knowing what to do, the words of this warning, enjoining him not to worry, often came back to his memory and sustained him.

Returning to Madras, Salim had the pleasant surprise of finding a letter from the Sacem, informing him of a new payment of royalties, this time not only coming from France, but also from Great Britain and from Canada. The few private recordings that he had made for French television, as well as the background music he had composed for a British company just before leaving Paris, were bearing fruit, providing him with the financial tranquility he needed to continue to live in India and undertake new travels.

Practical considerations.

Salim had the experience of his childhood in the East and, during the years that he lived in India, he was strict about taking a series of precautions that sometimes seemed excessive, if not exasperating, to some of Westerners that he had to mix with.

It is remarkable that, despite his extremely fragile health, he did not pick up any parasites in almost seven years spent in India. Such a result implied a discipline that he never slackened: no raw vegetables, disinfect all fruit before peeling it, systematically boil water, even for washing up, and keep all food in glass jars, because of the rats, the red cockroaches, or other disease-carrying insects. Many times, he saw Europeans, irritated by these precautions, obliged to undergo emergency repatriation on medical flights.

It is true that there are sometimes Westerners (Salim particularly remembered an Australian, pupil of a Theravada Buddhist monk, who had already been living in India for fourteen years when Salim met him in the Himalayas) who, surprisingly, are lucky enough to possess a natural immunity to all ordeals and who, without taking any precautionary measures, are practically never ill.

To the problems linked to the climate and the poverty of the country, were added risks due to a lack of scruples on the part of ignorant people. Scandals, even in the medical and pharmaceutical fields (such as a trafficked drug becoming a fatal poison) were, at that time, widespread in India. Most of the time, the people incriminated had not considered the consequences of their actions. In this vein, one of the Madras daily newspapers reported one day that a sumptuous wedding, bringing together a large number of guests, had resulted in nearly one hundred deaths and as many lifelong invalids, because the oil bought and used for the culinary preparations was engine oil.

During his travels in the interior of the country, Salim always carried a small pressure cooker, an electric hotplate and kettle, various nuts, white rice, yellow lentils, raisins (which he cooked with vegetables), ghee (clarified butter, to brown the vegetables), some mild spices, and some potassium permanganate to sterilize the fruit and vegetables that he bought along the way at each stage of his trek. These utensils and provisions accounted for a certain weight, which he had to accept encumbering himself with if he wanted, as far as possible, to protect himself and to protect his companion. The food was kept inside a light aluminum suitcase, bought in Paris, so as to keep the food safe from rodents—which one sometimes found even in hotels. As all his bags were secured with padlocks, even in hotel rooms, mercifully, he was never robbed. He nevertheless preferred to always carry his passport, his money, and his airline tickets on him.

The East may seem very romantic in films and documentaries, but the audience is often ignorant of the dangers and unpleasantness that prevail in these countries: illnesses of all kinds, dubious water, lack of doctors, lack of basic comfort, etc. Yet Salim did not experience existence in this country as difficult since, on the contrary, it was in the West that he felt foreign and isolated. He considered this part of the world as his real home and looked upon this country with love, but also with lucidity.

Living and dying in India.

Salim met in Madras, through a young French woman who had, for some days, followed a course of meditation under his supervision, a Theravada Buddhist monk of around sixty years of age, who invited Salim to come and drink a cup of tea with him. He was living, for the short duration of his stay, with some friends who lived at quite some distance from Besant Nagar.

Despite his habitual punctuality, on this occasion, Salim arrived very late for his meeting. In fact, on the way, in a spot at a little distance from any houses, an alarmed looking man stopped the taxi Salim was traveling in to beg him to agree to rush to the hospital an untouchable woman, who had just been knocked down by a car, which had immediately driven off. Salim immediately got out of the vehicle and got the injured woman into the back, along with the woman who was with her; then, promising him an extra payment, he got in beside the driver. The hospital was a very long way from the site of the accident and Salim, who turned his head from time to time to check on the condition of the poor blood-covered, trembling woman, was distressed without knowing what to do to help her. Upon their arrival at the hospital, he had her taken directly to a surgeon and, before leaving, placed a little money into the hands of the woman accompanying her. Still very moved, he thought how serious a problem it is in a country like India to rush a seriously injured person to the hospital when an accident of this kind occurs.

In such parts of the world, one sometimes witnesses certain situations that are so unexpected and moving it is impossible not to be shaken to the core of one's being and not to feel appalled. In this connection, Salim remembered that one day, while he was waiting in Calcutta for a train that was four hours late, he caught sight, at one end of the platform, of a poor skeletal untouchable, dying in his own feces. Hundreds of flies were circling around his glazed eyes, his half-open mouth, and his excrement. Salim saw that he was still breathing. Nevertheless, no-one paid him the slightest attention; it was as though he didn't even exist.

When Salim called out to a station employee and gestured to signal the presence of this unfortunate to him, the official, who apparently knew a little English, responded to him with incredible insouciance: "Oh!... that? There's a truck that will come and pick him up tomorrow morning, when he's dead"—as though it was a question of an unimportant object and the simple promise of its removal should reassure Salim. Salim learned that, in fact, poverty in Calcutta was such, and the number of unfortunates living and dying on the sidewalks so high, that, every morning, a truck drove around the city with the task of picking up the bodies that it found on its route.

Dreadfully moved and incapable of forgetting the sight of this man living his final moments on that platform, surrounded by general indifference, Salim could not help exclaiming within himself: "Oh, fabulous India, horrifying India!"

Paradoxically, he said to himself that, as Westerners do not encounter death on their streets, they always lack, to their detriment, a certain regard for life which they take as something due to them, which they find it normal to pass in comfort and abundance, and which should even last forever. Because, in the West, death is concealed, it ends up being considered as an abnormality which it is always possible to avoid. Surprisingly, the majority of people forget the appointment they have made with death, a fateful meeting that awaits them from the very moment of their birth.

Through his spiritual experiences and the understanding that he drew from them, Salim knew the importance of the final thoughts that occupy the mind of a dying person in determining the state to which he will gravitate after having quit his corporeal envelope. He saw, with compassion, that this poor untouchable had no-one at his side, at that critical instant, to help him turn his mind to thoughts of a spiritual order. Because of the difficulties that he had doubtless suffered during his whole existence, his daily subsistence would have become his only interest and a paramount demand which would not have left him any possibility of dedicating himself to higher aspirations.

Salim said to himself that Westerners who generally enjoy material security that would be unimaginable to this poor pariah, do not know how to use it to dedicate themselves, as they should, to a spiritual quest, which would constitute the only thing of worth in their existence, but, on the contrary, they worry only about their physical health and forever accumulate more material possessions, which they will, in any case, have to abandon when death stands before them, and they will find themselves naked and bare at that ineluctable moment when they must leave alone for a world which, as long as they remain what they ordinarily are, will be forever incomprehensible to them.

Story of a Theravada monk.

On his arrival, Salim told the monk the reason for his lateness and the monk showed, with sympathy, an immediate understanding. As they were alone, the monk, who visibly wished to confide in Salim, told him how, at the age of thirty, at which time he was a prosperous trader in Bombay, he was suddenly seized by an irrepressible desire to become a Buddhist monk. Without losing any time, he distributed all his possessions equally so that his family members would lack nothing, then he left, on foot, with nothing, for Burma, where there was a famous master of the Theravada school whom he had heard of. After a journey of many months, over the course of which he had begged for his food, confronted numerous dangers, and had fallen ill many times, he finally arrived, exhausted, at his destination. When, at long last, he reached the monastery, he prostrated himself at the feet of the master, asking to be accepted as a disciple. However, for some incomprehensible reason, the master refused his request and even firmly enjoined him to return to his home. The man explained at length all that he had left behind him in India and that he now had nothing, that he had undertaken a long and difficult journey and that he was in a condition of extreme fatigue. However, although he continued thus to plead his cause, his interlocutor would not allow himself to be swayed.

The monk explained to Salim the extent to which he was distraught at this unexpected welcome; he insisted, obstinately supplicating the master to at least permit him to stay at the monastery. It was only with a great deal of condescension that the master finally responded to him: "Very well, you can stay here, but it will be only as a servant; you will sweep my room, clean the toilets, wash my clothes, and cook for me, and that will be all!"

The man, happy to be able to stay within the master's circle, accepted without hesitation. Day after day, he saw him teaching the members of the monastery, without ever understanding why the master not only refused to teach him anything at all relating to the spiritual domain, but he would not even permit him to approach the others or to meditate with them. Despite his repeated requests, the master remained intractable, declaring that, if the man was not happy, he had only to leave.

In the end, he resigned himself to serving the master without expecting any more from him, while he saw, with sadness, the master go to the others to watch over their meditation and to guide them.

Fifteen years had passed in this way, when, one day, after having lost all hope of ever being accepted as a disciple by this master whom he admired so much, the master suddenly called him and, to his astonishment, declared: "That will do now; from now on, you will leave all these tasks and you will dedicate yourself wholly to meditation and to the teachings that I will impart to you". Subsequently, he became the main disciple of this master towards whom he felt a boundless gratitude for the manner in which he had, in fact, guided him throughout all this time without him having understood, putting, day after day, his faith and his tenacity to the test.

This story bears striking similarities to that of Milarepa, the famous Tibetan ascetic and mystic, who was also severely tested by his master Marpa before the latter would consent to take him as a disciple. However, Milarepa lived in Tibet in the twelfth century, whereas the story of the monk is contemporary. He told Salim that, with people who came to see him, he never used such methods, necessitating on the part of the disciple a profound respect for the master and for what he was trying to attain.

Dharamsala.

Before leaving for Paris, Salim had heard a great deal about Dharamsala, a town situated in the north of India, where the Dalai Lama and his compatriots had taken refuge after the invasion of their country by the Chinese.

Without knowing the reason, he had always felt mysteriously attracted by this region. Furthermore, the word Himalaya rang in his ears like a call that he was, one day, going to have to answer. As usual, he carefully packed his bags and his food provisions, then he took a flight to New Delhi. He then had to take a train as far as Pathankot, at the foot of the mountain range, and, finally, a bus to go up to Dharamsala.

The ascent proved trying; Salim found the driver's style abrupt and even, occasionally, very dangerous. Two or three times, on hairpin bends, he glimpsed in the distance, down below, carcasses of buses and cars which had come off the road to crash down into the ravines. As he was coming to the end of his journey, Salim had his breath taken away by the discovery of the vertiginous peaks of the snow-covered massifs which stood out against an intense blue sky, inspiring him with reverential wonder. He understood why the anchorites always preferred to live away from the world, among the inviolate heights, to practice their meditation.

When the bus arrived at its destination, Salim got off to collect his bags. The view of an enormous snowy peak emerging from behind the mountain he was standing on, plunged him, briefly, into one of those enigmatic states that he had already experienced many times before and, in a fraction of a second, his whole being was flooded with a mysterious silence, in the course of which, he felt the absolute certainty that the movement he had just made to take his suitcase and the emotion that he felt on seeing the peak standing before him, had already taken place in an inexplicable past. He stood transfixed for a moment and, as he did every time this impression seized him, he asked himself: "When, but when, have I lived this same situation, made this same movement and felt this same feeling, as this is the first time in my life that I have been here?"

He remained, as he did every time, perplexed in the face of such a question, trying to understand the origin of these memories and, above all, what aspect of himself was remembering them.

On this subject, Salim told me that, in certain circumstances, the experiences that he had lived were so powerful, so impressive and imbued with mystery, that they were practically unbearable. Sometimes, an indescribable feeling of an eternal 'nowness' dominated these experiences, arousing in him the vivid sense that everything is, was, and will be forever. He added that consciousness in a human being and in the Universe could never be explained in a tangible way; after the dissolution of matter, consciousness continues to subsist, with its memories and its unfathomable experiences that the manifest world can neither grasp nor apprehend.

As Salim felt very tired, he went into the first hotel he could find near the bus stop. The room was not very clean and, moreover, it was very cold. All night long, he heard a rat constantly and at full speed going up and down a long dirty curtain at the other end of the room. But the rodent had chosen a bad time to try to impress its public with its acrobatic talents, as Salim was not at all in the mood to give it the admiring attention that it doubtless merited. So, to show its displeasure, it took its revenge by, from time to time, attacking with its teeth the aluminum case holding the precious provisions necessary for Salim's stay in Dharamsala.

The following morning, the first thing that Salim did was to change his hotel. After having performed his ablutions with hot water from the bucket that had been brought to him, he began to meditate. He then went out to see if he could find some eggs, fruit, and vegetables to buy.

Dharamsala is divided into three parts. The lower part of the mountain is principally peopled by Indians who have difficulty bearing the cold that reigns higher up. The median zone, where Salim was staying, is occupied by Tibetans. As for the highest part, it is only inhabited by a few hermits, isolated from the world.

On his route, Salim was surprised and moved when crossing the path of some elderly people who were incessantly repeating the famous mantra "Om Mani Padme Hum", while continually turning small prayer wheels that they held in their hands. There were also, mounted on plinths against the walls of some houses, large prayer wheels that passers by set in motion with a movement of their hands. The majority of the Tibetans were dressed in dark red outfits and, among them, were a number of monks. The dwellings were very simple and in the Tibetan style. What struck Salim the most, was that, everywhere he went, he encountered an atmosphere evoking the Sacred.

After having bought the fruit and vegetables that he had succeeded in finding that day, he went straight back to his hotel to put them in his room. Then, having asked the way of the hotel manager, he set out with the aim of going to see the Dalai Lama's palace and visiting the surrounding temples.

There was no road at that time, just some narrow trails. The Tibetan pontiff's palace was some distance from the spot where Salim was staying and at a much higher altitude. After a long walk, he finally came to a sort of square where stood the Dalai Lama's dwelling. It was an imposing building, constructed in the Tibetan style. A little further on was a magnificent temple, inside which a religious ceremony was taking place; it was being celebrated by monks reciting sacred texts accompanied by sounding of gongs, by tinkling of bells, and by rhythms beaten on wooden drums.

While Hindus often make access to their sanctuaries difficult for Westerners, whom they consider to be untouchables, the Tibetan Buddhists showed no reticence on Salim's entrance into their temple; quite the contrary, he was even greeted with looks and smiles, which made him feel that he was welcome.

So as not to disturb anyone, he stayed a little apart, tranquilly sitting in a state of profound contemplation, immersing himself in the devotional atmosphere that was emanating from the place, while the statues of Buddha, which were glowing in the faint light of butter lamps placed before them, invoked in his being mysterious and elusive memories. He felt like he belonged to this place and the possibility of a return to the West seemed to him like a veritable exile.

Barely an hour later, he heard some hustle and bustle outside; suddenly, another group of monks, including the Dalai Lama in person, entered the temple. Salim was impressed by the deference shown by everyone to the Dalai Lama, bowing in veneration as he passed. Such devotional respect, so deep and sincere, elevates those who carry it within them.

Despite it being the most favorable season to visit Dharamsala, and despite it being quite warm in the sun and the sky being a constant blue, scattered with a few small clouds, it was, nevertheless, quite cold in the shade and even more so in his unheated room when Salim got back to his hotel later in the evening.

The next day, while he was walking in the neighborhood, looking for more Tibetan temples, he heard about a religious performance which was to take place two days later and last a whole day. On the day in question, he went to the spot early in the morning in order to reserve a place that would allow him to miss nothing of the spectacle. He had just settled himself when he saw a crowd of other spectators, all Tibetan, beginning to gather around the stage which was built in a semi-circle.

After what seemed to him to be a long wait, suddenly, the striking tones of immense horns and gongs broke out; the performance, picturesque and colorful, had just begun. The actors, men and women were all dressed in colorful costumes; some wore enormous, terrifying masks of dragon and Asura effigies.* Women were dancing performing graceful movements to emphasize certain developments in the action; their arms were covered with very long sleeves, in the Chinese style. A speaker intoned a text, supported by a musical formation whose members were playing conch shells, cymbals, Tibetan oboes, small flutes, small bells, and string instruments. From time to time, especially when they were accompanied by the demons and Asuras, the musicians succeeded in producing a very impressive noise by simultaneously hitting several gongs of various types, thus creating an atmosphere of reverential awe.

The story, according to what Salim, who didn't understand the language, could make of it, was that of Padmasambhava battling against evil entities who were opposed to the establishment of the Buddhist doctrine in Tibet. The decor was suggested by very simple accessories, appealing to the audience's imagination.

---

* Demonic gods.

Although already knowing the plot playing out before them, the spectators were no less absorbed and watched the drama with unflagging attention. They followed every gesture, every word, and every incident with intensity. The assembly watched in silence with an interest that did not, at any point, wane, although the performance went on until the evening.

In a particular place in the room, while a sung passage with a slight resemblance to Chinese music had just begun, with voices recalling the immense, faraway spaces surrounding the snowy mountains, Salim felt unexpectedly moved to the point where, without being able to explain why, tears ran down his cheeks. These specific musical tones, illustrating the destiny of these gods and these demons had caused mysterious silent memories to arise within him.

Every time it seemed to him that he had impressions linked to previous existences, these faded so quickly that afterwards they left only very vague and uncertain recollections. He retained only a feeling of something indefinable which never managed to take form in his mind.

He stayed in Dharamsala for a week before returning to Madras.

Is the Universe within oneself?

Thanks to the ever more subtle struggle that he pursued to remain permanently in a state of particular presence to himself, Salim succeeded in experiencing the strange feeling of being non implicated interiorly and, consequently of being "apart" from the manifestations unfolding before him.

He finally discovered, through a direct insight—and in a way that filled him with wonder and with reverential awe—that all that presented itself to his gaze was not outside of him, but, in some way, ordinarily impossible to conceive, within him; moreover, this strange observation extended to the whole Universe. This extraordinary experience, so unexpected, left such a strong impression on his feelings and his being that he could no longer accept relying so passively as he had in the past on what his sensory organs communicated to him.

Nevertheless, despite the privilege that had been accorded him to go through an experience as elevated as it was unusual, by way of which he had been able to access knowledge of an entirely different order than that which related to the world of the senses, he noted, with regret that, despite his efforts, because of the forces of habit and of gravity, he could not keep himself in this state which was, as yet, unfamiliar to him, and that, before realizing what had happened to him, Creation was once again, as before, outside of him.

Amritsar. Haridwar.

Salim, who had often heard about the beauty of the Sikh sanctuary of Amritsar, as well as that of Haridwar—famous for its countless temples and where the great Kumbh Mela gathers every twelve years[*]— was glad to visit these places, thereby escaping the intense heat of the month of May which pervaded Madras for the four or five weeks preceding the monsoon. He had an additional reason for going to Haridwar, because this journey offered him the opportunity of seeing Indira Devi again, having learned that she would be spending the month there.

His first stop was Amritsar. Despite the extraordinary beauty of its famous golden temple with its admirable architecture, Salim was struck, on seeing it, with an inexplicable feeling of unease, which did not leave him for the twenty-four hours that he stayed in the town. Despite all his attempts to overcome it, he could not rid himself of the feeling that some invisible menace, which he was incapable of defining, was hanging over the place; it was as though some unfathomable past was continually trying to clear a path to infiltrate the present. He had the constant feeling that an elusive memory was continually trying to form in his mind, without success. Unable to comprehend the reason for feeling this unrest and after having passed a very bad night, he was impatient and even glad to leave the place the following day.

---

[*] This religious event, which takes place every three years, swells to a greater size every twelve years.

He wondered once more: "What is time? Is it possible that the
past and the future exist somewhere in another dimension, ordinarily
inaccessible, and that it is only in exceptional circumstances, when
one finds oneself in a state of particular receptiveness, that inexplicable
memories or mysterious portents can find the conditions necessary
for their manifestation?"

He was very glad of the opportunity that presented itself of seeing
Indira Devi again and he awaited this reunion with impatience. He
had no-one in whom to confide and he hoped to be able to speak to
her privately for a moment in order to tell her about his questioning
and about some of the mystic experiences he had had and by which
he was perplexed.

On his arrival at Haridwar, he went to a sort of guest house to
reserve a room. As the room was not yet free, he entrusted his bags to
the manager and went immediately to visit Indira Devi in the large
house that she had rented on the other side of the river.

He felt great joy upon once again seeing the holy woman, the venerable Dilip Kumar Roy, Shri Kanta, and the fifteen or so members of
the ashram, mainly women, who had accompanied her from Poona.
Indira Devi welcomed Salim with her characteristic delightful smile.
Such love and goodness emanated from her person that he felt moved.
When she learned that he was waiting for his room in the nearby guest
house to be ready, she immediately suggested that he should, if he
wished, move into their dwelling, where there were some free rooms,
even offering him use of the kitchen to prepare his meals, because she
knew that he could not eat the extremely spicy food that was prepared
for her and the other ashramites. He was particularly glad of this
unexpected chance to be able to stay at her side and thought that, in
this way, it would be easier for him to find an opportunity for a tête-
à-tête with her about the things that had been hanging over him for
so long.

The vast dwelling was located on an island around which the river
separated into two branches which came back together downstream.

Opposite, stood a long line of temples. With the exception of some sannyasins who maintained them, there was practically no-one there. Salim thought that this was an ideal spot for his spiritual practices. Indeed, apart from his meditation in his room or sometimes outside, on the banks of the river, in a spot where he could not be seen, he was able to undertake his concentration exercises while walking within this area which perfectly suited his work. Moreover, the pleasant climate and the splendid view were favorable to sustained spiritual efforts.

In the mornings, the members of the household would sing bhajans; for the rest of the morning, the women who took care of Indira Devi busied themselves with household tasks and prepared lunch. Salim did his own cooking, but ate with the group. After lunch, Indira Devi, sitting at the water's edge, surrounded by the venerable Dadaji and a few other people, would recount anecdotes, always relating to spirituality. Sometimes, everyone would stroll along the bank until it was time for dinner. Salim would spend some time

Salim with Dilip Kumar Roy in Haridwar

in their company, then leave to meditate and to practice his various spiritual exercises which occupied a good part of the day.

By the pensive way Salim looked at her from time to time, Indira Devi must have felt that he was preoccupied by some problem; thus, when there came a moment when, by chance, she was alone and he asked to speak to her, she immediately arranged things so that they would not be disturbed. He finally had the opportunity to confide in someone whom he respected and who showed herself attentive and

Indira Devi and Dilip Kumar Roy in Haridwar

receptive towards him. He spoke to her at length, particularly about the experiences relating to time and to the future that he had had on various occasions, both in France and in India, but also other disturbing phenomena which sometimes occurred during his meditation (and which he preferred not to speak of in his books, for fear that his readers would be tempted to seek them out), as well as the mysterious and unusual dreams that he occasionally had.

She listened to him, saying nothing, with a very different attitude to that which she habitually adopted; she, who, ordinarily, was so cheerful and smiling, had become, on this occasion, very serious, her eyes cast down towards the ground, attentively listening to and considering every word he uttered. During the long silence that followed, while Salim was waiting for her to provide him with some enlightenment on the singular facts that he had just described to her, she lifted her head and gave him a look both serious and filled with compassion and tenderness. Finally, speaking very slowly, in a low voice, she said to him: "It is the fate of some people to suffer for that which they have been permitted to come into contact with and because of which they will remain alone and isolated for all of their lives, in a world which is not theirs".

This was certainly not the kind of response that Salim had hoped to receive, but, instead of offering him just any explanation, she had the honesty to let him know that she could not decipher the enigmas which he submitted to her.

Rishikesh.

As the town of Rishikesh is just a few hours away from Haridwar, Salim decided to go there and, in particular, to visit the ashram of Shivananda, who had, by then, been no longer of this world for some years. One morning, therefore, he rented a car for the journey (with a driver, as was usual in India) and he set out, without forgetting to take the precaution of taking with him a bottle of boiled water and some fruit. On the way, the vehicle suddenly had to avoid a dead buffalo, lying in the middle of the road. A group of vultures were perched on the body, but without eating it, apparently waiting for something. Salim, intrigued by their behavior, asked the driver, who spoke a few words of English, if he knew the reason for it. The driver gave him to understand that the rule among the species was that they should wait for the leader to begin to eat first.

Having arrived in Rishikesh, the beauty of the landscape that greeted him compensated Salim for the nausea that had inevitably afflicted him during the whole journey. On the banks of the Ganges, which was still turbulent at this point, he caught sight of some tiny huts, made graciously available to any who wished to stay in them for a while in order to dedicate themselves to meditation. The few people who he saw staying there were mainly adherents of "japa", a practice consisting of tirelessly repeating a mantra, the name of Ram or of another divinity.

The river could be crossed by a bridge, accessible by some steps, and a ferry, always heaving with passengers, at risk of sinking into the turbulent waters. On the other bank, on top of a small hill above the river, was the ashram of Shivananda. There was still a certain amount of activity, but the animator was no longer there and Salim saw nothing to interest him.

As one of the occupants of the cabins, with whom he had struck up a conversation, had told him of the existence of a hermit or guru living not far from there, in a spot difficult to access, Salim, intrigued, decided to go and visit him. On the way, he bought some fruit to give as an offering and set off to find the holy man, following the instructions he had been given.

After a while, the path progressively narrowed, becoming no more than a narrow, dusty track, between the rock face and the torrent below. Salim had to gather all his courage to be able to traverse this dangerous passage, pressing himself against the rock face and not daring to look down, especially since he was sensitive to vertigo. As his feet tended to slip on this slightly sloping strip of ground, he feared falling into the water and drowning, as he could not swim. He was relieved to reach more solid ground, where he rested for a moment before continuing on his way. He finally reached the spot where the so called hermit lived. He found a very fat Indian, surrounded by a dozen women, all Westerners. There may also have been men in his entourage, but Salim did not see any. He placed his offering before the guru, who regarded him with a certain amount of suspicion. As the master did not speak English, Salim asked one of his disciples what their sadhana consisted of: did they practice hatha yoga, meditation, japa, or some other technique? The woman replied, in a distinct American accent: "Here you must do nothing, only stay at his side and receive his vibration, which transports you". Such a naive affirmation proved sufficient for Salim, who immediately took his leave to confront once again the escarpment that he had to traverse in order to get back to the car.

On the way back, he saw again the scavengers still perched on the buffalo carcass, but, since the morning, they had completely stripped it. The smell emanating from the bones exposed to the sun was appalling. A few crushed vultures were lying here and there, as, strangely, these birds did not seem to understand the danger that cars represented to them and did not move when a vehicle approached.

When Salim returned to Indira Devi in the evening, she welcomed him with the quizzical smile she wore when she wanted to tease him, as though to say: "Well, what did you find over there? Haven't you learned your lesson yet?" Salim, who thought he had understood her unasked question, replied aloud: "I have already learned my lesson; I found nothing but some vultures eating a buffalo". With a graceful movement, she turned her head with a small amused laugh.

As the town of Dehradun was not very far away, Salim decided to go there to visit a Tibetan center located a little way outside the town. He saw nothing but some lamas and a rather voluminous library, which was of no use to him, as he never read.

Apart from these few excursions, he stayed, most of the time, in Haridwar, making the most of conditions that were particularly favorable to his spiritual practices. Sometimes, when he went out to undertake a concentration exercise outdoors, he felt Indira Devi's eyes on him, as she watched him from a window.

Upon his return to Madras, he thought again of what the holy woman had said, and he experienced, at one and the same time, a feeling of peacefulness and the impression of being more alone than ever. Some of his spiritual experiences had brought him a knowledge of the world that was completely different from that transmitted by his sensory organs. His meditation allowed him to access non spatio-temporal dimensions, through which he understood the interaction and interdependence of the Universe and of life at a level of complexity which remains ordinarily incomprehensible. At certain moments, he could directly feel the suffering of plants which human beings must, nevertheless, eat in order to survive. At other times, he reached states of such an elevated and mysterious mystic order that he always felt the impossibility of being able to tell anyone about them. However, he never sought these phenomena.

What was most important and the essence of a practice for him, was to access, by a tenacious effort of concentration, another state of consciousness that everyone carries within them, to recognize it, and to try, by all means, not to lose it—a state of consciousness of the greatest subtleness accompanied by a completely different feeling of oneself in a continually renewed "nowness."

He had realized that it is only in this unusual state that the human being can hope to liberate himself from his dependence on external stimulation to experience the sensation of his existence.

This is the reason that, although he recognized the value of the elevation one could feel in contact with some people who were really worthy of interest, he could not accept a passive approach where seekers imagined all would be bestowed upon them by way of a simple darshan. He remembered that the Buddha had struggled for long years to attain the supreme goal—"supreme goal which," he said to himself, "many speak of in India... but how many achieve it?..."

Nepal. Thubten Yeshe.

Apart from the beauty of the landscape, the visit to the ancient temples in the valley, and his encounter with a Tibetan lama, the week that Salim spent in Nepal offered little of interest to him.

Kathmandu is situated at the confluence of two rivers, on a plateau surrounded by high mountains. It is impossible not to feel moved and pervaded by a feeling of wonder in the face of the majestic peaks of the Tibetan Himalayas, visible in the distance from the Nepalese capital.

Salim was enormously touched by the kindness and helpfulness of the Nepalese. However, the hygiene conditions seemed even worse than in India; in the markets, flies swarmed to such an extent that, on some stalls, the fruit was completely covered with them.

After having visited the town and its temples, Salim went to a place six kilometers from Kathmandu, Patan, the age-old royal capital, where the impressive architecture of its ancient sanctuaries did not fail to dazzle him. He learned that the Chinese and the Japanese were inspired by these Nepalese roofs with their curved extremities, which are found all over Asia.

From a spiritual point of view, Salim only saw the external aspect of the Hindu religion, with its rites, its superstitions, and its blind beliefs.

Thupten Yesche

He happened to be on the spot in Kathmandu when more than three hundred buffalo had their throats slit in a day to satisfy the blood thirst of Kali, the Hindu divinity. He was shocked to see these poor creatures writhing in agony for at least fifteen minutes, while the blood ran from their slit throats like a scarlet stream. When he endeavored to make the person leading the "ceremony" understand the horror of such a massacre, the man responded with anger: "You are an ignorant, it's a ritual, it's a ritual!" This same type of cruel practice took place in India as well. In her travel journal, Alexandra David-Neel recounts that when she was in India, so many animal sacrifices had been carried out that she walked through a pool of blood that came up to her ankle.

Salim went, one day, to a Tibetan center, some eight kilometers from the capital, where he met Thubten Yeshe, a lama whose appearance was at once imposing and cheerful.

As always, the Tibetans had chosen an elevated site, offering a magnificent view. Strangely, apart from the lama and one or two monks, Salim saw only Westerners there. The master was a serious man, demanding a strict practice of meditation. Salim felt a great deal of respect for him and retained good memories of that place.

Both on entry to and exit from the country, Salim, who, as was his habit, had made up his provisions for the journey, had to deal with the tenacious curiosity of the customs officials, who did not understand why he kept food in his suitcase and insisted on knowing if it was for commercial purposes. He encountered great difficulty in getting them to acknowledge that the supplies were only meant for his personal consumption. While he was still arguing with them, he saw a Westerner in the clutches of these obstinate officials who wanted to cut the bellows of his accordion to check that there was nothing inside. Salim left without knowing how this story ended for the tourist musician.

Krishnamurti.

Back in Madras, Salim had the opportunity of attending a public lecture given by the famous Krishnamurti. As this was someone he had heard a lot about, he went with interest.

A large crowd had come, mainly made up of Indians, but also some Westerners. A quiver of expectation went through the room when Krishnamurti appeared and climbed slowly, with (it appeared to Salim) difficulty, onto the platform. He was an old man, with white hair, who seemed tense and extremely tired; without doubt, something exceptional emanated from his person. As soon as he began to speak, he became surprisingly animated and full of strength. It was impossible not to feel admiration for this man and his way of looking at life; moreover, he expressed himself with remarkable intellectual ease. The audience was generally quite attentive, but, every time he affirmed that the assistance of a guru was not necessary and neither was a Yoga discipline nor any meditation practice, some Indians protested loudly and heckled him. Indignant disciples took these detractors aside, which only amplified the hubbub in which the orator was imperturbably continuing his speech, only his gestures, marked by nervousness, betrayed his reaction.

Salim returned to listen to some other lectures, the content of which seemed to him to be intellectual, mainly dealing with psychological type questions and not leading to any practical directive or method.

When, later, Salim received pupils in Paris and in Belgium, it often occurred that people who came to see him were surprised by how demanding he was and his insistence on the necessity of making efforts during concentration exercises and meditation. Having read Krishnamurti, they thought they would be able to gain a sudden, or at the very least, rapid illumination, without having to make the efforts that Salim demanded of them.

So, Salim had to explain to them that what may have been possible for Krishnamurti, whose level of being was probably very elevated, was not possible for the majority of seekers, and that, for them, if they wanted to succeed in knowing a true spiritual experience, they would have to accept committing to assiduous concentration practice by way of various specific exercises, as well as subjecting themselves to strict meditation—without neglecting the indispensable necessity of knowing the various undesirable tendencies within them which barred their route and which were not necessarily identical from one person to the next.

Yercaud.

Just before the monsoon breaks, the May heat in Madras reaches its maximum extremes. The climatic conditions are much harder to bear than in Poona, which is at a higher altitude. The first year, Salim, unaware of how high the temperature could climb, stayed in Besant Nagar; despite his being used to scorching heat, he occasionally had the impression that "his blood was boiling in his head", and this was while he was in the shade, in his apartment. He couldn't help thinking with compassion of the poor Indians who were obliged to work in this implacable heat in order to earn their meager living; it was not unusual to hear of workers dropping dead due to having spent too long in such a furnace.

In the following years, he arranged to spend this time of year in cooler places. Thus it was that, in 1973, he went to Yercaud, a few hours by car from Madras, a green and mountainous place where he had the leisure of going for long walks. He was staying in a bungalow that some acquaintances from Pondicherry had lent him for the month.

As was always his habit, Salim would get up very early in the morning to meditate and to carry out his hatha yoga poses; he would then go out for a long walk while pursuing various concentration exercises. After having walked for a while, he arrived at an impressive sheer drop, overhanging a vast area. The contrast between the dryness of the plain, stretching as far as the eye could see, and the abundant exotic vegetation of the mountain was very striking.

Nowhere in the world had Salim heard birds singing in such a manner to greet the sunrise; it was an unforgettable symphony to his musician's ears, an ode to the glory of the sunlight which began to bathe all the surrounding countryside, announcing the rebirth of the day.

In this region, the approach of dusk was of a dreamlike splendor— especially when the reddening disc of our star was rapidly disappearing below the horizon which had taken on a fleeting blue-green tint.

Shortly after his arrival, while he was taking a new route on his daily walk, he was surprised to find, along his path, an old Christian monastery. Wanting to see if it was still inhabited, he took the initiative of entering. He met just one monk, an Indian Carmelite, very sincere, with whom he soon became friends. The religious man confessed to Salim that he suffered in his solitude, complaining that his superior had ordained that he should stay there so that the monastery would not remain unoccupied. During the conversation, he told his visitor that, not far away, there lived an extremely poor Indian family whose father only managed, with difficulty, to find a little irregular work here and there. He explained to Salim that he didn't know what to do to help these unfortunates, especially the twelve children, who never had enough to eat.

When he returned to his bungalow, Salim could not stop thinking of what the monk had told him about this family in need. There were so many similar cases in India! What could he do?

When, later in the day, he went to do some shopping, he noticed that the old caretaker, who looked after his bungalow and who lived in a small hut opposite, had a dog. The poor animal was extremely thin and his eyes were runny. No-one worried about him; furthermore, in such a remote spot, there was doubtless no possibility of getting treatment for him.

Once at the market, Salim began by buying some eggs; it was then that, suddenly, an idea came to him for helping the people the Carmelite had told him about. He also bought oatmeal (which couldn't be found in Besant Nagar), thinking that this would make a pleasant change from rice, which was the basis of his diet. He also bought milk and, thinking of the dog, made a few extra purchases, deciding to give him something to eat every day.

On his way back, Salim hurried to find the monk again, so as to tell him about his plan to help the family, with whom he had been continually preoccupied. He took from his royalties the sum of three hundred rupees, which, at the time and in that area, represented an appreciable nest egg, which he gave to the Carmelite, asking him not to give this money to the family's father, but rather to buy him around forty hens and some strong wire mesh to build a hen run so as to protect the poultry from foxes and other predators. Some of the eggs could be sold to the small hotels in the area as well as the local stores, and the rest could go towards increasing the number of laying hens. The monk, for whom these three hundred rupees were a gift from heaven, lost no time in purchasing the necessary items and taking them to the family. The poor man wished to immediately thank his benefactor, but Salim, who wanted to spare him any obligation, and particularly the worry of finding some sort of offering, refused this meeting. When he went back to Madras a few weeks later, he learned from a letter sent to him by the monk that his plan had worked wonderfully and that the family was now much better off. He also received a photograph of the parents surrounded by the twelve children that remained to them of the fourteen that the poor woman had carried.

Blind beliefs.

Since the first day of his arrival in Yercaud, at the end of every morning, Salim was surprised to hear, from his bungalow, playing at full volume, an old Western syncopated refrain, possibly dating from the nineteen thirties, played on the saxophone, accompanied by a sort of jazz orchestra. The same piece, which lasted around four or five minutes, was replayed, almost without interruption, for half an hour or more. Most intrigued, he made inquiries about the origin of this strange cacophony. What a surprise he had in discovering that it came from a Catholic convent located nearby. From a high point, he could see, by leaning over the rocks, the yard of the convent, in which some Indian nuns were busy taking a class of around twenty little girls in uniform who were doing gymnastics to this unexpected accompaniment. The mother superior, who was a Westerner, was there too, and Salim thought that he would like to meet this woman for a simple exchange of a spiritual nature.

One afternoon, therefore, he went to the convent, asking to speak to her. She welcomed him politely, offering him a cup of tea and some local sweetmeats. She was an Irish woman who had been living in India for many years. During the ensuing conversation, as soon as there was any mention of Hinduism or, especially, of Buddhism, she became suddenly hostile and always harked back to the same phrase: "Believe in Jesus and you will be saved!" Both she and the Indian nuns who were present at this interview, expressed an obstinate refusal towards any other doctrine than her own.

Salim could not help thinking that there were so many people in the world who blindly believed in Jesus, without that having been able to prevent the unleashing of terrible wars between Christian populations or even hatred between different branches of Christianity. He said to himself: "Belief... what belief? A blind and passive belief, whether in Jesus, in Shiva, or in any other divinity, cannot help anyone; only direct knowledge of the Sublime can bring human beings together in such a way that they realize they all issue from the same Divine Source".

And he could not help thinking of the words of the Buddha who said:

"Do not go upon what has been acquired by repeated hearing;
nor upon tradition;
nor upon rumor;
nor upon what is in a scripture;
nor upon surmise;
nor upon an axiom;
nor upon specious reasoning;
nor upon a bias towards a notion that has been pondered over;
nor upon another's seeming ability;
nor upon the consideration, 'The monk is our teacher.'
"Kalamas, when you yourselves know: "These things are bad; these things are blamable; these things are censured by the wise; undertaken and observed, these things lead to harm and ill," abandon them.' "
"Kalamas, when you yourselves know: 'These things are good; these things are not blamable; these things are praised by the wise; undertaken and observed, these things lead to benefit and happiness', enter on and abide in them. " (Kalama sutra)

Karmic chain of causes and effects.

As Salim had taken the initiative of regularly feeding his Indian neighbor's dog, the animal had quickly become attached to him. It was a very affectionate, but very timid animal, which never barked. It followed Salim closely, without making any noise, every time he went out on his daily walks.

One morning, when he was setting out to undertake his concentration exercises outdoors, the dog followed him as usual. Suddenly, the dog stood in front of him, placing its paws against his legs and preventing him from continuing. Salim, not understanding this behavior, tried to go around the dog, but the animal turned with him, always making itself an obstacle to his progress. Surprised by this attitude, Salim was thinking that the dog wanted to play when, suddenly, upon lifting his head, he was shocked to see, three or four meters in front of him, an enormous snake, half hidden in the foliage, which he would inevitably have collided with had the dog, who had sensed the presence of the reptile, not dissuaded him from advancing. Furthermore, as soon as Salim turned around and went back in the other direction, the dog tranquilly took up its place behind him as usual.

Salim, very grateful, said to himself that the action he had taken in feeding this animal, had proved to be a striking illustration of the karmic chain of causes and effects and that, on that day, the animal had, in all probability, saved his life. He also thought of that other dog, injured by a car, that he had taken care of in Poona some years before; on that occasion too, he had seen in action the process of karma, because it was through taking on this responsibility that he had had the opportunity of meeting Mr Dady.

New health problems.

The innovation that Salim had introduced to his culinary habits in replacing the rice with oatmeal had disastrous consequences for his health. He returned to Madras in a state of extreme frailty, without understanding the cause of his problems. Nevertheless, when he returned to his rice based diet, this being the most common cereal, his health progressively recovered. However, he began to experience a great deal of pain in his kidneys. He waited for a while, hoping that the pain would pass, but the situation worsened; he decided to go to a small local hospital where he was seen by a very amiable Indian doctor, who had, it seemed, undertaken his studies in the United States. After some X-rays, the doctor informed him of the presence of three stones in his left kidney and gave him some medicine to eliminate them. Not only did the remedy prove useless, but, after around three months, Salim also began to suffer from ocular problems, due to the side effects of these drugs. He was finally obliged to go to Paris, armed with his X-ray plates, to consult a surgeon friend. When examining Salim, this friend was horrified by the diagnosis made in India and the substances prescribed. He told Salim that he did not have any kidney stones, but he did have an acute inflammation, possibly as a consequence of his intestinal problems. Thanks to a new treatment that he gave Salim, a rapid improvement took place and Salim returned to Madras barely three weeks later.

Marital crisis and premonitory dreams.

On his return, he discovered that something had happened in his absence that would lead to the end of his marital relations and his life in India. Furthermore, he remembered having had, while still in Paris, two premonitory dreams, which had aroused in him an apprehension that he had been unable to shake off.

In the first dream, he saw taking place on his left the funeral of a child. The scene was in vivid color, creating a remarkable atmosphere. On the coffin, carried by a few people, were placed three or four enormous sunflowers. Salim's companion was following, without seeming affected in the slightest by the death of this child. While Salim was walking alongside the cortège, he was holding a vehement conversation with a man near him relating to England, as though he were afraid of going back there. Upon waking, Salim had remained pensive and troubled, thinking that he had understood the sense of this dream, which was, moreover, confirmed by another that he had shortly afterwards.

In this second dream, which, like the previous one, was in spectacular color, Salim found himself on an imposing cliff and, at his side, was his companion. In front of them, the sky's palette of colors was dazzling, composed of luminous tints never encountered in the tangible world. The solar disc seemed to be enormous and an astonishing bright red. Turning towards her, Salim said: "Oh, look, the sunrise!" But at the very moment he uttered these words, he was flooded with a feeling of consternation, because he realized that he had made a mistake; it was not a sunrise at all, but an alarming dusk... Then, looking down below, he saw hundreds of railroad tracks, crossing each other in all directions.

Upon waking, he remained transfixed for a long moment, because he felt that he had grasped the meaning of this strange dream, which did not belong to the category of ordinary dreams. He understood that the sunset was announcing, with indubitable clarity, the end of an important chapter in his life, and the railroad tracks were warning him that, afterwards, he would not know what to do or where to go.

Almost as soon as he got back to Madras, he found himself facing very painful marital difficulties, which caused him enormous suffering. It was at that time that Salim began to learn the Bharata Natyam, a form of Indian dance, which interested him very much and which, fortunately for him, took his mind, at least partially, off his problems.

Indian Dance and Music.

Madras is the southern center for Indian dance. Because of his artistic temperament, Salim particularly appreciated the beauty of this form of expression, which he thought was probably the most refined dance in the world. Moreover, Indian music has the most complicated rhythms in existence. In three months of intensive lessons, despite the fact that he was over fifty, Salim made progress that so enchanted his dance teacher that the teacher organized a show where Salim would perform in public for an hour.

The delicacy of the Indian culture was always a source of wonder for Salim. He enjoyed listening to the bhajans, which, not only spoke to him as a musician, but moved him deeply on a mystical level, as there was always something of the Sacred about them. He had the opportunity, in Madras, of listening to Subuh Lakshmi, one of the most famous bhajan singers, whom he had heard in Poona, when she had given a recital at Indira Devi's ashram. The evening had left him with an unforgettable memory; he very much appreciated the delicacy and sensitivity shown by some of the great Indian artistes. Subuh Lakshmi sang with her daughter; the latter knew her mother's repertoire so well that one had the impression of only perceiving a single voice when they sang together and it was a remarkable performance

Darjeeling.

Since coming back from his trip to Paris, Salim had to fight hard not to let the adverse conditions he was suffering at home interfere with his spiritual practices. Finally, in an attempt to save his marriage, he decided to go with his companion to the north of India, to Darjeeling and Kalimpong, with a view to visiting some Tibetan Buddhist masters.

Having arrived in Siliguri, they took the bus to Darjeeling. The distant mountain peaks appeared as the vehicle progressed in its climb. The beauty emanating from this awe-inspiring nature elevated the soul and detached it from ordinary contingencies. Upon arrival, Salim found a reasonably adequate, but expensive, hotel. They then had to present themselves to the local authorities to obtain a residence permit, as the spot was subject to certain restrictions because it was so close to the border.

The next day, going to a monastery that he wanted to visit, located around an hour's walk away, while he was busy admiring the countryside around him, Salim was suddenly flooded with a feeling of dread, to the extent that he had the impression his blood was turning to ice in his veins. On his right, he had just caught sight, on a rocky hillock, of three trees standing out against the sky—three trees that he recognized down to the last detail as being those that he had seen in a dream nine years before! The shock was even more striking for being so completely unexpected. He did everything in his power to conceal his emotion from his companion, who was at his side.

Profoundly troubled, he could not help once again interrogating himself about time and the future. "If the future already exists, "who" in himself knows it?" And, remembering his most recent dreams, Salim could not help feeling that he should expect to be obliged to take, probably in the near future, the decision to separate from his companion, which, until then, he had refused to contemplate.

The location of the monastery that he was going to had been given to him in Paris by a talented French painter of about fifty years of age. Arriving at the monastery, he had the pleasant surprise of seeing this artist, who, in the meantime, had become a Buddhist nun and had been living there for three years. He admired her endurance, because she lived in a small primitive cabin, standing near the temple, with no water nor any conveniences and, moreover, without any heating in a glacial cold.

She told him that a number of masters were present at the monastery, having come to attend a funeral ceremony as a tribute to a well-known Rinpoche who had just died. The rite was principally led by Nono Rinpoche, whom Salim had previously heard of.

Nono Rinpoche.

Nono Rinpoche was an adept of Tibetan hatha yoga. According to what Salim was able to learn, this discipline was much more powerful than the hatha yoga practiced in India.

When he met him, Salim saw straight away that this Rinpoche was a great yogi; his gestures were surprisingly delicate and fascinating in their grace, which demonstrated an absolutely exceptional knowledge of the various chakras and their locations within the human body.

Nono Rinpoche

For the first time since his arrival in India, he felt that, finally, he was before someone who inspired him with complete confidence.

Through a young Tibetan interpreter, Nono Rinpoche asked Salim a number of questions of a spiritual nature and, seeing that he expressed himself with difficulty and was undoubtedly unwell, he asked about his health. At that time, Salim was suffering from an infection affecting his ears and the joint of his jaw, he explained that the antibiotics prescribed to him by an Indian doctor, which he had been taking for a month, had not relieved it.

With a compassionate look that Salim was never able to forget, Nono Rinpoche asked the young translator, who spoke English fairly fluently, to suggest that Salim came back the next day so that he could give him something to cure him.

Feeling more and more drawn to this man, Salim returned to see him at the monastery, as arranged. To his surprise, Nono Rinpoche told him to stop taking his medicines, but, instead of replacing them with others, he gave him a very thin sheet of onionskin paper, on which were written sacred texts, which he had folded into the form of an envelope. He had placed inside it twenty one minuscule rolled-up morsels of paper, on which he had also written something and he asked Salim to swallow one every day. Salim, who felt great confidence in this Tibetan master, stopped, without hesitation, the treatment he had been taking until then and faithfully followed the Nono Rinpoche's instructions. From the third day, a distinct improvement occurred; on the twenty-first day, he was completely cured.

On another occasion, while Salim was walking in the monastery, Nono Rinpoche saw him and sent someone to fetch him. To the astonishment of Salim, who had absolutely no inkling of the reason for his being called, the master, with surprising kindness, began to teach him a mantra, the manner of reciting it, as well as the correct intonation and accentuation. Furthermore, Nono Rinpoche explained to Salim that if the mantra was recited in silence, it would have to be accompanied by breaths scanning certain syllables; if the aspirant was seated and alone, he must then say it out loud and accompany it with hand gestures and visualizations of specific colors. Salim, who was deeply touched and moved, did not know what to do to thank Nono Rinpoche, whom he had only known for a few days, for the confidence that he had shown in him, which he had not expected in the slightest when he first visited the monastery.

Drukpa Rinpoche.

Darjeeling rises in terraces from 1800 to 2400 meters, in the midst of vast tea plantations. Although Salim had gone there at the right time of year and was carrying a heavy coat and wearing several layers of sweaters and four pairs of socks, he suffered terribly from the cold. His failing health prevented him from eating properly and he always felt chilled. It goes without saying that the hotel, like the monasteries, was not heated.

Salim, who hoped to meet Drukpa Rinpoche, whose lamasery was too far from the hotel to be able to walk there, rented a jeep with a driver for an afternoon. The master received him with typically Tibetan kindness. Through an interpreter, Salim learned that the Rinpoche had to carry out the ordination of around ten children and that Salim might attend if he wished. The walls of the room where the rite took place were made of badly fitted planks which let in glacial drafts. Salim was completely frozen. He saw the children, aged from eight to

Drukpa Rinpoche

ten years, sitting on the ground, dressed in the style of Tibetan monks, with bare arms, indifferent to the cold.

After the ceremony, which was very long, Drukpa Rinpoche invited Salim into another room where he asked him all sorts of questions about himself and the reasons for him coming to India and, particularly, to Darjeeling. Tibetan hospitality brought forth tea and even, later in the evening, a dish of rice, which Salim dared not touch because of his state of health.

He noted that Drukpa Rinpoche was also not in good health; he coughed a lot and even seemed to be suffering from a serious pulmonary illness. During their whole conversation, the master remained so peaceful and calm that Salim was far from suspecting the tragedy that had just struck the community. It was only when he was leaving, when he had just offered, in an envelope, a little money to help the monastery, that he learned that the body of a Tibetan woman who had lived not far from there, was lying in the next room. The unfortunate woman, who was married and the mother of several children, had been stabbed that very day by a young Nepalese man in order to rob her of the small amount of money she had on her.

During the following years, Salim often thought of this Rinpoche and of the kindness that had been shown to him throughout the duration of their meeting, without the Rinpoche ever letting him see the pain he must have been feeling following this tragedy.

Chatral Rinpoche.

A few days later, Salim arranged to be driven by jeep to the monastery of Chatral Rinpoche. Visitors were welcomed by the strident sonorities produced by the numerous prayer flags which snapped

Chatral Rinpoche

ceaselessly in the wind, emitting continuous harmonic notes; as one approached, the sound became very acute, a little like that of a wind turbine. The building was perched very high, it was difficult to imagine a more spectacular view. In all directions, vast spaces spread out all the way to the snowy peaks standing out against the distant horizon.

Chatral Rinpoche was married and had several children. Salim saw one of them, a little girl, who was running around joyfully. The community, which chiefly lived on offerings, included a large number of monks who relied on the master to assure their subsistence. Salim later learned that Chatral Rinpoche went down to Siliguri, two or three times a week, to work there as a porter so as to earn extra money for his monastery. As there was no translator and the Rinpoche didn't speak a word of English, Salim had no way of exchanging any sort of conversation with him, but the Rinpoche's manner of being left a strong impression on him.

Khenpo Rinpoche.

Khenpo Tenzin Rinpoche lived in Ghoom. The monastery was difficult to access. Even the jeep had to stop before reaching it and Salim had to continue on foot. The passersby that he met on his way gave him helpful information, because everyone knew the lamasery. He was chilled when he arrived in sight of the modest buildings, to which new buildings were going to be added, which the monks were in the process of constructing.

Khenpo Rinpoche gave Salim the impression of having unusual strength. Unfortunately, the interpreter who attended their conversations spoke English very badly, which made the exchange rather arduous. Salim nevertheless returned to see this Buddhist master several times and the master always welcomed him with touching kindness, addressing him in Tibetan with words that Salim could not, alas, understand. During one of these meetings, the Rinpoche proudly showed Salim the buildings he was constructing in order to receive any visitors that might come wishing to work spiritually with him.

Salim retained a touching memory of this luminous man who seemed particularly well settled in his "hara". Salim felt such a warm sentiment towards him that, after he had left India, every month, for many years, he sent Khenpo Rinpoche a sum of money representing, in the context of that country, an appreciable assistance. In return, he regularly received kind little notes of thanks, written on the Rinpoche's behalf, in broken English.

These few Tibetan Buddhist masters whom Salim was able to meet, impressed him very much with the honesty of their spiritual approach and their true goodness.

During the two weeks or so that Salim spent in Darjeeling, he did not neglect to return to the monastery where Nono Rinpoche was temporarily staying. As soon as Nono Rinpoche saw him arrive, he would send his young interpreter to meet him. He confided to Salim, one day, while Salim was asking him about Tibetan hatha yoga, that the psychic forces unleashed by this discipline, in the way that he practiced it, could prove very dangerous for inexperienced people.

On that day, the Tibetan yogi, who wanted Salim to accompany him to Kurseong, wrapped Salim's coat around his leg, as though to make him, symbolically, his prisoner. Salim, who felt very strongly drawn to him, felt deep dismay, because he knew that it was impossible for him to accompany the Rinpoche at that time. When he left, Nono Rinpoche made him a gift of a small meditation bell, to which was attached, by a chain decorated with turquoises, a horn clapper. The little bell had an astonishing sound and vibration. He told Salim that this object had been in his family for three hundred years and that he was happy to give it to him. Salim felt very touched and promised to come back and see this man who had so impressed him.

Unfortunately, not long after his return to France, he was deeply saddened to hear of Nono Rinpoche's death; this master had apparently suffered the fate of many Tibetans when they descend to the plains, they cannot bear the heat or the air pressure, because their lungs are only adapted to high altitudes. Salim was afflicted for a long time by the death of the only person he had met in India into whose hands he had felt he could give himself in all confidence.

Kalimpong.

Leaving Darjeeling with a heavy heart, Salim rented a jeep very early one morning and left for Kalimpong. The car passed through places of great beauty, with impressive rock formations and great mossy trees, draped in tropical mists, abundantly maintained by a multitude of streams and small waterfalls.

On his arrival, he settled himself in a hotel kept by an elderly British aristocrat. The panorama offered by the terrace literally took his breath away. At the bottom of a vertiginous precipice, an intense blue-green torrent seethed; opposite stood the mountains of Sikkim, on the right, those of Bhutan, and, on the left, in the distance, the peaks of Tibet could be seen. Before this unforgettable spectacle, Salim, who felt a very particular elevation, understood only too well the reason for the yogis seeking out places of this kind to dedicate themselves to their spiritual practices.

The hotel owner, who was over seventy, was a widow and, although British, she had never left India. She took a shine to Salim and showed the greatest benevolence towards him. Once she knew of his health problems, she personally supervised the preparation of the meals, undertaken by a Tibetan in whom she had instilled strict hygiene rules. For once, during his treks in the country's interior, Salim was happy to be able, in all tranquility, to allow himself to be fed by someone else. The cuisine, which was, moreover, prepared in front of him, was delicate and extremely tasty.

He went to the nearby monastery, which stood at the summit of a mountain overlooking vast spaces. Inevitably, at such a height, it was exposed to a glacial wind which blew constantly. The Rinpoche was very ill and, although no-one had told him so, Salim sensed that he was dying. The monks nevertheless displayed great amiability and showed him around the monastery and, in particular, a room where two enormous statues of Buddha, around three meters high, stood on plinths. When Salim lifted his head and met the half-closed eyes of one of these statues, he felt strongly within himself the spiritual force of their timeless regard.

Residing permanently in the hotel was an old retired Indian general, melancholic, ill, and lonely, who never let slip an opportunity to converse with someone to pass the time. But what could he talk about, other than his poor warrior exploits that seemed of no interest to any-one? Apart from his military life, which he kept going over, the poor man had no other interests and Salim felt a great deal of compassion for him.

A large colony of Tibetan refugees lived in Kalimpong. They sold their craft products to tourists, such as their thick rugs, richly colored tankas, ritual bells, and other objects, many of which were linked to the Sacred. Salim only stayed a few days in this place where one naturally felt inclined towards meditation, before going back down to Madras, where he appreciated the heat of the plain.

During the whole of this journey, his thoughts had been continually monopolized by the marital problem that was tormenting him. One day, absorbed in his meditation, a strange feeling suddenly flooded his being and, in the same way as during his interview with Satya Sai Baba, a voice arose from a mysterious supernatural silence, speaking directly to his mind (and being simultaneously translated into English), saying to him: "Let her go!"

Pondicherry. Return to Europe. The decision.

Shortly after his return to Madras, Salim had to go to Pondicherry for a short stay. One early afternoon, not knowing what drove him to go out despite the scorching heat, he went for a walk by the sea, extremely troubled by the decision to be taken which was tearing him apart, yet, which he knew, deep down, to now be inevitable.

Still deep in his painful thoughts, he came to a place where his gaze moved involuntarily towards the foot of the cliff, when, suddenly with a feeling of consternation, he recognized the same three rounded rocks, rising above the waters, that he had seen in a dream nine years earlier. Surprised and distraught, he abruptly lifted his head towards the sky and, as the sun was still very strong, he protected his eyes with his arm, thus reproducing exactly the same gesture as in this strange prophetic dream...

When he returned to Besant Nagar, the climate at the end of March was already scorching. The visit to the Tibetan masters had changed nothing in terms of the adverse conditions Salim was suffering at home. He left for Paris, where he stayed for a while with some friends, then went to London, to his mother's house. He stayed there for a few weeks.

He had already bought his return ticket for Madras, but, towards the end of June, he canceled his return journey. He wrote his companion to tell her of his decision not to come back to India, his letter crossed her own asking him not to come back because she had taken the decision to live with someone else. Salim went back to Paris and began divorce proceedings, which were finalized in 1976.

India exercised such an imperious attraction over Salim, that he always regretted having to leave. The years he spent there were decisive for him spiritually. Although he had not discovered the master he had been looking for, he had found a particular spiritual atmosphere that was lacking in the West and which, all the time that he lived there, proved to be a precious aid to his sadhana.

Chapter 5

France 1974 - 2006

Return to Paris.

Arriving in Paris after having spent a few days with some obliging friends, Salim found, through one of his pupils, a small room to rent on Rue Octave Feuillet, in the sixteenth arrondissement.

After the years spent in India, during which he had enjoyed relative financial tranquility, he found himself once again, at over fifty years old, in a precarious situation. In fact, his main source of income had just dried up, as French television had suddenly removed the background music from all its televised news bulletins and Salim was now only receiving some meager royalties from abroad. Music was over for him, so he found himself, unexpectedly, obliged to give hatha yoga lessons to survive.

Salim 1974

Wanting to teach is considered, in spiritual traditions, as a sign that the person is not ready; it is circumstances that must drive him or her to do it, otherwise this desire, which one may believe to be legitimate, roots itself in the need, conscious or not, for recognition. Salim had no desire to teach and, had he not been pushed by necessity to find a way to survive, he undoubtedly would never have done it.

It was at that time, in December 1974, that the karmic connections which invisibly linked us together would manifest themselves. A friend with whom I practiced hatha yoga advised me to go and see this "yoga teacher", recently returned from India, who, she told me, was no ordinary yoga teacher. I was immediately struck by the depth of his gaze, by his voice, and by his manner of being.

Salim later told me that he had had, before our first meeting, a symbolic dream from which he understood that this meeting would be very positive for him.

Indeed, he was not an ordinary "hatha yoga teacher". He did not simply teach the postures. He strove to share with his pupils the essence of his own practice. He showed them specific exercises to tear away from oneself and experience a moment of true presence. He meditated with them; he helped them to recognize the "Nada", and explained to them the importance of this aid to concentration. Finally, Salim did not fail to impress on them the importance of self knowledge.

Journey to India.

As soon as the legal formalities relating to his divorce were finalized in July 1976, Salim put the few pupils that he had in contact with the Gurdjieff groups, then he immediately packed his bags and set off for England, firmly decided to go to Poona as soon as possible, there to be reunited with his friend Mr Dady, whom he had informed of his arrival by letter. He wanted to move to Mr Dady's leper colony and help him take care of these unfortunates, having the firm intention of never returning to the West.

It was about three in the morning when his plane finally landed in Bombay, after what had seemed to Salim an interminable and tiring journey. No sooner had he landed than his difficulties commenced. For some reason that he didn't understand, a border control official took his passport which he passed to some distant office and, before it was returned to Salim, he had to wait more than three hours, which seemed to him to pass with incredible slowness. Harassed by his health problems to which was added his jet lag, he was impatient to get to a nearby hotel, whose address he had. He therefore took a taxi which took an interminable detour of an hour to make a trip of five or six minutes at most, the driver claiming to be lost. As soon as he finally got to his room, he put his bags down without even opening them, threw himself on the bed and, exhausted, let himself drift into an uneasy sleep.

The next day, he bought his train ticket, with the intention of going to Poona the day after. In the evening, on his return to the hotel, he noticed that the restaurant was offering a rice based dish, which, he had been assured, was not too spicy and, as he felt very tired and far from recovered from his jet lag, instead of preparing his own meal, he made the mistake of ordering this dish. Barely half an hour after he had finished eating, he began to suffer from abdominal pains and to feel very feverish, then he began vomiting blood. He continued, every twenty to thirty minutes, vomiting more and more blood, while his fever continued increasing to the extent that he had the strange impression that his body was abandoning him.

Finally, he called the hotel manager, who called out a doctor, who, as soon as he saw Salim in this alarming state, diagnosed a serious case of food poisoning. Despite the treatment he prescribed, Salim continued to vomit blood for another thirty-six hours. Alone in his room, he was delirious with no-one to take care of him. The walls of the room seemed to sway incessantly; sometimes they even seemed to lean towards him, giving him a painful feeling of being crushed.

The doctor, seeing that he was a foreigner and unable to defend himself, took advantage of the situation to demand exorbitant fees for each of his visits, probably twenty times higher than the price of a normal consultation.

Salim was reduced to such a state of exhaustion that his organism had become excessively vulnerable; moreover, to add to his misfortune, he contracted an infection in his left eye that could have led to him losing it. In the midst of these overwhelming problems, the doctor, although dishonest, nevertheless proved to be a good practitioner. The injections and the medicines that he administered began to work relatively quickly, for Salim's eye as well as for his food poisoning. The doctor forbade him any other food than bananas which he had bought for him and which protected him against other complications.

After a few days, Salim felt so physically exhausted and weakened that he realized the impossibility of prolonging his stay in India.

Profoundly affected by this distressing realization, he was obliged to return to the airport to take the first flight to London. After an interminable wait, he finally obtained, at about one in the morning, a seat on an Air India flight.

Third and final part of Salim's premonitory dream.

He arrived at his mother's house in such a state of exhaustion that he needed a long period of convalescence before beginning to regain his strength. Still undecided as to his future, he went out towards the end of a December afternoon to walk a little and think things over. There was a thick fog and the glacial cold was penetrating. He had gone just a few steps when he said to himself, in anguish: "But, I don't want to go this way, I want to go where there is some sun!", and, suddenly, with a feeling of incredulous despondency, he realized that he had been plunged into the third part of the disconcerting dream he had had more than ten years before.

He could not help once again interrogating himself about the strange enigma posed by fate, asking himself: "Can the future really be known in advance? Does it exist somewhere, buried in the consciousness of the person who has already lived and apparently forgotten it? But, if that is so, lived when and in what time?" And the troubling idea of the potential recurrence of existence impressed itself on him with growing acuity.

Rue Turgot.

As soon as he was sufficiently recovered, Salim decided that as, for the time being, his health made a return to India impossible and neither the climate nor the atmosphere of England suited him, it would be better for him to return to Paris.

Through one of his pupils, he found furnished accommodation at a reasonable rent on Rue Turgot, not far from Pigalle, in that part of Paris where coach loads of tourists eager to experience the world of venal sex regularly arrive. The atmosphere of the place was the polar opposite of that he had known in India.

When he had lived, a few months earlier, in the little room on Rue Octave Feuillet, the conditions were uncomfortable, but he had been sustained by the hope of being able to return to India in the near future, whereas, during the seven years he spent on Rue Turgot, he had to accept the impossibility of his returning to that country, because, due to the almost total disappearance of his royalties, he was obliged to find ways of earning his living. The memory of those dramatic moments during which he had found himself so ill, left to himself in his room in the Bombay hotel, remained so vivid in his mind and he realized that, given the deterioration of his physical state, it was completely unrealistic for him to go away alone, with no-one at his side in case of difficulties. Thus he knew moments of despair seeing himself obliged to remain in Paris, where destiny had placed him. He remembered then the words that he had heard internally at Satya Sai Baba's ashram: "There will come a day when you will be placed in a situation where you will not know what to do ; don't worry, don't worry, don't worry, don't worry..."

Nothing belonging to the manifest world is permanent; he knew that no situation, no challenge, however difficult they might appear, was permanent. Only the Sublime Aspect of his nature which he had found within him was unchanging, the only unalterable support that brought him a peace not of this world.

When the memory of India came back too strongly to his mind, when his health and his material problems became too heavy, he used the power of thought, relying on phrases that he repeated within himself as a sort of mantra and which he invented according to the needs of the moment, such as: "What a wonderful day it is today, by Divine Grace, all that is wonderful, spiritual wealth, Light, health, etc. are coming to me." or as a prayer, which he linked to his respiration: "Infinite Source, Fill me with Thy Light, Give me the strength to think of nothing but of Thee." In one way or another, he always found something to do to prevent external conditions from interfering with his sadhana.

Apart from his spiritual practices, Salim drew great comfort from listening to music. Throughout the trials he underwent, listening to the works of certain great composers, such as César Franck, Brahms, Beethoven, or Debussy always helped him and proved to be nutrition as indispensable, if not more so, than earthly food.

After his return from India, it was particularly in the slow movements of Gustav Mahler's symphonies that he found support, as though this music called human beings to feel, towards their fellow beings as well as towards all living creatures, the compassion that is so tragically lacking on this planet.

Meetings with remarkable men.

It was around this time that the Gurdjieff groups decided to make a film about the spiritual quest of their master, inspired by the book "Meetings with Remarkable Men", a sort of autobiography written by G I Gurdjieff in the nineteen twenties and thirties and first published in 1963. Peter Brook was the director. He came to see Salim in Paris to ask him to write the music for the film. He offered him a large sum of money and to make available to him however many musicians he wanted for the orchestra, because he knew that Salim liked to write for a large orchestra, he also offered him the opportunity of conducting the music himself. It was a great temptation, for, as well as the financial gain, it would have helped his remaining published musical works to become known on the other side of the Atlantic. But Salim felt that he should not take up music again, he did not accept the offer, however attractive it was. Peter Brook tried again two weeks later, offering him even more money. In the meantime, Salim had had a dream which confirmed to him that, indeed, it was not desirable for him spiritually to accept; therefore he once again refused, because, as he later said to his pupils: "I don't want to be reborn doing the same thing. Music is over for me, all I want now is my spiritual quest and nothing else".

Spiritual work with Salim.

Salim began once again giving hatha yoga and meditation lessons. I was very glad to see him again so as to pursue the work I had already undertaken with him. Before meeting him, I already knew and regularly practiced hatha yoga; a great attraction to Japan had also drawn me towards aikido and Zen Buddhism. However, as soon as I began working with Salim, I felt immediately that his teaching found an echo in me in a very particular manner.

He helped me to understand that it was not enough to acquire a certain ease in the execution of the asanas or to demonstrate endurance in meditation. He put the emphasis on the necessity of invoking and maintaining during my practices a presence to myself that should result in a particular state that Salim taught me to find and to recognize through specific concentration exercises.

The intensity of concentration that was required of me was new to me; I had to fight to keep a different feeling of myself linked to a conscious knowledge of my own existence while I was performing hatha yoga postures, while meditating, or even while I was having to respond to the requirements of external life. I had to acknowledge that reaching this other state of being demanded a constant internal renunciation that was not at all easy to achieve and that had to be continually renewed. I also had to accept the evidence that this step represented a whole life's work. However, despite the difficulties I experienced, I felt that the efforts demanded of me were taking me the right way; such an approach was part of a pragmatic, rigorous method, which required neither belief nor the adoption of another culture.

When Salim returned from the brief trip to India that had ended so badly for him, I saw him so ill that I took fright at the idea that, if he left this world, not only would my work with him be interrupted, but others who had not had the privilege of knowing him would never be able to benefit from his spiritual experience which I felt intuitively to be infinitely precious. So, from that moment, I began to write down what I could remember from each of the lessons I took with him. However, I saw that these notes could only be personal and I realized that it was indispensable that Salim himself should commit to paper the fruit of so many years of work. Therefore, I pressed him many

times to write down what he had to convey, but he always responded
that he was quasi-illiterate, that he did not even know how to construct
his sentences and that what I asked of him seemed an entirely impossible task.

Visit to Japan. 1979.

It was at that time, through an English friend who had married a
Japanese woman, that Salim had the chance of going to Japan, where
he was invited for a stay of a month and a half. Knowing that the
country offered impeccable hygiene conditions and that he was only
going for a short time, he dared to undertake the trip. This friend,
who knew of Salim's interest in all things connected with spirituality,
had found him lodgings with a family, none of whose members,
unfortunately, spoke a word of English, but one of whom, apparently,
practiced hatha yoga.

In preparation for his journey, Salim began, some months before
his departure, to learn a few rudiments of Japanese. This language
proving very difficult, he was only able to acquire a limited vocabulary
which was, nonetheless, a great help when in that country and having
to communicate with people who spoke nothing else. This linguistic
barrier represented a significant obstacle to exchanges with the people
who accommodated him. The Kinoshita family, who offered him
hospitality, comprised, apart from the parents and their three children,
eight other members. They lived in a small, cramped house with
minuscule rooms. Salim had to share a small bedroom with a young
student of seventeen whose unremitting work rhythm was impressive
to see. Accommodation proving not only difficult to find in Japan
but also exorbitantly priced, Mr Kinoshita had had to work like a
galley slave for many years to acquire this modest dwelling and he
seemed worn out and emptied of all energy, even though he was not
more than forty-five years old.

His wife earned a little money giving hatha yoga lessons to people
with health complaints, whom she brought together in a group.

Strangely, she did not practice the asanas herself, contenting herself with finding them in books and then showing them to her pupils.

When she learned that Salim taught hatha yoga in Paris, she jumped at the chance of taking some lessons with him so as to acquire an elementary technical basis. Another member of the family was taking calligraphy lessons, but only with the aim of teaching it in the future.

Television played a great part in the lives of his hosts; their attention was constantly attracted by advertisements and by incredibly violent cartoons that the children of the household never failed to watch whenever they had a moment free.

Observing these children glued to the screen, Salim could only say to himself: "As in the West, they are constantly and insidiously persuaded that, without these dramas, without terror and without cheap, false heroism, their lives would be nothing. Over time, as in other industrialized countries, new generations will lose interest in real life and try to rid themselves as quickly as possible of all that they consider as merely unappetizing chores, so as to be able to get back as soon as they can to the dreams of artificial life offered to them by the television, to which they will become shackled like slaves."

Japanese politeness.

Although he had previously heard Japan spoken of as a center of Buddhism, Salim did not find there the same atmosphere marked by spirituality that, for him, gave India its unique character. Nowhere did he sense the devotional aspect so particular to the Indian attitude and which proves so important to a spiritual approach.

On the other hand, in comparison with India, the legendary cleanliness of the Japanese as well as their extreme politeness were pleasant advantages which enchanted him. He told me a very meaningful anecdote, reflecting the differences in mentality that can exist between different peoples. He went, one day, to a post office to buy stamps; upon entering, he went tranquilly to the end of the long line waiting in front of the appropriate counter. To his surprise, the people in front of him, seeing that he was foreign, gently pulled his sleeves and used expressive mimes to make him understand that he might simply go in front of them. Not wanting to abuse their amiability, he politely refused, but they insisted so much and so kindly that, finally, he could only accept and thank them with the usual "domo arigato". The contrast was so striking between this attitude and that generally adopted by Westerners towards foreigners.

Salim also had the opportunity on a number of occasions to enjoy the surprising politeness of café waiters, both to him and to the local customers. Furthermore, for the sake of cleanliness, every meal, or even just a drink, would involve the presentation of a hot, scented napkin. He was also particularly sensitive to the atmosphere of courtesy in which daily life took place; even in the supermarkets, where he accompanied members of the household, charming clerks invited him with delicacy to taste sweetmeats or treats that they were promoting.

On his arrival in the Kinoshita family, the lady of the house invited Salim to join them for a communal bath. In the spacious bathroom stood a large circular bathtub filled with very hot water, in which, after having soaped and rinsed themselves, seven members of the household could sit together and enjoy, in all simplicity, the joy of relaxation so precious to the Japanese. Salim, embarrassed, had to explain that it was not the custom in the West and that he would prefer to bathe alone. His wish was immediately accepted and his privacy respected.

He discovered the delights of Japanese cuisine, joining the family twice a day around a long low table, on which were lit four alcohol burners, to savor the dishes that Mrs Kinoshita had prepared and which she cooked quickly as they ate. She always offered, in a dozen or so bowls, an astonishing variety of delicacies whose aspect and flavor were enchanting. This did not prevent Salim from frequently falling prey to his usual intestinal crises.

When he was ill, his hosts, who did not understand his problem, would be rather impatient and inquire, with sometimes rather forced politeness, if the food they had served was not to his liking.

In the Fujisawa Temple.

During a walk, Salim discovered, on a hill close to the house, a small temple, whose upkeep was undertaken by a monk who came every day, very early in the morning. The rest of the time, the building stood empty. So, remarking that his hosts were not interested in spiritual practices, in order to avoid making them uncomfortable and on pretext of going for walks, Salim went to the temple at different times of the day to meditate there.

Sometimes, while he was resting tranquilly unmoving after his meditation, he would have strange spiritual experiences, difficult to translate into words.

One day, his gaze, which was resting on one of the trees planted in front of the temple entrance, suddenly retreated in an inexplicable manner inside his head so that the tree that he had been looking at seemed to him to be inside his own head and no longer outside of him. An inexpressible silence descended on him and on all his surroundings in such a mysterious way that the rustling of the foliage, the birdsong, and the sound of the wind totally faded. An enigmatic contact established itself between him and the tree to the point where it seemed that he and the plant were one, or rather, that his consciousness and that of the tree had fused to constitute One Single Consciousness. At that very moment, the tree, which was, or seemed to be, in him, said to him: "I am, I was, and I will always be". There reigned an extraordinary feeling of an "Eternal Nowness".

When, not long afterwards, he reflected on the experience which had occurred to him and which had been so troubling and so strange to customary sensory perception, he said to himself that, nevertheless, this tree, just like him, had known a beginning in the manifest world and that it would inevitably die one day, that no tangible creation could escape this fate once its time came. He then felt that this mysterious wordless declaration: "I am, I was, and I will always be" that the tree had expressed in him, could only draw its origins from the Mind of the Great Divine Knower that, so to speak, he had himself become.

Kabuki and kimono.

As he wished to get to know the Japanese cultural traditions, Salim one day asked his hosts if it would be possible to attend some artistic performances, such as the Kabuki or the Noh. Surprised by his interest in an aspect of their heritage that they, themselves, considered to now belong to the past, they nevertheless agreed to accompany him one afternoon to a theater in a town near Fujisawa.

The Kabuki is a theatrical performance that can last for up to eight hours and mixes dramatic intrigue with lighter, even comic aspects; Salim did not understand what was being said on the stage, but, from time to time, he looked discreetly at the other spectators who showed lively emotions and who even began to cry in concert when the heroine killed herself by committing "hara-kiri".

He also attended a performance of Noh theater; the performance presented the most austere of appearances and bathed in a dramatic atmosphere which was reinforced by the extreme slowness with which the actors advanced. While admiring the formal beauty of the piece and the dignity of the participants, Salim could not help being bothered by the omnipresent cult of suicide in practically all Japanese artistic fields, including traditional music.

"It is not the courage of putting an end to one's life that should be celebrated," he said to himself, "it is rather the courage of inner renouncement, to achieve inner death, but an inner death which leads to the True Life."

Salim had always intuitively sensed the importance of a country's customs, of the architecture of its edifices, the resonance of its language, and the manner of dressing and eating of its people. For him, it was indisputable that the buildings one lives in and that the eye continually sees, the linguistic sonority, and the type of clothes that one wears must exercise a considerable influence over the psyche.

When, one day, he was expressing his regret that the Japanese were abandoning their traditional clothing for a Western style of dress that he considered as banal and lacking in beauty, Mrs Kinoshita's mother invited him to take tea in the tiny studio that she occupied at the top of a modern building. To his surprise she received him in a superb kimono that she had donned in his honor. She even carried out for him a tea ceremony, scrupulously respecting the forms of the ritual, but without understanding the spiritual essence of this tradition which originally aimed to help the participants to find and maintain a state of silence and of inner presence. Salim was, nonetheless, very touched by her delicate attention.

Salim and Madame Kinoshita in front of Kamakura's Buddha

As it is difficult, given the barrier of language and of writing, to travel in Japan without the assistance of someone from the country, one of the members of the family had the kindness to accompany Salim to visit some famous sites, including Kamakura where he had heard that he would find a gigantic statue of Buddha. When he found himself before this imposing statue, barely coming up to its foot, he felt, with emotion, the force that emanated from it. He learned that, during an earthquake that had occurred in the distant past and had destroyed the whole of the town, only this colossal sculpture had miraculously been spared.

Kyoto, Kobori Roshi.

The city of Kyoto, which is located around five hundred kilometers from the capital, probably embodies the main part of what is left of the tradition of the land of the rising sun. In fact, the city has more than one thousand five hundred temples. Salim made a brief stay there, accompanied by Mrs Kinoshita. The simple beauty of these sacred edifices, so different from that of the Indian temples, is of a restrained splendor.

Salim's desire to visit this city was increased by his hope of seeing Kobori Roshi there, a master of Rinzai Zen whom Salim had met in Paris some years previously. He wrote him from Fujisawa and was very pleased to receive in return a letter written in English, inviting him to meet Kobori Roshi at his monastery.

As soon as he arrived there, and even though Zen was not his path, Salim was touched by the honesty that prevailed and struck by the almost military rigor that reigned there. He was very impressed by the efforts and the seriousness demanded of the Japanese monks, as well as by the profound respect that they showed their master.

Kobori Roshi

Kobori Roshi was a man of around fifty years of age whose astonishing inner strength could be seen at first glance. Upon Salim's arrival, Kobori Roshi was in the company of another master, Sochu Suzuki Roshi, who belonged to the Soto branch of Zen. The latter, smaller than Kobori Roshi, had, like him, extremely lively and brilliant eyes. Using the little English he had, he asked Salim about the reasons for his visit to Japan and his interest in Zen monasteries. After a few minutes, he took a piece of paper, wrote the address of his monastery, located near Mishima and, still in his rudimentary English, he said to Salim: "You come see me". He repeated his invitation many times—to which Salim could not, unfortunately respond—before finally leaving him with Kobori Roshi.

The latter was very amicable towards his visitor and ordered one of the monks to bring them tea and sweetmeats which they shared in silence. They then conversed in English—which the master spoke relatively well—for more than two hours. During the conversation, to Salim's surprise, the Roshi suddenly complained about his monks, deploring the meager results they obtained, despite their apparent determination. After having asked, out of respect for the master, permission to express himself freely, Salim spoke to him of the differences in levels of consciousness, intelligence, and being, which distinguish human beings, of the obstacle constituted by some of their undesirable tendencies, and the fact that, without them realizing it, even for those who have undertaken the step of entering a monastery, the true decision to commit oneself to a spiritual practice has not yet really been taken. At one point, Salim also referred to music and its influence on the human psyche.

Kobori Roshi, listening attentively, was very open and interested in the different subjects broached. At the end of his visit, when he had just taken his leave, Salim had gone only a few steps when Kobori Roshi called him back and, suddenly, to his great surprise, told him, with surprising simplicity: "I have learned something from you."

While recognizing the virtues of the Zen approach and admiring the exemplary rigor that reigned in the Japanese monasteries, Salim could not help remarking that it lacked the particular devotional character one encounters among the Indians and which is of vital assistance in supporting the seeker in all his practices. "For," he would say, "of body, feeling and mind, it is feeling that proves to be the most powerful force in spiritual research. The Buddha, who lived in India, bathed in an atmosphere considerably more devotional than that one finds in the Far East."

Salim liked to say that, in a spiritual approach, it is necessary to succeed in bringing together Japanese rigor and the profoundly devotional attitude of India.

After having left the monastery of Kobori Roshi, Salim set off, with Mrs Kinoshita, for Fujisawa. As soon as they got off the train, as his hostess had told him that she was hungry, Salim invited her to eat in a nearby restaurant. She ordered two vegetable and seaweed soups with noodles. They had just left the table when Salim began to feel the first symptoms of a crisis coming on, which, alas, he knew only too well. Once in a taxi, he gestured to Mrs Kinoshita that he was ill; but she could not understand what it meant for him, this journey which seemed to him interminable and throughout which spasms were tearing through his stomach. While she insisted on speaking to him and asking him various questions with the aid of a dictionary that she had brought along, he hardly heard her, so acute was his pain.

During all those years that he had to experience such situations, he met with so much incomprehension on the part of the people he mixed with that, subsequently, he felt it necessary to instill in his pupils the importance of learning to feel for one another. This faculty of empathy, which implies a certain distance from oneself in order to turn towards the other, requires a particular effort that must be deliberately cultivated.

Ongoing experiments.

Coming out of his meditation one day in the temple in Fujisawa, Salim realized, through a direct perception, not translatable into everyday language, that the continual changes that occur in existence and within the human being constituted, in fact, ongoing experiments which, unknown to humanity, proceed without respite—trials undertaken by the Divine Spirit, seeking to obtain from his Creation a result ordinarily very difficult to conceive of.

And Salim said to himself: "Should the human being not ask himself where this strange cosmic game is going? Towards what accomplishment? To obtain what? Why does this continual succession of births and deaths exist in the Universe?"

He later tried to make his pupils understand that, if a seeker wishes to know, through direct experience, the answer to these questions, rather than contenting himself with extracting them from a book (including Salim's own), he would have to, through assiduous work on himself, come to recognize his Divine Essence before death took possession of him.

Now, unlike involution, which, through the inexorable law of gravity, can only consist of a passive, downwards movement, true evolution must be undertaken in an active and voluntary manner.

"Indeed," he would add, "it is necessary for a human being to assist his Original Source in this mysterious experimentation, so enigmatic and beyond the grasp of the rational mind, by responding, through his personal efforts, to what It wishes to obtain from him: the recognition of Its Holy Presence in the Universe—but a conscious recognition which cannot take place in a human being without his consent and his active participation."

The end of the Japanese visit.

After a few weeks, Salim had made sufficient progress in Japanese to be able to make allusions in his exchanges with his hosts to reflections on existence which aroused their interest. From time to time, he played a game of chess with Mr Kinoshita, who was delighted to have someone to play with, or with the youngest child, aged nine, to whom he would show various tactics of the game. The whole family ended up adopting him. So, when his stay was coming to an end, the various members of the household kindly asked him, to his surprise, to stay with them.

Mr Kinoshita's father, who had taken a shine to him and who was bored all alone in his home in Kobe, offered him hospitality. At the same time, Mr and Mrs Kinoshita also had the astonishing generosity to suggest that he move in permanently with them, without him having to worry about financial problems. Although extremely touched, he could not accept, because, despite the pleasure he had taken in his stay in Japan, he preferred, if he couldn't return to India, towards which his heart still yearned, to return to France and to his pupils.

When the moment came to leave, everyone showed their emotions, especially the young boy with whom Salim had played chess, and who, crying, held on to his bags and wouldn't let go. Almost the whole family accompanied him to the airport.

Salim's first book : "The Way of Inner Vigilance", 1979-1983.

Upon his return from Japan, I renewed my attempts to get Salim to write down what he was teaching me, but he always said that because of the handicap that his lack of formal education represented for him, he did not even know how to start a book, never mind finish it. He had, nevertheless, shown me a few notes that he had taken over the years, while telling me that he could not see at all how it could be possible to make something publishable out of them. As he had, naturally, chosen English to write down these notes for his personal use, I suggested that he continue to use that language to develop certain themes, without worrying about a plan, simply approaching one by one the various aspects of his work that he wanted to expound. Although my level of English was far from being good enough for a task of this order, I promised to do my best to help him, telling him that, if necessary, I would find someone to help me.

After many hesitations, Salim began to draft a few paragraphs. As he thought without words, he had to find a vocabulary allowing him to translate inner understandings, intuitions, and experiences that were not ordinarily expressible. He had to patiently forge himself a tool, word by word, with much difficulty, crossing out and revising over and over the things that seemed to him not to be clearly enough explained or sufficiently described. Being far from mastering English, he had to resort to dictionaries, in which he searched for hours the terms that seemed to him to be the most appropriate, so as to avoid, as far as possible, any risk of misunderstanding on the part of his readers.

He worked to a rhythm that I could not follow. He could remain at his desk for sixteen to eighteen hours, battling obstinately to find the right words to express what he was trying, with so much difficulty, to convey. This represented, for Salim, who had no intellectual training, a task of herculean proportions.

The fact that I was not, myself, sufficiently expert in English did not help us. I translated into French everything he gave to me so as to check the structure, then we achieved, by using dictionaries, a first draft, which I typed (at that time, there were not yet any personal computers) and submitted to a friend who was an English teacher; her corrections led to more alterations from Salim, until, little by little, the text took shape. All of this evidently required an enormous amount of time; I was already very busy, both with absorbing professional responsibilities which often took me away on business trips, and with my children, adolescents at that time, who were unable to understand the interest I took in this work.

It took no less than six versions before the text was sufficiently settled on and we were able to organize it into a structure of forty-eight chapters. After four years of unremitting work, Salim sent the book, entitled "The Way of Inner Vigilance" to a London publishing house recommended to him by a friend. However, the publisher, considering that there were too many errors in the English, said that it was indispensable to have the text revised in its entirety by a professional whom he suggested.

This man undoubtedly knew the language and the rules of syntax very well, but he was not at all interested in the content of the book or in spiritual research. He was constantly saying to Salim: "We need to find more ordinary words and a more usual formulation", when a common and banal language was precisely what Salim did not want to express that which related to the highest human aspiration. Often, as he was not in agreement with the changes made, it was necessary to discuss every little detail. Finally, after all the work the book had demanded, Salim went to London for its launch. When he returned and gave me a copy, we felt very moved to be able to finally hold in our hands the fruit of all those years of hard labor.[*]

Teaching.

Salim felt acutely the weight of responsibility which fell to him in passing on the fruit of his spiritual work. He wanted wholeheartedly to be true and rigorous in the choice of his words. He had also shown

---

[*] The book was republished in 2010 by Inner Tradition with the new title : "The Law of Attention, Nada Yoga and The Way of Inner Vigilance".

the greatest scruples in writing his first book. To come to a truth of
being of a quality beyond ordinary reach, it was necessary, he would
say, that there should be, within oneself, less and less of oneself and
more and more of the Infinite, so that the Latter might take its proper
place in one's being.

He applied these same scruples in his work with his pupils, whom
he always received individually. Little by little, he stopped teaching
hatha yoga postures, instead teaching concentration exercises destined
to help seekers to recognize what a true state of presence to oneself
consists of—which, for him, was the basis on which a practice must be
built, a true spiritual work being unable to commence for an aspirant
before making the discrimination between the two aspects of his nature.

He said : "He who teaches should be capable of remaining conscious
of himself and connected to his Inner Source while teaching so as to
be able to perceive clearly, from this impersonal higher perspective,
when the pupil is truly present, and the degree to which he is so. He
should continuously take the aspirant by surprise when he is least
expecting it, and immediately make him see each time this special
awareness of himself has degenerated again. He should persistently
and patiently repeat this procedure until the aspirant really arrives at
an understanding of the implication of this mysterious sleep into
which he keeps disappearing, and the paramount significance of the
opposite movement that takes place in him when he is abruptly
awakened once more."

He would show a pupil how to recognize the Nada, the interior
sound that is a precious aid to concentration, which sustained him so
much in his own quest.

When he meditated with someone, he helped him, through direct
transmission, to sense a clarity of being and of consciousness that was
not habitual to him, everyone feeling this direct help from Salim
according to his degree of receptivity and level of being.

He finally unleashed in his pupils a psychic force, the shakti, which
had been awoken in him during the powerful experience of enlighten-

ment that he had had at the age of thirty-three. But, he would make it very clear to them that, when the awakening of this Shakti is unleashed by someone, the experience cannot have the same intensity. Someone for whom this Shakti has been awoken by an external intervention has not paid the price for it. He has only the possibility of feeling that something not arising from the tangible exists within him. This, in itself, is a great deal and will help him, but, if he doesn't accomplish any serious spiritual practice, this Shakti will fall back into the latent state it was in before this triggered awakening. A serious spiritual practice implies specific work on concentration in meditation, as well as in one's active life, without forgetting the struggle with undesirable tendencies, so the simple awakening of this Shakti does not, in itself, constitute an accomplishment.

Salim had to find comprehensible words for the beginners and try to help everyone with compassion, according to his levels of being, of consciousness, and of intelligence. The major problem facing seekers in the West, he noted, was that one lives in such spiritual ignorance that, in fact, one doesn't know what one is looking for. One may feel an indefinable inner call, but one does not understand how to respond.

He would emphasize the fact that speaking spirituality and living a practice are as different as night and day, as are thinking presence and truly being present with the whole of oneself, which requires an effort of an unusual kind. He reminded his pupils that he had seen many times in India, including in ashrams, people who spoke brilliantly on spirituality, but who acted in a manner not at all compatible with spiritual truths of which they had only an intellectual knowledge. He also insisted on the fact that people who were not committed to any spiritual practice could have a level of being and qualities greatly superior to those of an aspirant.

Sometimes the pupils were surprised at having to make efforts of concentration when they had heard elsewhere that it was absolutely essential not to make an effort. "After all", they would say to him,

"Did the Buddha not preach the 'The Middle Way'? Which certainly means that it is better to only make efforts with moderation!"

Salim would respond: "Such an interpretation of the words of the Buddha suits people who forget that the great being pronounced these words after fasts and excessive austerities that he had inflicted on his body and which had weakened him physically and psychically to the point where it had become impossible to continue to meditate. 'The Middle Way' applies only to the way in which one treats one's body; in other words, it advocates eating neither too much nor too little, sleeping neither too much nor too little, not making excessive physical efforts, but not remaining inactive either, and so on. The principle of restraint certainly does not apply to the efforts one must make in the course of meditation practices and during spiritual exercises. Quite the contrary, the Buddha continually exhorted his disciples to ever greater efforts, telling them: 'Make the most sustained efforts of which you are capable and be tirelessly vigilant'.

"If one suggests to young people who are studying musical composition or the piano to apply 'the middle way' to their apprenticeship, one may be certain that they will never be anything but very mediocre musicians. It is enough to examine the lives of great composers (such as Beethoven or Gustav Mahler) or great painters (such as Michelangelo, Rembrandt and others) to realize that what has caused their greatness arises precisely from the fact that they are all extreme beings. The lives of Milarepa, of Dogen, that of Ramana Maharshi, of Teresa of Avila, of Madame Guyon, or other great mystics must be examples for all aspirants. These exceptional beings were also extreme beings.

"I have so often heard spiritual teachers in India, and even in the West, say to their disciples: "No efforts, Everything is already here." Or better: "You are already a Buddha; effort comes from the ego wanting to grasp it." Such statements, if not simply deceitful, are at least the result of a dangerous kind of spiritual ignorance.It is true that "All is here," but does one really know the "All" that is here? And even if, after great effort, one should, through a real direct experience, arrive at knowing the "All" that is here in its immensity, can one remain with this "All" and be merged in It?"

For a number of years, Salim regularly went to Belgium to teach. During the three days he would spend there, he ate nothing, or very little, and felt constantly frozen, especially in winter. He had to content himself with frequent cups of tea to warm himself up.

The day's program allowed him to work with people both individually and collectively. He rose always at three in the morning to be able to meditate and carry out his hatha yoga postures before his pupils woke at six. After a breakfast taken in silence, everyone joined together in the meditation room for an hour long session. Salim would first gave some instructions, then lead the meditation for twenty to twenty-five minutes; the pupils would then undertake a slow walk of around ten minutes, during which, to retain their concentration, they carried out series of mudras. Then, they meditated again for around twenty minutes.

When they left to attend to the preparation of the meals and the dishes, throughout which tasks they had to continue accomplishing concentration exercises adapted to active life, Salim would take one of them to work one to one with him for fifteen to thirty minutes. Once the lesson was over, the pupil would call another who would take his place, which allowed Salim to adapt the degree of difficulty of the exercises to the capacity for attention of each. The individual sessions would continue in this way until ten thirty in the morning, the time of a new collective meeting taking place, like the last one, with two sessions of steadily guided meditation with an interval of slow walking accompanied by mudras. At eleven thirty, he would take more pupils one to one until lunch at one.

Lunch would take place in silence. At two thirty, an hour of meditation brought everyone together again, then individual lessons went on until dinner, with a break for another hour of collective meditation. From time to time, someone would bring a cup of tea to Salim, who spent all day in the meditation room, with the exception of mealtimes, during which he read spiritual texts to his pupils to stimulate them.

After dinner, while some pupils were doing the dishes, Salim would take a few more people for individual lessons before bringing all the participants back together for a final and short meditation followed by a question and answer session. At around eleven at night, he would withdraw to his room to meditate before going to bed at around midnight.

Sometimes, during the afternoon or the evening, he would tell a story with a spiritual meaning that he would then ask each of them to repeat in turn. This particular work was destined to make the pupils clearly perceive the force that gravity exercises in their phenomenal lives, for, as they took up the narration, it was surprising to note the extent to which deformations might creep in. Everyone had heard what he wanted to hear, or forgotten certain significant details, or involuntarily added an element bearing no relation to the original tale, and so on. Everyone could thereby remark, in a concrete manner, the difficulty that existed for each of them in being accurate.

Through this simple exercise, it was easy to see how the transmission of a truth is inevitably subject to distortions that progressively creep in, including into sacred texts which were orally transmitted in times gone by—distortions leading inevitably to misunderstandings, incomprehension, and frictions between human beings.

After these three days, Salim left instructions and indicated the spiritual work to be carried out in the pupils' active lives until his next visit. Finally, exhausted, he set off on his return journey.

Although often ill even before he left, he never canceled his journey, striving always to surpass himself in order not to disappoint the pupils awaiting him and, also, because he believed effort on oneself to be vital in spiritual practice.

Sri Lanka, Nyanaponika Théra.

Seven years had passed since Salim had left India in 1976 and he still hoped to rediscover the atmosphere of that country which he missed so much. We decided to go there for a brief trip, immediately after we were married at the end of 1983.

We wanted first to go to Sri Lanka as a center of Theravada Buddhism. We arrived in Colombo on Christmas day and, after a night spent in a guest house, we took the train to Kandy. Salim, who contemplated the luxurious vegetation with rapture, certainly appreciated the tropical climate, particularly after the cold of the Parisian winter.

We spent a week in Kandy, in a modest hotel located not far from the famous "Temple of the Sacred Tooth". We intended to visit a monastery recommended to us by the Sinhalese Buddhist Publication Society. After renting a car and driver, we set off. Finally, when we arrived at our destination, it was to find some modest buildings that were almost deserted; the manager of the site was apparently away and the atmosphere which reigned there was, strictly speaking, not at all that of a monastery; so the visit proved to be disappointing.

Nyanaponika Thera

Nyanaponika Thera, a hermit of German origin, lived in a hermitage quite close to Kandy; we asked to meet him. We had to obtain authorization from the Buddhist Publication Society to be able to approach him. His small house stood in the middle of an exotic forest, sheltered from all outside disturbance; the access route was even watched by a forest warden. The erudite anchorite received us with benevolence in a room filled with books from floor to ceiling. He had become famous in the Buddhist world for his translations, especially of the famous Satipatthana Sutta on the development of attention.

Madras, Chinmayananda.

Arriving in Madras, Salim hoped to revisit the place where he had lived for so many years. Only, the demographic growth that India had experienced, which had transformed cities with lightening speed, had so changed Besant Nagar that it was difficult for him even to find his way.

We went one evening to attend a performance of Bharata Natyam given at "Kalakshetra", the Indian dance center, which Salim was very moved to see again. As we knew we were staying for only a short time, we had brought a water filter and what was necessary to sterilize fruit, but we were not sufficiently equipped to cook as Salim had been during his previous journeys. We had, therefore, to eat out some of the time, taking the maximum amount of precautions. After trying a Chinese restaurant which offered dishes just as spicy as Indian cuisine, we came to content ourselves, for lunch and dinner, with ordering in the hotel restaurant the same non-spicy dish, consisting of a spoonful of fried onions and potatoes in batter, which, to my despair, made Salim continually ill.

We learned that Satya Sai Baba was passing through Madras for a lecture. Salim having told me of his wish to see this famous guru again, we went to the location, but we found only the crowd which was dispersing. We finally had the opportunity of meeting Chinmayananda, famous for his commentaries on the Baghavada Gita.

In going to Sri Lanka and Madras, Salim had firstly wanted to rediscover the atmosphere of India and he was also hoping to find opportunities for interesting exchanges in the spiritual field; from this point of view, the journey did not bring him anything that he was hoping for.

Karlfried Graf Dürckheim.

Karlfried Graf Dürckheim

When I met Salim in 1974, I was practicing Zen meditation with a disciple of Karlfried Graf Dürckheim in a dojo not far from Rue Octave Feuillet and where Dürckheim sometimes came when he was passing through Paris. Therefore, I arranged for Salim to have the opportunity of meeting him during one of his visits.

Some years later, when I was taking Salim to the mountains for a rest, we passed through Rutte to visit the center that Dürckheim, who was blind by this time, possessed in the Black Forest. He brought up India with Salim and, on this occasion, told us of his meetings some years previously, with Ma Anandamayi and Muktananda. He also spoke of the work he had written on the Hara, entitled, in English, "Hara, the Vital Center of Man" and which, at the time I read it, had fascinated me. When Salim said that, in his opinion, this vital center was a neutral force that one could develop, without necessarily having known enlightenment, I was very interested to hear Dürckheim declare that, since the time of writing his book, he had come to the same conclusion. They then spoke about psychoanalysis, Jungian and Freudian, which Dürckheim considered as a potential stage in a spiritual quest, perhaps necessary for some people who were overly disturbed; he nevertheless made known some distinct reservations relating to the confusion that sometimes existed between a spiritual practice and the Jungian notion of "individuation". Salim could only agree, because, he said, in Western psychology, no sort of therapy aimed to enable a human being to access the superior level of consciousness existing within him, whereas it is the experiential—rather than intellectual—recognition of this superior level of consciousness which constitutes enlightenment.

Puzzling spiritual experiences.

In his books, Salim mentions some of his spiritual experiences in order to enable a better understanding of what a practice consists of and also to encourage aspirants. Naturally, among the people who would come to see him, the majority were hoping themselves to have powerful spiritual experiences, but without realizing the necessity of being ready to be able to bear them. Salim would put them on their guard by explaining to them: "As these experiences cannot be compared or related to any known thing existing in the tangible world, they can subsequently be disquieting and disturbing.

If a seeker wishes to obtain Grace, it is indispensable, through assiduous work on himself, not only for his undesirable tendencies to be transmuted, but also for his levels of being and of consciousness to be sufficiently elevated, otherwise he will find himself submerged, even crushed, by these Holy manifestations".

Most of the time, Salim avoided speaking of the mystic phenomena that had occurred to him, because it is a temptation for an aspirant to want to seek them instead of remaining new and open to the present. Thus, most of the phenomenal experiences he had will remain, as he would say: "A secret between the Divine and him".

Salim often received the thoughts of people close to him, particularly those of his pupils, and often he would even see in his mind what they were doing or going to do, or he would know in advance the content of letters he was going to receive, but which had not yet been written.

He also received, in the streets, in public places or elsewhere, in a disconcerting manner, thoughts of the people around him. This was not particularly pleasant. Thus he could receive the kind of images that arise in the masculine mind when a young woman goes by. He could not help thinking, at such times, that if this woman suspected the crudeness of the fantasies that emerged in the heads of men and what she was reduced to at that moment, she would certainly not feel flattered by their looks nor desirous of attracting their attention.

Salim emphasized that, in such circumstances, a man did not understand the gravity of the wrong he did both to the woman and to himself in allowing himself to harbor such imaginings. "It must not be forgotten," he would add, "that a human being is a creature of habit and, through the repetition of the sort of thoughts he allows to traverse his mind, without being conscious of it, he allows them to plow their furrow ever more deeply in his being. If these thoughts prove incompatible with spiritual aspiration, this person closes to himself, without knowing it, the door to the Divine Light within himself."

Salim had, many times, spiritual experiences linked to food, which allowed him to better comprehend the importance of the daily act of feeding oneself.

One day when, while working on himself, he was just about to eat a few grapes, he was seized by an indefinable feeling. He remained immobile for a moment, contemplating the grape in front of him, when, suddenly, an enigmatic contact began to establish itself silently between him and the fruit. In a way that was impossible to describe, he felt the being of these grapes and felt, within himself, their fear. They were, in their own way, surprisingly conscious that the time had come for them to lose their lives. They lay before him, impotent and incapable of flight, and, for Salim, their fear in the face of imminent death was evident and incontestable.

He remained frozen in the same posture while inexpressible thoughts on the unfathomable mystery of Creation and of existence ran through his mind. At this moment, no doubt was possible for him concerning the fact that all the food human beings eat possesses a form of consciousness that is ordinarily impossible to comprehend and, consequently, it senses its life and fears its death.

Thus a human being finds himself in the unfortunate position of being obliged to suppress living things in order to sustain his own organism. But, as Salim received confirmation one day when cutting a tomato or, on another occasion, when he was about to cook some rice, these foodstuffs know, in their way, what death is and dread it. "That is the reason," he would say, "for the necessity, through a very particular inner attitude and respect for the sort of sensibility that these living entities possess, to be able to reassure them regarding the pain that they cannot fail to feel before bringing their lives to an end in order to eat them. The fact of remaining immobile for a few moments in silent prayer and joining oneself to the food that is going to be cooked or eaten helps the aspirant to become present and to be 'placed' in himself in a manner that is different from his habitual manner. Moreover, this awakens in him a sense of responsibility and respect for these entities which are about to be sacrificed in order to maintain his physical existence. Finally, this attitude allows him to calm the feelings of the food, which, at that moment, is going to lose its life and its individuality in the interest of the seeker, and, as far as possible, help to relieve its fear and pain."

However, it must not be concluded that, as all creatures suffer when one takes their lives, there is no difference between eating meat and satisfying oneself with a vegetarian diet. As Salim recalls in "The Way of Inner Vigilance", the level of suffering is not the same in a plant as in a mammal or a fish. Furthermore, if people who eat meat without wishing to think of the suffering of the animal had to slit its throat themselves, what would be their attitude then? Would they agree to do what is done behind the walls of the slaughterhouse ?

Salim wrote on this subject: "Because of the tremendous terror, physical pain, and moral agony dumb creatures must inevitably go through when faced with their bewilderingly precipitate and harsh death at the hands of humans, it is better to refrain altogether from eating animal flesh. For every piece of meat less that is consumed means in time one animal less will go to the slaughterhouse.

"At such an atrocious moment, these unfortunate creatures become intensely alert and concentrated. The feelings of terror, helplessness, and despair that they go through during these fearful instants—not to mention also the anger and hatred that they bear toward the people who are slaughtering them—are, in keeping with the violence of these moments, extremely powerful. These final terrible emotions that they take with them when dying inevitably infect their flesh and remain highly active in it, and when consumed by human beings—especially in the heedless manner in which they generally do so—it is bound to influence their inner state adversely and gradually fill them with sentiments corresponding to those that these ill-fated beings had in them at the time of their death."

When he was in the East, Salim had unbearable experiences from every point of view in seeing buffalo and other animals having their throats slit in the public square by men who, afterwards, talked blithely among themselves while witnessing the lengthy death throes of these unfortunate beasts without showing the slightest pity for them.

"Compassion! One has to feel compassion," Salim would exclaim, "towards all living creatures who, despite the fact that they do not possess the same level of consciousness or the same capacity for reflection as the human being, are no less aware of pain in all its reality and know what death means."

Moreover, Salim was always astounded when someone told him that a fish did not suffer when a hook tore through its palate and it was hauled out of the water. Many times, he had painful experiences feeling in himself the terror and the suffering of these mute creatures. "Even if one has not oneself been touched by perceptions of this nature, it is enough," he would say, "to observe the manner in which a fish twists and contorts itself in all directions and with all its strength when it is torn from its aquatic lair and thrown on the ground where it lengthily agonizes before dying, to realize that it is inconceivable that this animal is insensible to pain, to fear, and to death."

He told me one day of a strange experience that had occurred to him when he was living in his tiny room on the Rue du Cherche-Midi. Nelly Caron, the friend who greatly admired his music and who had enabled him to obtain that providential shelter, had come to pay him a visit. She had brought him some provisions, wrapped in paper, which she had put down in a corner of the room. After she left, he opened the packet and saw, to his grief, that, among the food contained therein, there was a piece of meat. Salim explained to me that he had been completely taken by surprise by the state he was suddenly plunged into upon seeing this piece of meat which, in an entirely accidental manner, had fallen into his hands.

He was seized with a terrible feeling of pity for the animal, whose silent cries, it seemed to him at the time, he could hear and so anguished were they that he remained troubled and unable to move. It was as though the poor beast wanted to be relieved of the dreadful suffering that it had been subjected to when its life was taken.

Salim did not know exactly how long he remained in this distant state, filled with compassion for the unfortunate creature while that mysterious sound, the Nada, vibrated in his ears in such a striking manner that he had the impression his head would not be able to bear it.

When he had, so to speak, come back to himself, at least half an hour had passed and, to his astonishment, the slice of meat, which he had held in his hands throughout this time, had become hard like stone; it was as though it was mummified. When, a few days later, he showed Nelly Caron what had happened to the meat that she had bought him, she was so surprised and touched that she asked him for permission to keep this strange relic, which he immediately gave to her, asking her not to bring him any more meat in the future. He also spoke of this troubling event with Mr Adie, who, after a moment's silence, told him: "There are things that occur sometimes in life that one cannot understand or explain at all". Then he remained pensive for a long time, looking at Salim.

On the subject of this phenomenon, Salim was eager to emphasize that it had happened independently of his will, that he had absolutely not sought it and that he did not, himself, understand in what mysterious manner this piece of meat had become mummified in his hands.

On another occasion, when he was coming back from the Saint-Eustache church, extremely hurt by the manner in which he had been received by the priest attached to this church, who didn't think it appropriate to play a mass written by a non-Catholic, he passed through the old neighborhood of Les Halles, plunged in thought, when his eyes suddenly fell on a vast warehouse opening onto the road, where hundreds of cattle carcasses were suspended. Through his mind's eye, so to speak, he suddenly had a vision of the panic-stricken spirits of these animals who, without understanding what had happened to them, were desperately trying to find their bodies in the midst of all these remains that burly workers, dressed in blood stained overalls, were manipulating with total indifference and insensitivity.

Communal illusions.

Many people meeting Salim for the first time came to see him full of illusions, as much about the knowledge they believed they had of themselves as their aspirations. Despite all that he had explained in his first book, they hoped to be able to rapidly attain enlightenment and liberation without too much effort.

Among the spectacular promises and false revelations dispensed by pseudo-masters, there is one that particularly fascinates people and which concerns past incarnations. Salim one day received a visit from a young woman who wanted to work with him and who told him that someone had "seen" that she had been Cleopatra in a previous life. Considering the exceptional destiny of this queen of Egypt who was a woman so out of the ordinary, who spoke seven languages, who sacrificed herself ceaselessly for her country, and who tragically ended up committing suicide at the age of thirty, how is it possible not to doubt such affirmations which aim only to impress credulous people?

Salim always made it clear to his pupils that previous incarnations did not interest him. Only the present was important and counted in his eyes, because, he would say, "The present is the inexorable result of what one was yesterday, the day before yesterday, last year, etc., and the way today is lived will determine, in just as unavoidable a manner, what will be tomorrow, next year, or all future existence, whatever form it may take".

He had himself, without having sought them, troubling experiences relating to past existences, but he understood that, even if he managed, through certain specific exercises, in going so deep within himself that he succeeded in reaching the secret regions of his consciousness and recalling some of his previous lives, these memories would have been much too sparse and confused. It would have been impossible for him to visualize the totality of his past actions and the consequences they had had and continued to have on his being, or even, as all is interconnected, the mysterious traces that they might have left on this planet, and to see in what way they might have influenced and still be influencing this globe, for better or for worse.

Writing a new book. The Dhammapada. Tibetans in France.

Because of the incomprehension he encountered with his pupils, Salim decided to write a new book, but, taking into account the difficulties that we had encountered in developing the English version of his first book, he saw that it was henceforth preferable to write directly in French; in this way, I no longer had to translate, but simply to correct his grammar.

At the same time, as he always deplored the fact that the transcriptions in French that he could find of the Buddist text "The Dhammapada" were not up to the standard of the English copy he possessed, he decided at the same time to undertake, with my help, a translation of this work.

We had the opportunity of attending a lecture in Paris on the theme of compassion in Buddhism, given by Kalu Rinpoche. The radiance that emanated from this remarkable man made a strong impression on us.

Without any doubt, this was the Buddhism that Salim felt closest to. Although these teachings have been externally subjected to significant modifications according to the country in which they are established, the fundamental points of the Dharma (the doctrine) nevertheless remain always alive: the necessity for meditation and concentration, the insistence on compassion and tolerance, a way of living in accordance with elevated aspirations, and, finally, an aim, the Awakening, which the human being can only attain by personal effort. All the aspects of the Eightfold Path had been put into practice by Salim before even entering into contact with the teachings of the Buddha.

Thinking of the incomprehension he sometimes encountered in people who came to see him on the subject of what an authentic spiritual path implies, Salim remembered a reflection addressed with mischief by an old Tibetan to some Westerners who had come to see him in India. "If there were an easy path, the Buddha would have found it. Who dares to think that he is cleverer than the Buddha?"

Nourishing his inner life.

Being only able to count on his own resources to find ways to nourish his inner life and feed his spiritual practices was a perpetual challenge for Salim.

The only spiritual works that he could really get interested in and that he re-read fairly regularly were The Dhammapada, The Bhagavad Gita (Sri Aurobindo's translation), "Practice of the Presence of God" by Brother Lawrence, The Gospels, and The Tibetan Book of the Dead (edited by W. Y. Evans-Wentz and Lama Kazi Dawa-Samdup) in which he found, when he discovered it, confirmations of spiritual experiences relating to death that he had had years before. Later, he found in "Living Time" by Maurice Nicoll an echo of his own questioning concerning time which particularly moved him; finally, he was interested in all that related to the Cosmos and the Universe and very much enjoyed watching documentaries on this subject which fascinated him.

Besides his sadhana, which, obviously, came first in his life, music remained his principal support. He liked to listen to recordings of Indian and Tibetan music that he had brought back from his time in India; for him, they expressed the Sacred and were situated "outside of time". The bhajans always spoke to him of an intense devotional feeling, while the Indian flute or the strange pentatonic Tibetan harmonies evoked in his mind the vast spaces of the Himalayan plateaus.

Concerning Western music, for Salim it was essential to find something other than technical ability. "When," he would say, "one listens to what the majority of composers have to say, despite the fact that they know their profession well and their works are pleasing to the ear, it is often just music for entertainment. There is so little music which addresses a human being to speak to him of another world, habitually inaccessible to him. The composer must have a vital message to convey, to awaken in the auditor an intense desire to penetrate the mystery of existence."

Over the years, the composers that Salim still liked to turn to became fewer and fewer; he could no longer give his attention to anything but an extremely internalized music.

He listened to cassettes, which allowed him to make mix tapes and to put together extracts of works he liked with the greatest care.

Every day, he listened to the Benedictus section of Gounod's St Cecilia Mass' which, because of its exceptionally devotional character, had become, as he put it, "his prayer".

Listening to certain extracts of Beethoven's work, such as the adagio movement of his Piano Concerto No. 5, he keenly felt that the great man was saying to his auditor, with infinite tenderness: "Yes, I know, I know my friend that you know solitude and I sympathize with you." Other passages of his music give off such force and such goodness that these can only be the expression of what Beethoven was in himself.

Salim always came back to the exceptional love expressed by the music of César Franck, particularly his work entitled "Psyché", as well as to the loving breadth of Brahms's symphonies, the heroic dimension of Richard Strauss's "An Alpine Symphony", and Chausson's symphony. At other moments, he needed to listen to Gustav Mahler's symphonies for the depth and compassion that emanate from them, or the adagio movement of Saint-Saëns's Symphony No. 3 for the extraordinary tenderness conveyed by this music.

Continuity was also an element of great importance to Salim, which is why he liked to listen to certain works by Respighi and also Satie's Gymnopédies, orchestrated by Debussy, or to Elgar's Cello Concerto.

When he was going through health trials that were too difficult, he preferred to turn towards a piece of descriptive music that was very close to his heart, written by Miklos Rosza for the film "Ben Hur", certain sequences of which illustrate the presence of Christ. Although only a composition for a movie, this music nevertheless gives off love of such an elevated nature and such an exceptional feeling of courage that Salim drew great comfort from it.

Following phenomenal experiences relating to non spatio-temporal dimensions that he had had, Salim also enormously appreciated listening to a work by Gustav Holst entitled "The Planets" (which so mysteriously evoked an infinite sidereal space), Paul Dukas's "La Péri", and several of Debussy's works including "Sirènes" for female chorus and orchestra, the orchestral version of "La cathédrale engloutie", and "Le martyre de Saint Sébastien". In the creations of these composers, Salim sensed what he had himself tried to make appear through his music, the expression of the existence of enigmatic and invisible universes, inciting the auditor to want to overcome the limits of the tangible world and to wonder about the mystery of life and of death.

The sense of mystery.

Salim was fascinated by the mystery of origins, where did we come from? where do we go after death? He always felt, cultivated, and nourished a keen sense of mystery in the face of the enigma of life and of the Universe. It was with astonishment that he noted the lack of this sense of mystery in his pupils.

In the West, scientific rationality such as it is taught in schools relegates metaphysical questioning to the level of children's fairy tales. Scientific discoveries should arouse fascinated wonder in the whole of humanity before the inconceivable Intelligence that is at the origin of the laws permitting the organization of matter and the emergence of a consciousness capable of self-questioning. Yet, in place of this dazzling astonishment which leads to the question of what this Supreme Intelligence expects of its Creation, scientific discoveries are immediately considered from a utilitarian angle and used with greed for profit, domination, or destruction.

The general state of mind in the West is that religion is outdated, useless, that the Universe is governed by chance and necessity, and that there is no point in petitioning a demanding God to implore his clemency. Spirituality is regarded with condescension or even rejected with suspicion.

However, the greatest scientists are well aware that mystery is everywhere, behind the immutable laws of Creation.

In a speech addressed to the League of Human Rights in 1932 and entitled "My Credo" , Albert Einstein said:

"The most beautiful and deepest experience a human being can have is the sense of the mysterious. It is the underlying principle of religion.... He who never had this experience seems to me, if not dead, then at least blind. To sense that behind anything that can be experienced there is a something that our mind cannot grasp and whose beauty and sublimity reaches us only indirectly and as a feeble reflection, this is religiousness....one cannot help but be in awe when (one) contemplates the mysteries of eternity, of life, of the marvelous structure of reality. "

Salim kept constantly alive within himself a state of questioning in the face of the mysterious deployment of the Universe. He liked to look at Hubert Reeves's work "Poussières d'étoiles" (Stardust) illustrated with fascinating images of stars and galaxies. He even copied out a passage that particularly struck him relating to the infinity of the Universe:

"Here is a computer generated reconstitution of the layout of the galaxies in the few billion light years of space that surround us.

"Each of these luminous points is a galaxy like our own, with hundreds of billions of stars, nebulae, planets, and, perhaps, civilizations. Vertiginous documents that show us, like no other image, the immensity of our Universe. And this is only a drop in a vast ocean. Our observations suggest that the Universe is infinite, that the number of galaxies is infinite.

"'Name a figure as big as you want', say the mathematicians, 'the infinite is bigger than that'. How many galaxies are there? A billion, billion, billion... billion? More. Always more. However long our

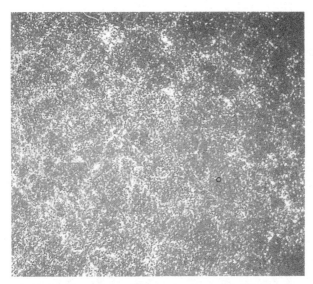

Computer generated reconstitution of the Universe

journey lasts, however far we go in space, the Universe will always remain the same. In the porthole of our spacecraft, galaxies will succeed each other indefinitely...

"Before this spectacle, what do you feel? Unease, anguish, exaltation, indifference? Everyone has his own way of feeling those situations that are beyond him."

Questioning time, is it circular or linear?

Because of inexplicable phenomena—some of which have been related in this book—which occurred to him repeatedly throughout his spiritual progression, Salim never stopped wondering about the nature of time which is normally accepted without question.

Approaching the troubling question of the future which seemed to him, in some strange way, already to exist and which, apparently, could be known by a certain aspect of oneself, he tried to penetrate the enigma of the many premonitory dreams that he had had, during which he had been present at events and scenes that he had only lived much later, or still other sorts of dreams, during which certain future situations had been revealed to him symbolically. When I asked him the reason

Chacun de ces points lumineux est une galaxie comme la nôtre, avec ses centaines de milliards d'étoiles, ses nébuleuses, ses planètes, et peut-être ses civilisations. Documents vertigineux qui nous rendent comme aucun autre l'image de l'immensité de notre univers. Et ce n'est qu'une goutte d'eau dans le vaste océan. Nos observations suggèrent que l'univers est infini, que le nombre de galaxies est infini.

"Nommez un chiffre aussi grand que vous le voulez, disent les mathématiciens, l'infini, c'est encore plus grand." Combien y a-t-il de galaxies? Un milliard de milliards de milliards... de milliards? Encore plus. Toujours plus. Aussi longtemps que durera notre voyage, aussi loin que nous allions dans l'espace, l'univers restera toujours semblable à lui-même. Dans le hublot de notre vaisseau spatial, les galaxies se succèdent, indéfiniment... Devant ce spectacle, quel est votre état d'âme? Malaise, angoisse, exaltation, indifférence? Chacun vit à sa façon, avec sa sensibilité, les situations qui le dépassent.

Hubert Reeves's passage about infinity of the Universe.

for these premonitions occurring most often during nocturnal dreams and not during the day, Salim responded that, in the course of the day, one is too busy responding to the call of external life; thus one is rarely sufficiently available and open internally to be able to receive these enigmatic messages and it is only in nocturnal sleep that the Great Knower in a human being can find a way to communicate what It wishes so mysteriously to convey to him and which may prove vital to him.

Moreover, thanks to an extrasensory perception that he had felt one day during a concentration exercise and which had shaken him, he remained convinced that actions and events that had taken place in the visible world continued to recur in other dimensions whose existence is not ordinarily suspected. "Therefore," Salim would go on, "should the aspirant not, knowing that nothing is ever lost and that his thoughts and actions are repeating themselves almost indefinitely in time and space, question everything that he is thinking and doing in the present?"

He often told me of his preoccupations concerning repeated experiences which occurred at the most unexpected moments; suddenly, in a fleeting instant, something mysterious would happen within him and, through a strange inner silence, he would be seized by the inexpressible certitude that what he was doing or living had already taken place in a past that had no connection with his current life. Perplexed, he would always ask himself: "As I know that I have never yet performed this action or lived this situation in my present life, where and when did this happen to me?"

It was following these disconcerting experiences that Salim acquired the profound conviction that time was circular and that, without one realizing it ordinarily, one was a prisoner of the recurrence of existence.

However, the Buddhist tradition states that, when the Buddha attained his final awakening, he remembered many of his previous lives; Salim, himself, had memories of situations and events that did not belong to this life or to places that he had known. In addition to this, Ian Stevenson's works on children who remember a previous life are very troubling. The published facts were collected over dozens of years with the greatest scientific rigor and include thousands of cases in a wide variety of cultures and countries. These children who remember a previous life sometimes give surprising details of elements that enable some trace to be found of the person they claim to have been in their previous incarnation.

How can these data relating to a linear time be reconciled with Salim's experiences of recurrence suggesting circular time? Experiences of recurrence which were too many and too powerful to be ignored. We spoke of this together at length.

The perception of time being directly linked to the level of consciousness, it is certainly a vertiginous question that cannot easily be grasped and which does not belong to ordinary binary logic.

Perhaps when an interest for something begins to become predominant in a person, a trace left in his being creates the conditions for recurrence. It is striking to see the assurance with which great beings, musicians, scientists, or mystics, throw themselves into the activity that is dearest to them—as though they had already done it; which may be explicable if they are in circular time, in other words, in a recurrence of the same existence. The intensity of their being has crystallized something in them which has traversed death, unlike the majority of people who remain subject to the vagaries of linear time.

On this subject, it should be noted that the cases collected by Stevenson were never remarkable personalities, whether in the fields of science, art, or spirituality.

On the other hand, one cannot fail to be struck by the repeated affirmations of the great conductor Karajan who declared on many occasions: "Nature will have to provide me with a new body, I need it to carry on my work". His ardent desire to be reborn in order to continue his musical work could only give rise for him to the very conditions of recurrence.

Is it possible, then, to advance the hypothesis that the more crystallization of a predominant interest there is, the more deeply it will leave its mark on the being of the person and attract the necessary conditions for the realization of whatever is dearest to him. It is in this way that, by deliberately cultivating an interest in a spiritual quest, an aspirant is leaving a trace within himself and creating for himself the conditions for recurrence.

His hope rests on the possibility of the circle of time becoming, for him, through assiduous spiritual practices and the transformation of himself, a spiral. From this perspective, recurrence appears as the necessary means to bring a human being to such an elevated level of evolution that ordinary mortals do not have the slightest notion of it.

Salim came to the conclusion that the flow of time is not the same for everyone, that it changes according to the degree of evolution of the human being himself, who must one day come, through the spiritual efforts he makes, to discover the Impersonal Aspect of his nature which alone can permit him to break the chains that keep him subjugated to time.

New broadcast of Salim's Mass.

In the fall of 1988, after twenty-five years of oblivion, a completely unexpected event occurred that filled Salim with joy. His Mass was broadcast over the airwaves of the France-Musique radio station during the program "Avis de Recherches" (Searching for...), after "Kamaal", another of his works for solo and orchestra, had been played on this same program the year before.

Salim discovers the reason for his intestinal problems.

During the long years that I watched, powerless, the ordeals that Salim endured with his intestinal problems, we had consulted leading medical experts, undergone scores of examinations, tried diets, cures, allopathic, homeopathic, and natural remedies, etc. without ever achieving any results.

It was only in 1989 that something happened which had decisive repercussions for his health. One night, at around two in the morning, while he was suffering one of his crises, which, as always, left him completely exhausted, Salim lay down on his bed and, to distract himself a little from the pain of the spasms that were tearing through his stomach, he switched on the radio to listen to the BBC which sometimes broadcast programs relating to the cosmos, galaxies, and stars.

Through a providential combination of circumstances, he heard an English doctor talking about an illness which he called "sprue" and which had apparently been discovered by a Dutchman during the Second World War. It was an allergy to gluten, the protein that is found in most cereals (wheat, rye, barley, spelt, oats) and which provokes in the subject terrible diarrhea which weakens him progressively to the point where, if he, not knowing the cause of his illness, continues to ingest gluten, he will end up dying from it. The doctor explained that the slightest trace of gluten in a dish was enough to provoke such crises.

Salim said to himself that, as no doctor had ever spoken to him of this allergy, it could not apply in his case. However, the description of the symptoms corresponded so closely to what he felt that he could not rule out this hypothesis. When, the following morning, he told me about what he had heard on the radio concerning this illness, we decided, albeit without too much hope, to remove from his diet any food containing gluten, that is to say pasta, crispbreads, etc. which his doctor had recommended as they were light foods suitable for his delicate stomach.

The results turned out to be surprising as, for the first time in fifty years, Salim felt an improvement whose cause was easily identifiable. This illness that had distressed him for all these long years and which had been an enigma for all the doctors he had consulted, finally turned out to be a severe gluten allergy, otherwise known as celiac disease.

When we spoke to the specialist who was monitoring Salim, he seemed little impressed, alleging (without suspecting the unusual resources that an intense spiritual practice might confer) that it was completely impossible to live to sixty-eight years old with this allergy and that, if, truly, Salim had been affected, he should have died of it long before.

Of course, his intestines, damaged by the interminable crises that he had suffered for so many years, remained extremely sensitive and fragile. A possible complication of celiac disease is the development of an intestinal cancer which is, in fact, what subsequently happened and carried Salim away in 2006.

The basic food of Asia being rice, in retrospect it seems understandable that during his childhood and his adolescence in the Middle-East, when he ate practically no other cereal, he didn't suffer from this problem, then later, in India, when he again took up this rice based diet, his health improved without the reason really being understood. On the other hand, as soon as he entered the British Royal Air force, in addition to the shock he suffered, the Western food, which included bread, wheat flour, and pastry, quickly made him very ill.

After this providential discovery, Salim was finally able to dare to go out in relative tranquility, without being haunted, as in the past, by the fear of being seized by one of his crises.

Preconceptions concerning spirituality.

It is common to hear that, if someone is supposed to be on a spiritual path, "God being with him", everything should turn out well for him.

Many times, Salim found himself facing people who, because of his health problems, doubted the authenticity of his spiritual path. Such people asked whether true spirituality should not be accompanied by riches, health, happiness, etc.? If one considers the terrible circumstances in which Christ left this world, He who said: "The Son of man has no place to lay his head", should it be concluded, giving credence to such reasoning, that God could not have been with Him?

A pupil one day said to Salim: "I have just read a marvelous book on positive thought; why don't you teach us that?" Salim responded that a practice of concentration and meditation was, by definition, positive and that no thought could be more positive than that which consists of seeking the Absolute in oneself.

The pupil told him that the book she had read (apparently written by an American evangelist) affirmed that, by the power of "positive thought", it was possible to be surrounded by material riches, to access a state of perpetual happiness, and even to die in good health. Why then did Salim have health problems? Was it not precisely because he was not using positive thought?

Salim responded that the sort of positive thought advocated by this author in his book would probably prove useful for people who wasted their time ruminating on negativities. However, before hoping for even partial results, such people should realize that people who recommended "positive thought" were basing it on the entirely erroneous postulate that a human being is sufficiently master of himself to be able to direct his mental processes according to his will. A long practice of concentration is indispensable to succeed in maintaining thought directed towards the same point. Consequently, would it not be better, instead of focusing on a utilitarian concentration in order that the world might respond to what one ordinarily hopes to obtain in terms of earthly goods, to deploy the necessary efforts to acquire spiritual riches which, alone, will prove to be useful after death?

The Buddha, who declared that life is suffering, must be, according to this simplistic theory, a pessimist who would undoubtedly have done better to devote himself to positive thinking...

As for the physical invulnerability assumed to be accessible through mental strength alone, in India too tales circulated and even reached the West giving the impression that, through the supernatural powers they developed, the great yogis were supposed to leave this world in the best of health and at the moment of their own choosing. This belief rests on the secret hope that everyone nourishes to die without suffering and the optimism that spiritual masters will find a simple recipe that can be followed.

The fact that the famous Ramana Maharshi, like Ramakrishna, died of cancer, or that Sri Aurobindo succumbed to a bout of uremia, has given rise to some criticism, even in India. Even among Buddhists, some maintain the belief that with enough practices they will succeed in keeping their bodies in good health forever.

Salim tried to explain to the people who came to see him that what a seeker attained spiritually was not destined to be used for earthly ends.

Western psychology has admitted what Eastern traditions have affirmed for a long time, namely that the physical and the mental are closely linked and that one necessarily affects the other. However, it is important not to go to the other extreme which consists of believing that once his mind has been purified of all negative thought, a disciple may live eternally in a body that will no longer be subject to the disintegration that inevitably awaits all tangible forms. In other words, as Salim liked to put it ironically: "No-one dies of good health!"

The aim of a spiritual practice consists, he would say, in finding in oneself what is unconditioned, beyond the tangible, which is not subject to birth or to death, and not to conquer the law of dissolution which inexorably applies to all that is manifest at the material level. The Buddha, addressing his disciples, told them:

"There is, O monks, an Unborn, Unoriginated, Uncreated, Unformed. Were there not, O monks, this Unborn, Unoriginated, Uncreated, Unformed, there would be no escape from the world of the born, originated, created, formed. Since, O monks, there is an Unborn, Unoriginated, Uncreated, Unformed, therefore is there an escape from the born, originated, created, formed." (Udhâna, VIII).

Furthermore, it must be understood that as a seeker progresses spiritually, he sees his sensibility become ever more refined. This is one of the reasons for some yogis preferring to retire from the world to take refuge in deserted places so as to no longer have to undergo the pressure of mental pollution which inevitably reigns in places of dense population.

Salim also experienced well-intentioned people saying to him: "God makes suffer those he loves". Salim, who did not accept this kind of gratuitous affirmation, would respond with humor: "Then ask him to love me a little less!"

Salim recalled modern science had shown that, on a physical level, the world is amazingly complex; how much more so, consequently, must the spiritual domain be. The mysterious causes that put some seekers in sometimes tragic situations are beyond common comprehension.

"Perhaps," he would say, "a person has, in some ordinarily inexplicable way, 'chosen' in advance, with the aim of accelerating his evolution, a destiny difficult to assume. And perhaps, through what he has learned in his suffering, he has been able to develop faculties permitting him to subsequently help other aspirants in a way that would not have otherwise been possible for him. However, suffering is no less real as well as trials."

It was precisely because he suffered physically in his body during so many years that Salim could not accept what he had heard so much in India: that it sufficed to say to oneself that one was not one's body to be liberated from it. He emphasized that no intellectual reasoning allowed a human being to tear away from the belief—profoundly crystallized in his subconscious from the day he had opened his eyes to phenomenal existence—that he is the body that he lives in. He can free himself from this belief which has been genetically conveyed to him from his earliest ancestors, only if he succeeds through intense meditation practices, in "dis-identifying" with his corporeal envelope in order to find the Impersonal in himself, which is free from time and from the tangible, and reveals itself as his True Nature.

Salim's other books.

In responding to his pupils' questions and seeing their difficulties, Salim saw the necessity for sharing more widely the understandings that had come out of his own path, to show others the exercises he had undertaken, to expose the difficulties he had encountered, and some of the spiritual experiences he had been privileged to have. When he was inspired to tackle a theme, he would write a first draft, show it to me, we would correct the French together, I would type it, he would work on it some more, and so on, six, ten, or even a dozen times, until the achievement of a definitive version which he would give a photocopy of to everyone who came to see him. In this way the texts built up and after a few months or years there was enough material to make up a new book.

It sometimes happened that when reading other spiritual works, I would find passages that were in complete accordance with what Salim was writing. When I showed him such phrases, he was very pleased and we developed, little by little, the habit of illustrating his writings with mystic quotations from all traditions.

Compassion and marital relationships.

In his book la Quête Suprême (The Supreme Quest), Salim conse-crated a great deal of space to theme of compassion, the cruel lack of which he deplored not only throughout the world, but also in his pupils and especially in their marital relationships.

On this subject, he never considered it beneath his dignity to share domestic chores, whether cooking (which he was more than good at), shopping, or housework, considering these activities as being part of his spiritual practices.

He often repeated that it was necessary to show love through actions and not simply in words. "No thought or action should be," he would add, "disassociated from the spiritual work of a seeker".

Salim quoted, in relation to marriage, the words of the great mystic Ramakrishna when one of his disciples came to complain that, in accordance with Indian customs, he was going to be married when he wanted to remain single to pursue his sadhana. Ramakrishna (who was himself married) asked him: "How much is one and one?" Surprised, the man responded: "Two, of course!" But, to his surprise, Ramakrishna told him: "Not at all, one and one makes eleven! A couple can create an enormous strength from which each draws benefits". "But such a relationship can only be envisaged," Salim would insist, "if each person learns to feel for the other; if one applies this simple maxim, the world will be metamorphosed by it".

There is not one line of Salim's books that he did not himself put into practice. I continually saw him making efforts, particularly to receive pupils, even when he was ill, without allowing anything to show, or going against himself in forcing himself, for example, to perform hatha yoga at over seventy years of age.

He never made these efforts through blind obligation, but because he wanted to make them, like an artist who works at his craft because he is passionate about what he does.

He always took great care to not allow the weight of his suffering to rest on me. When, before the discovery of his gluten allergy, he suffered intestinal crises almost every day, he nevertheless found the strength to joke about his pains, saying that a hundred thousand Red Indians were performing a war dance in his stomach and hitting his intestines with their tomahawks and, to make me laugh, he would then imitate their war cries. Indeed, Salim loved to laugh and joke and he often told his pupils or friends Mullah Nasruddin's funny stories.

The many headed dragon.

With the intention of helping his pupils, Salim came back many times to the particularly harmful tendency that exists in human beings to want, through laziness, to put off until later things that should be done at once, without concerning themselves with the problems (or even damage) that this delay may cause, both for themselves and others.

He tried to make them understand that this "later" was never ending, because one always finds pretexts for postponing until a later time things that should be done now; this is especially true in relation to a spiritual practice. Among the numerous stories that he had told them by way of teaching, there was one that was particularly significant in this context:

There was once a seeker who, one day, felt within himself the intense resonance of a spiritual call. So he decided to settle the business that attached him to this world and go on a quest to find someone able to guide him. He had heard of a great master and, wanting to follow his teachings, he went to him. Prostrating himself at the master's feet, he asked him humbly if he could aspire to the title of disciple. The master reflected for a moment, then responded:

"I will take you as a disciple, but on one condition. Not far from here lives a dragon. Tomorrow, at sunrise, you must go and kiss it on the mouth."

The seeker, surprised by this completely unexpected trial, replied with dread: "But he will devour me!"

The master retorted:

"If you do not agree to do what I ask of you, I do not want you."

As he ardently wished to become the master's pupil, the aspirant had no other choice but to do what was asked of him. So, at first light of day, he set off towards the dragon's cave. However, when he saw the gigantic size of the dragon, its blood-stained tongue issuing from its mouth with its terrifying teeth, he felt his legs give way beneath him. He went back to the master as fast as he could and, throwing himself at his feet, told him in a trembling voice that the task he had given him proved impossible. His interlocutor nevertheless showed himself to be inflexible and repeated that, if he did not kiss the monster, he could never benefit from his teaching.

The poor seeker passed a night of terror, haunted by the vision of the frightening mouth he had to kiss. He tried to imagine all sorts of ruses to approach the dragon, to skirt around it and to accomplish in a flash his terrible task. Finally, the sky was tinged with pink, announcing that the time had come to present himself once more before the monster. Alas, a horrible spectacle awaited him, because instead of a single mouth thrusting out an already sufficiently menacing tongue, there were now three heads presenting themselves to his view. He backed away, horrified, and ran to the master to tell him, in tears, of the transformation that had occurred in the beast.

The master contented himself with simply telling the aspirant that, as the dragon now had three heads, it was three heads that he had to kiss and unless he did he could not be accepted as a pupil. The poor aspirant returned to his dwelling and, despondent, threw himself on his couch and sighed. In his dreams, he constantly saw the three terrifying mouths rising before him to devour him. But day was already breaking and he had to set out again for the fateful cave.

Alas, three times alas, an even more horrifying picture presented itself to him. Each of these three heads had once again subdivided and the monster now possessed nine heads which, all, were watching him with furious eyes...

Through this Eastern tale, Salim wanted to make his pupils understand that, when they put off until tomorrow a task that they should undertake today, this task would become more difficult to carry out and would be more so again on the following days; concerning their spiritual practices in particular, by continually postponing the effort that was required of them in the present, this would inevitably become ever more difficult to make until, one day, they would feel overwhelmed because they had not agreed to do it at once.

Meditation.

When Salim was meditating, the whole apartment bathed in an indescribable silence which could be felt.

He described what he was experiencing in the following way in one of his books:

"He found himself plunged in a profound state of Self-absorption, with this strange and by now familiar sensation of having returned once more to his Supreme Source. The vast and sacred stillness in which he found himself immersed seemed at the same time a shattering silence. United with his True Being, he felt pervaded with a feeling of great melting tenderness, and he found himself transported to the exalted regions of himself, with this enigmatic Nada, as always, singing its ineffable song uninterruptedly in his ears. The whole room was bathed in an effulgent light as that of a mysterious flameless fire glowing with incredible brilliance, and all the objects about him seemed to have the most uncommon phosphorescent colors, surrounded by a most subtle and unearthly golden auric radiance. A great cosmic tranquility prevailed."

Lost Horizon.

It was with strong emotions that, in 1993, Salim saw advertised the television broadcast of an old American movie which had played a particularly important role in his life while he was still very young and before he had ever heard of any spiritual path; it was "Lost Horizon" by Frank Capra.

He told me that during the war, around 1943, while he was surrounded by airmen devoid of any elevated aspirations, this movie had been like a breath of fresh air coming from another world, a mysterious world which aroused in him he knew not what moving recollections.

The story, adapted from a novel by James Hilton, relates the strange destiny of a man who finds himself involuntarily ripped from his materialist environment and suddenly plunged into a paradise called Shangri-La, a place protected from human folly by the impassable mountain barriers of the Himalayas.

Although there is no question of spiritual practices, strictly speaking, this haven of peace located in Tibet is ruled by goodness and directed by a Belgian former priest who has become a lama. Giving in to the influence of contrary forces, the hero finds himself obliged to wrench himself away from his Eden. Realizing too late his tragic error, he then has to fight with unremitting tenacity and incredible courage to conquer a multitude of obstacles of all kinds before he is able to regain his lost paradise.

The movie played in the barracks theater for seven consecutive days so that all the men would be able to see it and, with the help of his friend Padre Strover, Salim managed not to miss a single screening. This evocation of Tibet, of the life of a lama, of a secret paradise... fascinated him in a way that he could not explain.

It was with the greatest joy that, shortly after the war, before he knew Mr Adie, he saw, while passing a movie theater on the bus, a poster for this same movie. The next day, having freed himself of all his obligations, he went to the movie theater and watched all the screenings. To the astonishment of the ticket office clerk, he came back every day until the program changed. From that moment, he never stopped looking in the papers for other screenings of this movie in the London theaters and, every time, canceling his planned activities for the week, he would go. He must have already seen it at least thirty times, but, although he knew it by heart, he couldn't help wanting to see it again so as to reawaken in himself that inexplicable silent memory that moved him to tears. This story was the clue to the existence of another universe that no-one around him at that time seemed to have the slightest idea of.

Moreover, what had impressed him most was the unremitting will and unwavering determination that this man had had to show to regain his lost paradise, a will and determination that Salim had never forgotten and which had, subsequently, a decisive influence on his musical work as well as on his spiritual practices.

Nearly fifty years after his discovery of this movie, despite the Hollywood flaws that had not struck him at the time and although he had, since then, found his inner "Shangri-La", Salim still felt just as intense an emotion upon seeing it again. Furthermore, when he heard the hero of the story declare, upon arriving in that heavenly country, that everything seemed strangely familiar, as though he already knew the place and the people, he could not help being troubled and struck by these words which mysteriously awoke in him his own experiences concerning time and the possibility of the recurrence of phenomenal existence.

Specific spiritual understandings.

"When someone ages," Salim would say, "if he succeeds in distancing himself from his body, he has the opportunity of acquiring an understanding of the greatest importance for him, to which he cannot come while he is still young and fiercely identified with his corporeal sensations which exercise too great a force of attraction on his being and his mind."

He confided in me on this subject that he often found himself in a strange inner state from which, contemplating his old worn body, he keenly felt the conviction of being totally "apart" from it and to be only temporarily inhabiting it. "This body is not part of myself, I am something other than this physical medium," and he would add: "In the most ordinarily inexplicable manner, I see with, so to speak, my mind's eye, the invisible aspect of my being which, at these unutterable moments, reveals itself to be the only Reality that exists for me in the whole Universe."

He sometimes remained unmoving for a long time in this state that he was always reluctant to quit, because his consciousness found itself amplified to a degree impossible to describe. The Nada vibrated in his head with such intensity that it seemed to him that nothing existed any longer in the Cosmos except this Primordial Sound and this extremely keen Consciousness.

In other circumstances, he reported being spontaneously seized by an impression so troubling that it aroused in him a strange reverential awe, because, he would tell me: "Just like a mysterious tree whose roots lose themselves in a vertiginous infinite, I experience the inexplicable feeling of being the last inheritor of a whole line of ancestors whose history stretches into the depths of a past so inconceivably distant that I am left profoundly disconcerted before the impossibility of imagining its beginnings!"

"And, when I undertake my spiritual practices, I have the feeling that I am not accomplishing them only for my benefit and that of the visible world around me, but also for all those invisible characters that inhabit me and are, themselves, awaiting their redemption. At such times, I cannot help feeling the heavy responsibility that falls upon me.

"Before this unfathomable mystery, does time not lose all reality? Does one not find oneself facing the strange phenomenon of an 'eternal nowness' in which the past and the future are forever converging?"

Final journey to India: Poona 1994.

Since his return from India, Salim had remained in contact with a doctor friend who lived in Poona; he always carried within himself nostalgia for the spiritual atmosphere of India and, particularly, for Poona as the two years he had spent there had been decisive for him spiritually. Thus, when Dr Barucha sent him, as he did every year, a card repeating his invitation to come and see him in Poona, we decided to attempt the adventure.

However, one cannot step twice into the same river; more than twenty-five years had passed, and in a country like India, the pressure for demographic growth is very strong; consequently Poona had become very different from the city Salim had known.

First, Bombay, deafening traffic in the streets and a crowd on the sidewalks, a crowd that flowed interminably. At every stop light, poor people held out their hands by the window of the taxi, a man with no legs, sitting in a wheeled cart, who, in order to come and request a few rupees, made his way perilously through the traffic which did not even slow down, another, his face disfigured and trembling, a woman with desperate eyes and a child in her arms, a little girl who looked at us with great, hungry eyes: what can be done in the face of such crushing poverty?

The train to Poona was in an unbelievable state of disrepair. Our journey was to last nearly two hours, passing dilapidated houses, buildings of two or three stories that seemed on the point of collapse although they had been built less than three decades before. After these buildings came kilometers of slums, slums without end, people squatting in nauseating runnels of water, an unimaginable degree of poverty. We passed trains heaving with people who were hanging from the doors, stations whose platforms were thronging with crowds, crowds everywhere. Immediately upon exiting the station, Salim was surprised by the activity that, at nine in the evening, still pervaded this town that he no longer recognized. Dr Barucha, at that time eighty-two years of age, who had come to meet us at the station with his driver, told us sadly: "There are more of us than there are mosquitoes".

The day after our arrival, we went with our guide to discover what had become of Poona. Salim had known a garden city, we arrived in a hive of activity with two and a half million inhabitants, infernal traffic, mainly rickshaws, scooters, motorcyles, and trucks; there were relatively few cars. Crowds everywhere, and poverty, the destitution of slums in some places, but less than in Bombay. When he asked where Mahatma Gandhi Road was, a large, shady avenue where he used to go to do his shopping, Salim could not believe his eyes upon discovering, in its place, a narrow, congested road, full of shops.

The following day, we took a rickshaw to go to Indira Devi's ashram. After having asked our way several times, we finally found it. Salim had known it isolated from any other buildings, surrounded by copses; he found it now jammed between houses, in a built-up neighborhood.

Indira Devi received us surrounded by twenty or so people (including some Westerners) sitting on the floor around the divan she was resting on; she welcomed us warmly, Salim was very moved. She was seventy-four years old, but seemed much younger; her hair was still black and her face without lines. People were arriving, greeting her, she welcomed them benevolently, others were leaving and asking for her blessing, she spoke to them with attention and interest. She received people in this way every day and, in the evening, bhajans were sung in the ashram's temple, which was closed during the day. She exchanged a few words with Salim on the changes in Poona over the previous twenty-five years and spoke of his books with praise. She was suffering badly with her asthma and frequently used an inhaler. She left this world a few months after our visit.

We visited Mr Dady, he was seventy-one; tall and thin, he too appeared younger than he was. He still lived in the same beautiful home, surrounded by a large yard and sufficiently distant from the city center to be spared the general trepidation. He told us that, fortunately, there were less and less people in the leper hospital as leprosy was dying out in India. Every afternoon, seven days a week, he and his sisters now took care of a veterinary hospital. Medical treatment was undertaken by a practitioner; Mr Dady fed and cared for the animals taken in: dogs, donkeys, cows, etc. The man was a kind of saint. He told us that he had taken into his own home, during the years that he had been taking care of animals, at least sixty-five dogs that had lived with him for a while before dying a good death and being buried in his yard. He always had with him seven or eight dogs, from the veterinary hospital who were generally of poor appearance. He invited us to a meeting the following Wednesday where he read, as he did every week, spiritual texts to a group of around ten people.

That evening we were invited to dinner with some friends of Dr Barucha who had read Salim's book "The Way of Inner Vigilance" and who asked him several questions about spirituality. A few days later, Dr Barucha took us to see a "saint" said to be ninety-five years old. Every square centimeter of the walls of the single room of the little house where he lived were covered with photos and images of saints, two armchairs decorated with flowers symbolized the thrones of Krishna and Rada, his companion. The wife of the "saint" was present, she was supposed to be ninety years old. A brochure showed the old man decorated with a supernatural light in the Indian naive style. The Indians who were present seemed to believe everything he said, with no critical thought.

We returned to see Mr Dady who was meeting with his small group. Salim spoke a little of his path to people who had only an intellectual knowledge of a spiritual practice and who were fascinated to see someone experiencing what they had read.

The train back to Bombay was even dirtier than the one from Bombay to Poona and, when it began to rain (it was the end of the monsoon and it rained every day), the rain came into the carriage and water flowed over the sari of the passenger next to us. In the middle of the compartment, a man with atrophied legs and deformed hands was dragging himself along and begging. When we gave him a bill, he placed it on his chest without looking at us and dragged himself on. The passengers were eating and drinking constantly, as boys came and went all the time offering drinks and food, but no-one gave him so much as a cent.

The aim of our journey—which was a sort of pilgrimage—was in a way achieved as Salim saw again the places and the people that had meant so much to him twenty-five years before. Now, India was only a memory for him.

The world is surprisingly perfect in its imperfection.

Even without taking into account natural disasters, illnesses, the implacability of nature, and the vicissitudes of existential life, being confronted with the terrible suffering brought about by incessant wars unleashed by men hungry for power, everyone is tempted, with good reason, to be appalled and to ask the eternal question: "If the All Powerful Creator is perfect in his Essence, why, then, is this tragic imperfection so rife throughout his Creation?"

Salim would respond: "Through a most paradoxical phenomenon, a human being, cut off from his Divine Source, needs all these misfortunes in order to experience the sensation of existing ".

He would add: "When looked upon with the right mind and positive inner attitude, it is impossible not to be filled with wonder and reverential admiration at the profound wisdom behind all these problems and hazards in life. Because of the human being's tendency to inertia, life in its seeming imperfections is indeed benignly perfect. In his present state, without these harsh conditions compassionately trying to awaken and urge him to look beyond himself and outer appearances to that which is concealed behind all these uncertainties, sorrows, and the impermanency of his physical existence, he would be lost, doomed to remain a wretched and forlorn creature."

"Suffering drives people to question the meaning of life, to feel for others, to go beyond themselves. Facility generates a tendency towards superficiality, lack of caring for the suffering of others, and weakness of character.

"The Creative Source cannot change the rules that It has established in the Universe. It leaves human beings with the choice to obey these laws, a choice that It cannot make in their place. If they had, from the outset, been made perfect, they would have no opportunity of recognizing their perfection which they must earn through their own practice.

"There is a reason for the existence of duality; without it, the human being would have no means of comparison; it is through duality that it is possible for him to recognize the Divine Aspect of his own double nature—just as he would not be able to appreciate and understand the day if there were no night, life if there were no death, happiness if there were no unhappiness. One cannot see and apprehend the light of the celestial bodies without the darkness that surrounds them. That is why the inferior aspect of the human being also has its place in Creation and cannot be blindly held in contempt or considered negatively as a useless obstacle in the path of the seeker; rather it should become the means of reminding him, every time he sinks into this aspect of his double nature, that he also carries within himself his Celestial Aspect which he needs to discover in order to finally immerse himself in It one day.

"All that is created in time and space cannot avoid living in duality. Paradoxically, it is not possible to overcome duality unless it is accepted as a necessity in the Universe and Creation; it is inconceivable to be able to comprehend something without its comparison with its opposite. If there were no inhalation, one could not imagine exhalation, if birth did not exist, one could not conceive of the reality of death; without creation, it would be impossible to understand dissolution.

"In order for the aspirant to succeed in overcoming duality, he has to begin by understanding it and recognizing its reason for being in the phenomenal world. As a method of comparison between two worlds, it proves indispensable in helping him to become conscious of himself in a completely different manner to the way he is habitually so that he may come one day, through assiduous efforts which he must agree to make, to find the place he is destined to occupy in the immensity of this mysterious Cosmos.

"Duality represents only a stage that cannot really be understood and overcome until the aspirant has succeeded in recognizing in himself, through direct experience, the Divine Aspect of his double nature.

"One day, he has to come to accept the complete loss of his customary individuality during meditation in order to be metamorphosed into his Divine Essence. After this supreme discovery, he will no longer argue with his fellow beings, whether he be man, woman, Christian, Jew, Muslim, Hindu, English, German, French, etc. He will realize in a manner that will shake him for eternity that he is really the Divine in the innermost depths of his being." Blasphemy? "No," Salim would insist, "It is a Holy Reality that forever erases in him the feeling of being separate and different from the other." And he would add: "Has one really understood the enigmatic and troubling words pronounced by Christ to help the world when He said: 'That they may all be one; as you, Father, are in me, and I in you, that they may also be one in us'?"

Overcoming the barriers of individuality.

Since his first encounter with Mr Adie in 1949, Salim had had many spiritual experiences through which his vision of the world had been fundamentally changed. It was a regular occurrence for him to overcome the barriers of individuality. He had thus acquired a special wealth, with no relation to the transient goods of this world. As a result of his efforts to remain intensely conscious and present to himself, he succeeded in really seeing what he was looking at. By maintaining for a sufficient amount of time this conscious manner of looking at, for example, a flower, he established between them a very subtle communion by way of which he grasped the kind of consciousness and particular feeling that this flower had of itself, the kinds of joys and fears that it felt, its kind of reaction in the face of the threat of imminent death, and so on. At these exceptional moments, he would notice that even an apparently inanimate stone had some form of consciousness. In reality Salim would say, there is nothing in the Universe that is not alive.

New spiritual experiences helped him to go even further. He pursued this work with pugnacity, yet with delicacy, finding from moment to moment what part of his efforts he still had to make and what part belonged to the Superior Aspect of himself to which he abandoned himself.

He had come to the point where he was so connected to this other state of being and of consciousness that he had, by tireless efforts, found within himself, that even if he wanted to forget it, he could no longer do so, because, he would say, this new feeling was now an integral part of his nature.

"I no longer believe blindly in an exterior Divinity, because I see now the Ineffable in me with, so to speak, my mind's eye and I feel It so keenly and so intensely that my whole being is shaken with it and filled with a feeling of limitless wonder and reverential awe."

When he looked back over his life, he remarked that the only moments that had engraved themselves indelibly on his memory where those where he had succeeded in giving himself wholly to his spiritual practices; the rest of his existence seemed to him, by contrast, like a dream devoid of meaning and of reality.

He ceaselessly encouraged his pupils not to project themselves into the future or to nourish imaginings of what they might attain spiritually, because, as he wrote in his book: "Pratique spirituelle et Éveil intérieur" (Spiritual Practice and Inner Awakening):

"Although, on a spiritual path, it may often be necessary to speak of a goal to be attained in order to try, inadequately, to explain the inexplicable, a serious seeker must, nevertheless, remember that in relation to his spiritual practices, the goal is always situated in the present.

One can, in a way, say that once he has committed to the Path, it cannot be to attain, one day, a final goal and then for everything to stop there—as is the case with ordinary things or worldly activities— because that would mean that the goal would be an 'end' in a sort of eternal death and afterwards there would be nothing. In reality, the goal and the present are indissociable in spiritual work; every instant must become the goal for the seeker, otherwise he risks giving himself all sorts of excuses to dream of a goal situated in a distant future and, in the meantime, without being aware of it, to carry out only a luke-warm spiritual practice that will come to nothing."

Holding a different feeling of oneself.

Salim resumed the essence of his teaching thus: "There exists in the human being a very particular consciousness in relation to which his customary consciousness is nothing but darkness. It is essential for him to discover this luminous consciousness that he carries in the depths of his being before death takes hold of him. It is an impersonal cons-ciousness of the greatest subtlety which pervades the whole Universe; furthermore, behind its tangible aspect the Universe is, in fact, simply a Vast Divine and Eternal Consciousness.

"The perfecting of his being can only be undertaken when the aspirant comes to find this Divine Aspect of his nature and remains connected to it; because, of himself, he can do nothing." It is for this reason that he must make incessant efforts so as to succeed one day in recognizing this Divine Source in himself and, finally, to remain continually connected to It, without ever losing It."

Salim constantly encouraged his pupils to ask themselves: "In what manner am I ordinarily lost to myself without knowing it? What that is precious to me is lost during the moments that I forget myself? Do I really know?"

And Salim would add: "A human being dies at every moment without ever realizing it. There is nothing that persists in him from one moment to another; so, how can he expect something in him to survive after his physical death?

"Furthermore, in the state in which one commonly lives, does one know one exists? is one really conscious of existing?

"When the seeker asks himself this question seriously and with intense sincerity, a totally different feeling of himself and his existence begins to rise up in him. He must realize the crucial importance for him of trying to constantly hold this unusual feeling of himself which is the means that will give access to the discovery of his Celestial Being. This is the reason that, in addition to his daily meditation, he has to, at the same time that he is busy responding to the demands of external life, try to hold interiorly the feeling of himself in a continual nowness. It is necessary for him to realize that this new feeling of himself held in a continual nowness is, in reality, Life and Force for him.

"If he hopes really to know what true work on himself consists of, the aspirant can try, with ardent sincerity to imagine in this very instant, that he is effectively living his final instant on Earth; what sort of feeling and what state of consciousness, that are not habitual to him, would then rise up in his being? It is precisely this new feeling accompanied by a strange interior awakening that he would feel at such a moment that he must try to maintain in himself.

"One often hears of enlightenment or of enlightened beings yet those who employ such terms do not really understand what they cover. Effectively there is a confusion in the mind of many aspirants on the subject of enlightenment, because either they believe that it is easy to attain—without realizing at the beginning of their commitment what is really implied by such work—and, when they encounter within themselves too many difficulties that they did not expect, they end up becoming discouraged and abandoning the pursuit, or, paradoxically, they do not accord it enough importance in their quest and, consequently, do not seek it."

"It is important to realize that there are various degrees of enlightenment, from a small change of state of being and consciousness, which can escape the seeker at the beginning of its manifestation in him, until the highest and so rare experience in which he acknowledges, without doubt, the Ineffable he carries within himself.

"Enlightenment may, after a more or less long practice of meditation, sometimes manifest itself very suddenly and at the most unexpected moment (all depends on the levels of being and awareness of the meditator), or slowly, in stages, as a subtle change of state of being and consciousness, accompanied by the beginning of an inner awakening which at first can remain misunderstood by the aspirant."

Spring 1996, death of one of his pupils.

One of his pupils, called Christian, whom Salim had not seen for a while got back in contact with him and told him, in despair, that, although hardly more than forty years old, he was about to die and that he needed Salim for this initiatory crossing. When he was hospitalized a few days later, Salim was able to speak to him by telephone; he reminded him to try to find and to hold the state of lucidity and of unusual consciousness of himself that Salim had tried to provoke in him in the past with the help of certain exercises. He emphasized as well the importance of departing while being at peace and in a state of benevolence towards the whole world.

A few hours before the end, Salim had the opportunity of murmuring to him by telephone precious words, indispensable at this crucial moment. He said, calling him by his name: "Christian, abandon yourself, do not resist. Accept, abandon yourself with trust..." The person who was at the dying man's bedside continued to repeat these same words until the end, which was serene and tranquil.

During several months, Salim continued his help by visualizing his pupil happy, smiling, at peace, bathed in divine light, until he felt that he had done all that was possible to help him.

October 1996 : an oneiric message for Salim.

On the night in question, I had a dream: I found myself in the home of Christian, Salim's pupil who had died some months before, the telephone rang, I hesitated to answer, this was not my home. As I was alone in the room and no-one picked up, I decided to answer and I then heard over the handset Christian's voice, which said to me: "No leave it, it's for me". I told Salim of this dream the following morning. He reflected on it during the morning and wondered if the message had not been destined to foretell someone's death. Indeed, he had noticed that, if he dreamed of a dead person, that meant the heralding of another death. During the afternoon, at an unusual hour for him, he was listening to France-musique. By chance, or rather not by chance, he heard the special program broadcasting the music of Berthold Goldschmidt who had died the previous morning at the age of ninety-four.

Berthold Goldschmidt
93 years old

The dream was astonishingly precise. I was in a pupil's house, that is to say in Salim's house as a pupil, and the telephone call that was not for me was announcing the death of his first composition teacher whom we had recently learned, thanks to the broadcast of a report on him, was still alive. Salim had studied with Berthold Goldschmidt for around four years and had learned much from him. He knew his profession as a composer well and demanded perfection. Like Salim, as soon as he looked at a score, he possessed the ability to hear in his head the diverse instruments of the orchestra, the harmony, and the rhythms in their smallest details. He was a remarkable conductor and pianist who could decipher any work that he played immediately and with ease. Sometimes Salim and he would play for their own pleasure works for the violin and piano. He was an extremely sensitive man who had suffered much from his cultural uprooting and the trauma of his flight from Nazi Germany; he could not fail to know that he had a great deal of talent and that made him sad over not being played in England after so many of his works had been destroyed in Germany. He had undergone, like Salim, the dictatorship of serial music and he had, little by little, given in to the discouragement and stopped composing for around twenty years. In the most miraculous manner, in the 1980s, the emergence of a renewed interest in favor of Jewish composers who were victims of the Nazis had allowed him the joy of hearing many of his works, including two of his operas, before he died.

Salim was moved by this death which reminded him of so many things in his past and, of course, which he felt linked to as a musician, for, even if he was no longer composing, he was and remained to his last breath a musician.

The abandonment of tonality in contemporary music.

After having fought in the past to create beauty in his music, Salim could not help feeling an infinite sadness when he heard on the radio (particularly on "France-Musique") all kinds of comments intended to justify the abandonment of tonality. According to these people, modern composers owed it to themselves to break the rules of harmony in order to be new, because, they affirmed, the possibilities of tonality were exhausted.

Salim would react to this kind of argument by retorting: "As long as there are human beings with varying aspirations and temperaments, they will always discover something new to express. One of the most significant examples in this regard is Gustav Mahler who, right up to the end of his life, constantly found different ways of using the same major and minor chords used by Beethoven in his music. Evidently, the more the number of great composers succeeding each other increases, the more difficult it proves to find new means of expression. From this point of view, Debussy was, so to speak, a "curse" to his successors, because, as they failed to reach his level or were no more than pale imitators, they tried to come up with a system that would not permit comparisons with great composers of the past."

Salim remembered an account of a lecture at the Collège de France, entitled "Le grand schisme de la musique contemporaine" (the great schism in contemporary music) given by André Lavagne, composer and winner of the Second Grand Prix de Rome (who wrote the column "La semaine du mélomane" [The music lover's week] in the French newspaper Le Figaro); during his talk, he used medical discoveries to demonstrate that the tonal principle is something other than an interchangeable system, it is based on biological foundations. The lecturer then demonstrated the implacable logic with which music, firstly atonal, then successively serial, concrete, electronico-serial, stochastic, becoming an art of the random, musical collages, leads to the absurd—such as a work constituted by the simultaneous recording of eight radio stations. "It is," he concluded, "a crisis of civilization with tragic consequences and the human being will only rediscover his image in music by shattering an icy universe, a world of incoherence and anguish, to find again a meaning for his own life from which flows the transcendent meaning of all artistic creation."

"It is precisely," Salim would say, "because current composers unfortunately no longer know the meaning of the word 'transcendence' that they take refuge in electronic sonorities, in random compositions, or in simple sound effects that they qualify as 'music'. Lacking genius, they try to be 'brilliant'. They don't understand the importance of arousing within themselves the inner silence necessary to pick up inspirations from a superior world."

Gustav Mahler spoke of composition as an "essentially mystic" act, he added: "Unknown sometimes by oneself, and through an inspiration coming from without, one sometimes builds something that one ceases to understand once the work has come into being."

Brahms once confided in Joachim, the famous violinist for whom he composed his concerto: "I have never written a note of music that wasn't given to me".

And Beethoven declared: "Nothing can be more sublime than to draw nearer to the Godhead than other men, and to diffuse here on earth these Godlike rays among mortals".

Salim could not help thinking that the world had become ill and mad, delighting in the ugliness that people devoid of any aesthetic sense poured over humanity, whether in the field of painting, music, or architecture.

All the incredibly difficult years in the Rue du Cherche-Midi remained always alive within him: the cold that had frozen him in the winter and caused him interminable colds, his intestinal crises that ripped through his stomach when he had to go and see a pupil (most often on foot for lack of money), the hunger that gnawed at him...

The money that he managed to earn often proved insufficient even to buy thirty-two stave music paper. After having given a lesson, he would regard the small sum he had just earned, torn by the dilemma that arose within him. The second movement of the unfinished piece was saying to him: "Me first," but his stomach was demanding: "No, I need to be satisfied first; you have given me nothing to eat for more than two days!" When the work in progress cried out to him: "I want to live!" his stomach would protest: "But I'm hungry!" This dispute would most often end with the victory of the music and, instead of satisfying his hunger, he would go and get the lined sheets which he needed so badly.

Thinking of this terribly hard time, Salim concluded that, finally, the composer who battles to transcribe in music the moments of elevation that he experiences acquires inestimable wealth which justifies his sacrifices, even if his work is never executed, because, ultimately, he has lived the experience of having written it and that is what is most important; his being finds itself thereby enriched in a manner that can never ordinarily be comprehended.

Listening intensely to the Nada.

One day, I went, as I did every morning, into Salim's room. He was, it seemed, listening to a music cassette, with the headphones on his ears, his gazed fixed on the ground. He didn't hear me. After having insistently made my presence known to him, he finally lifted his eyes. He explained to me that he was carrying out a concentration exercise consisting of concentrating on the Nada to the point of no longer hearing the music, which was, nevertheless, at a high volume on the headset. He told me that he had practiced this exercise intensely when he was in Poona. Around 1970, just when he was passing through Paris, before setting out again for Madras, he had the opportunity of receiving an invitation from a group of people who wanted to hear his Mass. While the work (which is thirty-six minutes long) was being played, he remained concentrated on the Nada with such intensity, from second to second, that he didn't hear a single note of his own music, him a musician! and his Mass too!—which was so dear to his heart. Only people who have tried a little to concentrate can understand the intensity that represents. It was through this power of concentration that Salim had so many unusual experiences.

When, through Indira Devi, he discovered the Bhagavad Gita, he found a stanza that touched him deeply:

"Among thousands, one here and there strives after perfection, and, of those who strive and attain to perfection, one here and there knows Me in all the Principles of My existence." (chap.7,3).

Later, he would say to his pupils: "I want to be one of those who knows the Absolute in all the Principles of its Existence. I don't wonder whether I will succeed, I don't think about it, I give myself completely, that's all".

The forge of destiny.

Among the various memories that he happened to mention in my presence, Salim told me of one particularly poignant one, relating to something that happened shortly after the memorable afternoon when the music critics closed the door of the world of music to him forever.

At that time, he was still living in his minuscule cell in the Rue du Cherche-Midi. It was very cold; it was still winter. He had just passed a sleepless night, stricken by an intestinal crisis that had continued to afflict him until late in the morning. He was completely exhausted and weakened.

He remained lying on his bed, his burning eyes fixed on the ceiling, saying to himself: "Who can I talk to? Who could understand how I feel? I feel so alone and lost in a world that has become insensible to everything that is noble and beautiful in life".

Despite his despondency, he continued to hear in his ears celestial music coming from another world, which called on him to give it life.

Between the music that constantly resonated within him and called to him with insistence, his empty stomach reminding him that he didn't have enough money left to buy food, and his intestinal pains which gave him no respite, he felt so miserable that he finally closed his eyes, trying to forget everything, to live the present moment, and to meditate lying down.

He had the impression that a long time had passed when he suddenly thought he had heard a light knocking at his door. His cell was so cramped that he only had to, while still lying down, stretch out his arm to open the door, asking himself who could be visiting him on such a cold day.

To his surprise, it was his friend René Zuber, the Gurdjieff film-maker, who was on the landing. He had come to ask Salim if he would like to accompany him to a small projection room to watch a short film about the steel industry that he had just made; he needed some background sound effects to punctuate a passage of the film and he had thought that Salim, who possessed an oriental drum (called a zarb), could improvise a percussion sequence for him. He added that he would be happy to pay him for this service.

Salim remained speechless for a moment, then, without knowing what he was doing, he grabbed his disconcerted friend by the arms, trying not to let him see the tears that were welling in his eyes and, for fear of his voice betraying his emotion, he simply nodded to indicate that he would be happy to be of use to him.

Although a close friend, René Zuber was far from suspecting the difficulties that Salim was struggling with simply to manage to feed himself. Indeed, as his mode of expression was music, Salim had difficulty in expressing what he felt and would practically never open up about his situation to anyone. René Zuber, who absolutely could not imagine how welcome his proposition was, given that it was going to allow Salim to earn enough to eat, did not understand the reason for his strange behavior. He looked at him for a moment in astonishment, then suggested they leave without more delay, as they were urgently awaited at the studio.

Chilled and very much weakened by his trials of the previous night, Salim entered the room which, to his great joy, was heated—so well heated, in fact, that it seemed to him to be a paradise.

The screening started immediately. While Salim was watching the images file past, seeing in a particular scene of the film an enormous metallic pincer seize a block of steel to carry it slowly to a glowing red furnace, he felt suddenly filled with an inexpressible mystic emotion, and he thought: "But that hurts... that hurts the piece of metal so terribly!" After having left it in the forge for a few minutes, the pincer took the white hot block up again, giving off bluish yellow sprays of sparks. Then, an enormous hydraulic hammer descended and began to hit the metal without mercy. Once again, Salim could not help saying to himself: "But, it's dreadful, it hurts so much!" It was as though he, himself, was feeling the metal's pain. Finally, after having undergone a series of hammerings, the steel, which had been curved and now presented an elegant tailored form, like a letter U, was plunged into water, probably to harden it.

The strange state that had taken hold of Salim throughout the film had conveyed to him a sort of teaching of inestimable value which, later, would have important repercussions in his spiritual work. While he was observing what was happening on the screen, he had understood with intense acuity that, just like this block of steel, he also had to accept constantly going through the burning fire of an assiduous spiritual practice if he wanted to have hope that a valid transformation might take place in his being.

Returning home, he found himself not only uplifted, but even transported into an ecstatic state, the complete opposite of the despondency that he had felt upon going out. When René Zuber, who had taken him home, wanted to pay him for the backing track he had improvised, Salim thought that it was really he who should repay René Zuber for the precious experience this little recording had allowed him to have.

Talking to me of this documentary, which, by a mysterious, providential chance, he had seen at a moment when he had most need of it, Salim told me: "The fire through which that piece of metal passed and the blows it received were, for it, the work of a few minutes, whereas the furnace of existential life that I have traversed and the blows that I have received have lasted all my life!

"But," he immediately added, "if I were given the chance to go back and start my life over, being able to choose a more comfortable existence, without the dramas and the suffering that I have had to endure, with, moreover, fame as a musician, but the price was that this facility would prevent me acquiring the knowledge I needed to accelerate my spiritual evolution, I would respond, without the slightest hesitation, that I would a thousand times rather go through the trials I have traversed again, with everything they have caused me by way of vicissitudes, physical pain, and moral solitude, than never to have known the inestimable spiritual experiences and understandings that I have been privileged to know and for which I have paid such a high price."

Recorded teachings:

Between 1998 and 2002, Salim regularly brought together a few pupils to spur them on in their practice. Some teachings were recorded on video. Below are a few extracts.

(Salim would often say "I" instead of "you" when addressing his pupils, because he preferred to avoid, as much as possible, expressions that unconsciously created a barrier between the other and oneself)

✤ *December 1998: Leaving a trace in oneself.*

Leaving a trace in oneself, so that, whatever a future existence may be, the trace that I have left in myself will be able to help me to move more quickly towards what is dearest to me, that is to say a spiritual practice.

Leaving a trace... memory signifies evolution, forgetting signifies

involution. You have to be so serious that this becomes the sole motivation of your existence. You have to succeed, when you apply yourselves to a spiritual practice, in being so exact and, above all, so whole. If you do not taste a moment when you are whole, at least once in your life, you will never know what it means to give yourself to the Infinite that inhabits you.

(Salim is reading an extract from "S'éveiller un question de vie ou de mort" [Awakening: A Question of Life or Death], chapter 13).

"The most ardent desire of a seeker must be never to find himself in a future existence as he is in the present, with his habitual thoughts going around without control in his mind, his changing desires gnawing at him, his sensuality and his interests in the ordinary things of existence, which weigh him down and bar the route leading to his emancipation.

If he wants to reach the end of his quest, the recurrence of the efforts he makes in the present—which can only leave a trace in him if they are sufficiently sustained and sincere—needs to become stronger than the recurrence of his not yet transmuted undesirable tendencies, otherwise the karmic predilection that he still feels regarding samsaric existence will continue to be wholly determining and will keep him shackled to it."

And Salim comments: "Thus the prodigious pianist (Evgeny Kissin), when he was eleven months old, could sing what his sister was playing on the piano. At a few months more than one year old, he sat at the piano and, with one finger he began to play. Then, later, when he came in from school, he didn't even take off his coat; only one thing counted for him: the piano.

A trace had been left in him of a previous life. He was seven years old when he gave his first concert.

I tell you all these things so that you might understand how important what I leave as a trace in me is."

⚙ *April 2001: The last thought.*

In a future existence, whatever form it takes, I want at all costs to remember only this spiritual quest and nothing else. It is truly necessary that, when we die, our sole and unique desire is our spiritual accomplishment.

I want to carry this desire with me so that, whatever my future, whatever form it takes and wherever it unfolds, I will already have something in me which will remind me of this desire: my spiritual accomplishment.

People who are subjugated to the pleasures of the senses, they will be reborn to find such pleasures again. That is not what one wants, even for an artistic goal. I don't want that; I don't want to be reborn for music, it has served its purpose, I don't want it to recontinue. That is why I stopped writing music so long ago.

One single goal, I must have a single goal, my spiritual accomplishment and that before all. And for that, I need to understand my enslavement to my senses. Without me knowing it, my senses govern me, the habit of this, of that. One wants more, always more, I have to always want my spiritual accomplishment more, that before all else.

Extract from "S'éveiller, une question de vie ou de mort", chapter 2: "Every evening, after his meditation, the aspirant must sit on his bed and rest for a while preparing himself before sleeping, because of the importance of the last thought that he is going to carry with him into his sleep and which will inevitably determine what the next day will be for him spiritually.

At the hour of his death, before entering into his last and longest sleep, how much more determining will be the last thought that he carries with him at this fateful moment, a last thought that, not only will determine the state he finds himself in when he quits this world, but also what his future destiny and future existence will be, whatever form this existence takes and wherever it unfolds.

Every evening, he must ask himself what he really expects from life, what this spiritual work means for him and what importance he must accord it. He needs to renew the decision to give himself wholly to what calls to him within himself and to appreciate the opportunity that is offered him to be able to work on himself spiritually. He has to realize that the day will come when this possibility will no longer exist."

What I have written there, I do myself every night before sleeping.

Because one cannot work on oneself without this form of existence; it is only this form of existence that provides us with the conditions that cause the tendencies one has within oneself to arise, the undesirable desires or even sometimes desires that are good and that one does not know one carries within oneself.

One needs this existence to accomplish something that one ordinarily does not know, that is why existence must not be fled, but must be faced, always faced, and one must work on oneself to transform certain tendencies, to be truer in oneself.

"Because, when this monumental moment comes, there will be no more tomorrows for him."

No, there will be no more tomorrows for him. Whatever the state in which one finds oneself or the conditions in which one is placed, it is essential to realize that, in any case, nothing is permanent. I must not stop this work...

I cannot make, on a spiritual path, the same sorts of efforts as those that suffice for external life. Why? Because these efforts in external life are extracted from me, whereas the efforts that I must make on a spiritual path must be made because I want to make them, because I understand the importance and the necessity of them.

I must continually stoke the fire that burns beneath a word called my interest. That is why all that I do in external life must now be in relation to my spiritual interest.

Always remember these words:

"I want never to forget these precious moments when my mind is turned towards something higher than ordinary existence.

I want to carry within me the memory of these moments in my death."

✺ *May 2001: Sense of mystery.*

What do I want? What am I trying to understand? All my life, I must continue to try to understand. One has never understood, never enough, there is always more to understand and yet more to understand.

The moment that I stop trying to understand, by an ineluctable cosmic law, I will start to die psychically.

You are missing the sense of mystery. It is truly necessary to realize that there are mysteries everywhere. This is the first time that I have gone out in a car since the last meeting. The leaves on the trees are very fresh, green. It is a miracle, how does the tree know the time has come, after the winter, for the sap to rise in all the branches and make each leaf?

Within the boundaries of our building, there are wisteria; those are my favorite flowers, so beautiful. What a miracle! It is extraordinary how the vine knows what color flowers to grow, at what moment, and what sort of perfume to emit, and I am intoxicated by all this beauty, but beauty that is fleeting, impermanent.

Life has to become a miracle, because it is true that we are surrounded by miracles, but that we do not see them.

Everything is mysterious to me. From my window, I see clouds moving, tree branches swaying in the wind, sometimes birds who fly past at such speed. The bird barely moves his wings, yet he flies so quickly; no human being could run so fast.

The other day, I saw a bird landing on a tree opposite my window; how did this bird, who arrived with lightening speed, succeed in beating its wings to glide between the branches without doing itself harm? For me, it was a miracle because there are many branches and many leaves on the branches of the tree.

If we were blind and someone suddenly gave us eyes, then, to see the blue of the sky, with its enormous clouds that move, that transform themselves, what a miracle if one really saw them for the first time; that is how one must be all the time; one must achieve this, then one begins to really live, to understand the mystery of existence. If one really saw the blue of the sky as though for the first time in one's life and, then, suddenly, a miracle, a bird flying so fast, seeing it as though for the first time in my life.

Do you really know how to really live? We have lost this faculty of really seeing, of really hearing.

If our practice is not approached with the sense of mystery at every moment, it becomes flat.

All my life, I must remain alert, I want to understand, I still want to understand, I have never understood enough, for all of my life.

March 2002: The image one has of oneself.

Without ever being conscious of it, everyone has an image of him/herself, which he or she does not wish to renounce and which closes the door of his/her evolution on another plane of being.

What do I mean by image?

(Salim points out two people in turn): If I had the power to transform you into so and so, would you accept? Vice versa, if I asked so and so, can I transform you into this person, would you accept?

Don't answer, just think about it.

I have an image of myself, I am deeply in love with this image without knowing it. Everyone has this problem, without exception.

This image that one has of oneself is closely linked to self-esteem. One does not see it, that's the tragedy of it. If ever one says of someone something that injures this self-esteem, then the person spends his time like a dog, licking his wound, in other words ruminating on the injury that his ego has received, you understand?

He or she cannot see, in his/her blindness, the self-consideration within him/herself and which is an obstacle to his/her spiritual practice.

How can this image one has of oneself be recognized? One takes oneself, unconsciously—all of this is unconscious—one takes oneself for someone special. "I am special", it is enough to look at photos of celebrities in magazines. "I am someone special".

Yes, one loves oneself, one has an image of oneself that one does not want to let go, one is special. There is no-one who does not have this problem. One takes oneself for someone unique and one must become simple, an absolutely simple being, to lose this image that one has of oneself.

I have suffered with this image of myself in the past. Someone attacked my music, I had an image of myself, self-esteem, how could my contribution go unseen? When there were meetings of composers, the ultra-modern composers would say with contempt: "This music is still tonal". So, I also, like all of you, have suffered from that. When I saw how it blocked the path, then I began, with invisible scissors, every time I saw this manifestation of self-esteem: snip (Salim mimes cutting something with scissors).

When I was living in Rue Turgot, opposite the building, at street level, there was a hat shop. One day, a woman came past, dragging a little dog after her, when, suddenly, she saw a hat in the shop window. She doubled back on herself, pulling on the dog's lead. She looked at the hat, then she went on, pulling the dog after her. Then, finally, she doubled back again, went into the shop, pulling the dog (who was not at all interested), and when she came out... the hat had bought the woman.

She was walking and admiring herself in the shop windows: I am a hat...

Another day, we were walking, a long time ago now, and there was a young man walking towards us, he had very long hair, he was proud of himself: I am hair...

The image that one has of oneself, he was forgetting that he was going to age one day, his hair would become white, he would lack energy, like I do today... If one could see the life of a human being speeded up, from birth to death, the crying baby, he gets married, he has children, that's it, it's over.

On another level, for the Infinite, our lives from our birth until our death, are nothing but a click of the fingers, a flash. At the level of the Universe, we are not even a virus.

This image one has of oneself, this self-esteem, it is the cause of all the misfortune that afflicts humanity. When one is absent to oneself, there is only reaction and self-esteem.

It is said, in Hinduism that the aspirant must become selfless for his emancipation, otherwise there can be no emancipation. What is liberation? One does not understand from what I must liberate myself, I must liberate myself from myself, from my mechanical reactions, then I attain the Absolute; what a paradox it is, to liberate myself from myself...

✦ *September 2002: Final teaching.*

Salim stopped teaching completely in September 2002 because of his state of health which had deteriorated too much. Nevertheless, he continued to work on his books until his last day.

Below are some extracts from his final teaching:

"Let each of you here ask himself: What have I been busy with since our last meeting... but ask yourself this with all your sincerity. What sort of thoughts have been turning in my head and monopolizing my attention since our last meeting. Were these thoughts really worthwhile spiritually?

What sort of desires have I had? Can these desires help me spiritually? Have they been able to help me spiritually?

Death awaits me, it is necessary to say this to oneself, death awaits me, inexorably. What provision have I made for this monumental hour? What am I going to take with me when this fateful hour arrives for me?

One sees the branches of trees sway, but one does not see the cause. What is the cause that makes the branches of a tree sway? Has anyone ever seen the wind? One sees the effect and one gives credit to the effect, but the invisible cause? It is the same thing for my life and the whole of this Creation, the Universe, this incredible cosmic manifestation with billions and billions of galaxies, which contain billions and billions of stars and planets. And our planet too, with all the various animals it contains, the trees the flowers, the animals, the human beings, you, me, one sees the effect and one does not think of the cause, the enigmatic cause that is the creator of this effect.

One gives credit to what is visible, to what one feels, to what one perceives with one's senses, what monopolizes all one's attention; the exterior fascinates our psyche and one forgets the cause. One must succeed, at least intellectually to begin with, in transferring this credit that one gives to what one perceives with one's senses, to the invisible. I need absolutely to know the Source whence I issued and into which I am going to be reabsorbed after my death, now, in this life; after death, it will be too late.

And, even if I come to recognize this Source, I will see how difficult it is to remain within this Source, how much the fascination of the exterior continues to have power over my psyche.

I am going to read you a quotation from St Thomas:
The disciples said to Jesus: "Tell us how our end will be."
Jesus said: "Have you already discovered the beginning   (that is to say, the Source from which you arose)
that you are now asking about the end?
For where the beginning is (the Source from which you arose)
there the end will be too. (it is into this that you will be reabsorbed)
Blessed is he who will stand at the beginning. (will stand, that is to say, will stay, on condition of having found it)
And he will know the end, (he will know what he is to be reabsorbed into when death takes him),
and he says at the end:
and he will not taste death.

Christ attached such importance to this discovery of what he called the beginning, the Source, and after that, he said: blessed is he who will stand, that is to say, will stay, at the beginning and he will not taste death.

The Tibetan Book of the Dead, I quote:
"O nobly-born, the time hath now come for thee to seek the Path [in reality]. Thy breathing is about to cease. Thy guru hath set thee face to face with the Clear Light; and now thou art about to experience it in its Reality in the Bardo state, wherein all things are like the void and cloudless sky, and the naked, spotless intellect is like unto a transparent vacuum without circumference or centre. At this moment, know thou thyself; and abide in that state."

At this moment, know thou thyself; and abide in that state... the last sentence of Christ... *Blessed is he who will stand at the beginning.*

When it is said : *"All things are like the void and cloudless sky, and the naked, spotless intellect is like unto a transparent vacuum without circumference or centre."*

This vacuity is not nothing and that is what you have to discover; it is the Source whence you issued; this vacuity is made up of an immense, immense Beingness-Consciousness, without beginning, without end, without shores, imbued with the breath of the Infinite...

One calls It a vacuity in comparison with the tangible which you know, but It is not nothing.

However, if one has not known this Beingness-Consciousness during one's life, one will fear it after death. As the Tibetan Book of the Dead says, one will wish to flee this state and seek the tangible that one has known.

Remember that your principal goal is to fight, to fight with the whole of yourself, with all your sincerity, when you meditate, when you undertake a spiritual exercise, whether in the street or at home, with all your being, in order to succeed in sufficiently tearing away from this secondary identity which is grafted onto you, onto all of us, and covers this essence, this Beingness-Consciousness imbued with the breath of the Infinite, call it what you will, one can call it Nirvana, one can call it my Buddha-nature, one can call it the Dharmakaya, but it is the same thing, this Enigmatic Source from which I arose and into which I will be reabsorbed after my death.

Remember that it is before all the quality of the efforts made that counts and not only their quantity.

One other thing that I want to say to you, which is so important, is on the devotional question. One needs Grace. We do our part, but one needs Grace, one cannot do it all alone. Something in me must be turned towards That which is higher, which one cannot name, with a deeply devotional feeling.

You must always keep in your mind that everything is mysterious, take nothing for granted, everything is mysterious. We are mysterious. The Cosmos is so vertiginous, we cannot even imagine it with our small and extremely limited minds; although it is visible, it is mysterious because of the Invisible which is the cause of this fantastic Creation. It makes one dizzy if one really begins to try to understand; one feels dizzy and one needs to feel this dizziness before the Incommensurable, to encourage us.

When you begin a spiritual exercise or meditation, you must set a timer, of course, and you say to yourself—as this Salim who is before you said to himself in the past—even if a hundred thousand scorpions walk over me, I will not move before the timer goes off and stops my meditation or, in the case of a spiritual exercise, in the street or at home, while I am cooking, washing myself, or whatever it may be, I will not interrupt the exercise before the time I have determined upon has passed; even if a hundred thousand scorpions walk over me, I told myself that in the past. You too, say what you want, but say something that moves you.

All that I have said to you today comes down to this: I want to know the Source whence I issued and into which I will be reabsorbed, I want to know it during my life so that I shall be tranquil when death comes, so that I shall not resist. In meditation, one can come to a point where one feels: I am going to be plunged into an incomprehensible emptiness, I must accept this plunge. One will discover at that moment that the emptiness is not nothing. There is no more tangible, there is no more movement as one knows it, there is another sort of movement, so fine, it is said that the Divine Spirit never sleeps, so fine, so full of life, Beingness-Consciousness, without beginning, without end, incommensurable, without shores, dizzying, imbued with the breath of the Infinite.

There is a reason for Creation; the Infinite wants its Holy Presence to be recognized, but the human being, such as he is ordinarily, with his limited intelligence and his limited level of being cannot recognize it.

It could be said that if beings provided with an out of the ordinary form of intelligence and a level of consciousness that one does not habitually experience do not arise from its Creation, to recognize its Holy Presence, then it is as though the Infinite did not exist.

Since our birth, so many things have happened around us, so many people that one has known, sad or pleasant events, people who have hurt us, those that we love and those that we do not; without realizing it, we carry all that in us and that takes up space in our being and leaves no space for other things. I must begin at certain moments to awaken myself sufficiently, to tear myself away from what I am habitually to see this immense crowd that I carry within me—I am talking for you now, aren't I?—each of you must begin to awaken himself to see the immense crowd that he carries within himself, a crowd that squeals, that shouts, that laughs, that protests.

I want to see them all, I want to begin to liberate myself from that, and I cannot if, during the day, I do not tear myself away from what I am and if I do not say to myself, in words: "Recollect yourself," because thinking "Recollect yourself," is not enough, one can think "Recollect yourself," and one does it superficially or even not at all.

It has to be said in words, I speak from personal experience in the past, I was obliged to say it to myself, I have seen that thinking of "recollecting myself" when I was lost in futile thoughts, in futile images, thinking "Recollect yourself, come back to yourself" was superficially done, or not at all, it is as though one believes that thought is enough, it is not enough. It is necessary to say to oneself: "Recollect yourself," gently, say it to oneself, within oneself of course. "Recollect yourself," then one will see that something becomes possible and when I repeat, "Recollect yourself," it begins to work...

When someone says something, thinks something, or does something, once it is said, thought, or done, he can no longer help wanting to re-say it, to rethink it, or to re-do it, so one will begin to say again "Recollect yourself, recollect yourself," and you will see that, when you are lost in thoughts that turn in your mind, when you are far from yourself, suddenly there will be a rapid movement of return towards yourself.

What I am saying to you, it is vital, it is a question of life or death. I have to wake in the morning from my nocturnal sleep so that I may realize I have slept and have—I believe—awakened. Yes, I am awake in comparison with my nocturnal sleep, but I sleep in another way and I know not in what other way I sleep, and my life passes, uselessly, futilely, without having made provision for the hour of my death.

When you succeed in staying with yourself for long enough in a state of inner silence, you will one day discover that this return towards myself is nothing less than the return towards the Infinite that I carry in myself, the return towards my Buddha Nature, towards Nirvana that I did not know I was already carrying in myself, this Enigmatic Source that is made up of Beingness-Consciousness imbued with the Breath of the Absolute.

And Salim concludes with this Bodhisattva vow that he formulated in the following way:

"Yes, I want to be a Buddha, I want to be a Christ, I want to be like him, he agreed to anything to help humanity!"

If one can continually hold on to the <u>feeling</u> of being with oneself, one will eventually come to <u>find God in oneself</u>.

If one can continually hold on to the <u>feeling</u> of being with oneself, one will eventually come to <u>find God in oneself</u>.

All spiritual practices can be reduced to the following few words: Each time one has, after a moment of inner absence, become inwardly aware and <u>present</u> again, one has, perhaps without truly understanding it at first, <u>come back to oneself</u>; or, in other words, one has <u>found</u> oneself again.

The problem is that, in the beginning of one's spiritual practice, one does not really realize that this <u>coming back to oneself</u> is, in very fact, <u>coming back to God in oneself</u>.

THE END OF THE PATH.

Salim's state of health had been deteriorating for a number of years; in fact, he was suffering from an undiagnosed cancer of the colon, which had resulted in a complete intestinal obstruction, and which was operated on one month after he had stopped teaching. We then left to live in the south of France, near my daughter, who had become our daughter since Salim had legally adopted her and whom he affectionately called Vidji.

Salim subsequently underwent several other operations and his body became for him, even more so than in the past, a crushing burden. An immense fatigue and constant physical suffering were the obstacles that he had to face with all the resources of his practice.

It might be thought that living with Salim was austere and burdensome, but it was not at all; he loved to laugh and even played some innocent practical jokes, which delighted him. Once, for example, as we were living in the countryside and there were donkeys on a neighboring property, he had recorded, without my knowledge, a donkey braying, which he imitated perfectly as it was something that he had known well during his childhood. He set the recording playing without me noticing it and, seeing my astonishment at the presence of a donkey in the garden, he began to laugh like a child.

A few weeks before he left this world, we were contacted via the internet by a Theravada nun in the Thai tradition of the forest monks, Ajahn Sundara, who told us that her master, Ajahn Sumedho, founder of a number of monasteries of that tradition in Britain was teaching listening to the inner sound and that he was referring to Salim's first book (the only one written in English, The Way of Inner Vigilance). Salim was very glad to learn that his book had been able to help make known this precious aid which had proved to be of such assistance to him.

Despite the deterioration of his body, Salim nevertheless continued to have new spiritual experiences and gain new understandings for which he had no words. He was now permanently in another state of being and of consciousness; there was very little difference between his meditation and other moments of the day.

He deplored that aspirants did not realize the importance of their quest for others, when this understanding gives a completely different dimension to this spiritual adventure.

"The human being," he would say, "is, without commonly suspecting it, so profoundly connected to the Universe, which he is indissolubly part of, that the battle he fights to surpass himself is, in the most enigmatic way, the battle of the Universe itself. So, in a manner ordinarily incomprehensible to the mass of humanity, his evolution to a superior plane of being and of consciousness is, in fact, the evolution of the Universe."

Once Salim told me very simply that he had known in his meditation a state where he had become the All.
That brought to mind the words of John of the Cross:

"To arrive at being All, desire to be nothing [...] for to go from all to the All, you must deny yourself of all in All."

and also the beginning of the Gospel according to Thomas:

"The one who seeks should not cease seeking until he finds.
And when he finds, he will be dismayed.
And when he is dismayed, he will be astonished.
And he will be king over the All." (logion 2, 1-8)

Salim expressed this experience in his work, Dans le Silence de l'Insondable (In the Silence of the Unfathomable), in the following way:

"It is only when one is absorbed in deep meditation that one can lose oneself; and in losing oneself, in the most astonishing manner, one FINDS ONESELF AGAIN! Oh, Wonder of Wonders!

Moreover, it is only when one is plunged into intense meditation that one succeeds in dying to oneself; and, in dying to oneself, to what one is ordinarily, one is reborn and, in this very way, one meets and one KNOWS the Infinite, God, the Absolute, Nirvana, within oneself! Oh, Wonder of Wonders!

In addition, it is only during deep meditation that one can come to lose the false identity that has been grafted onto oneself; in losing this false identity, one immerses oneself in the Infinite and one becomes ONE WITH IT! Oh, Wonder of Wonders!

Finally, it is only when one sinks into intense meditation that one comes to lose what one possesses by way of knowledge, by way of obsessive desires, by way of beliefs, and that one becomes empty; in becoming empty, one becomes in this very way the ALL! Oh, what Hope! Oh, Wonder of Wonders! Oh, Miracle!"

Salim had a deeply religious temperament and remained always in a state of wondrous adoration before the mystery of the Infinite which revealed itself to him.

Despite the crushing weight of a body which could no longer go on, he never ceased working on himself; furthermore, he would never have been able to do otherwise, as it had become second nature to him. So as not to be defeated by his state of exhaustion which brought an irresistible somnolence, he repeated mantras of sorts that he invented or phrases/prayers to sustain himself.

He distanced himself more and more from the events of this world and had only one remaining desire: to help others as long as he still lived. He continued to joke, to do his best to help me, sharing the music he liked, work on his books, interesting himself in all that related to the Cosmos, the stars, the Universe.

He would say: "Despite the spiritual experiences and the understandings that I have been privileged to know, and despite the long work that I have accomplished on myself during so many years, I can only insist on the fact that there are mysteries that it is not possible to grasp the full scope of in this form of existence. In this domain which surpasses human understanding, as long as one has breath left, one must always go further on, there is always more to know and more to understand.

It is necessary to succeed, at the hour of one's death, in being alone with oneself and the Absolute, alone with oneself, in a state of silence and of deep inner contemplation. It is necessary to succeed in remaining in such a state; I can humbly say that I have succeeded to a very great extent..."

He was, of course, as he had always said, "tragically human" and, sometimes, he would go through very difficult times. Moreover, he wanted to leave his mortal body, but he said: "Undoubtedly something must be wanted of me, as I am still here".

During his final stay in hospital, he continually told the care workers and nurses how much he loved them, which touched them deeply, to the extent that they wanted to know who he was. This was in no way an affected attitude on Salim's part, he really loved them, with a spiritual and infinitely compassionate love for their poor lives deprived of what was essential.

He knew that this hospitalization would be the last and he was going to face the most important moment of his existence. He had often written in his books that death was an initiation, because the dying person rediscovers, in all its purity, the original Source from which he arose at the time of his birth.

Salim had already known this state during his enlightenment at the age of 33 and, from then on, he had never ceased pursuing his practice with the most passionate sincerity, so as to achieve a state of permanent awakening. Despite that, he said with humility that he had not achieved the ultimate liberation. And death was the door offering him the opportunity of achieving the Supreme Goal.

This demanded a superhuman effort and unfailing concentration, as the Bardo Thodol says:

"That Voidness is not of the nature of the voidness of nothingness, but a Voidness at the true nature of which thou feelest awed, and before

which thine intellect shineth clearly and more lucidly. (..) In that state wherein thou art existing, there is being experienced by thee, in an unbearable intensity, Voidness and Brightness inseparable... Be not distracted. The line of demarcation between Buddhas and sentient beings lieth herein."

This line of demarcation was what Salim wanted with all his being to cross. He did not want to be distracted or disturbed by whatever or whoever it might be at the fateful moment that was so important to him. He had given us very precise instructions concerning this.

Vidji had brought the large photo of Buddha that decorated his bedroom and we put it up opposite his bed; some devotional music that Salim liked (Fauré's Requiem and Brahms's secular choral works) was playing on a loop very quietly; the care staff left us completely in peace. We remained in this peaceful atmosphere, in meditation, until the moment that Salim's breath stopped.

There is something so mysterious in breath that stops. In the West, it is common to have never seen someone die, yet this is an essential lesson in life. This ceasing of breath in a living being is a sacred mystery which we felt deeply. All night, the room was bathed in an intense spiritual atmosphere.

Salim's body was cremated three days afterwards and it was only then that, still according to his instructions, I made the news of his departure known to the people who knew him, thereby avoiding the possibility of this crucial moment for him being disturbed by emotional reactions.

Salim's life was a permanent miracle of will and inner strength drawn from somewhere other than ordinary human capacities. During all the years that I knew him, he was so deeply unified within himself that he remained the same in any circumstances, whether teaching his pupils, cooking, listening to music, or even joking. Permanently connected within himself to the Superior Aspect of his nature, he became free from the look of others, not worrying about preserving an image of himself. The only thing that counted for him was to help his pupils to understand how one habitually sleeps within oneself without knowing it and, in comparison, how to know and appreciate another state of being and of consciousness. Without hiding from them the difficulty of this inner awakening, he encouraged them ceaselessly.

"One gains spiritually drop by drop. One recollects oneself, one loses oneself, no discouragement, never be discouraged, a drop more, a drop more, and, one day, a threshold is crossed. Afterwards, nothing can stop us; on the contrary, the drops will fall more and more rapidly until, one day, there it is, overflowing. And at that moment, the Absolute gives us our reward in a cloudburst, I can assure you of that...

"No sincere effort is ever wasted, but, in the beginning, effort, effort... always with understanding. Life is a great adventure, but it all depends on the respect one has for it, the way one considers it, and the use one makes of it.

"Behind all the griefs of existential life, behind all its worries, behind all its incessant movement and change, behind all its moral and physical suffering, there is an Immutable Reality.

"To know this Reality before the mists of death descend upon him and put an end to his life is the most precious treasure that a human being can ever find.

"One single instant imbued with this Reality, one single moment lived in this Reality, one single second when the seeker's consciousness touches just the edge of this Reality is worth more than all the pleasures and all the wealth of this world multiplied by a thousand times one thousand—even if such pleasures and such wealth could last an eternity!"

EDWARD MICHAEL'S MUSICAL WORKS::

Listed by publisher, title of work, duration, performance dates.

Editions RICORDI :

- *Mass* for mixed choirs, two string orchestras, celesta, harp, glockenspiel, and
  percussion.. 36 ' - 1955 -
  1956. O.R.T.F. (French public service broadcasting) National Orchestra
  conducted by Eugène Bigot.
  1963.O.R.T.F. National Orchestra conducted by Eugène Bigot.
  1967. Radio Berlin.
  1968. Repeat broadcast of the 1963 performance .
  1988. Repeat broadcast of the 1963.performance

- *Fata Morgana,* symphonic poem for orchestra. 8'30 - 1958 -
  1960. Radio Liège. Orchestra conducted by Victor Clovez.
  1961. Radio Lille. Orchestra conducted by Victor Clovez.
  1962. Radio Lyon. Orchestra conducted by Raymond Chevreux.

- *La Vision de Lamis Helacim,* (Lamis Helacim's Vision) symphonic poem for
  large orchestra 10' - 1961
  1962. Théatre des Champs Elysées. National Orchestra conducted by
  Manuel Rosenthal.

- *Le Jardin de Tinajatama* (Tinajatama's Garden) for orchestra. 10' - 1958 -
  1960. Radio-Lille. Orchestra conducted by Victor Clovez.
  1961. Radio-Lyon. Orchestra conducted by Raymond Chevreux.
  1962. Radio-Bruxelles. Orchestra conducted by Louis de Froment.
  1965 Hambourg Allemagne
  1968. O.R.T.F. Orchestra of Nice conducted by Paul Mule.
  1969. O.R.T.F.. Orchestra of Nice conducted byVictor Clovez.

- *Sonatine* for flute and clarinet. 11' - 1964 -

- *Elegy* for orchestra. 5'30" - 1957 -
  1959. Radio-Lille. Orchestra conducted by Victor Clovez.
  1960. Radio-Lyon. Orchestra conducted by Victor Clovez.
  1961. Radio-Bruxelles. Orchestra conducted by Victor Clovez.

- *Elegy* reduction for Martenot waves and piano - 1957 -

Editions CHOUDENS :

- *Rapsody Concertante* for violin and orchestra 14' - 1946 -
>   1967. O.R.T.F. Orchestra of Lille conducted by Raymond Chevreux.

- *La Reine des Pluies,* (The Queen of the Rains) choregraphic poem
>   for large orchestra. 8' - 1962 -
>   1963. Radio Lille. Orchestra conducted by Raymond Chevreux.
>   1963. Australia.

- *Le Festin des Dieux* (The Feast of the Gods) for orchestra. 6' - 1962 -
>   1967. O.R.T.F. Orchestra of Lille.

- *Chant d'Espérance* (Song of Hope) for cello and piano. 18'30
>   1971. Cité des Arts, Salle Edmond Michelet
>   with Frédéric Lodéon (cello).
>   1998 Bruxelles and Liège - piano Isabelle Aubier
>   cello Didier Poskin
>   1999 Paris and Belgium - numerous concerts (CD)
>   2000 Belgium numerous concerts

- *Initiation* for string orchestra . 18'30 - 1959 -
>   1968. Orchestra of Lille conducted by Victor Clovez.
>   1969. O.R.T.F.. Orchestra of Nice conducted by Paul Mule.

- *Little Antique Suite* for flute, violin, cello and piano. 19 ' - 1960 -
>   1962. Switzerland. Ensemble of Paris. .
>   1971. Cité des Arts, salle Edmond Michelet.

- *Trois Rituels* (Three Rituals) for two oboes or two Martenot waves
>   and percussions. 12 ' - 1962 -

Editions TRANSATLANTIQUES

- *Kamaal,* symphonic work for narrator and orchestra. 40' - 1956 -
>   1958. Ecole Normale de Musique, conducted by the author.
>   1961. Radio-Strasbourg. Orchestra conducted by Marius Briançon.
>   1962. Salle des étudiants, rue du Docteur Blanche, Paris.
>   1987. France Musique, repeat broadcast of the 1961 performance

- *Les Soirées of Tedjlah* (Tedjlah's Evenings) for mezzo soprano (vocalises),
two flutes, piano and string orchestra. (mention Vercelli Prize). 20'1959
>   1960. public concert conducted by the author.
>   1961. Salle de l'école Normale de Musique with Noémie Perugia
>   conducted by the author.

-*Nocturne* for flute solo or Martenot waves and orchestra
(prix Lili Boulanger). 6'30 - 1955 -
1959. Radio-Paris. Orchestra conducted by Raymond Chevreux.
1960. Radio-Lille. Orchestra conducted by Victor Clovez.
1961. Radio-Lyon. Orchestra conducted by Raymond Chevreux.
1961. Radio-Bruxelles. Orchestra conducted by Raymond Chevreux.
1968. O.R.T.F.. Orchestra of Lille conducted by Victor Clovez.
1969. O.R.T.F. Orchestra of Nice conducted by Paul Mule.

- *Trois Tableaux* (Three Pictures) symphonic work for orchestra 11'30 1961
1962. Radio-Lyon. Orchestra conducted by Raymond Chevreux.

- *Le Rêve d'Himalec* (Himalec's Dream) for orchestra. 13' - 1946 -
1964. R.T.F. Orchestra of Lille conducted by Victor Clovez.

- *Chant Arabe* (Arab Song) for two Martenot waves. 5 ' - 1958 -
Between 1958 and 1971
Numerous performances on radio and télévision

- *A Travers un Vitrail* (Through a Stained Glass Window) for Martenot waves
and piano. 4'30 - 1958 -
Between 1963 and 1971
Numerous performances on radio and télévision.

- *Psaume* for male choir. (diplôme Vercelli). 8' - 1956 -

- *Little suite* for female choir.(or two soprano and two alto) 6' 1956

UNPUBLISHED WORKS:

ORCHESTRALS WORKS :

- *L'Oracle* (The Oracle) Archaic Symphony for string orchestra.
Four mouvements - 33' - 1959 -

- *La Quête of Koussouda* (Koussouda's Quest) for harp and string orchestra
Five mouvements - 12'30 - 1960 -

- *Scherzo* for orchestra ("The Dionysia"). 12'30 - 1942 -

- *La légende de Gampong* (The Legend of Gampong) for narrator and orchestra
(text and music by Edward Michael). 30' - 1963 -

- *Au Seuil of Persépolis* (On the Threshold of Persepolis) for orchestra. 6' 1962

- *Trois Mondes* (Three Worlds) symphonic work for large orchestra.
Three movements 14' - 1962 -

- *Les Eléments* (The Elements) for large orchestra. Four movements - 11' - 1962

- *Symphony* for large orchestra. Three movements. 30' - 1948 -

- *Concerto* for violin and orchestra. Three movements. 30' - 1948 -

- *Druze Suite* - Three pieces on ancient modes for orchestra 11'

CHAMBER MUSIC :

1998 release, in Belgium, of a CD with the following pieces :
- *Les Pléiades* (The Pleiades) for soprano and piano (eight movements)
      based on poems of A.E. Hausmann. 12'
- *Cinq Stèles Antiques* (Five Ancient Monuments) for celtic harp or piano. 12'
- *La barque enchantée* (The Enchanted Craft) for piano 6'
- *La légende de la fée d'un ruisseau* (The Legend of the Fairy of the Stream)
      for piano 3'20
- *Sonata* for violin and piano. 19'
(as well as *le Chant d'espérance* for cello and piano published by Editions Choudens)
- for all these pieces :
      1998 Bruxelles and Liège numerous concerts (CD)
      1999 Paris and Belgium numerous concerts
      2000 Belgium numerous concerts.

- *Sur l'océan of la fatalité* (On the Ocean of Fate) for soprano and piano 6')
- *Au Pays de Bharata* (In Bharata's Country) for piano
      eight movements. 25 1970
- Various pieces for piano, for Martenot waves, for flute and piano etc.
- *Evocation mystique* (Mystic Evocation) for flute solo
      or Martenot waves 4' - 1962
- *Gurumati* for Martenot waves, piano and percussions
      Three movements - 10' - 1961
- *Two English folk songs,* for soprano and piano harmonized
      by Edward Michael. 6' 1973 -
- *Six English folk songs* for soprano and piano harmonized
      by Edward Michael - 16' 1950 -
- *Three English folk songs* for mixed choirs harmonized
      by Edward Michael. 8' 1949 -
- *Rite de la Lune* (Rite of the Moon) for oboe or
      Martenot waves solo. 10' - 1960 -

- *Deux Esquisses* (Two Sketches) for flute
(or Martenot waves) and piano. 8 ' - 1960 -
- *Danse Méditative* (Meditative Dance) for piano.
- *Deux Danses Sacrées* (Two Sacred Dances) for piano.
- *Danse d'amour* (Dance of Love) for piano. 1960
- *Suite of Noël* (Christmas Suite) three easy pieces for viola and cello 10' 1953

ILLUSTRATIVE MUSIC FOR DOCUMENTARIES, FILMS OR TELEVISION PROGRAMS.

Registered in Great Britain :
- *Quatre rituels* (Four Rituals) for orchestra.
1967. Hilversum. Orchestra of Holland conducted by the author.

- *Sur le Mont Gelboe* (On Mount Gilboa) for orchestra.
1965. O.R.T.F. Orchestra of Lille conducted by Paul Bonneau.
1966. O.R.T.F. Orchestra of Lille conducted by Raymond Chevreux.

- *Sept préludes symphoniques* (Seven Symphonic Preludes) for orchestra.
1967. Hilversum. Orchestra of Holland conducted by the author.

- *Nathan le Prophète* (Nathan the Prophet) for orchestra.
1964. Recording conducted by the author.

- *Quatorze Esquisses Pittoresques.*(Fourteen Picturesque Sketches)
1967. Recording conducted by the author..

Registered in France :
- *La Tragédie of Masada* (The Tragedy of Masada) for large orchestra.
1969. ORTF Radio-France symphonic Orchestra
conducted by Alain Kremski.
The work was released as a vinyl record by Montparnasse 2000.

Music for radio program.
- *Les Récits of Belzébuth* (Beelzebub's Tales) descriptive piece of music for
choirs and orchestra for a radio program broadcasted in 1957
conducted by Louis de Froment.

- *L'Eclosion* (The Hatching) descriptive piece of music for orchestra
broadcasted in 1963.

Made in the USA
Las Vegas, NV
29 April 2022

48198869R00243